D0687709

THIS IS NO LONGER THE PROPERTY
OF THE SEATTLE PUBLIC LIBRARY

HOLY HUMANITARIANS

Holy Humanitarians

AMERICAN EVANGELICALS AND GLOBAL AID

Heather D. Curtis

Harvard University Press Cambridge, Massachusetts • London, England 2018

Copyright © 2018 by the President and Fellows of Harvard College

ALL RIGHTS RESERVED

Printed in the United States of America

First printing

Library of Congress Cataloging-in-Publication Data

Names: Curtis, Heather D., author.

Title: Holy humanitarians : American evangelicals and global aid / Heather D. Curtis.

Description: Cambridge, Massachusetts : Harvard University Press, 2018. |
   Includes bibliographical references and index.

Identifiers: LCCN 2017042044 | ISBN 9780674737365 (alk. paper)

Subjects: LCSH: Christian Herald (Firm) | Christian herald. | Humanitarian assistance,
   American—History—20th century. | Evangelicalism—United States—History—
   20th century. | Christianity in mass media—History—20th century.

Classification: LCC BR525 .C86 2018 | DDC 361.7 / 50973—dc23

   LC record available at https://lccn.loc.gov/2017042044

For David D. Hall

teacher, mentor, friend, fellow pilgrim

and for my parents

CONTENTS

HOLY HUMANITARIANS

INTRODUCTION

On a steamy summer day in July 1866, fourteen-year-old Louis Klopsch stood in the middle of the Beaver Street cigar shop in Lower Manhattan, his body covered with blood and drenched in sweat. Just after he had opened the store for business, an excited Klopsch told his employer, four men had tried to steal a large quantity of cigars. Not "the kind of chap to let such a proceeding go on without a protest," the boy attacked the would-be robbers with a piece of broken glass, and a desperate fight ensued. Eventually, he succeeded in driving the thieves out. Although the store was a mess, Klopsch was unharmed, and his grateful employer offered him the "handsome sum" of twenty-five dollars as a reward for his heroism.[1]

Several days later, the burglars were back—this time in greater force. Undaunted, the courageous Klopsch grabbed a crowbar and beat the six intruders until he had "broken the skulls" of two men and chased them all off. Now the shopkeeper became alarmed—perhaps these criminals intended personal violence against him. He called the police. When the investigators searched the premises, they discovered a suspicious sac containing traces of blood hidden in the water closet. Putting this piece of evidence together with their doubts about Klopsch's story, the police questioned the boy again. Realizing that he had been caught, the young man confessed to having "gone to a butcher's shop, filled a bladder with blood, and, returning to the store, scattered it about the floor and walls."[2]

The tales of the attempted robberies were entirely false. Klopsch was arrested on a charge of malicious mischief and after a brief incarceration was released into the care of his physician father, who blamed his son's exploits on drinking too much strong coffee and reading newspapers that filled his mind with imaginings. He "thinks to be something large," the elder Klopsch lamented, like the characters he encountered in the "liar books" that an irresponsible aunt had given him to read.[3]

Despite his prodigal adolescence, which included several more run-ins with the law culminating in a two-year term in Sing Sing State Prison for forgery and insurance fraud, Louis Klopsch did become "something large."[4] By the time of his death in 1910, Klopsch was hailed as "one of the historic figures in the annals of civilization"; a "friend of all humanity" whose "genius in the organization of benevolences" made him "the greatest inspirational force in the Christian homes of America" and "a blessing to mankind." As a pioneer in pictorial journalism and proprietor of the New York–based weekly newspaper the *Christian Herald* from 1890 onward, Klopsch took advantage of new printing and photographic technologies to publicize humanitarian crises at home and abroad. By deftly combining vivid images and graphic narratives of suffering near and far with appeals to biblical injunctions about almsgiving and to deep-seated millennial expectations about the United States' role as a redeemer nation, Klopsch induced readers to open their "hearts . . . hands . . . purses . . . and granaries" to "feed the hungry, to send or carry aid to the sick, and to spread the Gospel message everywhere."[5]

With Klopsch at the helm, the *Christian Herald* became the most widely read religious newspaper in the world and "a chosen channel of individual and collective benevolence for the Lord's people of all denominations," raising millions of dollars for the suffering and needy of every land through a relentless succession of relief campaigns. For his work as "an almoner of nations in distress," Klopsch was awarded the Kaisar-i-Hind Medal of the first class by King Edward of England in 1904 and was decorated in 1907 by Emperor Meiji of Japan with the Order of the Rising Sun. His biographer called Klopsch's life story a "Romance of a Modern Knight of Mercy" and predicted it would inspire future generations of good Samaritans: "The voice that is silent yet speaks as with a thousand tongues through the good works that go on."[6]

AN ALTERNATIVE ACCOUNT OF
AMERICAN HUMANITARIANISM

A century after Klopsch's admirers prophesied that "he started some streams of work and influence that will flow on and on forever," I stood in the middle of the Bowery Mission on the Lower East Side of Manhattan, my body covered with city grime and drenched in sweat. It was a steamy summer day in July 2011, and I was helping serve dinner to two hundred or so homeless New Yorkers participating in the Mission's residential recovery programs. With my hair tucked in a net and my plastic-covered hands struggling to hold the slippery utensils sliding between my perspiring fingers, I clumsily dished up mashed potatoes, baked chicken, and green beans for the hungry women and men who came through the line. Most were patient with my fumbling, and a few came back for seconds. After all had been served, I followed the crowd from the dining hall into the chapel, where the nightly worship service was about to begin. Settling myself into a pew toward the back of the building while the praise band started to play, I looked up. Prominently placed above the pulpit hung a plaque commemorating Louis Klopsch's role as president and patron of the Bowery Mission from April 1895 until his death in 1910: "IN LOVING TRIBUTE TO LOUIS KLOPSCH . . . A TRUE SERVANT OF GOD AND HUMANITY. HIS WORKS DO FOLLOW HIM."[7]

From the time of Klopsch's passing to the present, the Bowery Mission's ministry to homeless and hungry New Yorkers has provided men, women, and children "caught in the cycles of poverty, hopelessness and dependencies of many kinds," with free meals three times a day, as well as shelter, clothing, and medical care. Klopsch's legacy lives on in this faith-based organization, which strives to see "lives transformed to hope, joy, lasting productivity and eternal life through the power of Jesus Christ." Although Mission staff consistently refer to Jesus and his teachings as part of their work, they offer services to anyone in need, regardless of recipients' beliefs, and they accept volunteer help and donations from people of "all different faiths, or no faith at all." Through their expansive outreach programs, the Bowery Mission's leaders have made their enterprise one of the most well-known charitable ventures in and beyond New York City and built a broad base of financial support from individual donors, philanthropic foundations, corporate sponsors, and several government agencies.[8]

Although the Bowery Mission has become a prominent fixture on the nonprofit landscape, the origins of this renowned organization and its connections to a much larger history of humanitarianism remain relatively unknown. Despite his extraordinary contributions to the fields of domestic charity and foreign aid, Louis Klopsch has been mostly overlooked by scholars and subsequent generations of philanthropists. Several studies do mention the *Christian Herald*'s involvement in international disaster assistance campaigns at the turn of the twentieth century, but few historians have recognized the newspaper as a major force in shaping the humanitarian sentiments and habits of the American public during a period of increasing globalization and U.S. expansionism.[9]

In part, this omission results from the fact that the relief and development work of rival aid agencies such as the American Red Cross (ARC) and large philanthropic institutions like the Rockefeller Foundation eventually overshadowed the *Christian Herald*'s endeavors. The vast archives of these competing organizations and their leading lights—celebrated figures such as Clara Barton, Frederick Taylor Gates, and John D. Rockefeller—have provided scholars with abundant materials for charting their participation in the development of American humanitarianism.[10] Meanwhile, other than copies of the newspaper itself, some laudatory biographies of Klopsch and his associates, and a few accounts scattered in government documents or other periodicals, records of the *Christian Herald*'s remarkably effective efforts to engage American Protestants in massive international relief campaigns and a wide array of domestic charities have not survived.

This paucity of sources makes chronicling the *Christian Herald*'s seminal role in the expansion of American benevolence challenging. Recovering this history, however, provides a corrective to scholarly narratives that stress the increasing secularization of philanthropy during the Progressive Era. According to many studies, the rising influence of scientific authority and emphasis on professional expertise resulted in the decline of traditional modes of religious charity around the turn of the twentieth century. Some historians have argued that with the establishment of corporate foundations, the growth of the welfare state, and the development of the humanitarian aid industry in subsequent decades, alleviating suffering became the province of wealthy donors, government officials, and trained social workers rather than the responsibility of local congregations, benevolent organizations, or Christian missionaries. Other scholars point to the United States' becoming more religiously heterogeneous, allowing secular relief and development agencies to gain an advantage over sectarian charities and eventually to dominate the fields of domestic philanthropy and foreign aid.[11]

By telling the forgotten story of the Bowery Mission's benefactor and his efforts to assuage affliction both at home and abroad, this book offers an alternative account of American humanitarianism. Examining the benevolent enterprises of Louis Klopsch and his colleagues illumines the unfamiliar but fascinating figures who fostered a tremendously popular faith-based movement with an enduring influence on the practice of philanthropy. Although the *Christian Herald*'s relief campaigns may have been eclipsed by enormous charitable foundations, professionalized social work, and state-sponsored aid programs, the newspaper's grassroots, volunteer, and unapologetically evangelical approach to relieving suffering has remained compelling for a considerable portion of the American population to the present day.

Studying the role of popular religious media in shaping the development of humanitarianism highlights how and why ordinary people have engaged in efforts to aid the afflicted. Because so many scholars have focused on the work of corporate charities or government agencies in providing assistance for those in need, histories of American philanthropy have typically emphasized the contributions of business tycoons, social elites, and political officials in founding prominent institutions—leaders such as Andrew Carnegie with his various foundations for the advancement of education, Jane Addams with her settlement work at Hull House, and Herbert Hoover with his missions to aid starving Europeans after World War I through the American Relief Administration. Some accounts have analyzed the intellectual influences of social gospel theorists such as Walter Rauschenbusch or economic philosophers like Richard Ely. This book brings into view a different cast of characters. Tracing Louis Klopsch's transformation from duplicitous convict to "captain of philanthropy" and proprietor of the world's premier religious newspaper shows how an entrepreneurial publisher, his enterprising partners, and a diverse community of readers from all across the United States and every walk of life participated in the making of humanitarianism during a transitional period in American history.[12]

As the account of Klopsch's youthful escapades suggests, his spectacular success in arousing sympathy for the poor, the downtrodden, and the distressed is anything but a straightforward saga of heroic self-sacrifice for the sake of suffering others. Like many tales of benevolent campaigns on behalf of "those less fortunate," this history exposes how instances of exceptional generosity have been bound up with personal self-interest and broader political agendas; how charitable engagement has been shaped by a mix of sincere religious convictions, shrewd business calculations, and complex cultural presumptions; how even the best intentions often produce tragic outcomes; and how the practice of philanthropy has always involved the exercise of privilege, prejudice, and power.[13]

A VEHICLE OF EVANGELICAL BENEVOLENCE

Klopsch's journey from ignominy to global influence began in earnest after his release from prison in 1877, when he returned to Manhattan and began to seek new outlets for his "very active brain" in the printing and publishing business. In the following years, he found a solid footing in the industry.[14] By the summer of 1884, he was back at Sing Sing—this time as a convert to evangelical Christianity and a leader of the children's assemblies at the Methodist camp meeting that gathered in a grove not far from the penitentiary. Putting his lively imagination to work, Klopsch proved very popular with the young people, who "delighted to hear him tell his interesting stories."[15]

Through his evangelical activities, Klopsch came into contact with the "philanthropic labors" of the Reverend Stephen Merritt, pastor of the Jane Street Methodist Church in New York City. In 1886, Klopsch married Merritt's daughter, Mary—a sympathetic partner who shared his enjoyment of children (they had four) and supported his growing enthusiasm for combining religious journalism with Christian charity. Around this time, Klopsch also formed a partnership with the well-known preacher Thomas De Witt Talmage, editor of *Frank Leslie's Illustrated Sunday Magazine* and pastor of the "undenominational" Brooklyn Tabernacle—the largest church in the United States, with a seating capacity of five thousand, an even more extensive membership, and a national reputation.[16]

Like Klopsch, Talmage exhibited a proclivity for sensationalism that got him in trouble with authorities. Back in 1879, while Klopsch was trying to establish himself as a respectable businessman, Talmage was put on trial by fellow clergyman who accused him of dishonesty, deception, and "improper methods of preaching which tend to bring religion into contempt." Undaunted, Talmage defended himself with aplomb. "When I am called a sensationalist, I take it as a compliment," he declared. "God helping me, I will make it more true." When Klopsch, who also "did not object to being called sensational," came into contact with Talmage during the 1880s, he recognized a kindred spirit. The two men struck up a warm friendship and eventually became close collaborators in a campaign to expand how American Christians imagined humanity and extended charity to the afflicted in the United States and around the world.[17]

During a trip to Europe and the Holy Land in 1899, Klopsch and Talmage solidified plans to purchase and produce the American edition of the *Christian Herald*—a popular British weekly newspaper founded in 1876 by the Reverend Michael Baxter, a preacher and philanthropist with many connections to the transatlantic evangelical community. In 1878, Baxter had sent an agent to the United States to begin publication of a New York version of the periodical. By the time Talmage and Klopsch approached Baxter about acquiring the *Christian Herald*, the American paper had achieved a respectable circulation of approximately thirty thousand. It had "much in it of value," the partners believed, but "if it could be dedicated more especially to readers of the United States, its

Thomas De Witt Talmage and Louis Klopsch. From the *Christian Herald,* December 4, 1895, 811. Courtesy of the Christian Herald Association, New York.

usefulness would become greater." When they returned to New York in early 1890 after successfully negotiating with Baxter, Klopsch and Talmage embarked on their new venture with verve.[18]

From the outset, Klopsch and Talmage "had two leading purposes in view" for their project. First, they strove to make the *Christian Herald* the most successful religious paper in the world by creating a cohesive community of readers bound together by "broad evangelical" sentiment. Second, they planned to accomplish "many good works through the agency of the *Christian Herald*," with the hope that their publication would become "a medium of American bounty to the needy" around the globe. Within several years, the partners made impressive progress toward these interrelated goals. Circulation increased exponentially during the first decade of their leadership. By the turn of the twentieth century, the newspaper had almost a quarter million subscribers—nearly double the amount of its closest competitor among religious periodicals (the *Sunday School Times* had approximately 140,000). It was on par with or well in excess of other literary and illustrated weeklies, including *Collier's* (circulation 263,131), *Leslie's Illustrated* (70,300), and *Harper's* (whose subscription base totaled somewhere between 40,000 and 75,000).[19]

The *Christian Herald*'s readers came from all across the United States as well as from other nations and included members of large, historic churches such as the Baptists, Congregationalists, Episcopalians, Methodists, and Presbyterians, as well as participants in nondenominational organizations such as the American Sunday School Union, the Christian and Missionary Alliance (CMA), Christian Endeavor, and the Young Men's Christian Association (YMCA). The newspaper's international scope and expansive reach among a wide range of American Protestants made the publication unique among religious periodicals during the late nineteenth century and well into the twentieth century, when its circulation reached a peak of nearly half a million subscribers.[20] "The establishment of the *Christian Herald* marked the beginning of a new epoch in the history of religious journalism in America," Klopsch later reflected. "It was something new to have a journal so broadly evangelical as to commend itself to all Christian denominations, as well as to those outside the denominational pale; which knew no sect or creed antagonisms, but treated all alike on the generous plane of Christian brotherhood."[21]

By adopting this innovative, ecumenical editorial policy, Klopsch and Talmage hoped not only to expand the *Christian Herald*'s circulation but also to bolster American evangelical solidarity amid growing discord. Throughout most of the nineteenth century, "evangelicalism" had generally referred to a loose, transatlantic alliance of Protestant believers who prioritized conversion, warmhearted piety, revivalism, and the reform of society. Within the United States, participants in this powerful tradition claimed responsibility for ensuring the success and stability of American political institutions, economic order, social relations, and spiritual health. Through revival campaigns, media productions, and charitable enterprises, the evangelical "united front" worked to shape every aspect of American life.[22]

By the 1890s, however, new trends in theology, biblical criticism, evolutionary science, sociology, and psychology were creating fissures in this broad-based coalition. Many evangelicals feared that increasing dissension would undermine their cultural authority and the United States' identity as a "Christian nation." Concerns about rising immigration, deteriorating race relations, escalating labor unrest, the expansion of imperialism, and other unsettling issues exacerbated these worries. Within this context, Klopsch and Talmage proclaimed that their newspaper would refuse to publish articles on controversial doctrinal subjects or divisive political topics. Instead, the *Christian Herald* would embrace "the widest catholicity" and seek to promote spiritual cohesion among its constituents. "Through the instrumentality of an undenominational journal," one contemporary observed, Klopsch and Talmage aimed to "gather together the scattered fragments . . . and bind them in a great, united, happy family circle of Christian believers."[23]

One of the most powerful strategies for fostering harmony among an increasingly fractious evangelical community, Klopsch and Talmage argued, was to engage people of diverse theological perspectives and social backgrounds in a common enterprise of serving others. Participating in cooperative efforts to aid the afflicted, they believed, would enable individuals to set aside doctrinal differences, denominational preferences, regional disputes, social prejudices, class antagonisms, and cultural disagreements. By joining together to uplift the downtrodden, American evangelicals would also help ensure the ongoing stability of the nation's political institutions, economic achievements, social values, and international reputation.

With these broader aims in mind, Klopsch and Talmage endeavored to make the *Christian Herald* a vehicle of evangelical benevolence. Shortly after acquiring the newspaper, they started to solicit their subscribers' support for a wide range of charitable enterprises. Drawing on their shared passion for drama and spectacle, the partners barraged readers with reports of humanitarian crises around the globe as well as on

American soil. Soon, they moved beyond merely chronicling catastrophes to actively spearheading relief efforts by collecting contributions and taking a direct role in distributing aid. In the spring of 1892, the *Christian Herald* publicized its first official campaign to alleviate affliction: a food fund for famished peasants in Russia. Over the next several years, Talmage and Klopsch organized many more efforts to ease suffering of all sorts. During the winter of 1894, they encouraged readers to help families in New York City made destitute in the recent economic downturn. The following year, they solicited assistance for Armenians displaced by political violence in the Ottoman Empire. Next, they partnered with the federal government to rescue Cubans from starvation. From 1897 through the turn of the century and beyond, they engaged in massive fund-raising efforts to provide for victims of famine, earthquake, warfare, and flood in India, China, Scandinavia, Macedonia, Japan, Italy, and Mexico. At the same time, they offered ongoing support for ministries to the poor and downtrodden throughout the United States. By the time Klopsch died in 1910, the *Christian Herald*'s subscribers had donated over $3.3 million (equivalent to approximately $82.4 million in 2017) to domestic and international humanitarian causes.[24] Only the ARC, which became a quasi-governmental entity in 1900 and was subsidized after 1905 by congressional appropriations, rivaled the *Christian Herald*'s achievements as a relief agency during this period. No other grassroots charitable organization—religious or secular—came remotely close.[25]

In their efforts to establish the *Christian Herald* as the nation's foremost provider of humanitarian aid at home and abroad, Klopsch and Talmage enlisted the support of political leaders, influential businessmen, missionary agencies, and reform organizations. From the outset, they sought endorsements from ambassadors, secretaries of state, senators, congressmen, governors, and presidents. Talmage boasted that he counted Grover Cleveland and William McKinley as good friends, and Klopsch never failed to publicize commendations of the *Christian Herald*'s benevolent work from Theodore Roosevelt, William Taft, and other high-ranking officials. The partners also proved adept at cultivating relationships with prominent figures in other nations. When they traveled to Russia in conjunction with the *Christian Herald*'s first international humanitarian campaign for famine relief, for example, the two men were honored by the imperial family. Later they would interact with diplomats, heads of state, and royals from Great Britain, China, Denmark, Finland, Italy, Japan, Norway, and Sweden.[26]

Soliciting support for their aid efforts from powerful businessmen such as department store magnate John Wanamaker and bankers at Drexel, Morgan & Co. was also a priority for Klopsch and Talmage. At the same time, they insisted that almsgiving was not only the pursuit of a privileged elite but a popular practice in which every evangelical—no matter how humble—ought to participate. For this reason, the partners sought to join forces with missionary agencies and benevolent organizations striving to lessen suffering through outreach and reform. During their time at the helm of the *Christian Herald,* Klopsch and Talmage worked closely with well-known religious leaders, including James Barton, who served as the foreign secretary of the American Board of Commissioners on Foreign Missions (ABCFM); Frances Willard, president of the Woman's Christian Temperance Union (WCTU); and William Booth, founder and first general of the Salvation Army.[27]

By fostering such an expansive network of influential contacts, Klopsch and Talmage aimed to give the *Christian Herald* "the highest imaginable prestige, and put it upon a pinnacle of popularity as an organ of widespread humanitarianism such as no other publication in the world has ever before enjoyed." Their extraordinary success showcases the vital part they and their many collaborators played in inspiring American Protestants from diverse backgrounds to extend compassion across national borders, racial and ethnic barriers, and religious boundaries. Through their energetic outreach and inventive methods, these evangelicals created a novel and extremely influential channel for the exercise of faith-based benevolence within and well beyond the United States.[28]

DEBATES IN EVANGELICAL CHARITY

By analyzing the strategies Klopsch and Talmage employed to arouse sympathy, raise money, and provide relief for suffering people around the world, this book offers a fuller account of how evangelical media and its consumers contributed to the development of American humanitarianism. Exploring the *Christian Herald*'s efforts to alleviate affliction also brings into focus the various social forces, cultural norms, theological motivations, and political dynamics that shaped—and limited—the meanings and methods of evangelical charity during a pivotal period in the history of philanthropy.

When Klopsch first acquired the newspaper in 1890, for example, concerns about poverty and vice in urban settings were proliferating as income inequality spiraled, violent conflicts between capital and labor became more frequent, and revolutionary movements such as communism and anarchism gained popularity. Anxieties about the widening gap between rich and poor continued to escalate in the aftermath of the devastating financial downturn of 1893. As unemployment and privation reached unprecedented levels, evangelicals engaged in heated disputes with social Darwinists and proponents of "scientific philanthropy" about the causes of the social crisis and the proper conduct of charity. Were the poor responsible for their plight, or were broader structural conditions to blame? Would "indiscriminate almsgiving" encourage pauperism rather than inculcating moral virtues such as industriousness and sobriety? Did the destitute have to be worthy to receive aid? If so, what criteria determined who was deserving?

Debates about how to contend with poverty and unemployment in the United States also affected how *Christian Herald* readers viewed their responsibility to assist sufferers in other regions of the world. With increasing globalization, American evangelicals were encountering people of diverse political, ethnic, and religious affiliations more regularly than in any previous period. For visionaries like Klopsch and Talmage, these interactions presaged the dawning of a new, divinely ordained age of international unity. By aiding the afflicted of every nation, they contended, participants in the *Christian Herald*'s relief campaigns would help foster solidarity among God's children all around the world and in so doing help usher in Christ's kingdom of universal peace and goodwill.[29]

Although most American evangelicals agreed that alleviating distress was a scriptural duty, they often argued over whom, when, and how to help. Should assisting Muslim survivors of a catastrophic earthquake in Constantinople take precedence over rescuing Armenians from the "Christian-hating Mohammedans" who were slaughtering them? At what point did the United States have an obligation to act as the Good Samaritan toward neighboring Cubans suffering under Spanish rule? Was it right for evangelical philanthropists to support military intervention as a mode of humanitarian action, or was feeding the hungry and clothing the naked the only appropriate expression of Jesus's compassion?[30]

These controversies over how best to aid the poor and oppressed in distant lands reflected deeper disagreements about the United States' global mission. While some evangelicals celebrated American expansionism as a God-given opportunity to extend freedom, democracy, prosperity, and Christian civilization around the world, others worried that imperialism undermined the gospel message of harmony and equality among people of every tribe and tongue. Still others questioned whether the United States was really qualified to liberate or uplift the downtrodden in other nations when so many within its own borders were subject to political exclusion, economic exploitation, and racial violence.

The *Christian Herald*'s efforts to engage readers in campaigns to relieve suffering at home and abroad reveal how assumptions about race and ethnicity, gender and sexuality, civilization and citizenship, national identity, international politics, and religious belonging influenced evangelical charity during this crucial phase of American history. By examining how Klopsch and Talmage wrestled with the dilemmas and tensions that accompanied their attempts to care for strangers in distress, this book aims to put contemporary debates about faith-based humanitarianism in broader historical perspective.

As I worked on this project, I had the privilege of interacting with many people engaged in serving others through the Christian Herald Association as well as through evangelical charities such as Bread for the Hungry, the Salvation Army, and World Vision. Colleagues at these organizations attested that many of the theological, social, and political conundrums that perplexed their predecessors in the fields of domestic philanthropy and foreign aid remain vexing and unresolved. Ongoing deliberations about welfare and immigration policies, best practices in poverty relief, the ethics of international aid, the propriety of faith-based diplomacy, and the enduring entanglement of humanitarian intervention with American imperialism continue to make assuaging affliction a complex, contentious, and challenging process. The story of the *Christian Herald*'s charitable campaigns provides a wider frame for reflecting on these current difficulties and disagreements. By recounting this history, *Holy Humanitarians* invites us to consider how racial prejudices and gender biases, nationalist ambitions and capitalist aspirations, class discriminations, and religious antipathies have influenced efforts to extend Christ's compassion from Klopsch's time to our own day.

1

A RELIGIOUS PAPER THOROUGHLY HUMANITARIAN

"My entire theology has condensed into one word, and that a word of four letters, and that word is 'help,'" the Reverend Thomas De Witt Talmage told his parishioners one frigid Sunday morning in January 1879. "How shall I help the people?" In an era of intensifying urbanization, ongoing instability in world financial markets, escalating immigration, expanding unemployment, labor unrest, rampant poverty, and rapid globalization, his was a pressing question for American evangelicals. Since accepting a call to the Brooklyn Tabernacle ten years earlier, Talmage had been experimenting with ways of applying the Bible to the problems of contemporary society through passionate (some said sensational) sermons, public lectures, and forays into journalism. These efforts earned him fierce detractors who dismissed him as a "mountebank" or a "buffoon" and tried to have him defrocked. Yet Talmage's fervent attempts to reach the masses and to offer help for all who were "finding life a tremendous struggle" won praise from fellow evangelicals seeking to alleviate affliction at home and abroad amid the turmoil of the Gilded Age.[1]

For admirers such as the former felon and aspiring publisher Louis Klopsch, Talmage's determination to address the "hunger and suffering and want and wretchedness" that plagued the modern world proved particularly inspiring. Talmage's call for sympathy with the downtrodden especially appealed to a young man who had been forced to quit school at an early age to help support his struggling immigrant family. When Klopsch's escapades landed him in prison, he came face-to-face with men for whom crime had seemed the only means of providing food for their wives and children. These experiences shaped Klopsch's perspective on affliction in profound ways, drawing him to Talmage and causing him to question the popular notion that the poor were to blame for their plight.[2]

Throughout the nineteenth century, many Protestants insisted that indigence was the product of indolence, intemperance, or iniquity. Wealth came to the worthy who worked hard, stewarded resources wisely, and lived virtuously. Although mishaps might sometimes cause unmerited hardship (especially for widows and orphans), most often the destitute were responsible for their distress.[3]

By the time Klopsch found his way to the Brooklyn Tabernacle after his release from jail, some evangelicals had begun to challenge these assumptions. The scale and severity of the social crises Americans confronted in the decades following the Civil War prompted a number of Protestant leaders to recognize the role of structural conditions in the production of poverty. A financial panic in 1873 provoked a devastating economic depression throughout the United States, resulting in unprecedented unemployment, heightened tensions between employers and workers, and a massive railroad strike in 1877. That same year, federal troops withdrew from the Southern states, leaving African Americans vulnerable to increasing violence and discrimination. Meanwhile, financial and social hardships overseas fueled massive migrations to the United States, crowding American cities and pressuring labor markets and neighborhood infrastructure.

Although the nation's economy improved after 1879, conflicts between capital and labor continued—coming to an explosive head in the Haymarket Affair of 1886. This incident exacerbated concerns about the rise of socialist, communist, and anarchist movements in Europe and on American soil, aggravating fears of revolution but also undermining confidence in the fundamental tenets of laissez-faire capitalism. Within this tumultuous context, evangelical leaders like Talmage began to acknowledge that inequality and indigence were not simply the result of individual moral failings but the products of broader social forces. Rather than condemning the poor, Talmage insisted, Christians ought to empathize with those whose misfortunes and "evil surroundings" contributed to their distress, dissipation, or even delinquency.[4]

For Klopsch, an ex-convict with scant education and few social advantages trying to make good in a volatile economic environment, Talmage's gospel was good news. Klopsch was attracted to the Brooklyn Tabernacle for obvious reasons. In the 1880s, he became actively involved as a Sunday school teacher and a trustee. During this period, he also worked to cultivate both a personal and professional relationship with his popular pastor. After achieving some success in the publishing world, Klopsch approached Talmage in 1885 with a proposition to syndicate the minister's weekly sermons to several hundred newspapers. Eager to expand his audience (and also to supplement his income), Talmage agreed to the "plan of a world-wide pulpit." Within several years, his messages of sympathetic service to the poor were being printed in over three thousand periodicals and reportedly reaching twenty million readers in the United States and other English-speaking countries, as well as being translated into several foreign languages.[5]

Emboldened by this achievement, Klopsch began to consider ways that he and Talmage could capitalize on their partnership and exercise an even greater influence on evangelical conceptions and practices of philanthropy. By the time the two friends departed for the Holy Land in October 1889, Klopsch had devised a plan. Rather than solely reprinting Talmage's sermons in other newspapers, he and his pastor would produce their own periodical. Convinced that popular media could play a crucial part in educating American evangelicals about the plight of suffering people in their own neighborhoods and around the world, Klopsch arranged to purchase the *Christian Herald* and persuaded Talmage to serve as editor.[6]

In the several years following their acquisition of the *Christian Herald*, these two entrepreneurial publicists cultivated common perspectives on poverty as well as shared habits of relieving affliction. Confident in the coming kingdom of God, the partners enthusiastically embraced modern journalism's innovative technologies and sensational tactics to advance Jesus's reign of righteousness, justice, and charity within and beyond the United States. "How shall I help the people?" Talmage asked in 1879. From 1890 onward, he and Klopsch would work out a variety of answers to this question in the columns of the *Christian Herald*.[7]

Beginning with a spring 1892 campaign to feed starving Russian peasants, Klopsch and Talmage strove to make their publication an "instrument by which . . . God's people all over the country could work out their plans for the betterment of humanity." During this initial foray into foreign aid, they developed fund-raising techniques, established operational procedures, and articulated theological motivations to guide future relief efforts and to distinguish the *Christian Herald*'s humanitarian enterprises from other philanthropic endeavors. By presenting their approach as exceptionally reliable and explicitly religious, Klopsch and Talmage worked to establish the *Christian Herald* as a major force in American aid abroad at a time when the United States was playing a more prominent role in world affairs.[8]

Encouraged by their ability to cultivate compassion for overseas sufferers, Klopsch and Talmage turned their energies to escalating concerns about the plight of the poor and working classes at home. As debate intensified about how to solve the social crisis, these evangelicals encouraged readers to support a variety of legislative measures, reform movements, and religious enterprises designed to mitigate the adverse effects of laissez-faire capitalism among the nation's most vulnerable populations. When an economic downturn in the autumn of 1893 resulted in widespread unemployment, the *Christian Herald* announced the opening of a food fund to help the hungry and homeless in New York City.

Although this relief campaign was a great success, the newspaper's coverage of the financial crisis exposed ongoing disagreements among American Protestants about the causes of poverty and the proper conduct of charity. When proponents of scientific philanthropy criticized the *Christian Herald*'s efforts to assuage suffering, Klopsch and Talmage insisted that no one was beyond redemption. Uplifting the downtrodden, they contended, was a religious duty that blessed the afflicted but also united evangelical benefactors at a time when this community was increasingly challenged by doctrinal controversy, social diversity, and regional discord. Through its humanitarian mission, these publicists proclaimed, the *Christian Herald* not only would bind up the wounds of the brokenhearted struggling to survive amid the profound dislocations of modern life, but also would help heal the divisions that threatened to undermine evangelical unity in this fractious era.

A NEW MEDIUM FOR EVANGELICAL AID

Klopsch and Talmage chose an auspicious time to experiment with evangelical media as a means of influencing perceptions of poverty and practices of philanthropy. In the months leading up to their acquisition of the *Christian Herald*, a terrible disaster highlighted the role popular publications could play in stimulating concern for those who were suffering. On May 31, 1889, the South Fork Dam on the Little Conemaugh River failed, unleashing a torrent of water on Johnstown, Pennsylvania. At least 2,200 people were killed in the flood and the ensuing fires, which engulfed the small frame tenement houses by the river that were home to the employees of Cambria Iron and Steel Company and their families. The tragedy resulted in the worst loss of civilian life in American history to that point and created an outpouring of sympathy for the victims.[9]

When Talmage visited the devastated area shortly after the flood, he was shocked by the desolation and took up a collection among constituencies in Brooklyn and New York that ultimately amounted to $95,905 (according to his records). Newspapers moved quickly to publicize the catastrophe through graphic accounts of the "awful holocaust," and called on readers from across the nation to contribute to relief efforts. Donations poured in to various charitable agencies, including the fledgling American Red Cross (ARC). For Clara Barton, the Johnstown calamity offered an opportunity to build her organization's reputation as a civilian relief agency that was especially well equipped to deal with disasters of this magnitude. "Sickness, sorrow, and destitution, in the proportions existing there," one reporter argued, "can be alleviated only by systematic, well-organized effort; and this is precisely what Miss Barton's experience fits her to supply." As Klopsch worked to formulate plans for his own charitable enterprise, he aimed to combine this emerging emphasis on efficiency with the demonstrated power of popular journalism to invoke sympathy for sufferers. The lessons of Johnstown showed that a well-run newspaper with a wide circulation could serve as an effective vehicle for inspiring compassion and easing affliction.[10]

Klopsch's confidence in the capacity of modern periodicals to arouse concern for the distressed arose in part from his convictions about God's work in the world. Like many evangelicals of the era, Klopsch and Talmage interpreted advances in science, engineering, commerce, education, government, and—perhaps most importantly—popular media as harbingers of Christ's coming kingdom. This postmillennial optimism bolstered their assurance that an innovative religious newspaper dedicated to humanitarian causes could hasten the extension of justice and mercy around the globe. Although Protestant leaders since Martin Luther had deployed print technologies to promote their message, recent improvements that allowed for faster reproduction of text, a wider range of visual imagery, and more efficient distribution methods had revolutionized the publishing industry and helped make popular journals more pervasive than ever. As a result, these evangelicals believed, the newspaper had become "the most important agency for influencing the public mind" and "making the world better."[11]

Motivated by these millennial expectations, Klopsch and Talmage set out to make the *Christian Herald* a potent force for advancing God's kingdom. During the first few months after they acquired the newspaper, the partners took several steps they hoped would move them toward this goal. In his initial greeting to subscribers, Talmage acknowledged that the *Christian Herald* had already accomplished a great deal under previous management. In fact, longtime associate editor J. B. Fernie, who had moved to New York from London in 1878 to help establish the American version of the newspaper, maintained his post under the new leadership. Although they valued Fernie's experience, Klopsch and Talmage also believed it was time to recruit some additional talent. First, they hired George H. Sandison, a successful newspaperman who worked for Joseph Pulitzer's influential *New York World*, to serve as managing editor. Over the next several years, Klopsch and Talmage also enlisted well-known journalists such as William Willard Howard and Sylvester Scovel, along with popular authors and hymn-writers like Amelia Barr, Fanny Crosby, Marion Harland (Mary Virginia Terhune), and Margaret Sangster, to write for the publication. At the same time, they expanded the newspaper's art department to include famous illustrators such as Albert Hencke and, eventually, professional photographers. With this staff in place, Klopsch and Talmage contended, the *Christian Herald* would be better positioned to address the challenges of modern society and help usher in the millennium.[12]

Harnessing the power of the press for these purposes was especially urgent, they argued, given the competition religious periodicals faced from secular publications advancing a very different agenda. As proponents of "new journalism" such as Pulitzer and William Randolph Hearst strove to "reach the masses with entertaining, low cost, and visually stimulating newspapers," many evangelical leaders worried that the content and style of these increasingly successful publications degraded the tone and character of national discourse. Because they pandered "to the tastes of bad men and worse women," Talmage warned, unscrupulous editors were undermining public morality. Rather than allowing tabloids such as Hearst's *New York Journal* or Pulitzer's *New York World* to monopolize the marketplace of ideas, he urged, religious publishers ought to consecrate the printing press to "high and holy objects." Within this context, the *Christian Herald* would serve as a vehicle for promoting "the Lord's cause" not only by steering public opinion in the right direction but also by motivating a community of constituents to participate in "great political, and social, . . . and moral enterprises" such as breaking "off a million chains," standing "for liberty against all oppression," and fostering "an all embracing sympathy" for suffering people around the globe.[13]

To attract readers away from salacious periodicals and instead engage them in good works that would expand Christ's kingdom to the ends of the earth, Klopsch and Talmage eagerly employed many of the same innovative editorial practices, printing processes, and visual technologies that helped make their secular competitors so successful. Soon after acquiring the *Christian Herald,* the partners declared that their paper would be full of "compressed news," "vivacious" anecdotes, and "vivid pictures" that would appeal to a wide audience. By including up-to-date coverage of current events, entertaining serial stories, adventurous tales of missionary life, and "even a little romance," these publicists aimed to provide a compelling alternative to the tabloid magazines as well as to somber and old-fashioned religious journals that emphasized doctrinal disputation or failed to keep up with contemporary topics. Although some observers worried that these editorial methods hewed too closely to the controversial tactics promoted by Hearst and Pulitzer, Klopsch and Talmage argued that spectacle and drama were legitimate means of advancing an evangelical agenda. Amid the intensifying competition provoked by sensational journalism, they insisted that gripping headlines, stirring stories, and attention-grabbing images were indispensable techniques for publicizing distressing situations and exposing "wrongs that ought to be righted" both in and beyond the United States.[14]

During their tenure at the *Christian Herald,* Klopsch and Talmage continued to face criticism from naysayers concerned about the propriety of their innovative approach to religious publishing. Catering to the public's appetite for entertainment, opponents cautioned, could compromise Christian values of sincerity and sobriety. Competing with secular journals, others warned, might lead to the embrace of a questionable commercialism. Klopsch's decision to deploy modern marketing strategies was a case in point. Instead of eschewing advertisements, as many religious periodicals did, the *Christian Herald* included a large section promoting products and services. In addition to showcasing Bibles and spiritual texts, the newspaper publicized patent medicines, dress patterns, premier typewriters, baking powder, preferred securities, stove polish, insurance plans, pianos, pipe organs, and rustproof corsets. For some evangelicals, these endorsements signaled the *Christian Herald*'s concession to worldliness, but Klopsch insisted that the revenues they provided offset production costs so that subscription fees could be kept low, making the publication more affordable for a larger number of readers. In his view, critics of the *Christian Herald*'s business practices or editorial policies failed to recognize that "the limitations with which religious journals were supposed to be surrounded" had become obsolete in the fast-paced, high-stakes world of modern media.[15]

Talmage agreed that current demands necessitated a more entrepreneurial form of Christian journalism. "Our ambition," he announced in his initial greeting to *Christian Herald* subscribers, "is to be spiritual, enterprising, and wide-awake evangelical." Although Talmage saw no conflict among these categories, some of his contemporaries were uncertain about blurring established boundaries between religious publishing and the popular press. Since Talmage had already been charged with bringing "religion into contempt" through his questionable preaching methods, detractors feared that his foray into evangelical journalism would also cast opprobrium on the cause of Christianity. Pointing to Talmage's proclivity for self-promotion, some cynics assumed that his stint at the *Christian Herald* was just one more crass publicity stunt. Others took an even darker view. Remembering that Talmage had been put on trial for "falsehood and deceit," the minister's harshest critics would eventually accuse him of profiting from the *Christian Herald*'s philanthropic projects.[16]

Financial gain was, in fact, an integral aspect—even a stated goal—of the *Christian Herald*'s benevolent enterprises. Klopsch's first notice to the newspaper's readers explained that he and Talmage had taken on this venture as a means of making money to defray the cost of erecting the new Brooklyn Tabernacle. Talmage's church had burned to the ground during a thunderstorm on October 13, 1889—just two weeks before he and Klopsch departed for the Holy Land. This was the second time the church had been destroyed by fire during Talmage's pastorate (and it would not be the last). To rebuild, Talmage needed at least $150,000. Why not enlist the *Christian Herald*'s subscribers to help fund-raise for this purpose, Klopsch suggested. Perhaps this proposition helped persuade Talmage to accept Klopsch's offer to become editor in chief: not only would this position augment Talmage's celebrity, it would also help him solve his financial problems. In February 1890, Klopsch announced that proceeds from all *Christian Herald* subscriptions obtained over the next twelve months would be donated to the Tabernacle building fund. This project, Klopsch declared, would be "the first of many good works which he hope[d] to effect through the agency of the *Christian Herald*."[17]

The new Brooklyn Tabernacle—a mammoth structure that could seat six thousand worshippers—was dedicated on Sunday, April 26, 1891, with great fanfare. The *Christian Herald*'s first charitable appeal had been a success. Despite the acclaim that accompanied this achievement, doubts about Talmage's integrity continued to plague him during his career as editor of the *Christian Herald*. Even after his death in 1902, "his ethical standards were seriously questioned." When the value of the minister's estate—$300,000, all of which he left to his heirs (a curious choice, some said, given his stated commitment to philanthropy)—was made public, one journalist joked that his fortune "recalls the old pun of the clergyman who said he was much devoted to the law and the profits." Another quipped that the "snug sum" Talmage had accumulated showed that "it pays to serve the Lord!"[18]

While Talmage was always a tempting target for faultfinders, Klopsch also found himself the subject of scrutiny on several occasions. Some found his ambition unseemly—chafing at his relentless efforts to "put his personality and his paper in the foreground," as one opponent put it. After Klopsch's death in 1910, a former employee familiar with his business dealings demanded a public inquiry into the publisher's accounting practices at the *Christian Herald,* claiming that the "charity funds collected through the agency of that periodical were all deposited into Dr. Klopsch's own private bank account" against which "the philanthropist might check at will for the expenses of himself" or of the periodical. Although no formal investigation took place, auditors did discover that the Klopsch estate owed more than $110,000 to various *Christian Herald* charities. His heirs made the transfers without a fuss, and most observers concluded that there had been nothing nefarious in the publicist's practice of mingling his personal funds with those of the periodical he owned and operated. While some expressed dismay that this world-renowned humanitarian left his family an estate valued at almost $900,000 without making any charitable bequests, others defended his remarkable work on behalf of the afflicted and lamented efforts "to cloud the memory of one of the great philanthropists of the age."[19]

Klopsch began building this reputation in the months following the dedication of the Brooklyn Tabernacle. Having successfully enlisted the cooperation of the *Christian Herald*'s readers in this first charitable campaign, he and Talmage sought additional avenues for making their newspaper "a mighty power for good." With so many people suffering—from the flooded banks of the Little Conemaugh River, to the impoverished neighborhoods of Lower Manhattan, to the far ends of the earth—the opportunities to expand the *Christian Herald*'s humanitarian mission seemed endless.[20]

In August 1891, American media outlets received word of an ominous crisis occurring on the other side of the globe. A serious famine was causing terrible suffering in Russia. "In many districts, peasants are dying of hunger, while the survivors attempt to sustain life on grass, boiled in water," the *Christian Herald* reported. The newspaper continued to carry accounts of the worsening conditions over the coming months. By February 1892, an estimated forty million people throughout the empire were starving. Although the Russian government and many of its private citizens were making "almost superhuman efforts" to aid the afflicted, the relief they offered amounted to "little more than a drop of comfort in the wide ocean of human woe." With an empty treasury and the "government credit in a wretched condition," the tsar's resources for feeding his people had reached their limits. Unless help came from outside sources, Russia's starving millions would perish.[21]

While some skeptics balked at the idea of aiding a "despotic power like Russia," whose "selfish and inhuman government" kept "the peasantry . . . in an unprogressive and dependent condition," Klopsch and Talmage insisted that American evangelicals had an obligation to help the famine sufferers. Although they recognized that political decisions and long-term structural factors had contributed to the crisis and needed to be addressed, they argued that emergency assistance was a moral and spiritual necessity. This "calamity is one that awakens universal sympathy, and imposes a duty on Christians everywhere," the editors proclaimed. In mid-March, they announced that the *Christian Herald* would open a relief fund for the starving peasants. Readers who were "ready to extend the hand of the Samaritan to Russia" could send their donations directly to the paper, which would use the money to purchase food supplies. Talmage and Klopsch each gave $100 to get the collection off to a good start.[22]

Over the next several weeks, contributions came in from across the country, and the fund grew beyond expectations. Encouraged by the response to their appeal, the partners set the ambitious goal of sending a million pounds of flour to Russia. The first installment shipped out in April on the steamer *Conemaugh* along with donations collected by the Citizens' Famine Relief Committee of Philadelphia. Two months later, a second shipment totaling more than fifteen hundred tons of flour, corn, potatoes, and other cereals was loaded onto the *Christian Herald* relief steamer *Leo* at the Atlantic Dock in Brooklyn. Klopsch and Talmage announced that they would both travel to Russia at their own expense to superintend the distribution of supplies. When the ship arrived in Saint Petersburg in mid-July, Russian authorities had prepared a lavish reception for their American guests, including an audience with the imperial heir, Tsarevich Nicholas. Later in the trip, Talmage was summoned to a meeting with Tsar Alexander III himself, who warmly thanked the American people and *Christian Herald* contributors for their generosity toward his suffering subjects.[23]

Thrilled with the welcome they received from both starving peasants and the highest ranks of the nobility, Klopsch and Talmage declared their Russian famine relief campaign a success far in excess of anything they had anticipated. Having rubbed shoulders with royalty and raised over $32,000 to purchase more than three million pounds of foodstuffs, they returned home full of enthusiasm for their publication's prospects as a means of extending evangelical charity to foreign nations. "We feel honored in the fact that the *Christian Herald* has been made the channel through which these magnificent donations have been sent," they wrote. "No newspaper ever undertook such a work with more gratifying results." Although this claim was exaggerated—in fact, the *Northwestern Miller,* a Minneapolis-based trade journal, had collected an estimated $200,000 and shipped approximately 5.6 million pounds of corn and flour to Russia during the summer of 1892—the *Christian Herald*'s entrance into the arena of international aid did represent a pivotal development in the history of evangelical humanitarianism. During this first foreign relief effort, Klopsch and Talmage pioneered techniques for interesting American Protestants in the plight of distant strangers that would shape evangelical responses to distress at home and abroad in years to come.[24]

From the outset of the Russian aid campaign, the *Christian Herald* employed several strategies for eliciting compassion for famine sufferers on the far side of the globe. As they prepared to announce the opening of the relief fund, Klopsch and Talmage began to barrage readers with increasingly riveting accounts of peasants' distress. "Every mail brings additional details of the terrible famine in Russia, a calamity that eclipses

any of the same character during the present century," one article announced in early February. "Whole families—parents and children—lying
huddled together, and half frozen and numbed in body and brain, some
already beyond human aid. . . . Roots, grasses and other substitutes for
food dried and pulverized to make 'hunger bread' till the poor body falls
fever-smitten and the pestilential typhus follows on the heels of famine
and finishes its work." Klopsch and Talmage hoped reports like these
would awaken "the divine sympathy which every Christian feels for
those in affliction" and prompt all to come to their aid. If these stories
were not enough to arouse concern for Russia's starving millions, the
publishers trusted that images could help incite readers to action. "Today
we present a still more striking picture in which the artist, with realistic
pencil, has depicted the interior of a cottage of Russian peasants," they
declared in an early account of the disaster. The drawing portrayed a
family, "helpless and starving, huddled together awaiting relief or—at the
worst—death to end their misery."[25]

The confidence these evangelical publicists expressed in the power
of heartrending narratives and images to evoke sympathy for distant sufferers was rooted in long-standing assumptions about the role of print
media in stimulating humanitarian sensibilities. Beginning in the late
seventeenth century, Enlightenment philosophers such as John Locke,
David Hume, Frances Hutcheson, and Adam Smith began to develop a
new theory of ethics that located morality primarily in the emotions and
encouraged individuals to practice virtue by identifying with the distress
of strangers. Reading stories that aroused affections by detailing the ago-
nies of the afflicted became an important avenue for fostering moral
sentiments and inspiring social movements to alleviate various forms of
misery. Proponents of sentimental ethics also argued that images were
an essential means for developing compassion and motivating reform.[26]

Over the course of the nineteenth century, the exponential growth
of evangelical revivalism and the emergence of Romanticism—both movements that stressed the primacy of feelings—helped further the culture
of sensibility and fuel the production of humanitarian literature and pictorial representations designed to encourage compassion for new categories of sufferers. During the abolitionist agitations of the antebellum
era, for example, antislavery advocates drew on this ethic of "sentimental
sympathy" to demonstrate the shared humanity of enslaved Africans.

Combining harrowing accounts and gruesome illustrations of the injuries of the oppressed would, they believed, incite benevolent action on behalf of these afflicted others.[27]

By the 1890s, evangelical leaders like Klopsch and Talmage had fully embraced the belief that print media were a crucial means of advancing humanitarian projects, and they eagerly employed emerging technologies of popular journalism to interest their readers in the affliction of famine-stricken peasants. As an enterprising publisher always ready to adopt modern methods, Klopsch exploited innovations such as the Kodak portable camera—which enabled travelers, missionaries, and newspaper correspondents to document catastrophes in foreign lands. He also took advantage of advances in halftone printing techniques, which facilitated the mass reproduction of original photographs, to fill the *Christian Herald*'s pages with pictures and expose subscribers to the suffering of distant strangers.[28]

The graphic descriptions and illustrations of Russia's woe generated an outpouring of sympathy for the hungry peasants, just as Klopsch and Talmage hoped they would. "My heart aches when I read of those starving people," one reader wrote. "How I pity them," another proclaimed. Subscribers explained that narratives and images of famine's horrors not only roused their emotions but also moved them to respond. "My wife showed me a copy of the *Christian Herald* containing an account of the Russian sufferers, and the matter worried me so that I felt I had to do something," reported a reader who donated $60 to the relief fund. A group of boys from the Presbyterian Orphanage of Paschalville, Pennsylvania, "were touched" after reading stories of the distress and took up a collection totaling $2.76.[29]

As contributions accumulated, Klopsch and Talmage articulated the principles that guided the relief effort. First, the partners promised to account for all monies collected in the columns of the *Christian Herald*. "Every offering, no matter how small, will receive acknowledgment," they declared. Whether a well-off merchant sent $60 or a group of needy orphans gave $2.76, the paper would print the news. Second, they insisted that this was "a blessed work in which all should share." Since each mite mattered— even a nickel would buy a loaf of bread—every subscriber, whether poor or rich, young or old, ought to participate. Finally, Klopsch and Talmage pledged that every penny, dime, and dollar sent through the *Christian*

Starving peasants during Russia's famine. From the *Christian Herald,* April 13, 1892, cover. Courtesy of the Christian Herald Association, New York.

Herald would reach Russia "in full and unimpaired value." When questions arose about the best methods of distributing aid, both men determined to travel to Saint Petersburg to make sure that the newspaper's donations were delivered to suffering peasants in the interior provinces.[30]

Through these fund-raising strategies, Klopsch and Talmage sought to establish the *Christian Herald* as an accessible and reliable instrument for extending evangelical charity abroad. Their success depended in part on the familiarity of their tactics. Several other agencies, including a number of prominent newspapers, had adopted similar practices to engage the American public in foreign aid campaigns. Over a decade earlier, in fact, the *New York Herald* had first popularized the notion that periodicals could serve as benevolent organizations. In February 1880, the journal's proprietor, James Gordon Bennett, announced the opening of a relief fund for Irish famine sufferers. In his appeal, Bennett promised to publish the names of all donors, solicited offerings of any amount, and vowed to distribute contributions promptly and properly. He also gave $100,000 out of his own pocket.[31]

Although some critics condemned Bennett's campaign as a vulgar publicity ploy, others commended his newspaper for providing a great public service. "The *Herald* has discovered a still more important field in the capabilities of the journalist," one commentator observed, "to wit, its power to enlist popular sympathy in behalf of the suffering." Talmage noted at the time that "the effect of Mr. Bennett's gift this week has been electric beyond all description." By the early 1890s, several other publications, including the *New York Evening Post* and the *New York Tribune,* had entered the field of philanthropy. When famine struck Russia in the fall of 1891, midwestern periodicals such as the *Northwestern Miller* in Minnesota and the *Davenport Democrat* in Iowa were among the first to organize relief efforts. The *Christian Herald*'s foray into foreign aid built on these precedents but proposed a new departure.[32]

Klopsch and Talmage suggested that as a journal with national rather than regional ambitions, their publication was specially positioned to reach a wide range of readers from all sections of the United States. Throughout the Russian relief campaign, they repeatedly underscored the broad scope of the *Christian Herald*'s appeal. As offerings arrived from across the nation, the newspaper published the names or initials of every donor, including their city and state of residence whenever possible. These lists confirmed that gifts came from all corners of the country and almost every place in between. Letters from subscribers also indicated that the *Christian Herald* was successfully drawing in new groups of contributors. "I am so glad that a way is opened for those in the rural districts not able to join in the collections in the cities, to bestow their mites to alleviate the terrible sufferings of those poor people," wrote a woman from Fayette, Iowa.[33]

The *Christian Herald*'s status as a religious publication also set its charitable ventures apart from the philanthropic endeavors of newspapers like the *New York Herald* or the *Davenport Democrat*. For the first time, an avowedly evangelical journal undertook an unequivocally Christian work of relief. Whereas the editor of the *Northwestern Miller*, William C. Edgar, appealed to his constituents not "as Protestants or Catholics, as Christian or Hebrews," but asked them to help the famine-stricken "simply . . . in the name of humanity," Klopsch and Talmage couched their entreaties in explicitly theological terms. "Send on to us your contribution," they demanded. "We are sure you will be faithful. Then, when your day of distress comes . . . the great Judge will bend smilingly to you in memory of this generosity and say: 'I was naked and ye clothed me; I was hungry and ye fed me; inasmuch as ye did this to poor starving Russia, ye did it unto me!'" From this perspective, aiding distant strangers was an act of obedience to God, "who commanded his children to feed the destitute and clothe the naked."[34]

By donating to the *Christian Herald* relief fund, Klopsch and Talmage contended, readers engaged in a devotional discipline of imitating "that Saviour who fed the hungry multitudes on the slopes of the Galilean shore." Through this spiritual practice, American evangelicals served as agents of divine blessing to the afflicted. "Who can deny that every loaf given to Russia 'In His Name' carries with it a benediction?" Sacks of flour were transformed into conduits of God's grace. "Lift up your heads, ye perishing thousands of Russia, while we put upon your lips this solemn sacrament of bread in the name of the Father, and of the Son, and of the Holy Ghost," Talmage preached at the send-off service for the first shipment of grain. Charity, in this view, was a sacred work that honored Christ, advanced personal holiness, and served suffering humanity.[35]

The *Christian Herald*'s theological approach to foreign aid appealed to American evangelicals who sympathized with the distress in Russia but were uncertain what channel to choose for their offerings. When these aspiring almoners discovered that the *Christian Herald* was collecting donations, the editors noted, they responded at once to the appeal. "We know from the hundreds of letters that have covered our table daily,"

Klopsch and Talmage declared, that contributors to the relief fund "esteemed it a precious privilege to give in such a cause." Indeed, donors regularly expressed their gratitude to the journal for acting as a medium of evangelical charity. "I have longed for a way to give to God," a woman from Woodland, Michigan, wrote. "Your paper opens ways to help various causes, and I hasten to begin."[36]

By framing famine relief as a spiritual discipline, the *Christian Herald* succeeded in attracting a diverse constituency of American evangelicals to participate: "Children and octogenarians, the manual worker and the student, the business man and the invalid, mothers crowded about with household cares, poor working-girls and the daughters of the rich—all classes and conditions of men and women, who believe in and desire to follow Him who went about doing good even as he had opportunity, have hastened to send their offerings." Gifts also came from a host of evangelical associations, including the Young People's Society of Christian Endeavor, women's aid organizations such as the King's Daughters, and Sunday schools from across the nation. Leaders from a variety of denominations also lent their support to this overtly Christian relief campaign. Evangelical luminaries such as Baptist pastor Russell Conwell of Philadelphia and Methodist minister Stephen Merritt publicly praised the *Christian Herald*'s efforts to "extend the hand of the Samaritan to Russia in her need." Heartened that their first humanitarian venture had garnered such widespread backing, Klopsch and Talmage commended contributors for following Jesus's teachings. "Probably there has never been a more remarkable spectacle of disinterested Christian charity than this," they declared.[37]

Even as they insisted that selfless devotion to Christ motivated their subscribers to participate in benevolent work on behalf of God's poor, Klopsch and Talmage never hesitated to highlight other incentives for engaging in international almsgiving. Throughout the Russian relief campaign, they suggested that extending humanitarian aid to distant sufferers offered evangelicals opportunities to play pivotal roles in augmenting American political, economic, and cultural influence abroad. In this era of increasing globalization, they argued, *Christian Herald* readers could reinforce diplomatic ties between the United States and other countries by assisting foreign nations facing domestic crises. Since Russia would "accept no official aid from other governments," and the U.S. Congress remained divided over whether appropriating funds to feed Russia's starving people was politically expedient or constitutionally permissible, Klopsch and Talmage contended that private citizens, philanthropic agencies, and religious organizations had a responsibility to cultivate "cordial international relations" between these long-standing allies by delivering relief. "The friendship of two great nations may be strengthened and made deep and enduring by the exercise of Christian charity," they proclaimed.[38]

Sending foodstuffs and financial aid overseas also showcased American affluence in an era of intensifying international trade. "What a blessing that this Russian appeal comes at a time when our barns are full of wheat and our cribs are full of corn!" Talmage intoned. Sharing this abundance with "old-world people in their distress," he implied, displayed the growing wealth of the world's "youngest Christian nation" and demonstrated that the United States was able to provide sustenance for less fortunate countries.[39]

In addition to fortifying diplomatic ties and expanding commercial markets, evangelical almsgiving enhanced the United States' international reputation. By sending food to Russia's famished peasants, contributors to the *Christian Herald*'s famine relief campaign provided proof of their country's outstanding generosity. "In this most beneficent work," Talmage and Klopsch maintained, "the American nation stands alone, for no other nation has contributed to the relief to any perceptible extent, and Russia profoundly and gratefully appreciates the fact." Through "this manifestation of Christian brotherly love and charity so cheeringly, lovingly and generously bestowed," evangelicals had helped establish the United States as the world's most munificent almoner.[40]

As relief efforts for Russia's starving millions wound down in the late summer of 1892, Klopsch and Talmage congratulated their readers for undertaking this "Christlike mission" of succoring distant strangers. Although the editors acknowledged that many other agencies had extended American philanthropy abroad during the previous months, they also underscored the unique contributions *Christian Herald* subscribers made to this enterprise. Certainly citizens' relief committees, trade journals like the *Northwestern Miller,* and aid organizations such as the ARC were to be commended for their admirable work on behalf of the hungry peasants, Klopsch and Talmage maintained. Yet evangelicals deserved special praise for bringing theological principles to bear on the practice of international humanitarianism. Through their generous self-sacrifice in submission to God and imitation of the "Saviour's . . . service to the poor," thousands of Christians from across the United States sent "a solemn sacrament of bread from nation to nation." Foreign aid, from this perspective, was an outward and visible sign that made manifest the sacred realities of "Christian brotherhood" binding American evangelicals to their neighbors on the other side of the globe. Klopsch and Talmage anticipated that this distinctively spiritual approach to humanitarian assistance would put their newspaper at the forefront of a new movement of global solidarity. With the help of the *Christian Herald* and its nationwide community, they hoped, the United States would soon inaugurate a new era of universal sympathy and international friendship among diverse peoples all around the world.[41]

THE GOSPEL OF WEALTH AND THE PLIGHT OF THE POOR

Buoyed by their foreign aid accomplishments, Klopsch and Talmage sought ways for the *Christian Herald* to help the less fortunate in their own country. Surely, the publicists reasoned, if they had succeeded in stirring up sympathy for famine sufferers in a faraway land, they would be able to foster compassion for the destitute and distressed closer to home. As they prepared to close the Russian relief fund in May 1892, the partners identified a group needing assistance right on their own doorstep. Military veterans, they discovered, were having trouble cashing their quarterly pension checks without paying exorbitant commissions to unscrupulous money dealers or saloonkeepers.[42]

Having served as a chaplain during the Civil War, Talmage was especially eager to combat this injustice. On May 4, 1892, the Christian Herald Check-Cashing Bureau opened in the basement of the pension office on Canal Street in Lower Manhattan. Klopsch provided all the capital necessary for paying out the checks at face value and staffing the operation out of his personal funds. The venture proved so popular among veterans that Klopsch and Talmage repeated it over the next three quarters in the hope that wealthy readers would replicate the benevolent work in other cities. Since few seem to have acted on this suggestion, the partners concluded that perhaps this type of assistance should come under government auspices rather than continue as a private charitable endeavor.[43]

Lobbying both the state and private citizens to take responsibility for relieving suffering among the needy became an increasingly regular practice as Klopsch and Talmage expanded the *Christian Herald*'s charitable mission within the United States. Although evangelicals of their ilk did not yet envision the establishment of government-sponsored welfare programs such as social security or unemployment insurance, they did support legislation they believed would better protect the poor against the machinations of mercenary capitalists who cared only for the accumulation of wealth.

By the summer of 1893, a developing crisis in financial markets was making the need for such regulations more apparent than ever. In May, the *Christian Herald* began to chronicle the looming threat of a panic on Wall Street resulting from the failure of several large investment firms. During July and August, the paper reported, severe market instability provoked "a wave of financial and commercial depression which . . . swept over the country, carrying down banks and corporations . . . shutting down the mines and closing up factories and industries that gave employment to many thousands of workers." In the wake of this catastrophe, Talmage penned an editorial blaming the disaster on "godless speculators" and calling for a purification of the commercial code.[44]

Talmage's plea for legislative action in response to the financial crisis of 1893 reflected his growing concern about the consequences of laissez-faire capitalism not only for American society but also for the global economic order. From the beginning of their time at the *Christian Herald,* Klopsch and Talmage had devoted considerable attention to this issue in the pages of the periodical. A few weeks after assuming management of the newspaper, for example, they published an account of the International Labor Conference that had met in Berlin from March 15 to 29, 1890. This gathering "for the amelioration of the condition of workingmen," the reporter observed, had exposed the "wrongs and miseries" of the laboring classes resulting from increased industrial competition and a lack of regulation to ensure fair wages and employment conditions. "The doctrines of political and social economy . . . that rule the world in our day," the author declared, "are opposed to any government interference with the relation between employers and employed." Unchecked, "the law of supply and demand" had left workers in all nations vulnerable to exploitation from greedy industrialists who built up great fortunes by paying laborers a pittance. Passing legislation "to prevent oppression, to protect the weak and poor from the cruel selfishness and rapacity of the rich and strong" was necessary to counteract these "doctrines of the devil" and ensure a just society.[45]

Talmage reiterated these arguments in a sermon preached and published in May 1890, just after workers throughout Europe and the United States took to the streets in demonstrations commemorating the Haymarket Affair. "That diabolical law of supply and demand," he proclaimed, "will yet have to stand aside," making way for "the law of love, the law of cooperation, the law of kindness, the law of sympathy. The Law of Christ." Those who relied on "the robber-firm of Supply and Demand" to regulate the economy were unrealistic and failed to appreciate the danger of escalating class antagonism. "It is the mightiest, the darkest, the most terrific threat of this century," Talmage warned. Only a Christianized social order, he suggested, could avert the looming menace of "a hemispheric war" between capital and labor. Without "some radical change," the gap between rich and poor would continue to grow and the shrinking middle class "upon whom the nation has depended for holding the balance of power and for acting as mediators between the two extremes" would disappear altogether. "We all see that there needs to be a redistribution of property," Talmage declared in another sermon several months later.[46]

Despite Talmage's claims about consensus, not everyone shared his confidence that legislation could solve the problems of wage inequality and oppressive working conditions. In fact, a number of the minister's contemporaries rejected his critiques of the economic system. Steel magnate Andrew Carnegie, for example, put forward a very different vision for dealing with friction between capital and labor. Several months before Talmage and Klopsch took over the *Christian Herald,* Carnegie published an essay entitled "Wealth" in which he contested the assumption that increasing income disparity was cause for dismay. "The contrast between the palace of the millionaire and the cottage of the laborer," he declared, "is not to be deplored, but welcomed as highly beneficial"—an inevitable outcome of the law of competition that governed society. Although he conceded that this law might be "hard for the individual," Carnegie insisted that it was best for humanity as a whole because it ensured the "survival of the fittest." Warning that those who interfered with the laws of individualism, private property, wealth accumulation, and competition threatened to undermine "the foundation upon which civilization itself rests," Carnegie rejected proposals for radically restructuring society through regulation. To ensure the "future progress of the race," he concluded, "the laws of accumulation will be left free; the laws of distribution free."[47]

Rather than requiring employers to raise salaries for workers who would surely squander the additional money "in indulgence of appetite," Carnegie queried, why not allow successful capitalists to return any surplus riches to the "masses of their fellows" in forms "calculated to do them lasting good"? Public parks, free libraries, educational institutions, music halls, art galleries, bathhouses, and churches offered "the best means of benefiting the community," he contended, because they "place within its reach ladders upon which the aspiring can rise." Donating to these institutions would enable the "man of wealth" to act as "the agent and trustee for his poorer brethren, bringing to their service his superior wisdom, experience and ability to administer, doing for them better than they would or could do for themselves." "Such in my opinion is the true Gospel concerning Wealth," Carnegie concluded, "obedience to which is destined some day to solve the problem of the Rich and the Poor, and to bring 'Peace on earth, among men Good-Will.'"[48]

Carnegie's "Wealth" energized debates about the causes of poverty and the proper responses to social conditions. Among partisans of laissez-faire capitalism, Carnegie's proposal "met a cordial reception." Social Darwinists also found his propositions about racial progress and philanthropy congenial. Some religious leaders endorsed aspects of Carnegie's "Gospel" as a modern reiteration of the Puritan work ethic that linked true Christianity with the values of industry, thrift, and stewardship. But others, including Talmage, Klopsch, and their colleagues at the *Christian Herald,* found most of Carnegie's message deeply troubling. Although they praised his efforts to deal with social inequality by building libraries and music halls, these evangelicals concluded that Carnegie's solution to "the great problem of our day" was not, in fact, "a solution at all." Admonishing millionaires to live modestly and give generously during their lifetimes was admirable but not nearly adequate to address wage disparities and unjust labor policies. Only fundamental structural changes could remedy the troubles embedded within the economic system.[49]

By autumn 1893, the inadequacy of Carnegie's approach had become increasingly apparent to evangelical leaders struggling to respond to the widespread misery of men, women, and children affected by the market downturn. As unemployment mushroomed in the months following the panic on Wall Street, the *Christian Herald* warned that the nation was facing a humanitarian crisis of unprecedented severity. While Talmage and Klopsch continued to press lawmakers to enact reforms that would redress income inequality and improve working conditions for the laboring classes over the long term, they also urged fellow believers to take immediate and more direct action to lessen affliction among victims of the financial depression. "During the present winter," they observed in January 1894, "the amount of suffering among the poor has been greatly increased and the numbers of the destitute have swelled beyond all previous proportions." To help alleviate the distress, the *Christian Herald* invited readers to contribute to a food fund for the hungry multitudes thronging the streets of New York.[50]

Donations sent to the newspaper, the editors announced, would support relief efforts at the Eighth Avenue Mission, run by members of the nearby Jane Street Methodist Episcopal Church, where Klopsch's father-in-law, the Reverend Stephen Merritt, served as pastor. For about a decade, Merritt had ministered to Lower Manhattan neighborhoods, where his "ready sympathy with the poor and struggling were felt throughout the streets and homes." Believing that the gospel was "the true and only remedy for the sorrows and miseries" he encountered in his pastoral work, Merritt determined that the church had to offer tangible help to people at the "lowest depth" of New York society—those with "barely enough rags to cover their forms" who dwelt in the city's vermin- and disease-infested tenements. With the support of some parishioners, Merritt opened a night mission on Eighth Avenue that provided medical assistance for the sick, distributed clothing to those in need, and welcomed all comers—even those "low and vile beyond conception"—to enjoy a cup of hot coffee and bread.[51]

By early January 1894, the Eighth Avenue Mission had been feeding over two thousand hungry people daily for several weeks. These included

CHRISTIAN HERALD
AND SIGNS OF OUR TIMES

COPYRIGHT 1894, BY LOUIS KLOPSCH.

VOLUME 17.

REV. T. DE WITT TALMAGE, D.D., Editor.
Offices, Bible House, New York.

NEW YORK, JANUARY 24, 1894.

NUMBER 4.

PRICE, 5 CENTS.
Annual Subscription, $1.50.

THE FRIEND OF THE HOMELESS.

Rev. Stephen Merritt's Great Work Among the Destitute in New York—Feeding Crowds of Famishing Men at the Eighth Avenue Mission Hall before Daylight every Morning, and Supplying the Hungry Mothers and Children in the Afternoon.

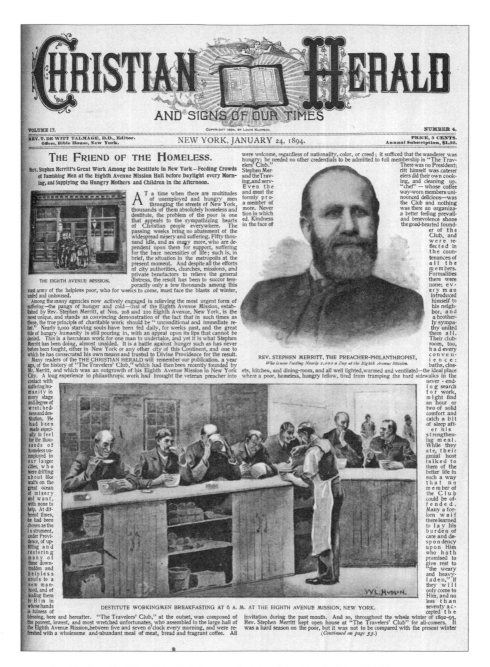

THE EIGHTH AVENUE MISSION.

AT a time when there are multitudes of unemployed and hungry men thronging the streets of New York, thousands of them absolutely homeless and destitute, the problem of the poor is one that appeals to the sympathizing hearts of Christian people everywhere. The passing weeks bring no abatement of the widespread misery and suffering. Fifty thousand idle, and as many more, who are dependent upon them for support, suffering for the bare necessities of life; such is, in brief, the situation in the metropolis at the present moment. And despite all the efforts of city authorities, churches, missions, and private benefactors to relieve the general distress, the result has been to succor temporarily only a few thousands among this vast army of the helpless poor, who for weeks to come, must face the blasts of winter, unfed and unhoused.

Among the many agencies now actively engaged in relieving the most urgent form of suffering—the pangs of hunger and cold—that of the Eighth Avenue Mission, established by Rev. Stephen Merritt, at Nos. 208 and 210 Eighth Avenue, New York, is the most unique, and stands as convincing demonstration of the fact that in such times as these, the true principle of charitable work should be "unconditional and immediate relief." Nearly 2,000 starving souls have been fed daily, for weeks past, and the great tide of hungry humanity is still pouring in, with an appeal upon its lips that cannot be denied. This is a herculean work for one man to undertake, and yet it is what Stephen Merritt has been doing, almost unaided. It is a battle against hunger such as has never before been fought, either in New York or any other city of this Continent, and one to which he has consecrated his own means and trusted to Divine Providence for the result.

Many readers of the THE CHRISTIAN HERALD will remember our publication, a year ago, of the history of "The Travelers' Club," which had then been recently founded by Mr. Merritt, and which was an outgrowth of his Eighth Avenue Mission in New York City. A long experience in philanthropic work had brought the veteran preacher into contact with suffering humanity in every stage and degree of wretchedness and destitution. He had been made especially to feel for the thousands of homeless unemployed in our larger cities, who were drifting about like waifs on the great ocean of misery and want, with none to help. At different times, he had been chosen as the instrument, under Providence, of uplifting and restoring many of these downtrodden and helpless souls to a new manhood, and of leading them to Him in whose hands is fulness of blessing, here and hereafter. "The Travelers' Club," at the outset, was composed of the poorest, lowest, and most wretched unfortunates, who assembled in the large hall of the Eighth Avenue Mission, between five and seven o'clock every morning, and were refreshed with a wholesome and abundant meal of meat, bread and fragrant coffee. All

were welcome, regardless of nationality, color, or creed; it sufficed that the wanderer was hungry; he needed no other credentials to be admitted to full membership in "The Travelers' Club."

Stephen Merritt and the Travelers, and serving, and meat the formly prominent a member of more. Never tion in which ed. Kindness in the face of

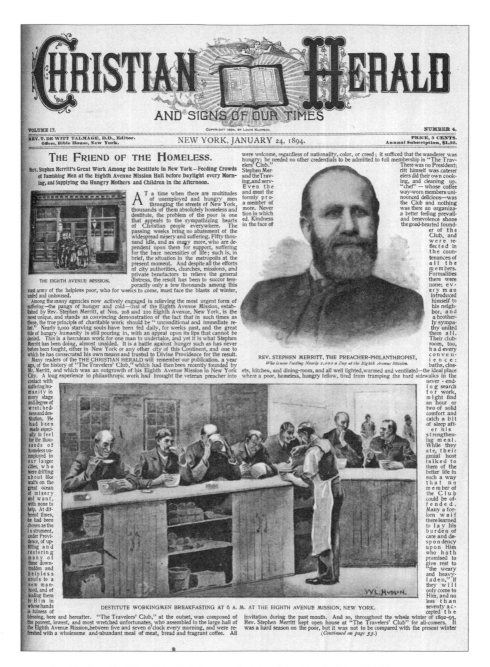

REV. STEPHEN MERRITT, THE PREACHER-PHILANTHROPIST,
Who is now Feeding Nearly 2,000 a Day at the Eighth Avenue Mission.

There was no President; Merritt himself was caterer elers did their own cooking, and cleaning up. "chef"—whose coffee way-worn members uniformly pronounced delicious—was the Club and nothing was there an organization a better feeling prevailed and benevolence shone the good-hearted founder of the Club, and were reflected in the countenances of all the members. Formalities there were none; every man introduced himself to his neighbor, and a brotherly sympathy united them all. Their clubroom, too, had every convenience: baths, closets, kitchen, and dining-room, and all well lighted, warmed and ventilated—the ideal place where a poor, homeless, hungry fellow, tired from tramping the hard sidewalks in the never-ending search for work, might find an hour or two of solid comfort and catch a bit of sleep after his strengthening meal. While they ate, their genial host talked to them of the better life in such a way that no member of the Club could be offended. Many a forlorn waif there learned to lay his burden of care and despondency upon Him who hath promised to give rest to "the weary and heavy-laden," if they will only come to Him, and no less than seventy accepted the invitation during the past month. And so, throughout the whole winter of 1892-93, Rev. Stephen Merritt kept open house at "The Travelers' Club" for all-comers. It was a hard season on the poor, but it was not to be compared with the present winter

DESTITUTE WORKINGMEN BREAKFASTING AT 6 A. M. AT THE EIGHTH AVENUE MISSION, NEW YORK.

(Continued on page 53.)

Rev. Stephen Merritt and the Eighth Avenue Mission. From the *Christian Herald,* January 24, 1894, cover. Courtesy of the Christian Herald Association, New York.

regular participants in Merritt's Travelers' Club—a group of chronically homeless and unemployed men of "all nationalities, creeds, colors" who met at the Mission for a meal between five and seven every morning—as well as many who had just lost their jobs in the recession. After serving breakfast to all who came to be fed, Merritt sent wagons around to local markets, restaurants, and hotels collecting surplus food to be distributed at the afternoon Women's Club meeting. For the past several months, Merritt had been paying all expenses of this ministry (about $10,000 so far) out of his own pocket (which was deeper than that of many of his peers since he ran a very successful undertaking business in addition to working as a pastor). But now, the *Christian Herald* reported, the work had extended far beyond Merritt's ability to fund it. Believing that his father-in-law's efforts to relieve suffering deserved support, Klopsch determined to help by giving from his personal resources and encouraging evangelicals across the country to do the same. "There is no stronger test of the sincerity of a Christian's love for the Master than his sympathy for the destitute," the paper intoned. Therefore, "we invite the attention of readers to this relief work as one that especially calls for their hearty Christian cooperation. Contributions may be addressed to the *Christian Herald*."[52]

Recognizing that subscribers might receive appeals for funding from other philanthropic agencies, the *Christian Herald* promoted Merritt's ministry as the most well suited to the challenges of the present crisis. "The Eighth Avenue Mission . . . stands as a convincing demonstration of the fact that in such times as these, the true principle of charitable work should be 'unconditional and immediate relief.'" All the credentials any applicant needed to become a member of the Travelers' Club, the paper reported, "were those of a hungry stomach, an empty pocket, and orderly behavior. . . . Following his Master's example, this hospitable man welcomes all who come, and when he expects that they are unworthy, he prays all the more earnestly for them." Imitating Christ, Merritt believed, meant helping others regardless of their willingness to help themselves.[53]

Merritt's unqualified refusal to segregate the "deserving poor" from "indolent tramps" ran counter to a powerful current in late-nineteenth-century philanthropy. Building on long-standing assumptions about the connections between moral character and financial stability, proponents of scientific charity asserted that aiding the "unworthy" only perpetuated poverty. During the 1870s and 1880s, leaders of this movement established Charity Organization Societies in Great Britain and the United States to promote the proper administration of assistance. These agencies worked to coordinate efforts among various benevolent associations in order to reduce redundancy. They also developed processes for determining who deserved help. Rather than doling out alms to panhandlers on the street, distributing free food at city missions, or allowing homeless vagrants unlimited access to shelter, these societies required the needy to apply for aid. Trained investigators interviewed candidates, asking questions about their work habits, health, spending patterns, housekeeping, children's education, and even religious practices. Sometimes "Friendly Visitors" would call on supplicants in their homes to confirm that the information they provided was accurate and their needs genuine. Petitioners judged worthy might receive actual monetary assistance, while those found wanting were usually offered advice or training in self-support. If their charges refused to accept their counsel or rejected the imposition of middle-class norms, charity investigators often deemed them intractable participants in a "vicious and willful pauperism" that would only "increase in proportion to the relief provided."[54]

As scientific discourse gained cultural authority, and anxieties about poverty and social disorder escalated during the late nineteenth century, the organized charity movement became increasingly influential in American society. By the time Carnegie published his essay on wealth in 1889, critiques of unconditional almsgiving were widespread. When Carnegie chastised practitioners of "so called charity" who gave assistance to "the slothful, the drunkard, the unworthy," proponents of scientific philanthropy welcomed his condemnations as an affirmation of their efforts to distinguish the deserving from derelicts. Although some practitioners of this investigative approach objected to Carnegie's claim that beggars were "irreclaimably destitute, shiftless, and worthless" miscreants who ought to be allowed to go extinct for "the improvement of the race," most agreed with the principle that aiding the improvident promoted dependency rather than inculcating industry and thrift.[55]

Although ministers like Merritt rejected the tenets of scientific philanthropy, many evangelicals found the movement's denunciation of indiscriminate aid difficult to disclaim. Even Talmage and Klopsch, who were attuned to the structural dimensions of indigence and inequality, worried that "charity which simply relieves immediate necessity tends to pauperize, instead of cultivating the spirit of independence." Articles in the *Christian Herald* often reflected this apprehension. When, in November 1892, Klopsch devised a plan to provide Thanksgiving dinner for poor families in Lower Manhattan on behalf of the newspaper's subscribers, he was careful to assure readers that meals were distributed to "destitute but deserving Christian Homes . . . not beggars." To identify "God's poor," Klopsch sent out a commissioner to visit the east and west sides of the city and make a thorough inquiry of which families were in need of help.[56]

When he repeated the experiment the next year, Klopsch again insisted that "those who were bidden to this Thanksgiving feast were . . . not the lazy idle nor the professional tramp but the deserving poor." This time, however, his conception of the worthy had expanded to include not only Christians but the "hunger-stricken refugee Russian-Jewish families" of the Lower East Side as well as "the waifs and strays of poor fallen humanity" who haunted "the vilest part" of the city. Rather than collecting names of eligible families through systematic investigation, Klopsch sent a bread wagon out into the streets and admitted that "it was no easy task selecting the deserving." Although he remained committed to the rhetoric of scientific charity, the exigencies of the economic downturn prompted Klopsch to revise his practices to provide relief for a wider circle of sufferers.[57]

As the financial depression worsened, Talmage openly questioned whether the investigative techniques of scientific philanthropy made sense in such dire conditions. "The methods of the charity organizations are excellent in ordinary circumstances," he stated, "but in a crisis like this, they are too slow." Rather than making hungry families wait until they had been properly investigated, relief agencies ought to offer assistance immediately, with "no restrictions . . . and no questions asked." In a January 1894 editorial entitled "Help All You Can," Talmage took aim at critics who complained that providing aid unconditionally would benefit the undeserving. "Indeed, indiscriminate charity is a bad thing," he admitted, "but I notice that those persons who write and talk very much about the dangers of indiscriminate charity never give anything." In fact, he charged, "most of this talk of indiscriminate charity is to cover up personal stinginess." Scientific methods gave misers an excuse for their selfishness and a platform for holding themselves superior to others. True Christianity required believers to sympathize with the afflicted, not to judge them. "Are you very much afraid that the 'unworthy' will be helped?" Talmage asked. "I say better by mistake feed fifty lazy scoundrels than let one good and worthy man or woman or child for whom Christ died freeze or starve."[58]

Evangelical ministers like Talmage and Merritt recognized that their support for immediate and unconditional relief would provoke controversy in a community already wrestling with competing claims about the causes of poverty and rival remedies for solving the social crisis. They were right. In the face of escalating censure, these pastors mounted a vigorous defense of their methods. Jesus himself, they argued, was reproached for associating with sinners, "and if he had limited his salvation to those who were worthy of it, very few would have been saved." Stinginess and scientific charity did not reflect the spirit of the gospel, which offered grace to all regardless of merit.[59]

One of the most forceful retorts to critics of indiscriminate almsgiving came from Reverend J. B. Hawthorne, who pastored a Baptist church in Atlanta. In "The Army of the Unemployed," which appeared in the *Christian Herald* under the heading "sermons worth reading," Hawthorne offered a strident critique of philanthropic schemes that ran contrary to the Golden Rule. Although he affirmed that "the science of sociology" might be useful in exposing injustice and oppression, Hawthorne complained that many of the discipline's conclusions contradicted the law of love revealed in the scriptures. He especially denounced the idea that "every idle man without a visible means of subsistence is a pariah, a loafer, a liar, a reprobate, and therefore unworthy of human respect or sympathy." Even if that were true, he contended, the Bible taught Christians to empathize with the downtrodden and help relieve their burdens. "If Jesus Christ pitied and blessed publicans and harlots, what are you and I that we should despise a penniless and sore-footed tramp begging bread?" Hawthorne demanded. Having compassion for the destitute and working to ameliorate their sufferings, he implied, would awaken Christians to the social forces that kept so many in a bondage worse than "African slavery." Just as their abolitionist forebears had fought to liberate the captives from oppression, so should contemporary evangelicals work for "the vindication of human rights, the redress of human wrongs, and the uplifting and strengthening of the great principles of human brotherhood."[60]

Convincing American evangelicals to engage actively in efforts to alleviate affliction and overcome oppression was precisely the goal that Klopsch and Talmage hoped to accomplish through the *Christian Herald*. However, achieving this aim without alienating a substantial segment of their constituency seems to have been challenging. Even as they published aggressive defenses of indiscriminate almsgiving, the partners sought to assure proponents of scientific charity that they were doing all they could to circumvent the risks of "spontaneous generosity" in their own philanthropic enterprises. While they extolled Merritt's relief work among "all comers" at the Eighth Avenue Mission, for example, they also proposed supplementing his efforts with a more systemized approach to distributing aid. Rather than donating money from the *Christian Herald*'s food fund directly to the Travelers' Club, Klopsch planned to reduce the number of people Merritt served by searching out "with the aid of experienced district visitors . . . the most urgent cases of destitution in the homes of Christian families."[61]

Within a few weeks of opening the food fund, the newspaper reported that its investigators had identified hundreds of "really deserving poor." The *Christian Herald*'s agents had recorded the names and addresses of these individuals so Klopsch could send provisions directly to their homes. The "district visitors" also gave out coupons that needy families could exchange for heating supplies and a daily loaf of bread. In this way, Klopsch explained, "care is taken that the charity shall not be diverted from the really needy or that it shall become promiscuous." Just a month after Talmage came out in strong support of "immediate and unconditional relief" as the most practical method of relieving suffering, another editorial in the *Christian Herald* declared just the opposite: "It is through such organized agencies as the Food Fund, where every dime and every dollar reach the mark, and not by indiscriminate charity, that the greatest good is to be accomplished."[62]

These striking inconsistencies in the *Christian Herald* indicate that American evangelicals remained deeply divided about the nature of poverty and proper modes of philanthropy despite the editors' efforts to create consensus. Perhaps even Klopsch and Talmage disagreed. That they made room for disparate—even competing and contradictory—perspectives within their publication suggests that they were striving to capture and retain the attention of diverse constituencies. To become "the most successful religious paper in the world," the *Christian Herald* had to reflect a generous "catholic spirit" and, as Talmage put it in an early essay outlining his editorial principles, allow "people to do things in their own way." Showcasing Talmage's emotional entreaties for spontaneous alms-giving alongside Klopsch's systematic schemes for identifying "God's poor" may have been a deliberate strategy, designed to demonstrate how evangelicals could embrace divergent views and practices while remaining committed to a common mission.[63]

EVANGELICAL CHARITY AND CHRISTIAN UNITY

As they continued to carry out relief work among the destitute during the economic crisis of 1894, Klopsch and Talmage increasingly stressed the unifying benefits of Christian benevolence. In mid-February, they re-printed an article written by Lyman Abbott, the theologically liberal pastor of Plymouth Church in Brooklyn, that urged Christians to set aside doctrinal disagreements such as "whether Moses wrote the Penta-teuch" in order to help the poor. Rather than judging fellow Christians, Abbott wrote, we can "unite with them to carry food to the hungry and fuel to the cold." The church, he implied, ought to concentrate on char-ity—the "most important lesson of Christian love"—not on policing theo-logical orthodoxy.[64]

Klopsch and Talmage agreed that charity offered a powerful means of promoting harmony among Christians beset by doctrinal discord. During the 1880s and 1890s, new methods of biblical interpretation challenged traditional accounts of creation, miracles, and even the divinity of Jesus, and threatened to divide Protestants into opposing camps. Although Tal-mage was known as a defender of conventional orthodoxy, the *Christian Herald* rarely mentioned theological controversies. Instead, the paper high-lighted successful efforts to create cohesion through philanthropy. In April 1894, for example, the editors announced that the *Christian Herald*'s food fund had "brought together, in the closest bonds of love and sym-pathy, thousands of Christian people in all parts of the Union, each of whom felt a personal responsibility for the success of the work."[65]

Participating in a shared enterprise of relieving suffering, Klopsch and Talmage implied, enabled individuals to overcome doctrinal differences, denominational preferences, and even regional prejudices that still rankled decades after the Civil War. Just as theological bickering jeopardized evangelical solidarity, lingering sectional animosities imperiled the tenuous connections between Northern and Southern Christians in this era of increasing tension over racial segregation. "After thirty years," Talmage lamented in an 1891 Decoration Day sermon, "the wounds and sorrow are still fresh, the losses hard to bear." Although progress had been made, North and South still needed to be brought into closer harmony. By engaging donors from different parts of the country in a common project of providing relief for destitute New Yorkers during the financial depression, the *Christian Herald* would help achieve this broader goal of national evangelical unity.[66]

To strengthen the bonds among dispersed groups of American Protestants, Klopsch and Talmage also commended the charitable endeavors of evangelical agencies all across the United States. Since taking over publication of the *Christian Herald,* they actively solicited stories about fellow believers engaged in efforts to "raise the fallen," assuage affliction, and advance the kingdom of God. Alongside editorials extolling Merritt's Eighth Avenue Mission, for example, the newspaper printed articles praising congregations in other cities that were ministering to the homeless and unemployed. Profiles of urban churches like the Congregational People's Palace in Jersey City, Bethany Presbyterian in Philadelphia, and Ruggles Baptist in Boston highlighted the practical programs these congregations were piloting to promote the welfare of the poor. The People's Palace, for example, assisted local tenement residents by providing bathing facilities, medical care, a clothing distribution center, day care for working mothers, a coffee shop, temporary lodging, a bank, and vocational training.[67]

Although most of the "institutional churches" the *Christian Herald* publicized were located in the Northeast, the editors also endorsed a variety of urban ministries in cities throughout the country. Some of these organizations focused on basic physical needs for food, clothing, shelter, and safety among penniless people struggling to survive in filthy, decrepit, crime-ridden slums. Others offered opportunities for education, employment, and even financial counsel. Klopsch and Talmage were especially intrigued by the settlement house movement. By moving into crowded urban neighborhoods where every resident was affected by poverty, the *Christian Herald* reported, leaders of this new initiative sought to follow Jesus's "example of self-abnegation in the interest of the poor." Thanks to the "wonderful magnetic personality of . . . Miss Jane Addams," who founded Chicago's Hull House, the movement was bringing "Christianity incarnate" to bear on the social and industrial problems of modern city life.[68]

Even as they devoted significant attention to urban ministries, Klopsch and Talmage recognized that many evangelical missionaries and philanthropists were working to relieve distress and uplift the downtrodden in rural areas. Articles describing efforts to establish educational institutions for poor children in Appalachia and on the western frontier appeared regularly in the *Christian Herald*. The editors also celebrated endeavors to provide industrial and religious training for African Americans throughout the South. Farm colonies sponsored by the Salvation Army, they contended, exemplified a "comprehensive and practical scheme" for combating unemployment by relocating idle workers from cities to agricultural regions that needed their labor.[69]

By familiarizing their readers with a variety of benevolent enterprises, Klopsch and Talmage hoped to cultivate shared responsibility for alleviating suffering and reforming the social order among American evangelicals. Since many of the ministries the *Christian Herald* championed were sustained entirely by voluntary offerings, the editors urged their constituents to support these charitable ventures through prayer and financial gifts. Sometimes, the newspaper provided an address to which money should be sent. But often, Klopsch offered to accept contributions and pass them along to the appropriate agency. Periodically, the *Christian Herald* published a list of donations to "Good Causes Helped," detailing the names of benefactors and the organizations they had sponsored.[70]

Evangelical leaders appreciated the *Christian Herald*'s munificence toward so many philanthropic endeavors. At a May 1894 celebration honoring Talmage's twenty-five years of pastoring the Brooklyn Tabernacle, admirers came from all across the nation to praise his benevolent work. "Clergymen without distinction of race or creed"—including an array of Protestants, a rabbi, and a Catholic priest—attended the international reception and paid tribute to Talmage's career of public service and the philanthropic projects through which he was "always contending for a united people and a united country." Speakers at the event noted that Talmage's benevolence was not "confined to his own country" but global in scope: "a world-resounding protest where there is oppression, bread where there is famine." Through the *Christian Herald,* several attendees remarked, Talmage had helped relieve starving people in faraway Russia as well as hungry Brooklyn families who were sitting in the Tabernacle's pews. "Wherever humanity is suffering his heart goes out in sympathy to the afflicted of all races and creeds," one presenter proclaimed. This generous spirit, participants in the celebration maintained, had made possible the gathering of an incredibly diverse crowd to fete Talmage's achievements, and it was this same broad-minded munificence that had inspired so many evangelicals from different backgrounds to join together in the *Christian Herald*'s campaigns to lessen affliction both at home and abroad.[71]

By the time they closed the food fund in the late spring of 1894, Klopsch and Talmage were confident they were making great progress toward the goals they had established when they first acquired the *Christian Herald.* Circulation had increased from 30,000 to over 150,000, indicating that the periodical was well on its way to becoming the most widely read religious newspaper in the world. These subscribers, who came from all across the nation and every evangelical denomination, had participated enthusiastically in the *Christian Herald*'s campaigns to relieve suffering within and beyond the United States. Indeed, in the years since he and Talmage had assumed control of the periodical, Klopsch wrote, they seemed "to have been Divinely led into a field of philanthropy so wide and far-reaching as to embrace the sympathetic co-operation of its readers in every clime." Although not everyone agreed about the causes of affliction, and some debated how best to cope with social crises, natural disasters, and economic calamities, thousands responded to the gripping stories and graphic images of distress they encountered in the *Christian Herald* by sending donations to the newspaper "in the name of Jesus."[72]

As they looked to the future, Klopsch and Talmage strove to capitalize on these early accomplishments in the arenas of domestic charity and foreign aid. A few weeks after announcing the end of their campaign to alleviate hunger among New York's poor, they requested their readers' permission to apply the balance of the food fund—almost $5,000—to establishing a summer retreat for "the little folks of the tenements." On June 15, the Christian Herald Children's Home at the Mont-Lawn estate, in Nyack-on-the-Hudson, New York, welcomed its first one hundred guests—all "city waifs" who had been helped by the newspaper's relief efforts during the previous winter. Through this ministry, which would become Klopsch's favorite charity in the coming years, the *Christian Herald* provided American evangelicals with a permanent channel for uplifting the downtrodden in the nation's largest and most diverse metropolis.[73]

The children's home at Mont-Lawn. From the *Christian Herald,* July 19, 1899, cover. Courtesy of the Christian Herald Association, New York.

Several months later, the partners announced another opportunity for subscribers to participate in ongoing service among the destitute. When the Bowery Mission—an organization that ministered to "the waifs and strays, the wrecks and derelicts of humanity from all parts of the world" who found themselves in New York City's most notorious neighborhood—was in danger of closing due to financial difficulties, Klopsch assumed responsibility for keeping the agency solvent on behalf of the *Christian Herald*'s constituents. Moving forward, he worked diligently to bring the needs of the Bowery Mission to the attention of evangelicals across the nation, reminding readers through regular reports that "there

The Bowery Mission. From the *Christian Herald,* December 30, 1896, cover.
Courtesy of the Christian Herald Association, New York.

is no depth of human misery and degradation so low that it cannot be reached by the love of Christ." By involving themselves in this enterprise, Klopsch contended, the *Christian Herald*'s subscribers would not only extend a helping hand to "the human drift-wood of the great city of New York," but also work to foster "spiritual kinship, reaching across a Continent," among American evangelicals of diverse backgrounds.[74]

With the help of this nationwide community of believers, Klopsch and Talmage also endeavored to expand the *Christian Herald*'s international relief efforts. Their success in cultivating concern for famine sufferers in Russia; for the destitute men, women, and children of New York; and now for the "poor, degraded human wrecks" who showed up at the doors of the Bowery Mission fueled the partners' faith in popular media as a means of fostering compassion for the afflicted. As they worked to engage readers in evangelical charities like the Mont-Lawn Children's Home and the Bowery Mission, Klopsch and Talmage were simultaneously on the lookout for opportunities to relieve suffering overseas. In the late summer of 1894, a calamity in Constantinople gave these enterprising publicists a chance to advance their worldwide humanitarian aims.[75]

2

COSMOPOLITAN COMPASSION

Just after noon on a balmy day in July 1894, American missionary Albert Long was enjoying a respite from his professorial duties at Robert College in Constantinople when he heard a sudden rumbling, grating, and grinding. "This terrifying noise was followed by a rising and sinking of the grounds," Long later recalled. "Then came . . . the crash of falling walls, the crumbling of chimneys and the falling in of vaulted structures centuries old, groans and cries from the wounded, piercing shrieks of women and children, and the roar of an insane crowd calling out in most of the languages of Europe and Asia." Within minutes, vast portions of the ancient city and many of its surrounding villages lay in ruins. More than a thousand victims were buried under the rubble, and many more survivors were left homeless and helpless.[1]

News of the Constantinople earthquake traveled rapidly, reaching American media outlets in time for publishers to print next-day reports of what some called the worst European calamity in two hundred years. Over the next several weeks, relief organizations formed in London and Paris to help Ottoman ruler Abdul Hamid II cope with the aftermath of the disaster. Despite these efforts, suffering in the city remained intense. By late August, many inhabitants were still camping out in open lots, business was at a standstill, and children were going hungry. With winter on the horizon and a growing realization that the government's resources were inadequate to meet survivors' needs, missionaries like Long appealed to their constituents in the United States. "The sight of all this is indescribably pitiful . . . and the misery and want of most of the unfortunate victims is beyond description," wrote American minister G. N. Shishimian in a letter urging supporters at home to extend assistance.[2]

When reports such as Shishimian's reached the *Christian Herald* headquarters, Klopsch cabled Alexander Terrell, the American minister to the Ottoman Empire, asking for more details. Terrell confirmed that conditions in Constantinople urgently warranted relief, indicated that all European governments had already contributed, and expressed his hope that "Christian America" would join these efforts. Chagrined that the United States was lagging other nations in offering assistance, Klopsch quickly reached out to several prominent philanthropists, businessmen, and "natives of Turkey" now resident in New York to organize a fundraising campaign for the earthquake victims. With Klopsch serving as president, the Turkish Relief Committee began its work on September 13 by issuing a public appeal urging people to send donations to the *Christian Herald*. The newspaper would forward monies received to Terrell and acknowledge all gifts in its columns.[3]

Generous contributions were soon flowing in, and other newspapers volunteered to receive offerings at their offices. Although the committee celebrated large donations such as the $1,000 gift from the banking firm Drexel, Morgan & Co., Klopsch reminded his constituents that even the smallest aid would be welcome. "It is within the power of every reader of the *Christian Herald* to help in this great work of charity," the journal proclaimed. In keeping with his goal of drawing American evangelicals into a cohesive community through the practice of benevolence, Klopsch invited "the cooperation of all our friends in every State of the Union, in this work of Christian sympathy" for "those whom the Gospel of Jesus teaches us to regard as brothers."[4]

The Constantinople earthquake of 1894 was a significant event in the development of evangelical almsgiving, expanding evangelical understanding and practices of charity beyond conventional boundaries. Although Americans of all backgrounds had participated in campaigns to alleviate distant suffering during several previous crises, earlier endeavors built on existing political, ethnic, and religious affinities with distressed communities. When the Greeks and other subject groups rebelled against Ottoman rule beginning in the 1820s, for example, many American citizens compared the revolutions to their own nation's fight against British tyranny and argued that the United States ought to support movements for freedom from oppression in other parts of the world. Similarly, after devastating potato crop failures contributed to widespread starvation in Ireland during the 1840s and 1880s, recent immigrants helped stir up sympathy for their former countrymen among the American public. Although some Protestants expressed unease about collecting funds for Irish Catholics, most set their prejudices aside when pressed to perform the sacred duties of Christian charity. During the Russian famine campaign, Klopsch and Talmage had repeatedly stressed the long-standing friendship between these two great "Christian nations." The *Christian Herald*'s appeal for the stricken population of Constantinople, by contrast, called on evangelicals to aid earthquake victims without "distinction ... on account of the nationality or creed of the sufferers." Deftly combining biblical injunctions and appeals to national interests, the partners urged American evangelicals to espouse a broad and self-denying charity that assisted the afflicted "whatever their color, race, or religion."[5]

Even as the *Christian Herald* collected contributions for the Turkish sufferers, however, events were unfolding in the Ottoman Empire that ultimately foiled efforts to foster a cosmopolitan ethic among evangelicals in the United States. Several hundred miles east of Constantinople, in the remote, mountainous village of Sasun, escalating conflicts between Armenian nationalists and Ottoman military forces erupted in violence that caused widespread devastation throughout the region. Reports that the sultan's troops had brutally slaughtered at least ten thousand Armenian men, women, and children began to circulate in the British and

American newspapers in early November 1894, provoking a public outcry on both sides of the Atlantic. Organized protests, calls for investigation, and pleas for international intervention to protect Armenians from further persecutions soon followed.[6]

Within this volatile context, convincing American evangelicals to continue aiding Abdul Hamid II became untenable. As accounts of ongoing atrocities against Armenians proliferated over the next two years, evangelical leaders like Klopsch and Talmage largely abandoned their attempts to promote a more inclusive humanitarianism among their constituents. Instead, the aggressive campaigns they mounted to aid Armenian survivors stressed the religious, racial, and cultural distinctions that set these fellow Christians apart from the "barbarous" and "fanatical Muslims" who were massacring them.[7]

Analyzing the narrative and visual strategies the *Christian Herald* employed to differentiate the "despotic, infidel Turk" from the "industrious, peaceable, and law-abiding" Armenians whose only desire was "to serve God" shows how evangelical efforts to alleviate affliction abroad became entangled with other political projects, social agendas, and religious ambitions during this era of intensifying globalization. Although some Protestants continued to insist that "human suffering makes brothers and sisters of all mankind," many evangelicals became convinced that "Christian America" had a special obligation to aid those who shared their democratic ideals, economic aspirations, and theological heritage. Assisting the faithful Armenians in their struggle against the "tyrannical" Ottoman Empire was a way for the United States to spread freedom, middle-class values, and Christian civilization around the world without engaging in direct military action or becoming enmeshed in alliances with other nations.[8]

Promoting this understanding of international humanitarianism proved a remarkably effective tactic for enlisting American evangelicals in foreign aid work. According to one historian, citizens of the United States raised approximately $300,000 to assist survivors of the Armenian massacres of 1894–1896. Readers of the *Christian Herald* were responsible for at least one-fifth of that total, contributing $63,868 to the newspaper's Armenian relief fund—almost double the amount collected during the Russian famine, and more than twenty times the sum donated for the Constantinople earthquake sufferers.[9]

Although linking Christian charity with American nationalism helped popularize international almsgiving among evangelicals, this strategy caused some consternation within the broader humanitarian community. When Klopsch enlisted Clara Barton as an agent of the *Christian Herald*'s Armenian relief campaign, she accepted the money he offered but ultimately expressed unease about partnering with patrons who politicized the practice of charity or encouraged her to privilege some sufferers over others. Because the American Red Cross (ARC) was committed to the principle of neutrality enshrined in the Geneva Convention of 1864, Barton was dedicated to assisting both Christian Armenians and Muslim Turks. Eventually, the tensions between her impartial approach and the particular expectations of evangelical benefactors like Klopsch resulted in a rift that would trouble future attempts to create a "collective culture of humanitarianism" in and beyond the United States.[10]

"A HELPING HAND TO THE TURKISH SUFFERERS"

"'In His Name' comes a loud cry for succor across the Atlantic once again," the *Christian Herald* proclaimed in September 1894. Following the campaign for Russian famine relief, the newspaper had continued to build its reputation as an effective instrument of evangelical charity through efforts to ease affliction during the economic crisis of 1893–1894, the subsequent opening of the Mont-Lawn Children's Home, and the acquisition of the Bowery Mission. When reports came in about the earthquake that destroyed so much of Constantinople and its environs, Klopsch and Talmage urged their growing network of subscribers to respond to appeals for aid. "The same humane, Christian spirit which has inspired the generosity of Americans in the past will prompt them now to extend a helping hand to the Turkish sufferers," they confidently declared.[11]

Even as they stressed the continuities between the Constantinople relief campaign and previous humanitarian endeavors, Klopsch and Talmage acknowledged that this latest effort was breaking new ground. For the first time, the *Christian Herald* encouraged American evangelicals to expand their concern beyond Western civilization. Unlike Russia, which most considered a friendly nation and an enduring ally of the United States with whom Americans shared a cultural and religious heritage, the

Ottoman Empire represented the epitome of "oriental despotism" long known for its violence, barbarism, and decadence. For centuries, Christian Europe had battled to liberate the Holy Land from the "infidel Turk" who had conquered the Byzantine Empire and continually threatened to push farther north into new territories. Although Ottoman rulers respected Christians and Jews living within their jurisdiction, offering them protection as well as limited political rights and religious freedom, most Europeans stressed the sultans' oppressive actions against non-Muslim populations, who were subject to heavy taxes, military conscription, and other deprivations.[12]

During the Enlightenment, European critiques of Turkish cruelties intensified as philosophers such as the Baron de Montesquieu contrasted the tyranny of the sultans' rule with the emerging ideal of republican government. In the nineteenth century, as the Ottoman Empire declined, American and European detractors increasingly distinguished between "the Occident" and "the Orient." Western civilization, in this view, was progressive, rational, industrious, and humane. The Ottoman East, on the other hand, remained backward, fanatical, decadent, and vicious. The sultans' brutal repressions of independence movements among insurgent minorities—many of whom were Christian—lent credence to the perception that "Mohammedan Turks" were unenlightened despots hostile to the modern values of liberty, equality, and self-determination. Reports of Ottoman atrocities against Bulgarian rebels in the late 1870s, for example, provoked outrage throughout Europe and the United States, prompting many to brand the sultan and his Muslim subjects as implacable enemies of humanity and Christian civilization. By asking American evangelicals to help Abdul Hamid II alleviate the suffering in Constantinople, Klopsch and Talmage were urging their coreligionists to set aside deep-seated prejudices in the service of Christian charity.[13]

To accomplish this goal, the partners employed all of the strategies that had proven successful in broadening evangelical understandings and practices of almsgiving during the Russian famine relief campaign. The *Christian Herald*'s reporting of Constantinople's disaster included gripping headlines, heartrending stories of misery, and vivid illustrations of desolation designed to stir up sympathy. Klopsch and Talmage again promised to account for every offering in the newspaper's columns, encouraged donations of any amount, and claimed that all gifts would

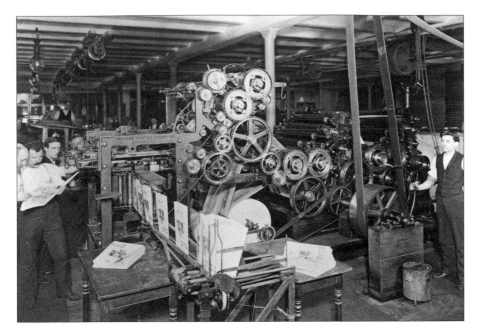

The *Christian Herald*'s press room. Courtesy of the Museum of the City of New York.

reach the earthquake victims promptly and efficiently. They also stressed the theological and devotional dimensions of assisting the Turkish sufferers. "Charity is a sacrament," they proclaimed, "and right giving, in the name of the Giver of all good gifts . . . is one of the highest privileges a Christian can enjoy." Finally, the editors insisted that helping the "unfortunate people of Constantinople" would advance the interests of the United States by affording "evidence of its practical claim to be regarded as a humane nation." Through their generosity, American evangelicals would help demonstrate that their country was "not to be outdone in deeds of Christian charity" by the European nations that had "been quick to respond to the call for aid."[14]

In addition to deploying these now-familiar fund-raising methods, Klopsch and Talmage used some new tactics to encourage American evangelicals to sympathize with those they had always viewed as enemies. Rather than reviling the sultan as a tyrannical foe, the *Christian Herald* praised Abdul Hamid II as an enlightened ruler devoted to the welfare of his people. "Under him," the paper reported, "Turkey has made marked advances. He has fostered education, the arts and sciences, and is doing his utmost to promote the best interests of the Empire." Unlike previous potentates who had destroyed ancient Christian sites, the current sultan had granted land and facilities for the erection of churches in Jerusalem. This generous liberality indicated that Abdul Hamid II was distinguishing himself from his forerunners in his treatment of non-Muslim communities.[15]

Klopsch and Talmage also suggested that the Ottoman ruler was forging a new path in his interactions with other nations. They repeatedly reminded *Christian Herald* readers that Abdul Hamid II had given a large donation to flood sufferers in Pennsylvania during the Johnstown calamity of 1889. In addition, he had worked to establish positive relations with the U.S. government. "The Sultan has always shown the most friendly feeling not only towards this country and its diplomatic representatives but to all Americans who have visited the Empire," the *Christian Herald* reported. By aiding this "humane ruler" in his time of need, Klopsch and Talmage contended, American evangelicals would help strengthen the bonds between the United States and the Ottoman Empire by "further breaking down the old barrier of antagonism that has existed for generations between Moslem and Christian."[16]

As the crisis in Constantinople worsened, Klopsch and Talmage sought to convince their readers that fostering peace and goodwill through evangelical charity was a worthy enterprise. Sometimes they stressed pragmatic considerations: Unless Americans helped relieve Turkish sufferers, they warned, painful consequences such as an outbreak of cholera might threaten all of Europe. Preventing the spread of plague by assisting the afflicted would place Ottomans in the debt of evangelical almoners. A generous gift on behalf of American Protestants would also have a positive effect on the sultan's attitude toward foreigners, especially Christians and missionaries working in the region. "By responding to the appeal," Klopsch insisted, "you will thus not only afford direct aid to the earthquake sufferers . . . but you will be opening up new opportunities for missionary influence and usefulness, and advancing the standard of the Gospel in a distant land." Philanthropy, from this perspective, was a form of evangelism.[17]

Even as they emphasized the practical benefits of aiding the earthquake survivors, Klopsch and Talmage maintained that relieving human suffering was a Christian duty. "The Samaritan did not stop to question the poor bleeding wayfarer before binding up his wounds, nor did the Saviour of the world withhold his human pity and his rich divine mercy from the Syro-phoenician woman," they reminded their readers. By grounding appeals for the Turkish relief fund in scriptural mandates to offer charity to enemies and outsiders, Klopsch and Talmage encouraged American evangelicals to embrace a more cosmopolitan ethic that extended sympathy to suffering others "regardless of race [or] creed."[18]

The *Christian Herald*'s campaign to cast Abdul Hamid II and his fellow Muslims as worthy recipients of compassion was part of a broader effort to usher in "an age of international goodwill and kindly deeds." Klopsch and Talmage believed that evangelicals could play a leading role in advancing harmony among all people through their philanthropic enterprises. The confidence that Christians could help bring about Christ's millennial reign of righteousness and peace set these two leaders apart from many of their contemporaries. During the latter decades of the nineteenth century, a number of prominent evangelicals began to embrace a premillennial view of history that predicted Christ's imminent return to earth after a period of chaos and decay. From this perspective, human efforts to ameliorate social problems, promote peace, or even alleviate affliction were ultimately futile. "Humanitarian schemes of benevolence . . . may do some good," New York City pastor A. B. Simpson proclaimed, but they were "certainly not God's highest thought for . . . the world." Instead, he declared, preaching the gospel was "the only remedy for all human ills and wrongs." Although the *Christian Herald* itself was founded by an ardent premillennialist who continued to prioritize evangelism over philanthropy in the British version of the newspaper, Klopsch and Talmage generally promoted a more optimistic, postmillennial stance that affirmed endeavors to further the kingdom of God on earth through both preaching and humanitarian reform.[19]

From the beginning of their tenure at the helm of the American publication, the partners put forward a range of arguments to persuade readers that charitable ventures were part of a divine plan for fostering international unity. According to the *Christian Herald,* evidence for the dawning of a new era of universal brotherhood rooted in benevolent interactions among diverse peoples of all nations was everywhere. Developments in communication and travel technologies such as newspapers, telegraphic wires, and railroads, Talmage declared, were signs of the world's progress toward global solidarity.[20]

Talmage's experiences as an international traveler also confirmed his convictions about the necessity of cultivating a cosmopolitan ethic among American evangelicals. "A recent visit to Europe, Asia, and Africa has enlarged our sympathies," he wrote in an early editorial outlining the *Christian Herald*'s ecumenical principles. "We must remember that other people do not differ more from us than we differ from them." Klopsch's trip to Russia had a similar effect on his beliefs about the role of humanitarian work in nurturing friendly relations among distant strangers. "Before I came here Russia was 5,000 miles away, but I have so learned to respect and to love you that henceforth I must regard you as neighbors," he avowed. "Surely the feeling of international brotherhood between Russia and the United States will forever abide!"[21]

Perhaps the most promising indication that Christian charity was strengthening bonds among diverse peoples came during the 1893 World's Columbian Exposition in Chicago. The *Christian Herald*'s coverage of the Parliament of Religions held in conjunction with this larger event celebrated the gathering of representatives from many of the world's faiths to discuss vital topics such as the duties each had toward humanity. According to the newspaper's contributors, the Parliament revealed that all religious traditions were "allies rather than opponents . . . so far as morality is concerned" because each strove to eradicate sin, to elevate lives, and to encourage "kindness, charity, and helpfulness." Many speakers at the gathering, the *Christian Herald* reported, stressed the importance of love, compassion, and sympathy in promoting global solidarity, and challenged American evangelicals to behave generously toward distant sufferers in foreign lands. From this perspective, humanitarianism played an essential part in transcending divisions among people of different religions, races, and nations. Through the practice of international benevolence, the *Christian Herald* proclaimed, American evangelicals could advance the "new movement begun by this Congress" by replacing "the hatred and bigotry of rival creeds" with "a world-wide law of sympathy."[22]

The ethic of cosmopolitan charity promoted at the World's Parliament of Religions deserved the support of all Christians, Klopsch and Talmage maintained, because its principle of universal brotherhood was rooted in both biblical teachings and scientific evidence. For over a decade, Talmage had been drawing on scriptural passages and science to combat increasingly popular theories of polygenesis. "Some have supposed that God originally made an Asiatic Adam, and a European Adam, and an African Adam, and an American Adam," he preached in an 1879 sermon. "But that theory is entirely overthrown by my text (Acts 17:26), which says that all nations are *blood relatives,* having sprung from one and the same stock." Furthermore, he claimed, physiologists had confirmed that "the plasma and the disk in the human blood have the same characteristics" even among peoples of diverse "physiognomy or temperament." Scientific investigation thus substantiated the Bible's claims about human origins and provided support for the practice of global humanitarianism. Recognizing "chords of kinship" that united the nations, Talmage argued, would surely lead Christians to empathize with the vast majority of the earth's inhabitants who were "engaged in *a mighty struggle for bread.*" Since "we are all bound together," he wrote, "let us never restrain our sympathies or dam them back," but rather exercise "pity and compassion for the woes of the world."[23]

As American evangelicals began to put this humanitarian vision into practice during the Turkish relief campaign of 1894, Klopsch and Talmage praised their readers for extending "the generous hand of friendship and good-will to men of every race and creed." Several months after announcing their plans to aid the afflicted in Constantinople, the partners published an appreciative article highlighting the contributions their constituents made to this and other benevolent causes through the *Christian Herald.* In the five years since they had taken over as proprietor and editor, they observed, charity had become a prominent part of the newspaper's mission, just as they had initially hoped. By sending relief to the starving peasants in Russia and the earthquake survivors in the Ottoman Empire, American evangelicals had joined together in "great work for God and humanity" that advanced the gospel, expanded the influence of the United States in international affairs, and fortified the fraternal bonds among diverse peoples of all nations.[24]

This certainty that every "loaf of bread given 'In His Name'" served as "an evangel of peace" between Christians and Muslims, however, was soon severely tested by outbreaks of violence in the Ottoman Empire. As reports that the sultan's forces had slain thousands of Armenian

Christians reached the American public in the late fall of 1894, evangelicals began to express doubts about the cosmopolitan ideals of charity that they had only recently begun to embrace.[25]

ARMENIAN MASSACRES AND THE RISE OF TRIBAL CHARITY

Just two weeks after the *Christian Herald* celebrated the success of the Constantinople relief campaign, the paper published a troubling inquiry from a reader questioning the propriety of this effort. "Why do you ask us to send money to the Turkish Fund when the Turks are today killing and persecuting Armenian Christians?" asked D. W. Snow of New Bedford, Massachusetts. "It is terrible to think of the massacre of our brethren in Christ. . . . Why do you help them?" In their response, Klopsch and Talmage reminded Snow that "Christ tells us to bless them that curse you and do good to them that despitefully use you." Extending charity even to enemies was a basic Christian responsibility. At the same time, the partners seemed to recognize that asking evangelicals to overlook escalating reports of suffering among Armenian communities in the Ottoman Empire was a tall order. Rather than continuing to promote a cosmopolitan humanitarian ethic, Klopsch and Talmage justified their efforts to lessen affliction in Constantinople by highlighting the affinities between American donors and a subset of the earthquake survivors. "As there are many Christians among the sufferers," they wrote, "we continue the appeals."[26]

This shift toward a more discriminating approach to almsgiving presaged a major transformation in the *Christian Herald*'s charitable endeavors. Over the next several years, the newspaper concentrated exclusively on aiding Christians whose struggles for survival and freedom from oppression seemed to resonate with American ideals of religious liberty, political autonomy, and economic independence. As they rallied evangelical readers to assist afflicted Armenians, Klopsch and Talmage underscored the sufferers' common theological commitments, civic aspirations, and cultural values. At the same time, they abandoned their earlier attempts to improve perceptions of Abdul Hamid II and his Muslim subjects. Instead, the *Christian Herald* increasingly resorted to deeply entrenched prejudices against the sultan and "sons of Islam" to enlist subscriber support for humanitarian intervention in the region. By framing almsgiving as a strategic instrument in a global war between "civilized" Christians and the "wicked and barbarous" Ottoman power, Klopsch and Talmage persuaded a growing cadre of American evangelicals to provide foreign aid at a time when the United States was testing new tactics for extending its influence overseas.[27]

Although this approach helped consolidate evangelical support for international humanitarianism, the *Christian Herald*'s response to the crisis in Armenia ultimately hampered the newspaper's effectiveness as a medium of American philanthropy abroad. When Ottoman officials encountered the divisive and inflammatory rhetoric promoted in the *Christian Herald* and other publications, they became increasingly suspicious of aid workers and missionaries assisting sufferers in the region. After the *Christian Herald*'s designated relief commissioner was denied entry to the empire, Klopsch hastily shifted his support to Clara Barton, whose commitment to the cosmopolitan principles of neutrality and impartiality enabled her to gain access where evangelicals were no longer welcome. This partnership would prove a contentious one, eventually exposing tensions and disagreements that troubled efforts to expand the scope of American charity in this pivotal period.

When news about the violence in Sasun swept through the British and American press in November 1894, the *Christian Herald*'s Turkish relief campaign was in full swing. As a result, no reports appeared in the paper about the "Armenian outrages" or the public outcries against them until readers like D. W. Snow began to raise questions. Within several months, however, Klopsch and Talmage had shifted course dramatically. In January 1895, Talmage preached a sermon condemning the massacre and calling on civilized nations to denounce the sultan's diabolism and condemn "Mohammedanism" as a curse. By April, he and Klopsch seemed to have completely lost confidence that humanitarianism could help heal long-standing animosities between Muslims and Christians. The recent troubles in Armenia, the *Christian Herald* declared, demonstrated the hopelessness of attempts to reconcile Islam and Christianity in parts of the world "where the Moslem has a firm foothold."[28]

In the months that followed, American evangelicals expressed growing horror over the sufferings of Christian Armenians. Coverage of the intensifying crisis became even more inflammatory after conflict between Armenian demonstrators and government troops in Constantinople in the fall of 1895 caused a "frightful riot" in which many were killed. After this incident, violence erupted throughout the Ottoman Empire. From early October 1895 through most of 1896, the *Christian Herald* and other American publications carried heartrending accounts of the cruelties inflicted by "fanatical" Turks on "defenseless" Armenians.[29]

Although Klopsch and Talmage expressed some concern that these tales of affliction would trouble the sensibilities of their readers, their scruples rarely prevented them from printing sensational stories of "hideous crimes against Christians," including flaying alive, cutting to pieces, and even tearing out entrails. Women were "torn from their homes and outraged, and hundreds of young girls forcibly carried off, fiendishly used," all with the sultan's permission. These "diabolical measures," one author declared, furnished "conclusive evidence . . . that the Turk is at heart, and under all circumstances, a savage" who "holds in his breast no spark of generosity, no trace of fellow feeling or kindness for any who are not of his own race and faith." Although Abdul Hamid II may have tried to present himself as a civilized sovereign sympathetic to humanitarian concerns and ready to join the community of modern nations, one writer implied, his "brutal and fanatical . . . deeds of blood and rapine" showed that he was in fact just like all his predecessors: "an enemy of mankind . . . a stumbling block to civilization . . . and a menace to Christianity."[30]

The *Christian Herald*'s rehearsals of these familiar denunciations exacerbated suspicions about the sultan's intentions toward the Armenian populations in his territory. Some missionaries active in the region had long been warning that Abdul Hamid II's promises of reform masked a diabolical plan of exterminating Christian Armenians. Although political leaders in Europe and the United States had remained hopeful that the Ottoman leader would acquiesce to demands that he provide adequate safeguards and freedoms for minority groups, recent outbreaks of violence led diplomats to conclude that the sultan had decided on a policy of annihilation. "All civilized nations are in horror at the attempts of that Mohammedan government to destroy all the Christians of Armenia," Talmage declared in an incendiary sermon that decried the indifference of the Western powers in the face of the sultan's ongoing duplicity and despotism. Some might believe that the Turkish government's latest acts of oppression represented a departure, Talmage proclaimed, but "No, no! She is at the same old business." Throughout its history, he claimed, the Ottoman Empire had persecuted its Christian subjects while promising to protect them. Now the time had come to "stop the rivers of blood." "Why, after all the . . . lying on the part of the Turkish government, do not the warships of Europe ride up as close as is possible to the palaces of Constantinople and blow that accursed government to atoms?" he demanded. "In the name of the Eternal God let the nuisance of the ages be wiped off the face of the earth!"[31]

Although Talmage asserted that European nations must take the lead in any armed effort against the sultan, he also argued that the United States had a role to play in this impending holy war. Dismissing concerns that intervention on behalf of the Armenians would jeopardize the Monroe Doctrine, Talmage insisted that humanitarianism took precedence over worries about hemispheric security and obligated the United States to take action. Although he stopped short of agitating for direct American military engagement, Talmage maintained that the U.S. government should pressure its European allies to send battleships into Turkish waters to liberate the victims of "Mohammedan oppression." In the meantime, American citizens should work to help the suffering Armenians, whose only "crime is that they will not become followers of Mahomet."[32]

Talmage's call for humanitarian intervention echoed many other entreaties that appeared in the *Christian Herald* as reports of conditions in the Ottoman Empire poured in. The rhetoric of holy war appealed strongly to readers who viewed history as a contest between good and evil, civilization and savagery, freedom and coercion, rationality and fanaticism, republicanism and tyranny, kindness and cruelty, sobriety and sensuality. Placing the Armenian Christians and Turkish Muslims on opposite sides of these divides proved an effective technique for soliciting evangelical interest in the situation unfolding on the other side of the globe. For if the recent atrocities had exposed the "phenomenal inhumanity" of the sultan, these events also highlighted the fortitude of the Armenian people, whose loyalty to Jesus in the face of persecution warranted the admiration and aid of all Christians. "Not only are the Armenians our fellow beings," one writer intoned, "but they are the oldest Christian nation on the globe." Having converted to Christianity in the fourth century and endured oppression for hundreds of years, they had consistently "laid down their lives rather than betray their Master by accepting the fate of Islam." As "the Moslem war for the extermination of the religion of Jesus in Asia Minor" had intensified in recent times, the "martyr-roll" of this "simple, peaceful, pastoral people" was continually expanding. Unless "civilized nations" stepped in to assist the Armenians and protect them from further atrocities, one *Christian Herald* reporter warned, this "ancient Christian race" would perish.[33]

To prevent such a calamity, Klopsch and Talmage again organized a relief campaign. In September 1895, they announced that the *Christian Herald* was arranging aid for survivors of the massacres and invited readers to participate. Expressing growing frustration with the European powers for failing to take decisive action against the sultan, they insisted it was time for the United States to lead the rescue. "Whatever other nations may do," they declared, "let our people take a stand for Armenia, and thus demonstrate to the world that we are a compassionate Christian nation." By showing their solidarity with fellow believers through Christian charity, American evangelicals would help save Armenia from "Moslem cruelty" and "utter extermination."[34]

Assisting beleaguered coreligionists in their desperate battle for survival also gave *Christian Herald* readers an opportunity to defend the "right of this oldest Christian nation on earth . . . to live and worship in the faith of their fathers." Klopsch and Talmage suggested that as the world's foremost champion of democracy and religious liberty, the United States had a special responsibility to support the Armenian people in their ongoing struggle for political and religious freedom. Surely their heroic resistance to "Islamic despotism" and their aspirations for autonomy deserved support from "the Lord's people in our own prosperous and peaceful country—where each family can worship under its own vine and fig tree," one *Christian Herald* reporter wrote. Those who had experienced the blessings of liberty for themselves, Klopsch and Talmage contended, ought to help others who sought these same "God-given rights."[35]

Christian Herald readers responded to the appeals with alacrity and enthusiasm. Letters accompanying contributions to the relief fund show that many donors found the various rationales for humanitarian intervention presented in the *Christian Herald* compelling. Subscribers like the Reverend A. Humphreys of Ingleside, New York, expressed feelings of spiritual kinship with their "Christian brethren across the sea" and sent gifts

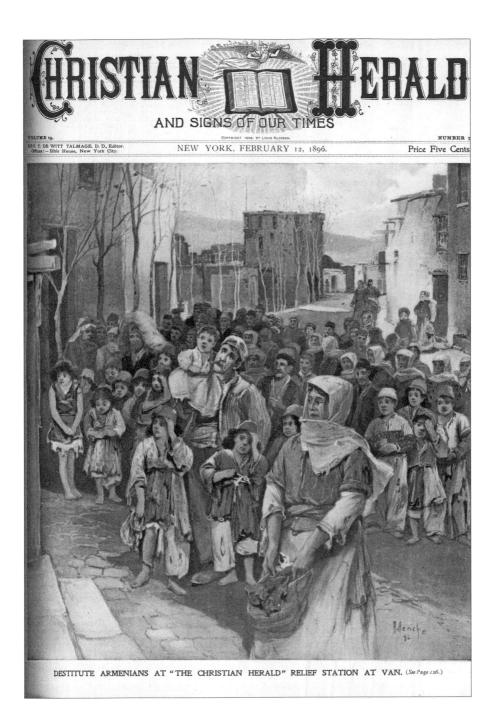

CHRISTIAN HERALD

AND SIGNS OF OUR TIMES

VOLUME 19.

COPYRIGHT 1896, BY LOUIS KLOPSCH.

NUMBER 7

REV. T. DE WITT TALMAGE, D. D., Editor.
Offices:— Bible House, New York City.

NEW YORK, FEBRUARY 12, 1896.

Price Five Cents

DESTITUTE ARMENIANS AT "THE CHRISTIAN HERALD" RELIEF STATION AT VAN. (See Page 126.)

The *Christian Herald*'s Armenian relief campaign. From the *Christian Herald*,
February 12, 1896, cover. Courtesy of the Christian Herald Association,
New York.

demonstrating solidarity. Others emphasized a sense of obligation to support the Armenians in their quest for religious liberty. "I thank God every day . . . that we can worship him unmolested," one reader wrote. Still others echoed the *Christian Herald*'s critiques of Ottoman political rule. "God hasten the time when a Christian government shall take the place of that rotten monarchy," declared M. Etzendams of Illinois in a missive accompanying his $10 offering.[36]

Within three months, Etzendams, Humphreys, and thousands of other readers had sent over $15,000 for Armenian aid—more than five times the amount the newspaper had collected to assist the Constantinople earthquake victims. "Once more," Klopsch boasted, the *Christian Herald* had served as "the means of stimulating a nation to activity" on behalf of distant sufferers. By publicizing Armenia's woes, the journal had successfully engaged Christians throughout the United States in "working together earnestly, harmoniously and prayerfully for a common purpose."[37]

"HAS GOD FORGOTTEN EDEN?"

Even as Klopsch celebrated the *Christian Herald*'s effectiveness at uniting American evangelicals in this shared humanitarian enterprise, he admitted that success had come at a price. Just weeks after dispatching the well-known journalist William Willard Howard to oversee the distribution of relief funds in eastern Turkey, Klopsch received a warning from the U.S. State Department that the sultan's government might view this envoy as hostile "in consequence of certain letters and articles he had written to the leading American newspapers."[38]

Prior to accepting the position as the *Christian Herald*'s relief agent, Howard had spent six months touring the devastated region of Armenia and reporting on suffering he encountered there. After agreeing to return to the area at Klopsch's behest, Howard published an account of his experiences in the *Christian Herald*. Like many other articles included in the journal during this period, Howard's piece highlighted the "wickedness and iniquity" of Muslim Turks who had wantonly massacred thousands of Christian Armenians and were subjecting survivors to persecution, torture, and starvation. "Soldiers of Sultan Hamid," Howard declared in a letter from the field, were "devils" who fiendishly hunted to death Armenian men, women, and children "whose only fault is that they follow Jesus Christ." Surely "America, the greatest Christian nation on earth," was bound by "ties of blood and race and religion" to stop this outrage and save the "ancient garden of Eden" and its inhabitants from being "utterly annihilated," he insisted. Although Howard's tribalist appeal resonated strongly with evangelical readers eager to rescue fellow believers, his rhetoric incensed Ottoman officials. When Howard finally arrived at the Turkish border in early December 1895, government agents prevented him from crossing into the sultan's domain.[39]

Howard's exclusion was a serious disappointment for Klopsch and Talmage, both of whom had worked hard to present the *Christian Herald*'s relief campaign as the most reliable and efficient means of aiding Armenia. According to the original plan, Howard was to partner with missionaries such as Grace Kimball of the American Board of Commissioners on Foreign Missions (ABCFM)—an organization with a strong and abiding presence throughout the Ottoman Empire—to allocate aid to sufferers who needed it most. This approach had several advantages. First, Klopsch noted, because the ABCFM missionaries knew the language, understood the culture, and were familiar with conditions on the ground, they were uniquely qualified to distribute assistance effectively. Second, since missionaries offered their services for free and Klopsch promised to cover all incidental costs from his personal resources, every dollar contributed to the relief fund would go directly to the field. Donors could be sure their gifts to the *Christian Herald* relief effort would be used economically, not squandered on salaries or other overhead expenses. Finally, ABCFM missionaries knew how to avoid attracting attention from the Turkish authorities. Unlike European missionaries who had been forced to abandon the field as conflicts between their governments and the sultan escalated, or representatives of the nationalist Armenian Relief Committee whose attempts to assist their fellow countrymen had provoked intense hostility from Ottoman rulers, American missionaries had earned the confidence of Turkish officials and could therefore distribute relief without molestation. For all these reasons, Klopsch and Talmage encouraged American evangelicals to choose the *Christian Herald* as the "only reliable and available" channel for aiding Armenia.[40]

When Howard was turned back at the Turkish border, Klopsch hastily assured contributors that the commissioner's recall would not impede the *Christian Herald*'s humanitarian efforts. In fact, he explained, the newspaper had been cabling collections from the fund directly to the American Missionary Committee in Constantinople and corresponding with individual missionaries like Grace Kimball for several months. Although Howard's involvement would have been helpful, the work could go on without him.[41]

Unfortunately, Klopsch's missionary partners were not so confident that they could continue to dispense relief on behalf of the *Christian Herald* since Howard's attempt to enter the empire had aroused the government's suspicions. Indeed, Howard's exclusion indicated just how tenuous the situation had become for American missionaries attempting to ease the suffering of Armenians in Ottoman territory. As foreign governments increased pressure on the sultan to end ongoing violence, and publications like the *Christian Herald* printed ever more vitriolic denunciations of Turkish atrocities, Ottoman authorities grew less tolerant of missionary humanitarianism. By November 1895, American missionaries were reporting that the sultan's forces were threatening to expel them from their stations and perhaps banish them from the empire altogether. Fearing both for their own safety and for the fate of the Armenians under their care, ABCFM officials began to propose alternative avenues of providing help.[42]

Just as Howard was trying to cross into Turkish territory, the Reverend Henry Otis Dwight of the Constantinople mission cabled ABCFM headquarters in Boston and reported that ordinary channels of relief were now blocked. He suggested that Clara Barton and the ARC be persuaded to enter relief work. Although the missionaries remained grateful for the remittances they received from the *Christian Herald* and would try to put the funds to use, Dwight explained in a letter to Klopsch, they were having difficulty getting money into the interior of the country due to the Ottoman government's growing distrust. "There is need of some great organization like the Red Cross Society, under international protection, to do the work of distribution in this terrible emergency," he declared. Only a religiously and politically neutral agency working under the auspices of an international treaty, Dwight implied, could effectively provide for the nearly half million people facing certain starvation in this climate of growing opposition to American missionary intervention.[43]

Taken aback at the turn of events and worried that involving the ARC in Armenian relief would overshadow his efforts to establish the *Christian Herald* as the nation's most effective humanitarian agency, Klopsch immediately wrote to ABCFM foreign secretary Judson Smith seeking clarification. When Smith confirmed that the ABCFM supported Dwight's proposal, Klopsch quickly shifted strategies. Rather than resist efforts to enlist ARC aid in Armenia, Klopsch threw his support behind the plan. During December and January, he wrote several times to Clara Barton, urging her to undertake this "mission of mercy" and promising to advertise her efforts to "the Christian community in such a way that thousands upon thousands of dollars will pour in." By working together, he suggested, the ARC and the *Christian Herald* could accomplish humanitarian work "more powerful and productive than ever before." "With Dr. Talmage backing us up in the pulpit," Klopsch enthused, "it is almost impossible to foresee . . . the eventual extent of our Relief fund."[44]

Although Barton agreed to oversee the distribution of aid in Armenia, the partnership with the *Christian Herald* proved rocky right from the start. Remembering that Barton had struggled to coordinate an efficient relief campaign during the Russian famine of 1892—prompting many charitable organizations (including the *Christian Herald*) to bypass the ARC in sending supplies to the starving peasants—Klopsch harbored doubts about her abilities. As soon as Barton accepted the invitation to help in Armenia, Klopsch began barraging her with questions about the timing of her departure (why had she not embarked immediately given the urgency of the situation?) and her readiness to take on the challenges that lay ahead (how would she deal with unforeseen difficulties?). He also interrogated her plans for working with American officials and missionaries in Constantinople (had she sought permission for her venture from the U.S. government? Did she intend to seek the advice of ABCFM workers who were so familiar with conditions on the ground?) and her reasons for believing she would gain access to the sultan's domain (was she really sure that the ARC would be allowed to enter Turkey?).[45]

Ever on the lookout for challenges to her authority, Barton chafed at Klopsch's intrusive inquiries. The ARC, she assured him, was wasting no time in preparing for this momentous mission. She was entirely confident that her staff was equipped to cope with any unexpected hindrances. Both the State Department and the ABCFM had already expressed unqualified support for her effort, and as a signatory nation to the International Red Cross treaty, Turkey would "scarcely refuse us an audience," Barton asserted. Since she and her workers intended to carry out the relief effort "in total conformity with the noble principles of . . . neutrality and humanity alone, with no regard for sect, race, nor governmental methods," she explained, the sultan's officials would have no reason to suspect their motives. Unlike the *Christian Herald*'s commissioner, Barton implied, the ARC would "enter the field . . . free from all racial or religious feeling or alliances" and therefore would have much greater success in gaining permission to assist the beleaguered Armenians. "In fact," she told Klopsch, "it is that feature of our organization which gives assurance to those in Constantinople who appeal to us"—ABCFM missionaries like Dwight and his colleagues—"that we may accomplish what they are unable to."[46]

Barton's insistence on maintaining—even emphasizing—neutrality in her work put her at odds with fund-raisers like Klopsch and Talmage, both of whom believed the success of their relief campaign depended on framing humanitarianism in explicitly religious, racial, and political terms that stressed the affinities between the Armenian sufferers and their American benefactors over and against the Turkish aggressors. Although the *Christian Herald* continued to proclaim support for Barton's mission as she and her staff readied themselves to travel to Constantinople, behind the scenes Klopsch redoubled his efforts to employ ABCFM missionaries as distribution agents. At the end of December, he wrote again to Judson Smith declaring his intention to expand the *Christian Herald* operation throughout Armenia by cabling funds to at least six new mission stations. He also encouraged readers to continue sending contributions through the *Christian Herald* since ABCFM missionaries who received their donations were "the only relief agents actually at work." When Klopsch heard in late January that the Turkish government might not permit the ARC to enter Armenia, he concluded that "the projected relief tour of President Clara Barton and her aids will probably have to be abandoned," leaving the field open for the missionaries who were successfully distributing the *Christian Herald* relief fund.[47]

In fact, Barton did gain entry to the Ottoman Empire in mid-February, and the ARC was able to conduct relief operations in several locales beginning in March. Despite her tenacity and determination to succeed, however, Barton and her assistants faced formidable challenges in this difficult, dangerous, and unfamiliar territory. In a letter to her nephew Stephen, who worked for the ARC in New York, Barton blamed her troubles on publicists like Klopsch, who continued to portray the sultan and his Muslim followers as monsters set on exterminating Christianity. "I see various foolish things published in the . . . home papers that reach us," Barton complained, "attacking all the people I have to work with in the most *religious* way. . . . Considering the thoughtless actions there, it will be a wonder if we ever succeed in getting anywhere or doing anything."[48]

Barton's worries about ineffectiveness were not unfounded. Although the ARC was able to distribute some agricultural supplies to Armenian farmers in the province of Harpoot and to provide medical assistance to survivors of massacres in two other communities, the agency's mission was not nearly as extensive as Barton or her supporters had expected. "In the end," historian Ann Marie Wilson has demonstrated, "the ABCFM handled the majority of the work carried out on behalf of the Armenians." Frustrated missionaries complained that the ARC had failed to take much work off their hands. American donors raised questions about Barton's competence and her loyalties, accusing her of collaborating with Ottoman officials and of ministering to Muslims as well as Christians.[49]

Although Klopsch refrained from publicly criticizing the ARC in the pages of the *Christian Herald,* he had privately raised all of these concerns in his initial correspondence with Barton back in December and early January. As his fears seemed to come to fruition in the following months, Klopsch tacitly withdrew whatever tepid support he had maintained for the ARC mission. In mid-April, he announced the official closure of the *Christian Herald*'s Armenian relief fund but encouraged readers to continue sending contributions directly to an agent of the ABCFM, who would forward them to missionaries in the field. At the same time, Barton determined to cut ties with fund-raising organizations she believed were inhibiting her ability to work effectively in this challenging context. "We will finish the field without further aid," she declared in a cablegram.[50]

Meanwhile, Klopsch and Talmage began shifting attention toward a new campaign to help Armenian refugees seeking asylum in the United States.

"Emigration is now generally conceded to be the only hope of the Armenian people," the *Christian Herald* reported in mid-May. Over the next several months, the newspaper joined forces with several other Protestant agencies—including the ABCFM, the Salvation Army, and the Woman's Christian Temperance Union (WCTU)—to promote Armenian resettlement. "There is probably no class of immigrants . . . more deserving of pity and assistance than the Armenians," one *Christian Herald* contributor declared. Like the Israelites wandering in the wilderness, another author maintained, Armenian exiles fleeing "the cruel fate decreed for them by the Turk" had been unable to find lasting shelter anywhere in Europe. "Who is to be the Moses to lead this persecuted people to a land of freedom and liberty?" The answer was clear: "America should glory in being the helper of the oppressed" and provide them with a permanent home.[51]

The *Christian Herald* urged readers to petition the U.S. government to extend special consideration to the growing streams of Armenian refugees arriving on American shores. Although immigration laws were necessary to prevent entry "of any who would be a burden upon or a menace to the welfare of the community," Armenians did not fall into this category. One observer insisted that the "thousands of natives of the ancient Eden" who had already immigrated to the United States had "in almost every instance proved acceptable citizens, successful merchants, and capable, self-supporting artisans or tradesmen." Despite having brought little with them to this country, all had prospered. Unlike other immigrant groups, Armenians eschewed "national clannishness" in favor of aggressive assimilation. "In a word," one editorialist concluded, "they are fellow Christians who deserve our warmest aid in their extremity. To welcome them is good business and an act of highest Christian charity."[52]

In addition to publishing articles that stressed the exemplary qualities of the Armenian people and imploring American evangelicals to advocate on their behalf, Klopsch committed to providing practical aid to refugees who arrived at Ellis Island "without friends and practically helpless in a strange land." The *Christian Herald*, he announced, would offer these vulnerable newcomers meals and shelter at a boarding house on Third Avenue until they could find employment or leave the city to join Armenians settled elsewhere. To expedite these outcomes, Klopsch encouraged subscribers who knew of any job openings to contact the *Chris-*

tian Herald office. He also collaborated with officers of the Salvation Army and the WCTU to devise a scheme for establishing agricultural colonies in the West and South—what he called "new and undeveloped sections of the country"—where the immigrants "would be a welcome addition to the population" rather than a threat to urban labor markets. Readers wishing to support these benevolent enterprises could again contribute to the newspaper's fund for Armenian relief, which reopened for donations in mid-August.[53]

For his energetic efforts on behalf of the exiles, as well as his ongoing support of ABCFM missionaries in the field, Klopsch received enthusiastic commendations from fellow evangelicals who appreciated the *Christian Herald*'s unequivocal stance toward the calamity in the Ottoman Empire. By clearly and consistently presenting the crisis as a holy war between faithful Christians and fanatical Muslim oppressors, the newspaper succeeded in engaging a broad segment of the American public in its relief campaign. Although this rhetorical strategy undermined Klopsch's attempts to partner with Barton and the ARC, the tribalist approach enabled him to cooperate harmoniously with groups such as the ABCFM, the Salvation Army, and the WCTU—all of which adopted similar frameworks for interesting their constituents in the plight of Armenian sufferers.

Leaders from these organizations expressed gratitude for Klopsch's unstinting support of their efforts to aid refugees fleeing "that accursed Turkish Empire" as well as those struggling to survive in their native land. "I wish to thank you and . . . your readers for the noble and generous way in which they came to the relief of . . . the many thousand suffering Armenian fellow Christians," wrote Grace Kimball. Commander Frederick Booth-Tucker sent a similar letter of appreciation for the *Christian Herald*'s help with feeding and sheltering Armenian exiles at the Salvation Army farm in Ramsey, New Jersey. Frances Willard, the indefatigable president of the WCTU who worked tirelessly to relocate refugees "escaping from the dominion of the Turk," thanked Klopsch for donating funds to her relief campaign and praised the *Christian Herald* for giving "more money to help the Armenian sufferers than any paper in the world." Like Kimball and Booth-Tucker, Willard recognized that the *Christian Herald*'s success was premised on its appeal among American evangelicals who believed they were fulfilling a sacred duty to assist their Armenian brothers and sisters in Christ as they suffered for the faith or sought asylum in the United States. For this audience, Klopsch's emphasis on the spiritual, political, and cultural affinities binding "Christian America" to oppressed Armenia held far more allure than Barton's pleas for impartiality and neutrality in the field of foreign aid.[54]

Although abandoning a cosmopolitan ethic in favor of tribal charity effectively established the *Christian Herald* as a major channel of evangelical almsgiving during the Armenian crisis, this approach would continue to trouble relations among leaders like Klopsch and Barton as they competed to shape U.S. foreign aid policy in the years to come. Indeed, just a few months after Barton returned from her Armenian mission, the American public began to debate options for responding to a catastrophe much closer to home. As Cuban rebels fought for independence, Spanish forces carried out brutal campaigns against insurgents and noncombatants alike, resulting in widespread misery throughout the island. When the *Christian Herald* and the ARC endeavored to collaborate in an effort to relieve starving peasants during the spring of 1898, the tensions between their divergent understandings of international humanitarianism came to a head in a confrontation that widened the growing gulf between evangelical almsgivers and their increasingly vocal critics.

3

WE ARE FIGHTING FOR
PHILANTHROPY

By December 1896, the crisis in Armenia appeared to be abating. Although there was "still much suffering," the *Christian Herald* reported, serious outbreaks of violence seemed to have stopped. Through the generosity of the Christian people of America, the newspaper declared, Armenian refugees were making their way to American shores, where they would find sanctuary and a new life of liberty in "God's country." Evangelicals ought to celebrate their contributions to this great work of charity and consider what other good deeds they might undertake as they strove to "cultivate more than ever before the love of men and concern for their welfare, which was Christ's prominent characteristic," Talmage and Klopsch proclaimed in a congratulatory editorial. "When before in the history of the world did the readers of any journal, religious or secular, do what the *Christian Herald* readers are doing for the persecuted Christians of Armenia?" they queried. Surely this "band of brothers and sisters" would continue a multitude of good works in the days to come. Indeed, over the course of the coming year, the editors declared, the *Christian Herald* would invite American evangelicals "to accompany it into new avenues of usefulness."[1]

Among the many opportunities to "feed the hungry, to sympathize with the sorrowing, to succor the oppressed," one would come to arouse the sympathy of Christians throughout the nation: the mounting "misery and death and anarchy" on the nearby island of Cuba. Since February 1896, General Valeriano Weyler had been conducting a ruthless war against insurgents fighting for independence from Spanish rule. Believing that the rebels were receiving widespread assistance from the civilian population, Weyler determined to root out the dissidents by forcibly relocating rural farmers and townspeople to urban areas where they would remain under strict army surveillance. Americans were quick to condemn the cruelty of Weyler's "reconcentration" policy. "At the present moment there is no other topic so universally and absorbingly discussed by the entire American people," the *Christian Herald* reported in January 1897.[2]

Recognizing that the general's orders prevented planters from cultivating their crops, the newspaper warned that devastating famine was likely: "Unless the military strain is relaxed and the land allowed to be used, great suffering is unavoidable." In the coming months, fears about the effects of Weyler's tactics became a reality. By June, Klopsch and Talmage observed that "almost every Cuban mail brings to this country some new and startling story of brutality inflicted upon the helpless Cuban peasantry by the Spanish troops under the name of military law."[3]

As reports of the indignities and increasing deprivation on the island filled the pages of the *Christian Herald* and other popular newspapers, public deliberations about how to respond to the growing humanitarian crisis intensified. Some advocated sending American troops to aid "downtrodden Cuba in her struggle for emancipation from Spain's cruel yoke." Others insisted that military action would violate the United States' long-standing policy of nonintervention in the affairs of other nations.[4]

Klopsch and Talmage proposed a middle ground between the extremes of armed invasion and ongoing isolation. "Although the policy of our own government is one of strict neutrality," they wrote, "this does not prevent the extending of practical sympathy and relief . . . through the *Christian Herald.*" From their perspective, the calamity in Cuba provided a perfect opportunity for American evangelicals to shape the development of U.S. foreign policy at a pivotal moment in the nation's history. "We are . . . no longer a third-rate power like Belgium, or Portugal, or Denmark today, but the equal of the greatest. We are to help set the fashion, as to when struggling nations should be encouraged," Talmage boasted. Given the United States' long-standing commitment to the ideals of freedom, democracy, and Christian morality, he argued, the country was uniquely positioned to influence global events by pursuing a foreign policy based on the Golden Rule. By offering alms to afflicted Cubans, Americans would not only prove their nation's worthiness as an emerging world power but also help determine the character of international relations by setting an example for other countries. Extending charity, rather than exercising military authority or remaining detached, was the way to promote a new global order of universal peace and goodwill.[5]

Evangelicals ought to be at the forefront of this effort to extend American benevolence abroad and advance the millennial reign of Christ in world affairs, Talmage asserted. "The first heart to respond to the cry of sufferers from drought, or flood, or earthquake, or cruelty," he declared, "should be the Christian heart." Over the past seven years, the *Christian Herald*'s readers had proved their faithfulness as good Samaritans, having already raised and distributed over $500,000 in humanitarian assistance. Having "become the bearers of embassies of love and succor to the afflicted and suffering throughout the world," Klopsch contended, the newspaper's subscribers were now poised to take a leading role in the expansion of U.S. aid overseas through the evangelical press. "Let the pages of religious journalism spread out the story of all such woes, and collect relief, and disburse alms all around our suffering world," Talmage proclaimed in December 1897 at a moment when the misery in Cuba had become too acute to ignore. "Religious journalism ought to become the aqueduct through which the Christian charities of the world should pour until there is no more hunger to be fed and no more ignorance to be educated, and no more nakedness to be clothed, and no more suffering to assuage."[6]

In keeping with this vision, Klopsch and Talmage began to make concrete plans for a new humanitarian aid campaign to help their island neighbors. Rather than simply raising money through newspaper appeals as they had in earlier relief efforts, this time the partners assumed a more ambitious role for the *Christian Herald* and its subscribers. When Secretary of State John Sherman issued a press release on Christmas Eve urging Americans to contribute money and provisions to Cuba, Klopsch immediately offered to collect donations through the *Christian Herald*. But he also offered to partner with the government in organizing a committee that would work alongside chambers of commerce, boards of trade, and other relief agencies—including the American Red Cross (ARC)—to coordinate fund-raising activities and forward contributions to the U.S. consul-general in Havana.[7]

Realizing "the need of orderly and concerted effort under well-directed control if timely assistance [was] to be given to the sick and needy," President William McKinley moved quickly to establish the Central Cuban Relief Committee (CCRC), which comprised three appointed members: Stephen E. Barton, nephew of Clara Barton and the second vice president of the ARC; Charles E. Schieren of the New York Chamber of Commerce; and Louis Klopsch, proprietor of the *Christian Herald*. The CCRC, which was authorized to act under the supervision and direction of the secretary of state in the name of the U.S. government, met for the first time on January 3, 1898, at the *Christian Herald* headquarters to devise a strategy for enlisting "the sympathies of the entire nation."[8]

Klopsch and Talmage were jubilant. Having recognized American evangelicals' "magnificent philanthropies in other fields," they exclaimed, the president of the United States was now inviting them to "inaugurate the relief campaign in stricken Cuba." By offering Klopsch a leadership position on the CCRC, McKinley had signaled his appreciation for the religious community in coordinating and shaping the nation's official policies of humanitarian aid. Over the next several months, Klopsch and his colleagues at the *Christian Herald* would take full advantage of McKinley's confidence as they strove to advance their vision of the United States as a redeemer nation divinely ordained to usher in an era of millennial peace by uplifting, protecting, and saving the world's oppressed and needy people.[9]

Central Cuban Relief Committee in session at the offices of the *Christian Herald.*
From *Report of the Central Cuban Relief Committee to the Secretary of State,*
Washington, D.C., c. 1898. Courtesy of Widener Library, Harvard University.

By capitalizing on a formal partnership between the federal government and their own faith-based humanitarian organization, these enterprising leaders hoped to secure the *Christian Herald*'s position—and by extension the standing of the broader evangelical community—as the leading provider of American aid and an influential voice in U.S. international affairs. With Klopsch at the center of the Cuban relief campaign, and the expansive constituency of *Christian Herald* readers engaged in the effort to alleviate affliction among the *reconcentrados*—civilians devastated by General Weyler's oppressive policies—evangelicals believed they could play a pivotal role in helping the United States fulfill its global mission of "assuaging human suffering and bringing the nations nearer to the Kingdom."[10]

Even as they celebrated their power to Christianize international relations, evangelical almsgivers faced a series of challenges in 1898 that hampered their efforts to promote world peace through philanthropy. As calls for military action in Cuba intensified after the explosion of the USS *Maine* in February, the *Christian Herald*'s mediating position became increasingly difficult to maintain. Klopsch, Talmage, and their associates continued to advocate for a diplomatic and peaceful resolution to the conflict so that aid to the suffering could continue, but their voices ultimately went unheeded. When war broke out between the United States and Spain in late April, these evangelical leaders were forced to wrestle with their assumptions about the connections among Christian charity, foreign policy, and American destiny. Dismayed by the prospect of losing their influence among government officials and the broader public—especially amid an embarrassing clash with Clara Barton that resulted in Klopsch's forced resignation from the CCRC—the *Christian Herald*'s editorial team chose to endorse the administration's declaration of war against Spain as an action "inspired by mercy."[11]

By expanding their definition of benevolence to encompass "righteous" wars of liberation, Klopsch and Talmage paved the way for American evangelicals to embrace the United States' subsequent military interventions in the Spanish colonies of Puerto Rico, Guam, Samoa, and the Philippines as expressions of humanitarianism. These conflicts, the editors proclaimed, were "God's way of . . . giving us what he intends to be our share in the enlightenment and enfranchisement of the whole world." In addition to the "work of feeding the hungry, clothing the naked, and saving the dying from death," they insisted, the United States was now called to "redeem," "civilize," and "Christianize" the people "brought under [its] protection."[12]

Although some constituents protested the newspaper's decision to sanction American imperialism as a form of Christian charity, many more welcomed this way of interpreting the nation's expanding empire. Subscriptions to the *Christian Herald* soared during the Spanish-American War and the ensuing conflicts in the Philippines. As the United States continued to extend its economic, military, and political power around the world, the concept of imperial humanitarianism replaced pacifism as the dominant framework through which American evangelicals came to envision the nation's global mission.[13]

"LET ALL HELP CUBA NOW"

"Cuba Needs Our Help," the *Christian Herald* declared in early January 1898. Since the start of the struggle for independence in the summer of 1895, the newspaper had been chronicling the rebels' progress in their fight for freedom, the harshness and brutality of Spanish military forces, and the devastating distress among the civilian population. By December 1897, suffering on the island had become so severe that President McKinley finally determined the United States must act.[14]

Resisting mounting pressure to send military support to the insurgents, the president instead proposed humanitarian aid as a solution to the crisis. In addition to issuing a Christmas Eve appeal for charitable contributions, the *Christian Herald* reported, McKinley and his State Department staff had "taken prompt action to make the relief movement a national one" by establishing the CCRC to supervise the collection and disbursement of donations. Klopsch's appointment to a leadership position on this important body, Talmage suggested, indicated that "the highest authority in the land—the President of the United States" recognized the crucial role American evangelicals had played in past efforts to alleviate affliction both at home and abroad. Now, government officials were counting on the *Christian Herald*'s proprietor and subscribers to make the Cuban campaign a success.[15]

Klopsch and Talmage accepted this charge with confident enthusiasm. Since taking control of the *Christian Herald* in 1890, the partners had repeatedly demonstrated their ability to stir up sympathy for distressed people both in and beyond the United States. The newspaper's graphic descriptions of famine in Russia, heartrending stories of financial devastation in New York City, and gruesome tales of massacre in Armenia had prompted "the Lord's people of all denominations" from every state in the nation to contribute generously during the *Christian Herald*'s previous relief efforts. The publication's innovative use of visual technologies to document the needs of distant sufferers proved especially effective in fostering concern for afflicted people in foreign lands.[16]

By acknowledging every donation in the columns of the *Christian Herald* and closing each fund-raising campaign with an audited account of collections and expenditures, Klopsch assured subscribers that the journal offered an efficient and trustworthy channel for their philanthropic endeavors. Given this track record, Talmage contended in January 1898, the newspaper was more than ready to take the lead in this latest humanitarian crisis. "We trust that the readers of the *Christian Herald,* ever prompt and cheerful in enterprises of humanity, and whose glorious benevolences have already gone abroad 'to the utmost ends of the earth' will take the cause of Cuba to their hearts and respond liberally and promptly to the call."[17]

Rescuing the *reconcentrados* from starvation, these publicists argued, offered American evangelicals an opportunity to prove that the president's trust in them was well placed and, even more importantly, to demonstrate that they were called by God to help make the United States the foremost champion of persecuted and impoverished people everywhere. "Not only the eyes of our government and nation," Talmage declared, "but of the whole civilized world are upon us." By invoking John Winthrop's famous sermon, *A Modell of Christian Charity,* Talmage connected the Cuban relief effort to a deeply rooted and increasingly popular image of the United States as a Christian nation divinely commissioned to uplift and protect the downtrodden. At a time when the European powers seemed to be abdicating responsibility to intercede on behalf of the beleaguered Armenians, Talmage charged, American efforts to lessen suffering "at our very doors" would present "Continental governments some splendid object lessons in practical Christianity." Because the United States remained unhampered by historical legacies of monarchy, aristocracy, ecclesiastical hierarchy, religious establishment, and warfare, Talmage had consistently argued, the American nation was better suited than Great Britain or other European empires to spread Christian civilization around the world through the practice of philanthropy. By extending "the hand of succor to these helpless and dying Cubans," he proclaimed, American evangelicals would advance both the "religion of Jesus Christ" and the United States' international reputation as a global power dedicated to promoting peace and prosperity among all nations.[18]

As fund-raising for Cuban relief got under way, Klopsch and Talmage praised McKinley for pursuing a humane foreign policy that avoided the pitfalls of apathy toward the afflicted, on the one hand, and aggressive interventionism, on the other. While it would be unthinkable to remain aloof from the terrible privations of the Cuban people, they implied, engaging in military action against Spain would undermine the United States' opportunity to foster goodwill in the international arena. "We hate jingoism and the spirit of conquest," Talmage had declared during the summer of 1897 when calls for sending American troops to assist the insurgents were growing louder. As a Christian nation, he argued, the United States ought to support the Cuban struggle for self-determination but only through peaceful means and always with selfless intentions that reflected the spirit of the Good Samaritan.[19]

Rather than entering into a bloody battle with Spain that risked embroiling the nation in the imperialist politics dominating international relations during this period, Talmage contended, McKinley had wisely chosen to summon "one of the grandest armies of consecrated Christian workers the world has ever seen . . . into active service." Over the past several years, participants in the *Christian Herald*'s campaigns to alleviate suffering in Russia, Armenia, and elsewhere had triumphed over the forces of famine, disease, and persecution through "peace and loving help and succor." Unlike "Caesar's famous legions and the Old Guard of Napoleon" who "maimed by sword and bullet," these veterans had "not slain their thousands, but saved them instead to lives of happiness and blessing . . . through heroic, self-denying effort." By enlisting the help of these evangelical humanitarians in Cuba, Talmage implied, the president and his administration had demonstrated their commitment to expanding American influence in international affairs through Christian charity.[20]

As Talmage and Klopsch expected, American evangelicals were quick to contribute to the Cuban relief campaign. Within five weeks, the *Christian Herald* had collected nearly $20,000 from donors across the United States. In his role as a member of the CCRC, Klopsch was in close contact with Fitzhugh Lee, the U.S. consul-general charged with overseeing aid distribution on the island. In response to Lee's appeals for specific items, Klopsch coordinated the shipping of one hundred hospital beds and $5,000 worth of food for children. He also promised to help recruit twenty-five nurses to travel to Havana and offered to guarantee their salaries for a period of three months. All of this was made possible, the *Christian Herald* reported, through the generous gifts of readers "who show a noble appreciation of Christian stewardship and the responsibility that comes with the power to help others." Through this good work, donors were not only "feeding the hungry, clothing the naked, and ministering to the sick" but teaching Cuban children that they had "kind friends in the 'great country not far away'" and offering "a striking and memorable object lesson to the entire world."[21]

Less than a week after the *Christian Herald* published this account celebrating American munificence and the effects the campaign was having on the United States' international reputation, an explosion aboard the USS *Maine* sank the battleship in the Havana harbor, killing two-thirds of its crew members and injuring many more. Although the cause of the blast was unknown, newspapers such as William Randolph Hearst's *New York Journal* and Joseph Pulitzer's *New York World* fueled speculation that Spain was responsible. As long-standing advocates of armed intervention in Cuba, Hearst and Pulitzer insisted that the sinking of the *Maine* was the last straw in a series of offenses perpetrated by the Spanish. In the weeks following the catastrophe, coverage of the incident and the subsequent investigation invigorated the public outcry against Spain and galvanized demands that the United States take military action in response.[22]

Klopsch and Talmage recognized that the loss of the *Maine* and the increasing public indignation toward Spain posed a significant threat to the Cuban relief campaign as a means of promoting international peace through Christian philanthropy. As the *New York Journal* and the *World* printed increasingly incendiary stories, the evangelical publicists lambasted the "mischievous efforts of malignant journalists to inflame the public mind." Accusations of Spanish treachery against the *Maine*, they contended, were "too horrible to be entertained without the most cogent evidence." Rather than allowing themselves "to be moved by the hysterical shrieking of journals which have stooped to falsehood and calumny," these evangelicals insisted, "the duty of all our citizens is to suspend judgment . . . until the court of investigation has finished its inquiries . . . lest false and unjust charges be entertained."[23]

Although some intemperate persons "would have liked to see our government declare war on Spain immediately after the disaster," the editors declared, the president and his advisers had thankfully recognized that this course of action would not serve the national interest. "Wars are barbaric," Talmage proclaimed in an editorial published in early March. "They may start about a technicality or a national misunderstanding, but before the first battle is over, the whole scene rolls back into the dark ages, and it becomes wholesale butchery, and war is only murder on a large scale." Although the destruction of the *Maine* was "one of the worst calamities of the centuries," he declared, "this disaster . . . was probably allowed to show us something of the horror of war, that we might be induced to keep out of it." Even if the inquiry into the cause of the explosion were eventually to show that "a wrong has been done us," the United States' government ought to "demand reparation with the majesty of a calm self-respecting nation" and in so doing increase the "respect of the world for the American character."[24]

During this period of tense waiting and warmongering, Talmage advised, "all those who know how to pray should be more and more earnest in petition for the reign of universal peace." He also encouraged American evangelicals to persevere in their efforts to assuage the suffering *reconcentrados*. In response to subscribers who asked whether aid to Cuba should continue given recent events and escalating hostility toward Spain, Talmage and Klopsch insisted that ongoing assistance was a Christian imperative. "Suppose it should be found that the blowing up of the *Maine* was the act of the Spaniards," Talmage wrote. "Would it improve the situation in the smallest degree if we were to permit 50,000 or 100,000 human beings to starve whom we might have saved—people who had nothing whatever to do with the disaster?" These "peaceful agriculturalists and village laborers," he maintained, "are innocent victims . . . whose very lives now hang upon our fidelity to [Christ's] teachings." Rather than allow themselves to get caught up in the clamor for revenge against Spain, Talmage argued, American evangelicals must remain committed to making the United States a redemptive force in the international arena. "It is not because we are a powerful nation that these sufferers have appealed to us for succor, but because we are a humane Christian people," he declared. Therefore, "in His Name, let us go forward, without hesitation, leaving the issues of war and peace in the hands of the great Disposer of events." Humanitarian aid to the Cubans must remain an integral feature of American foreign policy if the United States was to maintain its standing as the world's most faithful and fitting champion of the weak and oppressed.[25]

Fostering this image of "Christian America" preoccupied Klopsch and Talmage in the wake of the *Maine* incident. As the nation awaited the outcome of the government's investigation into the explosion, the partners sought to divert attention from deteriorating relations with Spain by focusing on the devastating misery in Cuba. Although the American people had already heard about "much of the terrible suffering" on the island, many remained skeptical that conditions were as awful as some reports claimed. "That such a calamity could occur within a half day's sail of an American port seems incredible," Klopsch and Talmage acknowledged, "and it is not surprising that the statement should have been called in question by many on hearing it for the first time." The increasingly sensational stories of abuse and oppression that appeared in hawkish newspapers like Hearst's *New York Journal* also raised suspicions about the accuracy of media accounts.[26]

Seeking to address these concerns, the *Christian Herald* assured its readers that the editors' close connections with State Department officials in Washington and Havana gave the newspaper access to the most current information. Talmage boasted that he had developed relationships with many leading political figures, including President McKinley, since accepting a call to pastor the First Presbyterian Church in the nation's capital during the fall of 1895. As a member of the CCRC, Klopsch corresponded with Consul-General Lee on a regular basis and also worked directly with members of the ARC—including Clara Barton, who arrived in Cuba to help with the distribution of relief in early February.[27]

In addition, the *Christian Herald* had engaged Sylvester "Harry" Scovel—an enterprising journalist who had traveled throughout Cuba reporting on the insurgency and the ruinous effects of Weyler's reconcentration policies since 1895—to prepare an illustrated pamphlet on the condition of the famine-stricken people. "This presentation of the actual case, by an eye-witness who has been among the sufferers and knows whereof he speaks," the editors declared, "is a complete, compact, graphic and accurate statement and will furnish all the information needful for those who are interested in aiding the work." Although Scovel had become famous as a correspondent for Pulitzer's *World*, Klopsch and Talmage suggested that he had returned to Cuba in January at their behest, traveling to the island "almost direct from the *Christian Herald* offices, in the Bible House." Scovel's letters, the editors suggested, "are written with a perfect knowledge of the facts and are therefore an accurate and trustworthy record. They constitute the first complete and undisguised story of the famine that has yet been published." Unlike secular papers that were circulating Scovel's dispatches and other sensational accounts to stir up public ire against Spain, the evangelicals intimated, the *Christian Herald* offered the American public an honest source of news aimed only to further the noble goals of the United States' humanitarian "mission of peace and succor."[28]

Despite these assurances of journalistic integrity, many Americans continued to express doubts about the extent of the suffering in Cuba. In late February, for example, Senator Redfield Proctor made an unofficial visit to the island to ascertain whether accounts of the affliction were accurate. Having "received through the mail a leaflet published by the *Christian Herald*" containing images of emaciated *reconcentrados,* Proctor reported, "I went to Cuba with a strong conviction that the picture had been overdrawn, and that a few cases of starvation and suffering had inspired and stimulated the press correspondents."[29]

Although many of the *Christian Herald*'s readers were confident the stories and photographs published in the newspaper were credible, some did raise concerns about the effectiveness of the relief effort. Dellis E. Francis, from Saginaw, Michigan, indicated that she had been reading about the crisis and had desired to help but first wanted to know how donations would make it to the *reconcentrados* given the worsening political situation on the island. "The ports are controlled by Spaniards," she noted, "and it has been explained to me that the Spaniards would get the largest share of whatever is sent." Before remitting the $20 his church had collected, Gus Johnson of Ann Arbor, Michigan, wanted to make sure the money forwarded through the *Christian Herald* would be safe, as many were afraid that "the Spaniards may in some way get it." Another subscriber from Iowa wrote that "one paper stated that the Cubans did not receive the supplies sent them, but that they were taken by the Spaniards."[30]

Seeking to allay these fears before they derailed the fund-raising campaign, Klopsch determined to undertake his own inspection of the relief work. After receiving approval for a visit from Consul-General Lee and encouragement from his CCRC colleagues, Klopsch requested a passport and letters of introduction from the State Department. He and his wife boarded a steamer bound for Havana on Saturday, March 5. The following Wednesday, they arrived on the island ready to tour the distribution facilities and ensure that efforts to ameliorate starvation and sickness among the suffering multitudes were indeed running smoothly.[31]

Over the next several weeks, the *Christian Herald* published detailed accounts of Klopsch's activities designed to reassure American evangelicals that the stories of affliction among the *reconcentrados* were reliable and that their attempts to aid the sufferers were not in vain. From the moment he set foot in Cuba, Klopsch resolved to visit "every centre of destitution that time will permit" in order to provide eyewitness reports of conditions and thorough assessments of the relief work. His inquiries affirmed that "frightful and wretched misery" prevailed in many parts of the island and that without the assistance of generous American donors, many innocent victims would have already perished. "It is indeed literally true that thousands have been almost 'snatched from the grave' by the opportune arrival of the food that came to them as though like manna to the children of Israel," the *Christian Herald* reported on March 16.[32]

The following day, Senator Proctor delivered a speech to Congress recounting the results of his own fact-finding mission in Cuba. "What I saw I cannot tell so that others can see it," Proctor told his fellow lawmakers. The distress was so intense that he simply could not describe it. Proctor also spoke of the relief effort "in the highest terms." "The American people may be assured that their bounty will reach the sufferers with the least possible cost, and in the best manner in every respect," he declared. With this official corroboration of the *Christian Herald*'s reports from one of the nation's most respected statesmen, the editors proclaimed, donors could be confident that they were "doing splendid service for Christ and humanity in the work of Cuban relief."[33]

Having received an endorsement from Proctor, as well as from several other prominent American statesmen who affirmed the widespread suffering and urgent necessity of relief after visiting Cuba, Klopsch moved quickly to expand the humanitarian mission beyond Havana and other port cities into the interior. Although he confirmed that aid delivery in many regions was progressing well, his thorough investigation of the provinces revealed that there remained "a very large Cuban territory as yet totally untouched by the relief work, and where the horrors of famine and disease are raging unchecked." Seeking to remedy this situation, Klopsch appealed to the American public to send more contributions. "Unless we can get, regularly and without a break, 300 tons of cornmeal and fifty tons of lard or bacon every week, we cannot give effective relief," he declared in a cablegram dated March 21.[34]

Reporting that both Consul-General Lee and Clara Barton "agree that supplies in greatly increased quantities are urgently needed," the *Christian Herald* urged American evangelicals to increase their giving. "Fifteen thousand dollars weekly will feed every starving man, woman and child in Cuba," Klopsch wrote. To ensure that adequate provisions reached the neediest towns, Klopsch proposed "to send a special steamer . . . to make a tour of the famine towns other than Havana along the coast" and arranged for "twenty-three railroad cars, loaded with food and a supply of medicine," to travel to different parts of the island. During his visits to various "centers of suffering," Klopsch also helped establish efficient relief stations, bakeries, and hospitals. Recognizing that U.S. consuls, local mayors, and others involved in distributing humanitarian assistance would require ongoing support after his departure, Klopsch "appointed three men to travel through the island, verifying the count of the needy, and seeing that supplies are properly received and handled, preventing fraud and generally aiding in the work."[35]

As he prepared to return to the United States at the end of March, Klopsch celebrated the results of his efforts to expand the relief work. "The whole island of Cuba is now covered by the new system which has been put into place," he wrote, and this method of distribution was proving a great success in carrying American charity to 296,000 destitute people in over four hundred towns and villages. It was no wonder, the *Christian Herald* reported, "that these suffering ones should look upon America as 'the home of angels,' since it has been their only hope of rescue." Nor was it any surprise that "in the recent addresses on Cuba delivered in Congress, the *Christian Herald* readers should have been recognized as the pioneers in this great humanitarian life-saving mission of the century." After all, "it was their contributions which enabled the *Christian Herald* to send Clara Barton to Havana with her Red Cross workers" and their generosity that "thrilled the whole country and induced our national government to aid the relief movement." American evangelicals, the newspaper proclaimed, could take credit for initiating, organizing, and leading this "sacred mission" of Christian charity, which showcased the United States' commitment to promoting peace and goodwill among all nations by alleviating the afflicted and uplifting the weak.[36]

As Klopsch boarded the steamer *Havana* bound for Tampa on March 30, his hopes for the ongoing influence of evangelical philanthropy on U.S. foreign policy were facing serious challenges on several fronts. "Amid many warlike rumors and gathering clouds of trouble on every side," Klopsch fretted that the humanitarian aims he had accomplished in Cuba on behalf of "Christian America" would soon be undone if hostilities between Spain and the United States escalated. On his way back to New York, Klopsch stopped in Washington, DC, to report to the State Department on the progress of the relief work. During his meeting with Assistant Secretaries of State Alvey Adee and William Day, Klopsch expressed his profound fear that a declaration of war followed by the closing of Cuban ports would result in deadly starvation for at least 150,000 *reconcentrados*, "thus destroying the very people who are now depending on our energies to save them." Upon hearing this concern, Day arranged for an interview with President McKinley and members of his cabinet so Klopsch could share his views. Since McKinley himself had initiated the campaign for Cuban relief and remained deeply resistant to war, Klopsch felt confident that his information might help sway the president to maintain peace despite mounting pressure from many within Congress for military intervention.[37]

Klopsch's audience with McKinley took place on the afternoon of Saturday, April 2. The following morning, accounts of the meeting in Sunday newspapers all over the country created a sensation. According to several prominent publications (including the *Morning Times* of Washington, DC, the New York *Sun,* the *Chicago Daily Tribune,* and the *San Francisco Chronicle*), Klopsch had strongly urged McKinley not to take up arms against Spain. "My words to the President," Klopsch reportedly told a New York *Sun* correspondent, "were: 'The pen that signs a declaration of war signs the death warrant of 150,000 *reconcentrados.*'"[38]

In addition to making this plea for peace on behalf of the afflicted sufferers, Klopsch had allegedly asserted that most Cubans did not consider their country capable of self-government and therefore preferred autonomy (home rule) to independence. "The better class of people in Cuba," Klopsch purportedly remarked, "would consider independence a terrible calamity" because they feared that "certain insurgents, who have for years been accustomed to lawless lives . . . would keep up the lawless-ness." Most worrisome to the majority of Cubans, Klopsch supposedly said, was the possibility that the "negroes" who made up "60 percent at least" of the rebel forces "would prey like vultures upon the property of their neighbors" if the country were to achieve full freedom. For all of these reasons, he reportedly told McKinley and his advisers, "a war at this time with Spain would be the greatest crime of the century."[39]

Klopsch's appeal for continued diplomacy that would enable on-going humanitarian work among the *reconcentrados* provoked a range of reactions among American statesmen, journalists, and the broader public. Those wary of intervening in the Cuban conflict praised Klopsch for providing the president with "the facts to sustain his argument in behalf of a policy of peace." But many advocates of military action con-demned the editor's attempt to avert a war. Some critics accused Klopsch of misrepresenting Consul-General Lee by telling the president that American officials in Cuba did not favor intervention on behalf of the insurgents. Some also speculated that Klopsch promoted a "peace at any price policy" to protect American business interests on the island—particularly those of Edwin F. Atkins of Boston, "the big sugar planta-tion owner of Cuba," who consistently counseled American lawmakers to maintain strict neutrality toward the revolutionaries so that the Spanish government would continue to respect the property of U.S. citizens.[40]

In fact, one article in the *Brooklyn Daily Eagle* alleged that both At-kins and Klopsch were present at the White House meeting with McKinley and his cabinet. According to Gonzales Quesada, the Cuban delegate to Washington, the *Eagle* reported, Atkins and Klopsch had "been sent by the Spanish authorities in Cuba" to oppose independence. By advocating for peace, Quesada declared, "Mr. Klopsch has been used as a mouth-piece for the Spanish" and ought to be exposed as "a hireling of the Spanish government." Rather than upholding American ideals of "char-acter, manhood, generosity, Christian principle," another detractor charged, Klopsch, who might be "an emissary of Spain," would instead "have the United States play into the hands of Spaniards, to assist in crushing the liberty-loving, freedom-aspiring Cubans." "No, no, Dr. Klopsch," this critic concluded, "you do not understand American character."[41]

Keenly aware that these accusations damaged not only his own reputation but by extension the *Christian Herald*'s bid to represent the United States internationally through evangelical charity, Klopsch vigorously contested the charges. On Monday, April 4, he telephoned the *Eagle* to insist that the newspaper's correspondent had misunderstood him and misrepresented his views. He also sent a letter to the editor of the *New York Tribune* requesting "the privilege of your columns to correct certain statements which have been wrongly attributed to me, in recent interviews, concerning my visit to Washington." "It has been asserted," Klopsch declared, "that I went to the National capitol with a 'peace-at-any-price' object, and in behalf of certain interests in Cuba." Avowing that he had never presumed to speak for Consul-General Lee on matters relating to Cuba, that he had no interests in Cuba beyond the mission of saving the starving *reconcentrados,* and that the idea the Spanish sent him to influence President McKinley was ridiculous, Klopsch insisted his anti-war stance was the logical outcome of his interest in the people he endeavored to keep alive through the contributions of the American people. Humanitarian concern, not personal political opinion or shadowy economic motivations, Klopsch avowed, inspired his efforts to persuade the president and his advisers to keep pursuing peace.[42]

Over the next several weeks, Klopsch and his associates at the *Christian Herald* continued to make the case that diplomacy was the best way to ensure security for Cuba's people and preserve the integrity of the United States as a benevolent force devoted to relieving suffering and protecting the vulnerable. "Should war now come," Talmage declared in an April 13 editorial, "the noncombatant peasantry of Cuba must inevitably perish. Their rescue from starvation by Christian America will have been in vain." Perpetrating such a terrible tragedy, he argued, would have a devastating effect on the United States' international reputation: "Shall it be recorded that our nation, which has already established a flawless fame for its humanity to the weak and the oppressed, knowingly gave over these *reconcentrados* to their fate? Or shall it be written down on the page of history that we chose the nobler part and gave them life? Which decision would be the better example to the world, and the greater honor to ourselves?" If the United States was to maintain its position as a global arbiter of goodwill, Talmage asserted, American leaders must not abandon the afflicted Cubans by engaging in a conflict that "will doom them to certain destruction." Only by staying on the "path of duty" and seeking "an honorable and lasting peace," he concluded, "can the deeds of a civilized and Christian nation be kept free from blot or stain."[43]

As the staff of the *Christian Herald* prayed that ongoing negotiations with Spain would avert an outbreak of war, they also sought to defuse another impending disaster threatening their efforts to promote international peace through evangelical almsgiving: the possibility that Louis Klopsch would lose his leadership position on the CCRC. Friction between Klopsch and the other two members of the committee—Stephen Barton and Charles Schieren—had been brewing since Klopsch arrived in Havana in mid-March. Although he went to Cuba with the support of these colleagues, Klopsch's activities on the island caused unexpected tensions that eventually provoked their censure.[44]

The trouble began the moment Klopsch disembarked in Havana and discovered that customs authorities were refusing to allow any aid provisions to leave the warehouse. Having found a box of jewelry among a shipment of relief supplies, the customs officers had become suspicious that Americans were attempting to smuggle valuable items to Cuba duty-free. As a result, they began to inspect all the consignments sent from the United States to make sure they contained no contraband. They ripped open boxes and left the contents strewn about, making the storage facility "a mass of confusion." Dismayed to learn that donations sent by American almoners were not being distributed to those in need but were rotting on the warehouse floor, Klopsch immediately acted to remedy the situation. On the morning of his second day in Cuba, he drove to the storage facility with a letter in hand from the Spanish governor indicating that the embargo had been lifted and disbursements could resume.[45]

Klopsch soon discerned, however, that disseminating food, medicine, and clothing quickly and efficiently was proving to be a great challenge. An inspection of the relief stations throughout Havana later that afternoon revealed a host of inadequacies: perishable goods piled on docks, appalling conditions at the municipal shelter, and thousands of people "walking the streets more than half naked, and many altogether so." Outside the capital, Klopsch was told, circumstances were even worse. All across the island, "provisions were rotting in warehouses, while the starving continued to starve and die."[46]

Distraught to find the relief work "at a standstill," Klopsch sought an interview with Consul-General Lee, who had been charged by the State Department with distributing supplies sent through the CCRC. During this meeting, which took place on day three of Klopsch's visit, Lee confessed that he "had been unable to give close attention to the details of relief work, owing to the heavy and exacting duties of the Consular office" and had largely turned over responsibility for disseminating provisions to the ARC. Although Clara Barton and her staff had worked hard since their mid-February arrival to meet the overwhelming need, it was clear to Klopsch that a better system was needed.[47]

After spending several days touring the countryside, Klopsch returned to Havana and arranged a consultation with Barton to propose a "more satisfactory . . . division of work." According to his plan, the ARC would "henceforth devote itself exclusively to hospital, asylum, and kindred work," which was funded through contributions from the *Christian Herald*. Responsibility for allocating aid to the afflicted in and beyond Havana would rest with a relief committee appointed by Klopsch and consisting of a local Cuban physician, an American who worked for the Western Railway of Cuba, and Consul-General Lee, who would arbitrate in case of any dispute.[48]

With this new method of organization in place, Klopsch believed the situation in Havana would greatly improve, and he could begin making arrangements for sending aid into interior areas of the island. The conversation with Barton, however, did not produce the outcome Klopsch had hoped for. What actually ensued was, in the words of one ARC employee, a "rumpus of a first-class dimension" as Barton and Klopsch engaged in a fierce battle for control of the relief work in Cuba and, by extension, for leadership of the United States' humanitarian mission.[49]

By the time Barton and Klopsch met for dinner at the Hotel Inglaterra in Havana on March 15, 1898, tensions between the two formidable personalities had been building for several years. Their attempted partnership during the campaign to aid victims of the Armenian massacres in the spring of 1896 had exposed serious differences in their beliefs about the purpose and practice of international philanthropy. From the beginning of that collaboration, Barton had bristled at Klopsch's apparent lack of confidence in her abilities. As she struggled to administer assistance to the afflicted Armenians, she blamed her ineffectiveness on publications like the *Christian Herald,* which cast the conflict in religious, racial, and political terms that undermined her claims to neutrality and damaged her relationship with Turkish authorities.

Barton's failure to meet expectations in Armenia fueled Klopsch's concerns about her approach and bolstered his commitment to positioning the *Christian Herald* as the nation's leading humanitarian aid agency. When Klopsch heard that Barton was seeking the president's approval to take charge of the relief effort in Cuba in the early winter of 1897, he quickly offered the State Department his own services as well as the financial support of the American evangelical community. Having secured a position on the CCRC and initiated the fund-raising campaign with great fanfare, Klopsch devised a plan he hoped would keep the ARC from usurping the *Christian Herald*'s status as the preeminent channel for extending American charity abroad.[50]

In late January, Klopsch wrote to Barton "as President of the American National Red Cross, whose object is to administer to the sick and suffering," asking her to go to Havana "to direct that phase of the American relief movement which has special reference to starving mothers and children and particularly the sick." By describing Barton's organization and its mission in Cuba in this circumscribed and explicitly gendered way, Klopsch sought to curtail her role in the broader campaign to aid the afflicted *reconcentrados.* Although he insisted it was "not his purpose or desire to in any way dictate or direct" Barton's actions in this hospital work, Klopsch's pledge to provide financial assistance in the amount of "at least Ten Thousand Dollars a month" for three months "to be expended specially for the relief of the sick women and children" would place Barton and her staff in his debt and enable the *Christian Herald* to claim credit for sponsoring the ARC's humanitarian activities in Cuba.[51]

Given her previous interactions with Klopsch, Barton hesitated to respond to his "noble and esteemed letter." But $10,000 a month was a lot of money, and she knew the need was great. On February 4, Barton accepted Klopsch's invitation but only after conferring with the State Department to ensure she had the government's approval for the mission and procuring letters of endorsement from the secretary of state and President McKinley himself. According to Barton's nephew Stephen, who served on the CCRC alongside Klopsch, the documents indicated that his aunt ought to be received in Havana not only as the representative of the *Christian Herald* but also as an agent of the U.S. government working under the direction of Consul-General Lee. In other words, Stephen later explained, Clara Barton went to Cuba under the auspices of the president and his cabinet to help with hospital work but also to "assist Consul-General Lee in the distribution of American Relief Supplies."[52]

After arriving on the island and finding the aid effort "in a state of chaos," Barton cabled the CCRC requesting reinforcements to assist in the monumental task of organizing the allocation of goods. The committee members agreed that she needed help and consented to send several ARC staff members. They also concluded that the relief work "would be very much encouraged and enhanced if a member of the Committee could accompany the supplies" and investigate "the precise conditions which we are called upon to meet and relieve." When Klopsch offered to make the trip at his own expense, Steven Barton and Schieren expressed approval, especially since his publication had "furnished such bountiful financial support" for alleviating the *reconcentrados*—far more, in fact, than any other contributing organization. Little did they know that his interactions with Clara Barton and her personnel would create so much controversy.[53]

As Klopsch and Barton sat across from one another in the dining room of the Hotel Inglaterra, they clearly held very different understandings of who had authority to oversee the relief effort and who was better suited to the assignment. Barton believed she had been commissioned by the State Department and Consul-General Lee to take charge of the aid distribution. From her perspective, Klopsch's proposal to limit her responsibility to caring for women and children in hospitals and orphanages was insulting and imperious. Although she admitted there had been problems with disbursing supplies when she arrived in Havana, Barton argued that the work had been well organized and systematized under her supervision. Based on what he had seen over the past several days, Klopsch disagreed. As a representative of the CCRC and a major donor to the cause, he claimed a duty to ensure that consignments were more efficiently delivered to the suffering *reconcentrados* and to help extend the humanitarian mission to neglected parts of the island. Furthermore, having understood that Barton "was to give her attention to hospital and orphanage work exclusively," Klopsch did not consider his attempts to promote a better distribution process an infringement on her jurisdiction but rather the restoration of a proper division of labor that would prove beneficial to all parties.[54]

Barton and her coworkers were not persuaded. The day after the dinner, her personal secretary, Charles Cottrell, fired off several letters to Stephen Barton demanding to know "what authority the Committee has given Klopsch." Complaining that Klopsch was "imbued with the spirit of dissatisfaction and fault finding" and had "antagonized everybody here by his bossy and insulting manners," Cottrell warned that Barton and her staff were likely to go home and let him "assume the burden of management" if the situation were to become any more unbearable. If Klopsch does have "carte blanche" to "regulate matters to his own satisfaction," Cottrell cautioned, "the Red Cross will have to take a back seat and . . . serve the purposes of 'the great organizer of the world.'" "I believe (and we all do)," Cottrell fumed, "that he is a liar and that he *started from New York* with the intention to break up if possible the Red Cross and have it withdraw leaving the entire field to the *Christian Herald*."[55]

Startled by these allegations, Stephen immediately cabled his aunt, urging her to "forbear, mindfully, serenely" while he investigated Cottrell's claims. At the same time, he sent a telegram to Klopsch begging him to "use moderation." To Cottrell, he composed a longer letter assuring the secretary that Klopsch's "impulsive and abrupt treatment of the Red Cross or anyone connected therewith, simply because their methods did not exactly correspond with his ideas, was not approved by me" and confirming that as a member of the CCRC, Klopsch had no authority whatsoever in "the matter of distribution, the State Department never having asked us to undertake that duty." Finally, he wrote to Fitzhugh Lee seeking to ascertain whether the consul-general had officially delegated responsibility for disseminating relief supplies and if so to whom. "We desire, as you can readily understand, to be perfectly clear in the matter," Stephen remarked.[56]

As Stephen awaited Lee's response, Klopsch tried to reassure his colleagues on the committee that all was well. "Let not your heart be troubled," he cabled to New York after receiving the chairman's chastising telegram. Meanwhile, he pushed ahead with plans to reorganize and extend the allocation of aid, announcing that several smaller distribution locations around Havana would be closed to consolidate dissemination from a central relief station. Having communicated with the railroad and telegraph departments, Klopsch also commissioned three trains to send supplies to "provinces where help was most needed."[57]

Incensed that Klopsch was interfering with what she believed was *her* commission from the U.S. government, Clara Barton determined to ask Consul-General Lee herself if the publisher "had shown any credentials and authority for his actions." Was it true, as Klopsch claimed, that the consul-general had recognized him as "the Commander in Chief" of the distribution effort? Lee's reply infuriated Barton. Since Klopsch was "the man who raised the money" and whose "orders to the Chairman of the New York Committee are obeyed," the consul-general declared, "*that is authority enough for me.*" Disgusted, Barton booked passage on the next steamer out of Havana. Leaving a few disheartened ARC workers behind, she boarded the *Olivette* for Key West on the afternoon of Wednesday, March 23.[58]

The following day, Lee affirmed his support for Klopsch in a telegram to the State Department reporting the work of relief was now "progressing most satisfactorily" and indicating he had been "greatly assisted by Mr. Klopsch." The consul-general sent a similar message to Stephen Barton, stating that he believed Klopsch "had every right to see what had been accomplished with the money," to investigate "whether the supplies reached those for whom they were intended," and to ensure that the system of distribution "was as perfect as possible to secure the purpose for which it was intended." Lee also issued statements to several American newspapers expressing his gratitude for Klopsch's "conscientious" work and declaring that "his labors here are now bearing abundant fruit." From Havana, Cottrell reported to Stephen that Lee had "endorsed everything that Klopsch has suggested and given him full swing." "We are defeated and humiliated," the secretary lamented. "With all authority gone and our forces so much disorganized, it seems useless to try to do much of anything." Klopsch's plan to drive the ARC from the field in order to "put his personality and his paper in the foreground," Cottrell concluded, had been a stellar success.[59]

Barton's sudden departure from Havana ignited a firestorm in the American media. Newspapers across the nation picked up the story and speculated about the reasons for her withdrawal from the relief work. Fearing publicity about the feud would undermine the CCRC's ongoing fund-raising efforts, both Barton and Klopsch tried to downplay their power struggle in conversations with the press. Although she "was intensely indignant" about the "derogatory statements . . . regarding internal dissension in the Red Cross Society, tardiness in supplying relief after its arrival in Cuba, and the stories of my own feeble health . . . or mental powers" that were circulating, Barton also repudiated rumors of a rivalry or rupture with Klopsch. "My return to this country is simply for the purpose of attending to my personal affairs and is not the result of any friction between myself and any member of the New York Relief Committee, as some newspapers in this country have claimed," she told reporters. "As to Louis Klopsch, I can say there has been no misunderstanding as far as I am aware." "In my absence," she remarked to one correspondent, "Mr. Klopsch will have full opportunity to attend to the relief work, and I wish him all possible success."[60]

Klopsch also vigorously denied reports of a rift with Barton and refuted claims he had criticized her work. "There has never been an unkind word between Clara Barton and myself," he insisted. "My relations with Miss Barton have always been very harmonious indeed." Although many of the nation's major and minor newspapers were printing front-page stories about the quarrel, the *Christian Herald* made no mention of any scandal. Instead, one article simply noted that Barton had left Havana for a time but promised to return soon.[61]

Meanwhile, the *Christian Herald* reported, the relief work was "progressing splendidly" under Klopsch's supervision: "Every detail of the system of distribution now in force has been planned by Dr. Klopsch with the active cooperation and cordial approval of General Lee." Contributors to the newspaper's relief fund could be confident that "the *Christian Herald*'s life-saving work in Cuba still goes on. No obstacle has yet arisen to interfere with this sacred mission which has been so divinely blessed and protected." This assurance would prove to be short-lived. For while Klopsch and Barton continued to deny their disagreements publicly, both were working behind the scenes to consolidate support for their claims to lead the nation's humanitarian relief efforts in and beyond Cuba.[62]

With the consul-general's backing, Klopsch carried out his plans for reorganizing the distribution in Havana and more remote areas. Lee used his influence with both Spanish and U.S. officials to "deprecate any attack upon Mr. Klopsch by friends of Miss Barton." Although Klopsch himself refrained from criticizing the ARC in print, his colleagues at the

Christian Herald did present his "side of the controversy" to the press as conjecture about the blowup with Barton escalated. Two days after Barton left Havana, George H. Sandison, the *Christian Herald*'s longtime associate editor, granted an interview to a reporter from the *New York Herald* in order to defend Klopsch against insinuations that he had gone to Cuba "to spy upon Miss Barton's methods" and had wrongfully interfered with her designated duties. Since Barton had undertaken relief work in Cuba at the behest of the *Christian Herald,* Sandison argued, Klopsch was entitled to ensure that the monies contributors had supplied were being well spent. When he arrived in Havana and found that "no one seemed to know how to distribute the accumulated supplies," it was only natural that Klopsch would draw on his previous experiences supervising aid delivery to develop a more efficient system. Why Barton should take offense at her benefactor's efforts to improve conditions Sandison could not understand. "We do not say one word against Miss Barton," Sandison declared. "She is a grand woman and none will deny the noble work she has done and is capable of doing." At the same time, he asserted, it was clear that trying to take on more than the hospital work for which she had been commissioned had proved too taxing for Barton and her staff, whose "old-time relief methods" simply failed to meet "the demands of the hour." "Without reflecting in any sense on Miss Barton herself," Sandison stated, "I am willing to say that modern methods conflicted with the old fogyism of certain members of the Red Cross who are her assistants." "I am positive," he concluded, "that when Dr. Klopsch is heard from, by reason of his experience and modern methods of application, the public will decide that he was right."[63]

On this point, however, Sandison would be proven wrong. For even as Klopsch was cutting through red tape to get supplies to the starving *reconcentrados,* Barton and her backers were mounting their own campaign to reinstate the ARC as the authorized distribution agent of American charity in Cuba. Cottrell continued to ply Stephen Barton with complaints about Klopsch, beseeching the chairman to intervene for the sake of his aunt and the reputation of her organization. "Klopsch has 'queered' us from A to Z and his baleful influence seems to penetrate everything we touch," Cottrell seethed in his letters from Havana. "This modern Mephistopheles will have to be entirely eliminated or nothing can ever be done that will reflect any credit upon the Red Cross." Rather than ceding the battle to Klopsch and the *Christian Herald,* Cottrell implored Stephen to fight for Clara and her coworkers. "I sincerely hope that you and her friends will be able to crush these contemptible conspirators and place the Red Cross in its position of preeminence over all other organizations of like nature in our country," he wrote.[64]

As his aunt headed home, Stephen determined to act on Cottrell's advice. On Friday, March 25, he sent a message to Clara indicating that he and Charles Schieren planned to meet her in Washington over the weekend, where they would "endeavor to get an interview at the [State] Department." On Monday morning, Clara Barton, her nephew, and Schieren met with Assistant Secretary of State Day. During the conference, Stephen Barton claimed, "Klopsch's name was not mentioned." Instead of complaining about any alleged interference from the proprietor of the *Christian Herald,* the members of the CCRC simply requested the committee "be made the agent of the government in both the collection and distribution of supplies." Day readily consented, officially granting Schieren and Stephen Barton power to appoint the ARC to allocate provisions with the full backing of the U.S. government. The committee immediately commissioned Clara Barton to undertake the responsibility, urging her to "return at once to the field and continue the work of relief."[65]

As Stephen Barton explained to a *New York Times* reporter, designating the ARC to supervise humanitarian intervention on behalf of the American people made sense, given the impending threat of war with Spain. As a signatory to the Geneva Convention (1864), he argued, Spain would be required to respect the right of the ARC to provide aid in conflict zones; therefore, "the relief work in Cuba thus protected will go steadily on, even though the two countries should be at war." With the unqualified support of the CCRC, the State Department, and the president, Clara Barton agreed to resume her work relieving the *reconcentrados.* "Glory to God! We are the People! hip, hip, hoorah!" Cottrell triumphantly proclaimed when he heard the news via telegram on Tuesday night. "Klopsch! rattttts! He leaves here tomorrow for New York; please meet him at the train with a club; you will know him by the tail between his legs."[66]

When Klopsch finally arrived back in Manhattan late in the evening on Saturday, April 2, he faced a barrage of critical questions concerning his relationship with Clara Barton, but also about his efforts earlier that afternoon to persuade McKinley to avoid war with Spain. Attempting to dispel rumors of his disloyalty to the United States and his disdain for the ARC, Klopsch immediately sent statements to leading newspapers clarifying his position on both of these issues. Over the next several days, he also repeatedly sought a private interview with Stephen Barton to share his side of the story.

Barton refused to meet with Klopsch in person, agreeing only to hear him out over the telephone. "Klopsch is very humble," Barton wrote to his aunt. "He denies absolutely any intention of interfering with or annoying you, he fully endorses our action in engaging you to represent the Committee, and in fact he almost implores us to listen to him and take him back into our confidence." Despite these assurances, Klopsch's fellow committeemen rebuffed him, and he was ultimately forced to resign his position on the CCRC and turn over all monies collected for Cuban relief by the *Christian Herald* to the treasurer, Charles Schieren. American evangelicals had lost their place at the helm of the nation's humanitarian mission in Cuba.[67]

Within a few weeks, it also became apparent that Klopsch's attempts to shape U.S. foreign policy in Cuba would fail to have any lasting influence. On April 11, McKinley delivered a long-awaited message to Congress. Rather than continuing to resist pressure toward armed intervention, the president requested authority to use military force to bring about "the instant pacification of Cuba and cessation of the misery that afflicts the island." Although deliberations continued for the next several days, conflict with Spain was quickly becoming inevitable.[68]

By April 20, Klopsch's fears about the effects of hostilities on efforts to aid the suffering *reconcentrados* had come to fruition: All relief work on the island was suspended as the consuls and remaining ARC agents were evacuated. Five days later, Spain and the United States formally declared war. Less than a month after Klopsch had celebrated the great advances American evangelicals were making by wielding the weapons of "bread and blessing" on Cuba's "fields of suffering," the *Christian Herald's* campaign to preserve peace through philanthropy had come to an abrupt, anticlimactic, and awkward end.[69]

Never one to accept defeat easily, Klopsch refused to relinquish hope that American evangelicals could remain in the vanguard of the United States' advancement as a global force for prosperity, goodwill, and universal harmony. Perhaps he and his associates had lost the battle to command American relief efforts in Cuba, but they could still rally their troops to lead the nation's fight against affliction, injustice, and oppression around the world. Just days after the outbreak of war with Spain, Klopsch and Talmage outlined a new strategy for evangelical engagement with American foreign policy. Rather than continuing to advocate for peace at any price, they acknowledged that God sometimes called Christians to defend the weak and vulnerable through military means. "There are times in the history of nations when it would be a sin and a shame to hold aloof from quarrels, and when interference by force would be a righteous course," they declared in an editorial published on May 4.[70]

Over the next several weeks, the *Christian Herald* printed numerous articles assuring American evangelicals that the situation in Cuba met the criteria of a just and necessary intervention on behalf of the afflicted. Even the staunchest pacifist could take comfort in the fact that the conflict with Spain was not an act of aggression or aggrandizement but rather a fight "forced upon us by considerations of humanity." "We did not want the Hispano-American war," Talmage insisted, and the U.S. government had done everything in its power to prevent an outbreak of hostilities. When Spain refused to stop mistreating the Cuban people, however, the American people had no choice but to accept armed conflict "as a last alternative." Like the Good Samaritan, the United States was coming to the aid of a suffering stranger; statesmen and soldiers were carrying out the Golden Rule. "It is quite true that Christianity is a religion of peace," Talmage asserted, but in this case, "God has put into our hands a sword" to "vindicate and deliver those that are oppressed." "We are fighting for philanthropy," he proclaimed. "We are binding the wounds of Cuba. We are being wounded for her sake." By obeying biblical principles of sympathy and self-sacrifice, the United States was fulfilling a divine mandate to extend the reign of Christ through "holy warfare."[71]

Once evangelicals could acknowledge that God was working through military force to bring about justice and righteousness, Talmage maintained, they would also be able to recognize other ways in which this war might prove beneficial for the expansion of Christ's peaceable kingdom. Not only was armed intervention an instrument of saving starving Cubans from physical suffering, but it was also an opportunity to bring political and religious liberty to subjugated people in all of Spain's colonies. "In Cuba as in everywhere else where Spain rules, there is oppression, cowardly wrong, and heartless cruelty," Talmage declared. For far too long, he argued, Spain had imposed its "tyrannical method of government" on unwilling populations who were now clamoring for freedom from the misrule of this "worn-out dynasty" that had not changed for centuries and refused to replace its "medieval" sensibilities with progressive ideas.[72]

In addition to denying political independence to its imperial possessions, Spain also allowed the Catholic Church to dominate these regions, thwarting the efforts of Protestant missionaries to evangelize or educate native peoples. As a result, most people in Cuba, the Philippines, Puerto Rico, and Guam remained "in heathen darkness," "entirely ignorant," and terribly impoverished. Peace-loving evangelicals, therefore, could embrace the conflict with Spain as a means "for the advancement of the sublime principle of liberty, which will yet encircle the earth," and for the extension of good government, economic opportunities, education, and the true gospel into these benighted territories. Although they may have "preferred the work of feeding the hungry, clothing the naked, and saving the dying from death," Talmage declared, "God has stirred up his people in this land to interpose on behalf of the down-trodden and enslaved" through "a righteous war."[73]

By interpreting the nation's military campaign against Spain as a divinely inspired "crusade of mercy," Klopsch and Talmage insisted that Christian charity remained the driving force of American foreign policy. From this perspective, the soldiers and sailors of the United States were emissaries of love bringing the "Gospel of human rights" to afflicted peoples. As American troops won rapid victories that left the United States in control of Cuba, Puerto Rico, Guam, and the Philippine Islands by the middle of August, the *Christian Herald* published numerous articles and editorials celebrating these triumphs as evidence that God had anointed the nation to extend freedom and enlightenment around the globe. Through these conquests of liberation, the "great American

Republic . . . will have made her civilization emphatic all over the earth," Talmage proclaimed. "And, henceforth the Stars and Stripes will carry this lesson of humanitarianism wherever it flies. And, if any other nation should inquire the secret of our success and glory, it is here: in the fact, that we burn to vindicate and deliver those that are oppressed. Spain represents the civilization of the Middle Ages. We represent the civilization of His kingdom."[74]

Indeed, these evangelicals argued, the United States was uniquely qualified to carry out this humanitarian mission because of the nation's long-standing commitments to democracy, religious liberty, equality, and progress. By embodying these ideals more successfully than any other country in world history, they asserted, the United States was especially suited to the task of advancing Christ's kingdom around the globe. "America is to be the world's civilizer and evangelizer," Talmage wrote. "Free from the national religions of Europe on the one side, and from the superstitions of Asia on the other side, it will have facilities for the work that no other continent can possibly possess. As near as I can tell by the laying on of the hands of the Lord Almighty, this continent has been ordained for that work. . . . Hear it! America is to take this world for God!"[75]

Other contributors to the *Christian Herald* agreed with Talmage's assessment. Presbyterian pastor Sheldon Jackson proclaimed that the Almighty had been preparing the United States to serve "as a base of operations for the conquest of the world" since the first settlers arrived on North American shores. Because the colonists came seeking "civil and religious liberty" and "laid enduring foundations" for these values in American life, he contended, the nation was better equipped than all others to "send out its beacon of light eastward to the sacerdotalism and formalism of Europe and the heathenism of Africa; westward to the dead conservatism of Asia; and southward to the benighted millions of the 'neglected continent.'" Although they continued to insist peaceful measures were the preferred method of extending Christian charity to the ends of the earth, ministers like Jackson and Talmage suggested that the conflict with Spain was a providential means of propelling the United States onto the global stage so that it could fulfill its manifest destiny.[76]

As the war drew to a formal close in the late summer of 1898, Talmage and his evangelical associates at the *Christian Herald* began to consider the nation's responsibilities toward the former Spanish territories that had "come under the dominion of the Stars and Stripes" during the past several months. In keeping with their convictions about the United States' humanitarian mission in these regions, most contributors to the newspaper initially assumed that the government ought to retain the islands in order to restore order, to provide for the needy (especially in Cuba, where starvation was still rampant), "to colonize and Christianize their population, and to give them good government and just laws." Because the people had suffered acutely under Spanish despotism for so many centuries, some argued, their capacity for self-rule was uncertain. To abandon them to their own fate under these circumstances would violate the principles of Christian charity. "We are in duty bound not to deliver them over to a tyranny which might be worse than that from which we have set them free," Talmage asserted. "The unkindest thing we could do would be to leave them liable to a calamity such as that which befell the man of whom Christ spoke, who being delivered from one devil fell under the tyranny of eight."[77]

Although Talmage remained unsure whether the United States ought to annex the acquisitions, grant them sovereignty but offer protectorate status, or keep them as colonies, he insisted that "we should not desert them." Some observers made an even stronger case for ongoing American obligations toward the island territories. Having rescued Cuba and the Philippines "from barbaric and clerical tyrannies," one pastor argued, the people of the United States were now "compelled to accept the consequences of their interference" by undertaking the "far more difficult task . . . of bringing the Cubans and the Filipinos up to the full standard of American citizenship." Through the Spanish-American War, he declared, the United States had taken its place "amongst the 'World Powers.'" From this exalted position, the nation should embrace its role as an empire divinely commissioned to promote "a higher conception of colonial expansion" that would ensure "the extension of the kingdom of God" to the ends of the earth.[78]

With these full-throated affirmations of war and imperialism as expressions of mercy, the *Christian Herald* encouraged American evangelicals to support the nation's policies of ongoing intervention in the islands at a time when opponents of expansionism were becoming increasingly vocal. Since the beginning of the conflict with Spain, anti-imperialists had been warning that retaining any of the territories conquered during the war would violate fundamental American values enshrined in the United States' founding documents. Although many critics appealed primarily to constitutional principles to support their arguments against the establishment of a formal empire, some also framed their dissent in biblical terms. Even as Talmage, Klopsch, and their associates were celebrating the nation's military victories as signs that God had ordained the United States to spread freedom, democracy, prosperity, and Western civilization around the world, some of their subscribers were questioning how they could reconcile war and colonialism with the gospel of peace and Christian liberty. "There must be a better way of ministering to the starving and oppressed Cubans than slaughtering thousands of our best and noblest young men," one correspondent wrote in early June. Several months later, another reader asked, "On what grounds are civilized and educated nations that quarrel and resort to killing, burning, and destroying justified, exalted, and applauded and upheld in so doing by Christian men and women when God says 'thou shalt not kill'?"[79]

As peace negotiations proceeded during the autumn of 1898, debates about the establishment of a formal American empire escalated, causing consternation among evangelical leaders like Klopsch and Talmage. They worried the growing discord could result in damaging rifts in their community that would ultimately undermine their ability to shape the nation's global humanitarian mission. Seeking to prevent ruptures within the ranks, the savvy publicists soon modulated their stance on military imperialism, admitting that the war and its aftermath had "given birth to many serious problems which could not be foreseen when our trouble with Spain began." Chief among these, they acknowledged, was determining what kind of governmental and economic relationships the United States should establish with Cuba, Puerto Rico, and the Philippines. Whether the Filipinos should be granted independence proved to be the most contentious issue in the coming months, as leaders of the revolution there protested "the intrusion of the United States Government on the sovereignty of these islands." As friction over the Philippines intensified, Klopsch and Talmage conceded that the situation was perplexing. "So many of our great statesman say that we ought to take full possession of the Philippine Archipelago, and so many of them say just the opposite, that we have come to think that the question is too big for us. We confess that we do not know what is best," they wrote in an editorial.[80]

Despite their uncertainty about how to resolve the question of Filipino autonomy, Klopsch and Talmage insisted that American evangelicals need not divide over the issue. As fierce debates about American imperialism continued to exercise the public during the spring of 1899, Talmage remarked that "fevered and angry discussion, in and out of Congress, is most inappropriate and bad." Instead, "equipoise, faith, prayerfulness, are the moods we should all cultivate." Whether the United States annexed the islands, held them under protectorate, or granted them independence was ultimately irrelevant, he argued, as long as evangelicals could unite to undertake "a campaign of moral and religious expansion . . . on [the] widest and grandest scale." Surely American military forces had "opened up a way for a kind of expansion we all believe in," he proclaimed. "The expansion of the knowledge and intellectual qualification of all those islandy [sic] regions is the desire of all intelligent Americans."[81]

Even more important than promoting educational uplift, Talmage argued, was the task of spreading the gospel by sending missionaries, Bibles, and pure literature (including newspapers like the *Christian Herald*) to the territories. Rather than wrangling over diplomatic questions, he advised, American evangelicals ought to focus on the prospects the islands presented for extending their faith into new regions. "Cuba and Puerto Rico and the Philippines are stepping stones for our American Christianity to cross over and take the round world for God," he declared. "We need a new evangelical alliance organized for this one purpose." Participating in this common mission would enable American evangelicals to spread their influence to the ends of the earth no matter what the outcome of the nation's deliberations over imperialism. Whatever the U.S. government decided about "the political destiny of those peoples," Talmage counseled, "let us join in a campaign of religious expansion— expansion of affection that can take all the world in."[82]

With this rallying cry, Talmage exhorted evangelicals throughout the United States to embrace the people of Cuba, Puerto Rico, and the Philippines as members of a growing global family drawn together through American missionary outreach. Emphasizing the evangelical dimensions of American expansionism enabled him to place the *Christian Herald* at the forefront of a national movement to incorporate the populations of Spain's former colonies within a universal fellowship of believers knit together by filial bonds of charity and sacred duty. The religious press, Talmage and his editorial associates argued, was the perfect instrument for enabling American citizens to "become better acquainted with the character and possibilities" of the people "brought under our protection." Through articles and images describing "scenes in our new colonial possessions," the *Christian Herald* would make known the many needs and great potential of the inhabitants of these islands, encouraging readers to see these former strangers not just as imperial subjects but as adopted family members or cherished friends. "These Puerto Ricans are our own brothers and sisters," Talmage declared in an editorial urging subscribers to provide relief to island communities following a devastating hurricane in August 1899. "They are now our own; we have adopted them, and to whom shall they turn in their direst need, if not to us?"[83]

Several months later, longtime contributor Margaret Sangster made a similar plea for the Filipinos. "Shall we not think of them as friends, these people in whom, by God's providence, we have become so vitally interested in these last days?" she asked. "A few years ago, the Philippine Islands were to our eyes only a group on the map and we had no concern either of ever seeing them ourselves or sending our sons and brothers there to fight or dwell or labor." But now that "war has cleared the way," Sangster wrote, "schools and churches and missionaries and teachers may bring them the best fruits of American civilization" and, even more importantly, "a knowledge of Christ as their Savior." To this end, the *Christian Herald* had commissioned a special edition of the Gospel of John printed in both English and Spanish so that the people of Cuba, Puerto Rico, Guam, and the Philippines would be able to read about "Jesus Christ in their own language—a privilege which, under the rule of Catholic Spain, they had never enjoyed." By contributing funds to this project, readers could help advance the knowledge of God and strengthen their connections with new members of America's expanding evangelical network.[84]

The desire to take advantage of opportunities to spread the gospel beyond American borders prompted a number of innovative evangelical publishing ventures. It was within this context that Klopsch conceived his idea for producing a Bible with Jesus's words printed in red ink. During

SUBSCRIPTION, $1.50 PER ANNUM
T. De Witt Talmage, D.D. Editor

NEW YORK, FEBRUARY 13, 1901

PRICE 5 CENTS
Offices: Bible House, New York

CHRISTIAN HERALD

CAPILLA
METODISTA
EPISCOPAL
DE PANDACAN

LA SIMIENTE ES LA PALABRA DE DIOS S LUCAS

THE FIRST PROTESTANT CHAPEL AND CONGREGATION IN THE PHILIPPINES

SEE PAGE 128

The first Protestant chapel in the Philippines—an example of the fruits of evangelical missions in the islands. From the *Christian Herald,* February 13, 1901, cover. Courtesy of the Christian Herald Association, New York.

the summer of 1899, he engaged a number of scholars to help with the project—the first of its kind (although other religious publishers would soon produce imitations). When the *Christian Herald* announced in July the production of the "Red Letter New Testament," the editors linked the innovation to the United States' mission to spread Christianity around the globe. "This nation can work wonders. It can be the means of converting the whole world. The eyes of other nations are upon it as at no previous time in history. If it upholds the Banner of the Cross its beneficent influence will be felt to the very ends of the earth," Klopsch declared in a letter advertising the new volume. When the Red Letter New Testament appeared later that fall, "it met with such instant success that soon the entire Bible was put into press." Eventually, the *Christian Herald*'s Red Letter editions were sent "all over the world," earning Klopsch accolades for helping "to make the Bible the most widely read book" on and beyond the North American continent.[85]

Many of the *Christian Herald*'s subscribers participated enthusiastically in the newspaper's various campaigns to draw the people of the recently acquired territories into their religious community. Some sent money to support the distribution of the Red Letter Bible and other gospel literature in the islands; others contributed to educational projects and missionary crusades. Still others sought to strengthen the bonds of affiliation through commerce. Indeed, connections formed through economic interactions, Talmage acknowledged, might prove even more influential than those resulting from other kinds of engagement. As local populations began to experience the blessings of "Christian civilization" and "American ingenuity"—such as "machinery to sow and reap" and technologies to cultivate natural resources—Talmage predicted they would increasingly desire to become part of the prosperous and progressive evangelical family. "The comfortable homes" of Christian converts among the islanders would serve as advertisements for the gospel to those who resisted more conventional forms of missionary outreach. "The Puerto Rican and the Filipino will come out from his uncleansed, and low-roofed, and uninviting kennel, and say to his neighbor of beautiful household: 'Why cannot I have things as you have them?'" Talmage declared. "And when he finds that it is the Bible, with its teachings on family life and personal purity and exalted principle and the church of God that proposes the rectification of all evil and the implantation of all good, he will cry out: 'Give me the Bible and the church and the earthly alleviations, and the eternal hope which have wrought for you such transfiguration.'" The advancement of trade, the growth of free enterprise, and the expansion of a flourishing modern economy, from this perspective, were also ways American evangelicals could help extend Christ's kingdom of peace, prosperity, and goodwill around the globe.[86]

Although Talmage's sanguine interpretations of American expansionism appealed to many of the *Christian Herald*'s constituents, some subscribers did raise questions about the ethics of this approach. As hostilities with the Filipino revolutionary forces became increasingly fierce, a number of readers sent letters asking the newspaper's editors to clarify how they could support ongoing military aggression in the archipelago as a missionary strategy: "Do you think God ever intended to drive men into his kingdom? Do you not think that if we would give them freedom, set before them a Christian example, and give them a helping hand, the influence we would exert would go far more toward bringing them out of heathenism than if we were to annex them against their will, riveting in their minds hatred for Christians? A taste of empire seems to lead to the fatal step of aggrandizement."[87]

In their replies to these and similar inquiries, the newspaper's editorial staff attempted to allay concerns by emphasizing the benevolence of American interventionism. Unlike other imperial powers, they insisted, the United States was not seeking to augment its territory through the acquisition of the Philippines. This conflict, like the previous one with Spain, was motivated solely by the nation's divinely inspired concern to protect the rights of the weak and liberate the oppressed. In this case, they argued, the native people were suffering under the rule of Emilio Aguinaldo, an influential leader in the rebellion against Spain who was now refusing to submit to American authority. Rather than recognizing Aguinaldo as the elected president of the First Philippine Republic, the editors of the *Christian Herald* referred to him as a "military dictator" concerned about his "own interests, rather than about the welfare of the country," who had "deliberately plunged his country into the war and precipitated hostilities" with the United States to satisfy his own ambitions. As the "Filipino Napoleon," one author reported, Aguinaldo possessed a lust for power and personal greatness that characterized the world's worst imperial tyrant. "He is like the man whom the apostle denounced who deceived the people with promises of liberty only to bring them into a worse bondage," the editors declared.[88]

By contrast, Klopsch and Talmage suggested, the United States was opposed to "ruling subject peoples, or . . . holding under our sway unwilling populations." "Our imperialism," they argued, "consists in such wise and benignant rule," that the Filipinos would surely "come to recognize the justice and beneficence of our government." Echoing the McKinley administration's rhetoric of "benevolent assimilation," the staff of the *Christian Herald* expressed their confident hope that the people of the Philippines would greet their American benefactors "not as conquerors but as allies and friends—instruments in the hands of Omnipotence to raise the benighted and neglected people to the full stature of a free and enlightened nation." Once American military forces defeated Aguinaldo and liberated the Filipinos from the "violence and anarchy" of his rule, these evangelicals declared, the people would have the opportunity to prove themselves "fit for self-government." Although the Philippines might remain under U.S. control while the people developed the capacities necessary for autonomy through the tutelage of American diplomats, businessmen, educators, and missionaries, the editors maintained, "there can be no doubt that . . . our government will give them independence" in due course.[89]

From this perspective, American military operations in the Philippines were working toward the longer-term goal of promoting democracy, free-market capitalism, educational enlightenment, and religious freedom around the world. Achieving these aims would have the even more important effect of creating conditions favorable for spreading the gospel to the ends of the earth. Although "imperialism has come to be an unpleasant word with us," one author asserted, American evangelicals could take comfort that the ongoing conflicts in the Philippines would ultimately help "usher in the imperialism of Christianity." In the present day, the signs were hopeful that "men of many creeds and of many races and tongues" were being drawn into "the kinship of the family of Christ." The war in the Philippines might have its downsides—as all hostilities did—but through this struggle and other forms of American expansionism, God's kingdom was advancing among all tribes and nations, and "a world-wide empire is being realized by the Prince of Peace."[90]

Although some readers of the *Christian Herald* continued to express concerns about the newspaper's endorsement of war and imperialism as divinely sanctioned forms of humanitarian intervention, most seemed to share the editors' convictions that the United States was conducting its policies "with the wisdom and magnanimity that should characterize an enlightened Christian nation, seeking not its own aggrandizement, but the moral and material elevation of mankind." Confident that the United States was a benevolent empire committed to exercising its power on behalf of suffering people for the sake of extending Christian civilization to the ends of the earth, Klopsch and Talmage urged American evangelicals to contribute to this project through their newspaper's ongoing charitable enterprises.[91]

Just as they had in Russia, Armenia, and Cuba, the staff of the *Christian Herald* would provide its subscribers with channels for aiding their neighbors in the United States' new "insular possessions." By subsidizing schools, starting businesses, sending disaster relief, sponsoring missionaries, and signaling their support for U.S. servicemen in these overseas regions, the editors averred, evangelicals could help integrate these foreign territories within an American empire that would ultimately set them free to become full participants in the broader "family of nations" and members of the expanding kingdom of God. Through these philanthropic endeavors, Klopsch and Talmage hoped, the *Christian Herald*'s evangelical almoners would remain an influential force in American foreign relations. Klopsch's clash with Clara Barton may have undermined his efforts to maintain an official partnership between his faith-based aid organization and the federal government, but in the long run, lending support to the nation's interventions in Cuba and the Philippines ensured that evangelical charity would continue to play a key role as the United States extended its global reach.[92]

But if a majority of the *Christian Herald*'s subscribers were swayed by the newspaper's lofty rhetoric about just wars of liberation on behalf of suffering and oppressed people, anti-imperialists were not so easily persuaded. Nor were the Filipinos fighting for their independence. Aguinaldo and fellow supporters of the First Philippine Republic were not about to trade one colonial master for another—no matter how "benevolent" the United States' supposed intentions. Rather than eagerly embracing American guidance and "protection," Filipino revolutionaries continued a fierce resistance against American occupation. The Philippine-American War would rage for several years and sorely test evangelical humanitarians' claims that the United States was advancing democracy, freedom, and prosperity through its "righteous empire."

4

ALMONER OF THE WORLD

"Famine sore. Help!" This desperate cable from American missionaries in Ahmednagar, India, arrived on Louis Klopsch's desk in mid-November 1899. The appeal confirmed the somber reports he and his staff had been receiving for several weeks about the impending food shortage in the western and central provinces of the subcontinent. The summer rains had failed to fall, and the autumn harvest had withered. At least thirty million people living in the vast region were in danger of starvation, warned the numerous missionaries who corresponded with the *Christian Herald*.[1]

The situation was especially dire because many parts of India had still not recovered from the devastating famine of 1896–1897, which took the lives of more than one million people and left thousands of orphans in the care of missionaries. During that disaster, American evangelicals had contributed over $400,000 in aid for the afflicted through the *Christian Herald*'s relief effort. With another catastrophe looming, missionaries begged Klopsch and his associates to initiate a new campaign for India's starving millions. "It is not strange that, as the dark shadow of this impending calamity begins to come over us again, the hearts of all connected with the suffering districts turn towards the *Christian Herald* as if prompted by a natural instinct," wrote James M. Thoburn, the Methodist missionary bishop of India who had helped distribute the newspaper's donations during the previous crisis. Since "the *Christian Herald* has become known throughout the world as the helper of those who chance to be in sore need," he explained, "I venture to appeal once more." Congregationalist minister J. E. Abbott, who was stationed in Bombay, made a similar supplication. "Surely the readers of the *Christian Herald* whose aid blessed so many two years ago will help again in the name of Christ and suffering humanity."[2]

The missionaries were not disappointed. Although Klopsch at first "felt reluctant to plead again for the same people" so soon, he quickly concluded that their plight was too piteous to ignore. By the middle of January 1900, the *Christian Herald* had collected almost $2,500 for "starving India" and had already forwarded double that amount to five missionaries working in the famine districts. For the next twelve months, the newspaper was replete with gripping headlines, graphic images, and heartrending accounts of the terrible tragedy unfolding on the other side of the globe.[3]

As the suffering escalated, Klopsch announced that the *Christian Herald* would spearhead an effort to "equip a Flying Relief Ship" to carry a cargo of American grain to Bombay. In March, Talmage made a personal appeal to the State Department requesting that the U.S. Navy charter a vessel for this purpose. Meanwhile, Klopsch cabled the British government asking for free transport for the supplies upon arrival. Both petitions were successful, and preparations began for filling the five-thousand-ton steamer *Quito* with "the life-saving gift of food . . . provided by American benevolence for the rescue of starving India." Contributions poured in from all across the nation, representing "the united offerings of every Christian denomination in the land" and the generosity of "railroads, business firms and corporations," grain merchants, elevator operators, and insurance companies that provided transportation rebates and services free of charge. By the time the ship was ready to sail, it contained "the largest cargo carried by any vessel, bound on an errand of mercy."[4]

As the *Quito* prepared to leave New York Harbor on a sunny afternoon in early May, an enthusiastic crowd gathered on the pier to offer prayers and blessings for the relief mission. They sang "My Country 'Tis of Thee" and listened to letters from President William McKinley, Secretary of State John Hay, and New York governor Theodore Roosevelt—all of whom sent their regrets at not being present to praise the "splendid work" of the *Christian Herald*. The assembly then turned its attention to the Reverend R. G. Hobbs, who offered this benediction: "This ship goes out of the harbor to a far-off land in the name of that God who made of one blood all the nations of the world: in the name of that Christ who died, that all men might be drawn into the bonds of a common brotherhood."[5]

The *Quito*'s departure was a high point in what became the most celebrated and successful international humanitarian campaign in the *Christian Herald*'s history. From the opening of the India famine fund in early 1900 to its official close at the end of the year, the newspaper raised a total of $641,072 (equivalent to $17,656,250 in 2017) for the starving multitudes in the form of freight refunds, grain contributions, cash donations, and other sources. In addition to the sizable sums they collected to provide sustenance, blankets, and medicine during the disastrous food crisis, Klopsch and his colleagues established a separate fund for the care of five thousand "famine waifs" at approximately sixty missionary stations throughout the subcontinent. Over the next several years, the *Christian Herald* sent a total of $557,000 ($15,340,760 in 2017) more to India for orphan support, making India famine relief "the greatest of all the foreign charities in which Dr. Klopsch engaged."[6]

Despite their initial hesitation about launching another fund-raising campaign after having so recently called on their readers to assist sufferers in this region, Klopsch, Talmage, and their coworkers soon recognized the new crisis as a chance to showcase the superiority of evangelical humanitarianism at a critical moment in the history of American foreign aid. By early winter 1899, the nation's relief and development efforts in its "insular possessions" were faltering. In Cuba, Clara Barton and the American Red Cross (ARC) had encountered numerous obstacles to delivering assistance to the starving *reconcentrados,* whose numbers had multiplied and whose suffering had intensified in the wake of the Spanish-American War (just as Klopsch had predicted). Escalating violence between the U.S. military and the forces of the First Philippine Republic led by Emilio Aguinaldo had stymied plans for promoting economic, educational, and missionary enterprises in the archipelago.[7]

At the same time, reports of atrocities committed by American servicemen against Filipino combatants and civilians were fueling anti-imperialist sentiment among several prominent evangelical leaders (as well as among the broader population). The catastrophe in India provided an occasion for directing public attention away from the humanitarian calamities unfolding under American aegis in the nation's new colonial territories. By conducting its most expansive and ecumenical international relief effort yet, Klopsch and Talmage hoped, the *Christian Herald* could reinforce evangelical solidarity and revitalize the United States' flagging reputation as the Almoner of the World.[8]

As they poured their energies into this ambitious endeavor over the course of 1900, the staff of the *Christian Herald* drew on a decade of experience in philanthropy, journalism, fund-raising, business management, political lobbying, and international networking to stir up sympathy for India's "famishing millions." Their expertise in these fields gave Klopsch and his colleagues remarkable insight into the kinds of narrative, visual, and organizational strategies that could unite evangelicals in a common effort to save "stricken India" and in so doing restore the image of "Christian America, the hope of the nations of the whole earth."[9]

Analyzing the diverse techniques these publicists used to foster compassion for India's afflicted people reveals the complex and ambivalent ways in which assumptions about race, gender, and American "civilization" shaped evangelical humanitarianism in this era of intensifying imperialism and globalization. At a time when critics of U.S. colonial policies were questioning the country's commitment to the ideals of freedom and self-determination, framing the *Christian Herald*'s relief campaign as a mission to liberate India's sufferers from the bondage of hunger—and especially to protect widows and orphans from the specters of slavery and sexual exploitation—enabled American evangelicals to imagine themselves as champions of emancipation who were carrying forward the abolitionist crusade set in motion by their antebellum forebears.[10]

Linking India famine relief with the war against chattel slavery in the United States also proved essential for encouraging evangelical donors to extend charity across religious and racial lines. With the exception of the quickly abandoned effort to aid Muslims after the 1894 Constantinople earthquake, the *Christian Herald*'s international humanitarian work had focused almost exclusively on fellow Christians who shared—at least tangentially—a common European ancestry with American almsgivers. Although a small number of famine victims in India had converted to various forms of Protestantism, the vast majority were Hindu; in the language of most missionaries, they were "heathens" who differed from their evangelical benefactors "in faith, race, and color." To make the case that these sufferers were "children of the same Father in heaven and hence brothers" deserving of Christian compassion, Klopsch, Talmage, and their associates employed a variety of rhetorical and visual tactics popularized by abolitionists to elicit empathy for blacks in bondage throughout the American South. Like the gruesome narratives and images of bodily distress that helped fuel antislavery sentiment in the antebellum period, the harrowing accounts and photographs of Indians in agony that appeared in the *Christian Herald* during the late 1890s played a major part in soliciting aid.[11]

Even as the heartrending depictions worked to broaden American almsgivers' vision of humanity and enlarge evangelicals' sense of responsibility toward racial and religious "others," some critics worried that the *Christian Herald* accomplished these goals by exacerbating rather than erasing distinctions and inequalities among believers of diverse nations. In the "Lord Jesus Christ," one India missionary reminded donors in the United States, "'there is neither Jew nor Greek, there is neither bond nor free, there is neither male nor female' . . . but all are one." From this perspective (and in the judgment of many scholars since), representations that emphasized the weakness and incapacities of India's stricken people reinforced the social, spiritual, and civilizational hierarchies that helped fuel the global expansion of imperialism while undermining efforts to promote Christian communities of equality.[12]

To subvert the imperial logics of economic dependency, racial inferiority, and cultural backwardness, some evangelical missionaries stressed the active and prominent role Indian Christians played in easing the affliction of their people. Stories and images of local believers such as the renowned reformer Pandita Ramabai, who established a refuge that eventually accommodated over two thousand famine sufferers, sought to affirm the agency, independence, and competence of Indian leaders in ways many evangelicals considered essential to the creation of an authentic, universal fellowship of faith.

Examining the diverse portrayals of Indian people that appeared in the *Christian Herald* during the famine exposes substantial tensions underlying attempts to unite American evangelicals in a shared enterprise of international benevolence. Ironically, at the very moment Klopsch and Talmage achieved their greatest success in making their publication "a medium of American bounty to the needy throughout the world," debates over the meaning and practice of evangelical almsgiving threatened to destabilize the entire project.[13]

Paying attention to the various renderings of Indian sufferers and relief workers in the popular press also elucidates the intercultural dimensions of humanitarian campaigns. Despite the *Christian Herald*'s emphasis on American leadership in international aid, accounts of the influence Ramabai and other Indian leaders exercised among missionaries and distribution agents assisting famine sufferers show that the extension of U.S. philanthropy abroad was not a unilateral process. Instead, the delivery of charity involved collaborative partnerships, reciprocal exchange, and sometimes strong disagreement among American evangelicals and Indian Christians striving to carry out biblical injunctions "to feed the starving and shelter the widows and orphans for His sake."[14]

"SAVING INDIA'S STARVING MILLIONS"

When reports of famine in India began to flood the *Christian Herald*'s New York headquarters in November 1899, accounts of the U.S. military's brutalities in the Philippines had been causing consternation among the American public for several months. In May, the Anti-imperialist League had published a collection of soldiers' letters detailing the ruthless violence with which U.S. forces were hunting down Filipino insurgents and the blatant disregard many showed for civilian life. According to one artilleryman, for example, a commanding officer had ordered his unit to "kill every native in sight" in retaliation for the apparent murder of an American soldier. As a result, "about one thousand men, women, and children were reported killed." Testimonies like this shocked the nation, prompting vigorous denials from many mainstream newspapers such as the *New York Times*, which denounced anti-imperialist sentiment as treasonous and insisted that the war was being conducted according to the principles of humanity.[15]

Despite the furor that erupted in the press over the *Soldier's Letters,* the *Christian Herald* remained silent about the accusations in keeping with the editors' policy of avoiding controversial and discouraging subjects that could divide the evangelical community and tarnish the country's reputation as a Christian nation. By fall, however, growing dismay over the situation in the Philippines was becoming increasingly difficult to ignore. In letters to the editors, some *Christian Herald* subscribers expressed concern about the amount of alcohol being imported to the territories and contributing to the chaos there. Other evangelicals complained that the ongoing instability in the region was delaying plans to send missionaries, whose task was already being made more difficult by the spread of "corruption, drunkenness and sin" among American soldiers. Such widespread viciousness and debauchery caused one reader to ask whether "the Philippine islands are more civilized than we are." Perhaps "they ought to civilize us instead of we them."[16]

In the coming months, evangelical dissension over the conduct of American troops in the Philippines would escalate dramatically. Although proponents of expansionism such as Talmage and Klopsch continued to express support for the nation's efforts to "pacify" the islands, evangelical anti-imperialists became increasingly vocal about their opposition to the war. One of the fiercest critics of U.S. military intervention in the region was the popular preacher and best-selling author Charles M. Sheldon, whose blockbuster novel *In His Steps: What Would Jesus Do?* (1896) had made him a household name among evangelicals across the country. As controversy about American imperialism intensified in the early winter of 1899, Sheldon determined to go public with his criticisms of U.S. foreign policy and its effects on the Christian community both at home and abroad. After several months of planning, Sheldon took over as editor of the *Topeka Daily Capital* in his home state of Kansas to conduct a one-week experiment in religious journalism. Sheldon used this opportunity to openly question the ethics of empire building sanctioned in the *Christian Herald*.[17]

The first issue of the "Sheldon Edition" contained a front-page article decrying the "war spirit" that was plaguing the United States like a dreadful disease, an editorial declaring "abhorrence of war as it is being waged today in the Philippines and everywhere else," an exposé of alcohol abuse and immoral behavior among American troops, and extracts from an address by Supreme Court Justice David Brewer openly criticizing imperialism. Rather than interpreting the acquisition of the Philippines and other colonial territories as a God-given opportunity to promote material prosperity, political liberty, and true Christianity among a destitute, benighted, and morally degraded population, the articles in Sheldon's newspaper argued that imperialism violated the principles of equality, self-determination, and religious freedom enshrined in the Declaration of Independence.[18]

Subsequent installments of Sheldon's daily went on to criticize the notion that the United States was particularly suited to "vindicate or deliver those that are oppressed." The government's disgraceful treatment of Native American tribes inspired little confidence in the nation's ability to respect the rights of "dependent races." Nor should American citizens assume that "all the influences going out from this Christian nation" would be "purifying, Christian, elevating." If history was any guide, the United States was likely to send "more hogsheads of rum than missionaries, more gallons of whisky than Bibles" to its colonial possessions. Indeed, the "civilization" Americans were exporting through "the exercise of brute force" in these regions, Sheldon charged, was not authentic Christianity but barbarism. The war in the Philippines, in his view, was not a mission of liberation to free a suffering and subjugated people from domination, but a "deplorable" act of aggression fueled by "commercialism and militarism." To disguise imperialism as a form of missions, philanthropy, or evangelical fellowship "under the cloak of patriotism" was to betray American ideals and abandon the most basic teachings of Christ, the prince of peace.[19]

The other major topic occupying Sheldon's attention as editor of the *Capital* was the humanitarian crisis unfolding in the British Empire. "The *Capital* knows of no more important news the world over this morning than the pitiable condition of famine-stricken India," Sheldon declared on the first day of his publishing experiment. India's plight remained a prominent concern throughout the week. Alongside articles and cartoons condemning American imperialism, Sheldon printed letters from missionaries in Bombay and Ahmednagar describing the terrible suffering they were witnessing. He also encouraged readers to send donations to the various agencies collecting funds for famine relief. "Let us all have a share in helping our brother man," he wrote, "for these 50,000,000 starving creatures are a part of that human family which Jesus taught us to love."[20]

Giving generously was imperative, Sheldon insisted, because God was sure to hold prosperous Americans accountable for the way they stewarded their growing wealth. "Must they starve? While Standard Oil Company makes millions?" Sheldon demanded. The $30 million John Rockefeller's corporation had just disbursed to its shareholders in dividends could save four million Indian lives, he argued. "America is rich," Sheldon concluded. "She is sinfully rich if she does not respond to this cry of a dying nation." Just as he urged the United States to live up to its founding ideals and Christian principles by decrying imperialism, so too did Sheldon implore American citizens to overcome the selfishness and greed that threatened to tarnish their character as a people and call down God's judgment upon the nation.[21]

When Klopsch learned of Sheldon's plan to shape public feeling on "the great social questions of the age" through a stint at the *Capital*, he commented that Sheldon's editorship would "doubtless be marked by the most radical and vigorous Christian policy" and pledged to follow the results "with intense interest." He immediately cabled the staff at the *Capital* to ask how his readers could subscribe to the special edition and also invited his constituents to suggest topics they hoped Sheldon might address. Once the experiment was under way, the *Christian Herald* provided extensive coverage of Sheldon's undertaking, highlighting the newspaper's appeals for India famine relief while downplaying Sheldon's anti-imperialist stance. In making "India's need the leading theme . . . as the foremost and most urgent topic for the consideration of Christian America," the *Christian Herald*'s correspondent declared, "Mr. Sheldon has given to the *Christian Herald*'s plea for India the grandest endorsement that could have been uttered or written."[22]

To capitalize on this common concern for India's afflicted, Klopsch took out a large advertisement for the *Christian Herald*'s relief fund in the *Capital* and also wrote a letter to the Topeka newspaper commending Sheldon for his role in advancing the aid effort. "You have contributed in a large measure to focus the world's attention upon the greatest catastrophe of the closing century," Klopsch declared. By presenting Sheldon as an ally in the monumental fight against famine, Klopsch and his associates endeavored to defuse the divisive effects of his crusade against American militarism and commercialism in the Philippines.[23]

Indeed, from the outset of India's crisis, Klopsch emphasized the opportunity for promoting evangelical solidarity through a broad-based humanitarian campaign that could unite American Protestants of different theological persuasions, political sensibilities, social classes, and geographic regions in a shared enterprise. More than any previous aid operation, the *Christian Herald*'s efforts to alleviate suffering in India had the potential to bring together these various constituencies, Klopsch and his colleagues argued, because the missionaries calling for help were themselves a diverse group with a demonstrated commitment to cooperating along ecumenical lines. Three years earlier, during India's 1897 famine, Methodist missionary bishop James Thoburn had organized an interdenominational committee comprising representatives from fourteen missionary societies working throughout the affected areas of eastern India to coordinate the distribution of donations from the *Christian Herald*. The consortium included members from large, historic Protestant churches such as the Baptists, Congregationalists, Disciples of Christ, Episcopalians, Lutherans, Methodists, Presbyterians, and Quakers as well as from smaller and more recent organizations associated with the Holiness and radical evangelical movements like the Salvation Army and the Christian and Missionary Alliance (CMA). By highlighting the harmonious collaboration among this coalition of missionary aid workers, Klopsch and Talmage had galvanized support for the *Christian Herald*'s 1897–1898 famine relief campaign across readers of every denomination and region throughout the United States.[24]

When disaster struck again just a few years later, Klopsch and his colleagues were confident they could build on this past experience to replicate their success now that the need to bolster evangelical unity was more pressing than ever. Soon after opening a new *Christian Herald* India famine fund in early 1900, the editors announced that an interdenominational missionary committee under the leadership of Bishop Thoburn would once more oversee the apportionment and disbursement of contributions. Donors could rest assured that this diverse group would operate with "a spirit of mutual concession and Christian regard for the needs of one another." This example of collaboration in the field, Klopsch and his associates intimated, ought to inspire supporters back in the United States to set aside their differences and join together in the common enterprise of saving India's starving millions.[25]

As gifts to the relief campaign accumulated, reports in the *Christian Herald* continued to underscore themes of cooperation and harmony among a broad range of constituents from a variety of backgrounds. "From nearly every section of the Union comes cheering news of the progress of the relief movement," one author proclaimed. "Every mail brings intelligence of enthusiastic work in churches, Sunday Schools, religious societies, and town and village communities." By the time the *Quito* sailed for Bombay in early May, the newspaper could boast that the ship's cargo represented "the united offerings of every Christian denomination in the land. . . . There is probably not a church organization or society in the land which has not shared in the life-saving work."[26]

To demonstrate the relief campaign's expansive reach, the newspaper published comprehensive lists of contributions received, providing as much information as possible about the giver (name, city or state, and/or affiliations with specific religious organizations). Some registers were more detailed than others, but all aimed to encourage the *Christian Herald*'s readers to see themselves as potential participants in a shared humanitarian endeavor that involved American Protestants of every persuasion, all ages, and various classes from across the United States. Although accounting records had featured in all of the publication's previous aid efforts, the India "honor rolls" far surpassed most prior lists in size and scope. Numerous issues of the journal during the 1900 campaign included as many as four consecutive pages of itemized donations.[27]

Alongside these registers of gifts from individuals, churches, and religious groups, the *Christian Herald* recognized contributions from chambers of commerce, private companies, and the U.S. government to this "work of a great international benevolence." Railroads, business firms, and corporations made the labor easier by offering rebates or free services, one article reported. Just as the previous Indian famine of 1897 had roused the enthusiasm of farmers, millers, merchants, and citizens, the editors declared, the current crisis gave American agriculturalists and commercial agents the opportunity to prove that Christian generosity was spread across all segments of society. At a moment when critics like Sheldon were loudly denouncing the greed that characterized the U.S. industrial system and fueled the nation's appetite for the acquisition of new colonies that could provide raw materials for increased production and new markets for exports, Klopsch and Talmage sought to cast American economic enterprises in a more positive light. By sending the fruits of the nation's bounty to famine sufferers in India, they contended, the United States demonstrated to the international community that its corn growers, grain distributors, transportation companies, and financial firms had both the wherewithal and the will to feed hungry people all around the world.[28]

Some proponents of the *Christian Herald*'s relief campaign conceded that India's food crises afforded an outlet for surplus American crops, thereby benefiting farmers by opening a new market for their grain. However, they simultaneously insisted that expanding trade into "the Orient" would ultimately serve the interests of both "our own people" and those whose local economies were proving incapable of providing adequate sustenance even in prosperous times. By God's grace, these evangelicals declared, the United States was uniquely positioned to meet the needs of poorer, less-developed nations. "There is no country in the world whose crops have been so richly blessed and so abundant in the last few years as our own," the editors asserted during the 1897 relief effort. "It is as though the bountiful Father had placed at our disposal this great opportunity in order that we might reach out with hands full of food and blessing, to those less favored than ourselves." But the opportunity, they insisted, brought with it "the gravest responsibility." Because God had made the United States "the land of plenty," American Christians now bore the "burden of duty . . . to save a helpless and prostrate people in their time of greatest need."[29]

By the spring of 1900, when anti-imperialists were vigorously denouncing the nation's conduct toward supposedly "dependent" populations in the Philippines, Klopsch and Talmage reiterated that the United States possessed an inimitable capacity and divinely mandated obligation to aid the afflicted around the world. "England is doing nobly," they declared in an advertisement printed in the *Topeka Capital*, "but she is not equal to the occasion, and America, with her overflowing, bursting granaries, must speedily come to the rescue or these millions will perish for the very lack of what we enjoy in superabundance." Although most articles in the *Christian Herald* commended the British imperial government in India for its efforts to alleviate suffering, the editors occasionally intimated that poor planning and mismanagement by English officials had contributed to the crisis. "If the money [the government] has spent in feeding the famine victims in 1897 and this year had been spent years ago in irrigation," they declared, "it would have made those famines impossible." Furthermore, because Great Britain was embroiled in a conflict in South Africa during the second Indian famine, many of the empire's resources "that would otherwise be available for India itself" were being "diverted into the war channel."[30]

Given England's "folly," Klopsch and Talmage implied, it was incumbent on the United States to take a leadership role in saving India's perishing millions. "Christian America" was "the hope of the nations of the whole earth," they had declared during the 1897 Indian famine. Now, at this crucial period in international affairs when Great Britain's ability to ease affliction throughout its far-flung empire was faltering, it was time for the United States to marshal its many agricultural, technological, financial, and spiritual resources "to prove to the world that the American people are, above all other nations, alive to the call of human suffering," as well as more capable than any other imperial power of eradicating distress in distant lands through humanitarian intervention.[31]

Making the case that God had equipped the United States to serve as the "Almoner of the World," Klopsch and Talmage believed, involved ongoing efforts not only to showcase the superiority and generosity of American economic enterprise in providing assistance to India but also to highlight the key role of the U.S. government in the relief effort. During both the 1897 and 1900 famines in India, they solicited support for the *Christian Herald*'s aid campaign from congressional representatives, state governors, and federal officials. On March 23, 1897, for example, Klopsch petitioned the House of Representatives to requisition a naval vessel for transporting grain contributions from New York to Calcutta. Within two weeks, Congress had granted the request by unanimous consent. This "magnificent act," Talmage proclaimed, revealed the "far-reaching humanity" of the U.S. government and confirmed that "once more our land will be the first to send substantial succor across the seas, to those in direst need."[32]

As the nation's foreign policy came under heightened scrutiny and critique during the Philippine-American War, highlighting the benevolent character of the U.S. government became increasingly imperative for evangelicals seeking to defend the country's Christian character. In April 1900, just after Sheldon had publicized his objections to American imperialism, Talmage made a personal appeal to the State Department requesting help in shipping donations to India. Drawing on funds remaining from Congress's prior appropriation for famine relief, the secretaries of the State and Navy Departments chartered the *Quito* to carry a cargo of *Christian Herald* relief supplies to Bombay. The action of these two officials "and the sympathetic co-operation of all with whom they are officially associated," Talmage asserted, would not only save many lives but also bolster the reputation of the United States, "adding new lustre to the fame of our Republic for international benevolence."[33]

As the "Famine Ship" prepared to sail, the *Christian Herald* published several front-page photographs of the vessel loaded with two hundred thousand bushels of grain representing "Christian America's gift to starving India." In contrast to the anti-war cartoons through which Sheldon and his editorial staff sought to expose the deadly violence perpetrated by American soldiers against the Filipinos, images of the corn-laden *Quito* made visible the concrete contributions of the federal government, and in particular the U.S. military, to the greatest humanitarian campaign of the closing century. The "spectacle of that steamer," Klopsch declared, offered a "startling object lesson . . . on the world-wide charity of the American nation." For evangelicals who worried that intervention in the Philippines was undermining the country's status as the standard-bearer of universal freedom and goodwill, pictures of the "noble ship" commissioned by government officials to carry "the life-saving gift of food" to a desolate and desperate people offered reassurance that the United States remained committed to its sacred mission of spreading the gospel of peace and prosperity across the globe.[34]

CHRISTIAN HERALD

AND SIGNS OF OUR TIMES

OFFICES: BIBLE HOUSE, NEW YORK   COPYRIGHT 1900, BY LOUIS KLOPSCH   VOLUME 23—NUMBER 20

Rev. T. De Witt Talmage, D.D., Editor   NEW YORK, MAY 16, 1900   PRICE FIVE CENTS

OUR FAMINE SHIP ON THE OCEAN

The "Quito," Loaded with 200,000 Bushels of Grain, Christian America's Gift to Starving India

ONCE more the readers and conductors of THE CHRISTIAN HERALD have been associated in the work of a great international benevolence, which has culminated in the sending of a Famine Relief ship to the starving multitudes in a distant land. Together they sent cargoes of food to Russia, to Cuba, and to India—the last-mentioned during the severe famine of 1897; and now, at the height of the most terrible famine of modern times, they have sent the good steamship *Quito*, with the largest cargo ever carried by any vessel, bound on an errand of mercy. Her **5,000 tons** of choice two-year-old American corn go to Bombay, where Dr. Klopsch will await the relief steamer's arrival and where, in conjunction with the Inter-denominational Missionary Committee, he will personally supervise its distribution, until the very last of the **200,000** bushels is sent out to the remotest centre of suffering.

This magnificent gift, which goes over the ocean wafted by prayer and blessing, represents the united offerings of every Christian denomination in the land—Presbyterians, Baptists, Methodists, Lutherans, Reformed Church, Disciples of Christ, Congregationalists, Episcopalians, Friends, Mennonites, Evangelicals and Moravians. There is probably not a church organization or society in the land which has not shared in the life-saving work. Little village communities and agricultural groups in the great corn-growing States have lovingly loaded up cars with corn and sent them on to swell the relief ship's cargo. It would not have been difficult to fill the largest steamer that ever floated, so generous was the sympathy, so noble the response. The Kansas State India Relief Committee is represented by 20,000 bushels; the Mennonites by 8,000 bushels, and the great host of good people belonging to all sects and denominations, make up the grand total of 200,000 bushels. It will afford all who have taken an active part in the benevolent enterprise additional satisfaction to know that their gift will reach Bombay at the very time when most needed, as our missionary letters assure us.

In the gathering of this great cargo it has been demonstrated that the spirit of Christian generosity is widespread in

America. Railroads, business firms and corporations in many quarters have combined to make the labor easier. The Postal Telegraph Cable Co. has franked all fund messages; the Pennsylvania, New York Central, Lake Shore, Delaware, Lackawanna & Western and West Shore railroads have been most liberal in their rebates; the elevator companies have also rebated charges; the Truesdell & McCord

erously opened, and all minds intent on forwarding the life-saving work and speeding the departure of the famine-ship.

As she lay at her dock at the West Central Pier, Brooklyn, while loading, the *Quito* was visited by thousands of interested persons from the city and suburbs. She is a fine-looking vessel, of iron throughout. Her commander, Capt.

Co., grain merchants, have given services at cost of actual outlays. Messrs. Johnson & Higgins, in insuring the cargo, contributed their commission to the Famine Fund. All hearts seemed to be gen-

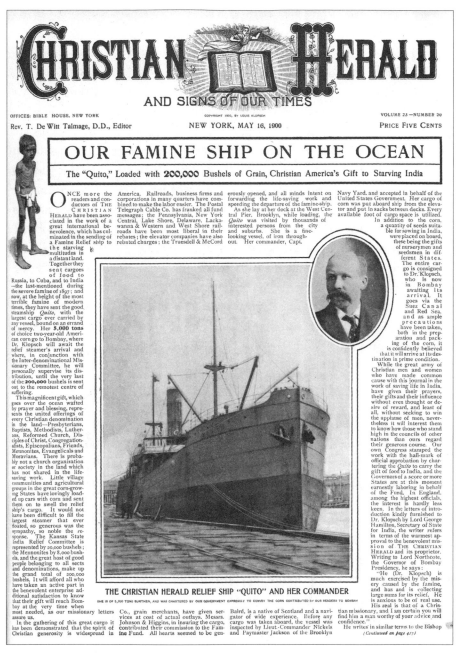

THE CHRISTIAN HERALD RELIEF SHIP "QUITO" AND HER COMMANDER

SHE IS OF 5,000 TONS BURTHEN, AND WAS CHARTERED BY OUR GOVERNMENT EXPRESSLY TO CONVEY THE CORN CONTRIBUTED BY OUR READERS TO BOMBAY

Baird, is a native of Scotland and a navigator of wide experience. Before any cargo was taken aboard, the vessel was inspected by Lieut.-Commander Nickels and Paymaster Jackson of the Brooklyn

Navy Yard, and accepted in behalf of the United States Government. Her cargo of corn was put aboard ship from the elevator and put in sacks between decks. Every available foot of cargo space is utilized. In addition to the corn, a quantity of seeds suitable for sowing in India, were placed on board, these being the gifts of nurserymen and seedsmen in different States. The entire cargo is consigned to Dr. Klopsch, who is now in Bombay awaiting its arrival. It goes via the Suez Canal and Red Sea, and as ample precautions have been taken, both in the preparation and packing of the corn, it is confidently believed that it will arrive at its destination in prime condition.

While the great army of Christian men and women who have made common cause with this journal in the work of saving life in India, have given their prayers, their gifts and their influence without even thought or desire of reward, and least of all, without seeking to win the applause of men, nevertheless it will interest them to know how those who stand high in the councils of other nations than ours regard their generous course. Our own Congress stamped the work with the hall-mark of official approbation by chartering the *Quito* to carry the gift of food to India, and the Governors of a score or more States are at this moment earnestly laboring in behalf of the Fund. In England, among the highest officials, the interest is hardly less keen. In the letters of introduction kindly furnished to Dr. Klopsch by Lord George Hamilton, Secretary of State for India, the writer refers in terms of the warmest approval to the benevolent mission of THE CHRISTIAN HERALD and its proprietor. Writing to Lord Northcote, the Governor of Bombay Presidency, he says:

"He (Dr. Klopsch) is much exercised by the misery caused by the famine, and has and is collecting large sums for its relief. He is anxious to be of real use. His zeal is that of a Christian missionary, and I am certain you will find him a man worthy of your advice and confidence."

He writes in similar terms to the Bishop

(Continued on page 417)

The *Christian Herald*'s famine relief ship *Quito*. From the *Christian Herald,* May 16, 1900, cover. Courtesy of the Christian Herald Association, New York.

If India's ruinous food shortage offered the United States an occasion to restore its image as the most effective global champion of oppressed and afflicted people in the wake of anti-imperialist condemnations, the famine also gave American evangelicals an opportunity to reassert their position as the nation's premier providers of foreign aid. After his embarrassing clash with Clara Barton and his subsequent dismissal from the government-sponsored Central Cuban Relief Committee, Klopsch was eager for another chance to prove the *Christian Herald*'s preeminence in procuring and distributing relief for sufferers around the world. Demonstrating the superiority of evangelical charity had become especially urgent at this juncture because Barton's ongoing efforts to secure a congressional charter for the ARC seemed to be gaining traction after her return from Cuba in the fall of 1899.

Despite many trenchant criticisms of the ARC's attempts to assist the *reconcentrados* both before and after Klopsch's visit to the island, Barton made the most of the publicity her involvement with the relief campaign had afforded. When she finally closed the ARC's Cuban operations, she received accolades from both government leaders and popular media outlets. Capitalizing on the public outpouring of praise, Barton renewed her appeals for official recognition of the ARC as the "agent for carrying out the obligations of the United States under the Geneva conventions"—a status she believed would finally establish her organization as the nation's only authorized agency for providing domestic and international aid on behalf of the federal government. Hoping to head off this troubling possibility, Klopsch determined to ensure that the *Christian Herald*'s 1900 India famine relief campaign would "eclipse all former benevolences of this character" and provide citizens of the United States the "greatest opportunity of the closing century to do good in the Master's name."[35]

To accomplish this goal, Klopsch continually stressed the federal government's endorsement of the *Christian Herald*'s aid efforts. As the fund-raising campaign gained momentum in the spring of 1900, for example, the newspaper printed a copy of a letter addressed to Klopsch from Second Assistant Secretary of State Alvey Adee. "Recalling your interest in the business of Cuban relief in 1898 and your efforts to assuage suffering in Russia, India, and Armenia," Adee wrote, "I take the liberty of sending you copy of a press item . . . expressing the willingness of the Indian Government to receive famine contributions from this country." Having recognized the *Christian Herald*'s crucial role in previous humanitarian crises, Klopsch suggested, Adee was now commissioning the newspaper to take a leadership position in this latest catastrophe.[36]

Several weeks later, after receiving word that the State and Navy Departments had approved Talmage's appeal for assistance in transporting supplies from New York to India, the *Christian Herald* celebrated the "prompt cooperation" of Secretaries John Hay and John Long in partnering with evangelical almsgivers in their "life-saving mission." At the *Quito*'s send-off service in early May, representatives of the newspaper's relief campaign read several letters from prominent federal officials—including the president of the United States—expressing enthusiastic appreciation of the *Christian Herald*'s efforts to aid the suffering people of India on behalf of the entire nation. "The success of this work is eminently gratifying to me," McKinley had written. Secretary of State Hay also sent a note "to testify to the interest I have taken in the work you have so nobly done." Given these indications of approval from the highest-ranking statesmen in the land, Klopsch and Talmage implied, contributors to the *Christian Herald*'s India famine fund could be confident that evangelical charity remained an essential part of the nation's international humanitarian efforts, despite Barton's attempts to consolidate the ARC's power at the expense of other philanthropic organizations.[37]

That the *Christian Herald*'s relief work in India was also receiving acclaim from foreign diplomats further strengthened the publication's position as a vital channel of American aid, the newspaper's editors contended. Both Lord Hamilton, the British secretary of state for India, and the Lord Mayor of London expressed to Klopsch and Talmage "warm admiration for American benevolence" and great appreciation for their efforts to help India's sufferers through the *Christian Herald*'s famine fund. The "philanthropic work done by the paper," Hamilton declared, not only was a great ministry to the afflicted, but also served to "bind the two hemispheres together in bonds of fraternal sympathy." Joseph H. Choate, the American ambassador to England, agreed that the *Christian Herald*'s India campaign was helping promote international harmony. These testimonies, the editors averred, confirmed that the charitable efforts of their readers on behalf of distant sufferers had "opened up new springs of good will between two great nations."[38]

Through their humanitarian endeavors, therefore, American evangelicals were exercising an important influence within the broader sphere of foreign relations. Although the ARC could claim stature on the international stage because of its status under the Geneva Conventions, Klopsch and Talmage had established productive relationships with the highest officials in England and elsewhere. From their first foray into relief work in Russia through this latest attempt to ameliorate starvation in India, these evangelical leaders had earned the trust and confidence of rulers around the globe. Given their successful track record and the "warm and fraternal feelings" their work had helped generate among nations, the editors implied, American evangelicals ought to remain at the forefront of U.S. international aid efforts.[39]

The *Christian Herald* also deserved recognition as the nation's leading humanitarian agency because of its proven capacity for effective fundraising and demonstrated ability to distribute relief through reliable channels. Unlike Barton, who had always been ambivalent about asking for money, Klopsch never hesitated to plead the cause of the afflicted and pressure his readers to open their purses on behalf of the suffering. Because of Barton's hesitancy, the ARC was frequently short on resources and had to rely on outside organizations for funding. According to its editors, the *Christian Herald* never failed to marshal adequate contributions to support its charitable operations. Moreover, because the newspaper's advertising revenues could help offset the costs of conducting humanitarian crusades, donors could be sure their gifts would go straight to people in need, rather than to defray overhead expenses. At the end of every relief campaign, Klopsch published audited financial statements detailing precisely how monies were allocated. Barton, by contrast, was a notoriously lax accountant and bridled when ARC board members demanded better bookkeeping.[40]

Perhaps the most important distinction between Barton's approach to international philanthropy and the *Christian Herald*'s methodology, Klopsch argued, had to do with means of distribution. Rather than employing paid staff members who had to travel long distances to unfamiliar regions where they would need to find housing, purchase food, and spend precious time acclimating themselves, the *Christian Herald* always sought local volunteers who knew the culture, understood the needs, and could disseminate supplies quickly and efficiently. Critics like Klopsch suggested that in both Armenia and Cuba, the ARC's structural and strategic disadvantages—not to mention Barton's stubbornness and incompetence—had stymied relief efforts and resulted in a waste of resources. During the Indian famine of 1900, Klopsch and his colleagues declared, the *Christian Herald* and its readers would have the opportunity to demonstrate definitively the superiority of the evangelical approach to foreign aid.[41]

Klopsch's confidence resulted in part from the success of the newspaper's 1897 India famine campaign. During that crisis, the Interdenominational Missionary Committee had distributed funds free of charge, "so that every dollar contributed [went] intact to the sufferers, with no deduction for cost or administration." With another catastrophe unfolding in 1900, Klopsch could remind readers how well this volunteer organization had worked during the previous disaster. "The care and faithfulness displayed by its members in 1897 is a pledge for like fidelity now," he asserted. Not only could contributors rest assured that every cent would be given to feed starving people, they could also trust the missionaries to allocate their gifts wisely, ensuring that monies would reach the neediest districts. All of the committee members, the *Christian Herald* reported, had a long experience in India and were appointed because of their intimate knowledge of the famine area. Given this expertise, they knew how to distribute relief supplies efficiently and economically to sufferers with "the most urgent need."[42]

When these afflicted people received succor directly from the hands of American missionaries, Klopsch and his coworkers asserted, they appreciated more fully "how compassionate are the people who bear the name of Christ." Aid delivered through evangelical agencies, in this view, not only was more cost-effective than relief distributed through government or private channels, but also served the paramount purpose of demonstrating "the love and kindness of the Christian religion." Although the staff of the *Christian Herald* expressed gratitude for the efforts of secular relief boards in raising funds for famine assistance, they also insisted that working through American missionary networks was superior because "the religious character of the distribution" revealed to recipients—and the broader world—"the true motive of the gift." Since "the American missionary is so obviously disinterested," the editors averred, famine sufferers would "understand that it was not political or commercial motives that had prompted the gift, but love for humanity, which is the product of the love of Christ." Within the British Empire, Klopsch and his partners implied, American evangelicals were better situated than their English counterparts to serve as almsgivers because they could present themselves and their humanitarian work as entirely altruistic—untainted by imperial ambitions or economic aims.[43]

Missionaries affirmed that their perceived neutrality and selflessness clearly shaped how beneficiaries responded to aid efforts. "There was," wrote Congregationalist Edward S. Hume, "a marked difference in the reception of funds by the famine sufferers. They regarded the relief they received from a secular committee as 'Girkar money,' that is government relief, implying only the government's recognition of its responsibility." When missionaries offered assistance, on the other hand, recipients "realized that the help was an expression of Christian compassion." This recognition, Hume hoped, would prompt many Indians of other faiths to view "the religion of Christ" not as a "meaningless profession" but as "a vital power." From this perspective, evangelical charity was an essential means of advancing the missionary enterprise in a difficult environment.[44]

The centrality of almsgiving for spreading the gospel in a context of calamity became a resounding theme in the *Christian Herald*'s India famine relief campaigns. "The two enterprises now go side by side—giving to India the bread of this life and the bread of eternal life," Talmage declared as the food crisis of 1897 began to escalate. By taking care of Indians' bodies, he argued, American missionaries would "accelerate" the salvation of their souls. Although he applauded the steady work of British evangelists such as William Carey, who first preached the gospel in the colony of Serampore in the late eighteenth century, Talmage asserted that these predecessors had faced serious impediments that could now be overcome through the agency of evangelical benevolence. "A stupendous obstacle in the way of Christianizing Asia has been the difference of language," he proclaimed, "but all those people understand the Gospel of bread." Many contributors to the *Christian Herald* agreed that humanitarian aid could help bridge the language barrier. "A gift coming from utter strangers," one author wrote, "proves, as preaching never could, that the religion of Christ is a religion of love and pity and helpfulness."[45]

As the *Quito* carried its cargo across the ocean to Bombay Harbor in June 1900, the editors predicted that the steamer would provide an "object lesson more potent than [the missionaries'] teaching." "Every bag of corn," they declared, "will be vocal with the message of the Gospel." Baptist minister A. C. Dixon affirmed this idea during the vessel's commissioning ceremony. "Our opportunity in India is to reach the soul through ministry to the body. . . . It is hard to teach religion in the abstract, to make people understand it as a theory when they are ready enough to accept it in demonstration," he observed. "Deed must interpret Christianity to the heathen. . . . We are going to batter down the walls of heathendom with the gospel of bread."[46]

Salvation Army Commander Frederick Booth-Tucker, who was also present on the afternoon of the *Quito*'s departure, agreed that the *Christian Herald*'s humanitarian endeavor was opening up a new era in world evangelism. "When a great vessel like this comes riding into port with a great cargo of corn straight from Christian America, she will be one of the best and mightiest missionaries you have ever sent to that country." By interpreting almsgiving as a more effective form of preaching and therefore an indispensable means of spreading the gospel in "heathen" lands like India, these supporters of the *Christian Herald*'s famine relief campaign sought to cement the connection between foreign aid and evangelical faith. Humanitarianism, in this view, was an essentially religious practice that ought not to be relinquished to secular agencies such as the ARC.[47]

Many evangelicals embraced wholeheartedly the *Christian Herald*'s proposition that international charity offered an unprecedented opportunity "to strengthen the stakes of American missionary effort" in Asia and elsewhere. But some found this proposal deeply troubling and worried about the practical effects of emphasizing philanthropy over preaching. What would happen to missionary budgets if churchgoers shifted their contributions to the *Christian Herald*'s relief campaigns while failing to fulfill their pledges to denominational organizations responsible for the maintenance of hundreds of overseas missions workers? Although Klopsch never suggested donors abandon their commitments to evangelistic work in favor of famine relief, critics like the Reverend A. B. Simpson of the CMA accused him of drawing attention and resources to humanitarian crises in a way that eclipsed and impoverished more conventional endeavors to spread the gospel. "Philanthropic schemes and social reforms are absorbing the interest and enthusiasm of thousands of redeemed men and women who ought to be giving their strength and wealth to the best things and not the second best," Simpson proclaimed in an address at the height of the 1897 Indian famine. Despite the fact that the CMA's own missionaries were among the beneficiaries of the *Christian Herald*'s relief fund, Simpson complained that "enormous sums of money" were being diverted to humanitarian efforts. Although he admitted that "these enterprises . . . have a place and a value," Simpson categorized "worthy charities" as "second and third class work" compared with spreading the gospel through preaching. Rather than wasting precious resources on side issues, Simpson urged American evangelicals to "let the world take care of them." Instead, he admonished, "let each of us purpose that henceforth, our time, our means, our sympathies, our influence, shall be wholly expended in the highest kind of Christian work, in the winning of souls, the evangelization of the nations," leaving philanthropic endeavors to other agencies.[48]

Simpson probably did not intend his comments as a direct attack on the *Christian Herald*'s famine relief campaign. Throughout both the 1897 and 1900 crises, the CMA expressed gratitude for the generous gifts its missionaries received from the journal's fund and praised Klopsch and his colleagues for "their beneficent efforts to relieve suffering and do good." Despite these acknowledgments of the *Christian Herald*'s "noble service," however, Simpson's vigorous and ongoing critique of the notion that humanitarianism was essential to the missionary enterprise clearly undercut Klopsch's attempt to unite American evangelicals through the practice of international almsgiving. Disagreements about whether philanthropy was an integral feature of evangelical identity and mission also made arguing for the *Christian Herald*'s premier status as an agent of the nation's foreign aid more difficult.[49]

As Simpson's views became widespread among certain segments of the evangelical community, Klopsch and his associates struggled to respond to questions about their emphasis on charitable activities in and beyond India. If humanitarianism was becoming controversial, some wondered, why not simply leave relief work to the ARC? Others asked whether it made sense to assist people who might be responsible for their own suffering: "Are the people so improvident that they do not sow their seed, at the proper season?" Perhaps most disturbingly, some detractors seemed to doubt the entire project of extending American philanthropy abroad: "Why have any interest in people so far away that it is evening there when it is morning here, their complexion darker, their language to us a jargon, their attire unlike that found in any American wardrobe, their memory and their ambition unlike anything that we recall or hope for?"[50]

As these various queries attest, Klopsch and the editors of the *Christian Herald* found themselves fighting an uphill battle on multiple fronts in the midst of what they had hoped would be a relatively easy campaign to establish the primacy of American evangelicals in the field of humanitarian aid. On one side they were working to thwart Clara Barton's ambitions to secure the ARC's status as the nation's official international relief agency. At the same time, they were contending with misgivings about the propriety of prioritizing philanthropy as a defining practice of evangelical mission from within their own ranks. As internal doubters threatened to destabilize the consensus they were working so hard to build, Klopsch and Talmage also had to cope with detractors who expressed indifference about or even hostility to the plight of distant, racially distinct, and culturally alien sufferers.

Rather than retreating in the face of these formidable challenges, the staff of the *Christian Herald* remained undaunted in their efforts to prove the preeminence of evangelical humanitarianism by making India famine relief "the climacteric, international charity of the nineteenth century." Marshaling almost ten years of experience in the field of philanthropic journalism, they deployed a number of well-tested and extremely effective strategies to convince both their critics and their constituents that aiding India's starving millions was an evangelical imperative best undertaken through the auspices of a religious newspaper with an established reputation "as a trustworthy channel for sending help to the suffering in all lands."[51]

From the outset of their efforts to promote the *Christian Herald*'s India campaign as "the grandest relief work of the century," Klopsch and his associates insisted that American evangelicals had a singular responsibility to lessen affliction among the famine sufferers because many of these desperate people were fellow believers entirely dependent on missionaries for support. When Indians converted to Christianity, the editors explained, they became outcasts among their own people and were therefore "likely to be excluded by their profession of Christ from any distribution controlled by Hindoos or Mohammedans who might not be careful to save the lives of relatives and friends who had exasperated them by abjuring the faith of their fathers." Indeed, during the 1897 famine, missionaries testified that converts were often turned away from both government relief works and poorhouses "with the remark that they must go to their Mission . . . for help." Many "were left to starve merely because they were Christians," one missionary lamented. The same was true in 1900. "Christian families—people who belong to Christ—are starving," the *Christian Herald* reported. "We may be quite sure that they will get no help from heathen hands."[52]

Given these circumstances, Klopsch and his coworkers argued, American evangelicals simply could not assert that preaching ought to take precedence over philanthropy or that delivering humanitarian aid was primarily the province of secular agencies like the ARC. The missionary enterprise, from this perspective, had exacerbated the suffering of converts who "in becoming Christians . . . had to accept ostracism" because of the caste system. Naturally, these believers would "look to the missionaries to help them in their dire extremity," and surely they had every right to "expect from them a practical exhibition of Christian charity," *Christian Herald* contributors argued. "God forbid that I should have to say to them that I can do nothing for them," declared the Reverend Richard Winsor of the American Board's Sirur mission. Succoring these "brethren in Christ when in such dire distress," another missionary affirmed, was "a responsibility that the Christians of America must feel." Klopsch and his associates agreed. "If the missionary is blamed for allowing men and women and children to starve to death at his door," they asserted, "it will be on us that the blame will fall." Allowing any one of these fellow believers to "perish for lack of food," they proclaimed, "would be an everlasting disgrace" to every American evangelical. Almsgiving in famine-stricken India was an obligatory outgrowth of the missionary endeavor that no conscientious Christian in the United States could ignore.[53]

Emphasizing ties of Christian brotherhood binding American evangelicals to Indian converts on the other side of the globe proved a relatively effective tactic for persuading donors to contribute to the *Christian Herald* relief fund. But some readers remained resistant to the idea of sending money to a far-off and predominantly "heathen" population with whom they shared so little in common. After all, only a tiny fraction of India's starving millions were followers of Christ. Most were Hindu, and many were Muslim. These critics contended that few, if any, showed sympathy for the missionaries' message and that the vast majority remained steeped in an idolatrous and backward culture that hindered their progress toward civilization and therefore contributed to their poverty and deprivation. Charity, from this perspective, could not bridge the vast spiritual, social, and spatial divides separating "Christian America" from "heathen India."

To counter these arguments, the editors of the *Christian Herald* employed several strategies they had been developing since their earliest forays into the field of foreign aid. One approach involved an attempt to elide the perceived religious and cultural differences between American almsgivers and recipients of humanitarian relief in distant lands. In their campaign to stir up sympathy for victims of the 1894 Constantinople earthquake, for example, Klopsch and Talmage had emphasized the shared lineage that linked American evangelicals of European descent with Turkish Muslims in a common "brotherhood of man." All tribes and nations, they proclaimed during the earlier disaster, were blood relatives united by chords of kinship into one human family whom Christ taught his followers to love. Every sufferer, therefore, deserved sympathy and assistance "regardless of race or creed." Although they largely abandoned this cosmopolitan ethic after thousands of Armenian Christians were massacred in the Ottoman Empire, contributors to the *Christian Herald* began to reiterate similar calls for a more inclusive approach to humanitarian aid as food shortages in India provoked widespread suffering among people of diverse faith communities and racial identities.[54]

In a sermon entitled "Hunger in India," for example, Talmage suggested that American evangelicals ought to be concerned about the calamity unfolding on the opposite side of the globe because the Indian subcontinent and its people were not as alien as some supposed. In fact, the preacher proclaimed, "our Christ was an Asiatic." Recognizing that "Christ was born in Asia, suffered in Asia, died in Asia, and ascended from Asia," Talmage asserted, should make the "Christian people of America" more attentive toward the cry of distress coming from the region.[55]

Some staff writers for the *Christian Herald* took Talmage's argument about affinities between Indian famine sufferers and citizens of the United States a step further. In response to a reader's query about the racial profile of the people of India, the editors stressed the common ancestry these populations shared with individuals of European heritage. According to ethnologists, they wrote, "the Hindus" belonged to "the great Aryan or Indo-European family of nations." The editors went on to explain that the "Aryan race consists . . . of two branches: the Western comprehending the inhabitants of Europe . . . and naturally their descendants in America; and the Eastern, comprehending the inhabitants of Armenia, Persia, Afghanistan, and the dominant race of India." All of these diverse peoples, they averred, were birthed by a single "mother nation"—as evidenced by "resemblances between the languages of all showing a common origin." Although the native inhabitants of India might differ from American evangelicals in appearance and habits, scientists had confirmed that they were originally of the same racial stock and therefore members of the same human family. The editors hoped that once Christians in the United States recognized these sufferers across the sea as their own kin, they would not hesitate to help their brothers and sisters in this time of desperate need.[56]

For those who might not be convinced by complex ethnological arguments affirming the hereditary ties binding Euro-American citizens to "the dense and dusky population of India," proponents of the *Christian Herald*'s famine relief campaign offered a different set of reasons why evangelicals ought to care for the distant strangers who "in race and religion and in moral ideas and social customs are widely separated from themselves." Bridging these divides, according to a number of contributors, did not depend on establishing a shared spiritual, ethnic, or cultural identity. Instead, aiding India's starving millions was a matter of theological principle and devotional practice. "The religion of Christ," one author explained, "includes a love that is world-wide." True Christian charity, therefore, could not be "limited to our household, nor to our own countrymen." Indeed "there is no limit to its operations. Neither distance, nor difference of race, nor unworthiness is to be a barrier." Like the good Samaritan who stopped to help a foreigner, this contributor contended, "the readers of this journal" ought to give generously to the newspaper's famine relief fund. "By this we show that we are Christ's disciples."[57]

The Reverend A. C. Dixon made a similar pronouncement during the *Quito*'s commissioning service: "Jesus Christ came to proclaim the doctrine of love that knows neither Greek nor Roman, Jew nor Gentile, bond nor free; his heart was big enough to take in all humanity." By sending a steamship full of food to feed the starving "heathen" of India, he declared, American evangelicals were fulfilling the ministry of the Good Samaritan and demonstrating that they were true followers of Christ. From this perspective, whether India's sufferers were descended from the same "mother nation" was irrelevant because, as another contributor put it, "though people may differ in faith, race, and color, yet they are children of the same Father in heaven and hence brothers."[58]

To bolster these theological assertions of "universal brotherhood" among all human beings, advocates of India famine relief reminded readers of biblical injunctions to help strangers and care for widows and orphans in their distress. The story of the Good Samaritan was a favorite, but contributors to the *Christian Herald* referenced a wide range of scriptural passages to make the case for extending compassion across religious, racial, and social boundaries. YMCA secretary George Sherwood Eddy quoted from the Gospels of Luke, John, and Matthew in an effort to convince American evangelicals that "these starving people are our fellow-men, each one your 'mother or sister or brother.'" Like the beggar Lazarus, who sought help from the rich man, Eddy asserted, India's afflicted were "laid at your gate, 'full of sores and desiring to be fed with the crumbs that fall from your table.'" Would the wealthy Christians of the United States act like the rich ruler who ignored Lazarus's desperate need? Eddy hoped not. Instead, he exhorted his constituents at home to show their love for God by obeying Jesus's commands in John 21:15–17 to "feed my sheep." By aiding their "fellow-men," Eddy concluded, American evangelicals would be succoring Jesus himself, as the Gospel of Matthew attested: "Verily I say unto you inasmuch as ye did it unto one of these, my brethren, even the least, ye did it unto me. For I was hungered, and ye gave me meat: I was thirsty and ye gave me drink."[59]

During both Indian famines, missionaries like Eddy frequently warned their supporters back home not to neglect "the stranger, and the fatherless, and the widow" (Deuteronomy 14:29). Citing biblical texts such as the Book of James, they defined aiding India's starving people as an expression of "pure religion" while insisting that failing to supply "those things which are needful to the body" to these brothers and sisters would result in severe judgment. "Faith, if it hath not works, is dead," the apostle had declared. In a plea that echoed the words of 1 John 3:17, Klopsch demanded, "Shall we shut up the bowels of our compassion and tell them that American money and American grain are for Americans only—that religion is one thing and charity quite another?" "Are we unjust stewards" who would refuse to share the vast resources God "has entrusted to our care" like the servant whose selfishness Christ condemned in one of his parables? "God forbid!" Klopsch exclaimed. Instead, he asserted, every reader of the *Christian Herald* ought to "join the Christian life-saving crew and to throw out to these starving people the life-line, before it is too late." By donating to the newspaper's relief fund, Klopsch and his coworkers implied, American evangelicals could become more like Jesus: a savior who rescued the perishing from certain death.[60]

Of all the biblical motifs the *Christian Herald*'s contributors referenced in their efforts to raise funds for India famine relief, the trope of the redeemer who possessed power to deliver a piteous people from destruction proved particularly compelling. Employing a rhetoric of rescue in the newspaper's philanthropic campaign enabled Klopsch and his associates to connect the work of humanitarian assistance to the broader project of saving "heathen India" that had captured the imaginations of American evangelicals for decades. Ever since the first Protestant missionaries had begun to send reports about their struggle to spread the gospel in the distant subcontinent, American Christians had envisioned India as a land in need of liberation. Stories of "hideous and barbarous worship as that of Juggernaut, or of Kali the black goddess of Calcutta" published in popular magazines like the *Christian Herald* reinforced the common perception of Hinduism as a "stronghold of ancient idolatry" that kept its followers "subject to the most slavish superstitions and ruled by priests whose whole duty is to keep them steadfast in their ignorant devotion to their heathen gods."[61]

Missionary narratives also lamented the "cruel and absurd bondage" of the caste system. Because this rigid and hierarchical communal structure prohibited social mobility, critics suggested, it promoted "fatalism, superstition, prejudice, and indolence," thereby preventing progress and miring millions in abject poverty. Within this oppressive context, observers contended, many seeking to cope with the inescapable misery of their situations had turned to addictive drugs like opium that, rather than offering true freedom, further fettered users to lives of deprivation and thralldom.[62]

According to most accounts, women in India were the worst off. Tales of the terrified bride as young as five years old "bought and sold for money, carried off forcibly from her childish home to dwell among strangers . . . the child-wife of a man who esteems women as a polluted, worthless race" abounded in popular writings about India throughout the nineteenth century. Imprisoned within "zenana" quarters or behind "the purdah" designed to keep women secluded, missionaries wrote, Indian women remained "absolutely subject" to despotic husbands, vulnerable to abuse, and barred from social life, proper health care, and basic education: slaves "in both life and death."[63]

By the 1890s, accounts of spiritual, social, and gender oppression in India had helped fuel widespread support for the American missionary enterprise "to bring the benighted millions into the light of the gospel." Conversion to Christianity, proponents of the evangelistic project urged, would set India and its people free from the multiple forms of slavery that kept them in bondage. "Our Jesus came to bind up the brokenhearted, to proclaim liberty to the captives—the opening of the prison to them that are bound—and to comfort all that mourn," Congregationalist missionary Mary Leitch proclaimed in an article promoting her work among the widows of Ceylon. That the United States had a singular role to play in India's emancipation was a common refrain among missionaries and their supporters. "America has done much toward redeeming India from its idols," wrote one such advocate. "It would almost seem as though India had been set apart by God in His wisdom to be wrested from darkness by His chosen servants as a special heritage of the present generation."[64]

During the food crises of 1897 and 1900, advocates of famine relief regularly invoked this influential assumption about the salvific mission of American evangelicals in their efforts to promote the *Christian Herald*'s India fund. Klopsch and Talmage frequently referred to the newspaper's aid campaign as a "great work of rescue," explicitly encouraging donors to think of themselves as deliverers of India's starving sufferers. "Let every reader take the question personally to his heart," Talmage exhorted: "How many lives can I save? How many of these poor emaciated brothers and sisters can I be the means of rescuing from death, and of calling back to strength and vigor, to hope and gratitude?" Collectively, "Christian America" possessed "the power to lift the shadow of bereavement from thousands of peasant homes in India" and "unquestionably prove herself worthy" of acclaim as the world's most bounteous and benevolent nation.[65]

At a time when critics were accusing the United States of betraying its commitment to the ideals of liberty and justice by forcibly subjugating the Filipinos, rescuing the perishing people of India offered American evangelicals a welcome opportunity to place themselves at the forefront of a "humane warfare against hunger and suffering." Contributors to the *Christian Herald*'s famine fund constituted a great relief brigade of self-sacrificing volunteers who had responded nobly and generously to "the call of duty," the editors averred. Unlike military officials who were being accused of committing atrocities against insurgent freedom fighters and innocent civilians in the Philippines, "the *Christian Herald* and its vast army of sympathetic readers" were "doing battle for the Lord" in a life-saving campaign that was alleviating affliction among India's oppressed people. "Our ship of conquest is not armed with guns of iron and steel and brass and copper," A. C. Dixon declared at the *Quito*'s departure ceremony, "but with bags and barrels of corn."[66]

With these weapons, American evangelicals were especially equipped to protect the most vulnerable of India's famine victims: widows and orphans whose social position placed them in danger not only of starvation but of suffering a "fate worse even than death by hunger." Echoing long-standing worries about the subjugation of Indian women, advocates of the *Christian Herald*'s relief campaign warned that young girls were at extreme risk of being sold into sexual slavery as a result of the food short-ages. "A singularly sad feature of this fearful distress," one contributor wrote at the onset of the 1900 famine, "is that unprincipled people in India are taking advantage of the straits of parents to purchase the na-tive children for immoral purposes." Several months later, a missionary reported that parents were offering their children for "as low as four cents each," highlighting especially his concern that "the Mohammedans are buying little girls at this price." Playing on negative stereotypes of rapa-cious Muslim men that had proved so effective in stirring up support for the Armenian relief efforts several years earlier, this commentator hoped to elicit a similar response to the India crisis by suggesting that lascivious Islamic predators were roaming the streets in search of starving young women with whom they could populate their harems. "Wicked men and women, like birds of prey, hover about the road to pick up these unhappy creatures and lure them away to lives of misery and shame," an-other correspondent wrote.[67]

As the calamity worsened over the course of 1900, rhetoric about the responsibility to rescue young Hindu widows and orphans from these terrible dangers became increasingly prevalent. American evangelicals, Klopsch and his associates insisted, possessed the power to provide defenseless women and children with places of refuge. By pledging to support an orphan sheltered at one of the many mission stations in India, the *Christian Herald*'s readers would not only fulfill the biblical com-mand to care for the fatherless but also further the cause of Christ in "that benighted and afflicted land." "Children are the hope of a country," the editors declared. By "rescuing and caring for the child-waifs," they wrote, "the Christian world might accomplish more toward the ultimate evangelization of India than by any other means."[68]

To facilitate this great "life-saving campaign," the newspaper estab-lished a program that enabled subscribers to "adopt" one of the nearly five hundred thousand famine orphans taken in by missionaries over the course of the crisis. Working with members of the Interdenominational Missionary Committee, Klopsch conceived a plan that he promised would provide ongoing support for at least ten thousand destitute children. Readers who committed to sponsoring an orphan at the cost of $15 per year, he explained, would "be put in personal and regular communica-tion with the little protégé, thus enabling the donor to have a direct, personal, living interest in the object of his or her benevolence." In every case, "foster parents" could designate the denomination they preferred and whether they wanted to provide for a boy or a girl.[69]

Klopsch suggested that through the *Christian Herald*'s adoption plan, contributors could establish intimate familial relationships with destitute children, creating "a bond of sympathy, humane and divine," that spanned physical distance and would ultimately eliminate religious and cultural differences as these "native dusky boys and girls" were "reared under Christian influences, and trained for Christian usefulness." In just three to five years, one of the scheme's promoters assured *Christian Herald* subscribers, "the adopted waifs will become self-supporting men and women, and will themselves become missionaries of the Gospel of Jesus Christ, of a higher civilization, of thrift and economy, of clean character and clean bodies."[70]

For American evangelicals dismayed that ongoing violence in the Philippines was hampering their hopes of liberating the islanders from Roman Catholicism and of promoting political enfranchisement, economic growth, and educational enlightenment, the "glorious work of child-saving" in India offered a chance to accomplish similar goals. By coming to "the rescue of the great army of orphans left homeless, bereaved and destitute by the India famine," Klopsch worked to advance the kingdom of Christ and the progress of Western civilization around the globe. The India orphan adoption plan was a surefire way of fostering the worldwide "expansion of affection" Talmage had hoped would characterize the extension of U.S. influence abroad. Surely, the *Christian Herald*'s editors concluded, every American evangelical who cared about spreading the gospel and liberating the oppressed ought to "have a share in this great work of child-redemption—the grandest work the century has afforded, and one upon which the religious future of India largely depends."[71]

To convince American evangelicals that they were responsible for the spiritual destiny and material well-being of an entire subcontinent, Klopsch and his editorial staff employed several persuasive publishing tactics they had developed and refined over the course of previous humanitarian campaigns. During both the 1897 and the 1900 Indian famines, almost every issue of the *Christian Herald* promoted the newspaper's relief efforts in bold, dramatic headlines designed to grab readers' attention through riveting allusions to the affliction of India's people. Some of the headlines confronted American evangelicals with direct questions about how they intended to respond to the tragedy unfolding on the other side of the globe: "Starving India's Pitiful Cry for Bread: What Will Christian America Do for India's Starving Fifty Millions? What Would Jesus Do?" or "Have You Adopted an India Famine Waif?" Others celebrated the generous and rapid response of the many readers who answered India's bitter cry, implying that those who were holding back were not fulfilling their Christian duty and were missing out on a great opportunity to serve God along with their fellow citizens: "The Whole Nation Helping India—Its Great Heart Touched by the Woes of that Famine-Stricken Land—Many Generous Gifts to the Relief Fund."[72]

Alongside these urgent appeals for relief donations and orphan adoptions, Klopsch and his production staff almost always included vivid images of people in distress that they hoped would help "make the pressing need known to the Christians of America" and move them to respond. Since the newspaper's pioneering experiments with the practice of "pictorial humanitarianism" during the Russian famine of 1892, the *Christian Herald* had remained at the forefront of this emerging trend. Over the course of the 1890s, Klopsch invested considerable resources in emerging technologies of photojournalism—purchasing state-of-the-art printing equipment, promoting the improvement of existing modes of newspaper production, and hiring well-known correspondents to travel to disaster sites so they could send back "exclusive" reports and pictures for the *Christian Herald*. While other popular journals and magazines such as William Randolph Hearst's *New York Journal* and monthlies like *Cosmopolitan* had also begun to integrate images of humanitarian crises into their pages by the time of the 1897 famine, none printed as many illustrations and photographs of the calamity in India as the *Christian Herald*.[73]

Convinced that graphic portrayals of suffering were powerful tools for eliciting sympathetic feelings, Klopsch packed his newspaper full of gruesome pictures of starving people. Images of "living skeletons," he and his associates believed, were one of the most effective means of bridging the geographic, social, and religious divides that separated American evangelicals from India's perishing millions. Although missionary entreaties, ethnological arguments, and biblical injunctions to care for widows and orphans all played a role in encouraging the *Christian Herald*'s constituents to accept responsibility for aiding distant and culturally different others, Klopsch and his associates believed that nothing proved more persuasive than photographs. "Arguments are soon forgotten," Talmage wrote in an article on the power of illustrations, "but pictures . . . are what produce the strongest effects."[74]

Missionaries and other firsthand observers of India's affliction concurred with Talmage's sentiments, frequently bemoaning the insufficiency of language to convey the horrors they were encountering. "I have no faculties for describing the awful sufferings of the poor people," one witness wrote. "Who can describe the suffering, woes, tears and groans which result in the lingering death of the multiplied millions?" During his own investigative "tour of the famine fields" in 1900, Klopsch repeatedly lamented his inability to depict the "scenes of desolation, of pain, of suffering, of hopeless despair, of heart anguish, of death" with which he came into contact. "Famine in India! How I dread to write about it! What pen can adequately portray the scenes which my eyes have witnessed?" he wondered. "How to describe it, so as to bring it within the grasp of the human mind, I know not." Despite many attempts to communicate the "abject misery" through detailed and vivid narratives that reported sensory assaults ("the heat was intense . . . the all-pervading stench from putrefying bodies impregnated clothes, hair and skin") and emotional anguish ("my heart almost sank within me"), Klopsch felt that words had failed him. "I was painfully conscious of the paucity of my vocabulary to do justice to the subject, and after I have written the worst, I shall feel that even then I have only faintly indicated the real condition of affairs." Convinced "no pen" could exaggerate the suffering and "word pictures" could only hint at the terrible reality of India's tragedy, Klopsch and other eyewitnesses hoped that images might more adequately portray the "shocking and revolting" situation and motivate American evangelicals to come to the rescue.[75]

And come to the rescue they did. Contributions to the *Christian Herald*'s famine relief funds in 1897 and 1900 far exceeded amounts collected for any of the newspaper's previous or subsequent charitable campaigns and easily outstripped the collections of all other humanitarian agencies. "Never before in the history of religious journalism have the readers of a periodical proved so conclusively the power of the religion of Christ

MISSIONARY PHOTOGRAPHS OF THE FAMINE SUFFERERS OF INDIA.

These realistic productions of the camera are the answer of the devoted American missionaries to those critics at home who have charged them with exaggeration, and who have even denied the existence of famine in India. These glimpses of suffering justify all the sympathy and help that have come from Christian America. We have reproduced only a few of many photographs of the same tragic character received by late mails. The scenes depicted above are: 1. Newly arrived famine children at the Meerut School. 2. Famine Children at Ahmednagar. 3. Some of the Meerut children after being cared for. 4. Famine children at the M. E. Mission Orphanage, Allahabad. 5. A pitiful group from Bilaspur. 6. More famine subjects at Bilaspur. 7. In the last stages of famine. 8. Famine adults and children. 9. A sufferer supported by Salvation Army officers (too weak to stand to be photographed).

"Missionary Photographs of the Famine Sufferers of India." From the *Christian Herald,* July 7, 1897, 531. Courtesy of the Christian Herald Association, New York.

Louis Klopsch during his tour of famine-stricken India. From the *Christian Herald,*
July 25, 1900, 610. Courtesy of the Christian Herald Association,
New York.

over the heart and life as have the readers of the *Christian Herald* in these
last two famines," Klopsch declared with exuberance.[76]

As conditions began to improve in the early fall of 1900, Bishop James
Thoburn singled out Klopsch and his associates for their leadership
in the national relief effort. "The power of a single newspaper," Thoburn
declared, "has been strikingly exhibited by the use made of the *Christian
Herald* in arresting public attention and stirring the public conscience so
as to bring it to bear in a practical way upon the duty of American Christians to the outlying parts of the earth." The graphic accounts of physical affliction illustrated by photographs of famine sufferers whose
"shocking ghastliness" told the "pathetic story of [their] urgent need" had
produced the desired effect: All across "Christian America," evangelicals

had "united so generously in this great life-saving work" of feeding the hungry, clothing the naked, and saving the dying from death.[77]

COMPETING VISIONS OF EVANGELICAL HUMANITARIANISM

In June 1901, the *Christian Herald* celebrated the great success of its India famine relief and orphan adoption campaigns with a cover image bearing the caption "America, the Almoner of the World." The illustration exemplified the editors' convictions about the United States' duty to aid destitute, persecuted, and helpless people of every tribe and nation. Surrounded by ragged children, veiled women, and poorly or half-clothed men of varying hues, the regally clad figure of America towers above her pitiable petitioners. In one hand, the solemn lady holds a book (a Bible?) while with the other she drops a measure of grain into the empty baskets at her feet. Sitting on the ground are a naked child and a gaunt, turbaned man representing the starving people of India. The burlap sacks that fill the space under America's outstretched arm are clearly labeled "Christian Herald India Famine Relief Work," making the source of the country's generosity apparent.[78]

Published amid ongoing controversy over war and military crimes in the Philippines, the image of "America, the Almoner of the World" promoted a more sanguine picture of U.S. international relations. By portraying the nation as a benevolent savior whose munificence extended to needy people of diverse religious, racial, and cultural backgrounds, Klopsch and his associates endeavored to showcase the United States' worldwide charity at a time when American activities abroad were under severe attack. As the overwhelming response to the India relief campaigns suggests, many evangelicals embraced this vision of "Christian America's" preeminent position as a redeemer of the poor and oppressed in foreign lands. For some of the *Christian Herald*'s constituents, however, the implications of representing the United States as a paragon of virtue, charged with the responsibility of rescuing, protecting, and superintending powerless people in India and elsewhere around the globe, seemed troubling for several reasons.

Missionaries such as the Reverend Marcus Fuller, who served as an executive member of the interdenominational committee that distributed the *Christian Herald*'s offerings, for example, often expressed concern

"America, the Almoner of the World." From the *Christian Herald,* June 26, 1901, cover. Courtesy of the Christian Herald Association, New York.

about humanitarian campaigns that fostered dependency among aid recipients rather than promoting self-sufficiency and autonomy. Fuller and his fellow missionaries suggested that instead of encouraging India's famine sufferers to rely on free handouts, relief agencies ought to provide employment through building and irrigation programs that would enable participants to earn money to purchase grain donated from the United States at "cheap rates, so as to help them without taking away their independence, and making paupers of them." "We wish to give as little gratuitous help as possible," Fuller's wife, Jennie, explained. Instead, missionary relief workers ought to "help the people to help themselves." From this perspective, images that depicted India's afflicted sufferers as utterly reliant on the charity of a dominant United States threatened to undermine the responsible practice of humanitarian aid.[79]

Given their worries about subverting the agency of relief recipients, missionaries like the Fullers also deplored that publishing heartrending images of "living skeletons" had become such an essential strategy for conducting a successful fund-raising campaign. "It seems a pity that intelligent people should need to have their feelings stirred by pictures," Marcus Fuller lamented in a May 1900 article describing the famine's toll. Although he did resort to sending photographs of people "lying by the roadside never to rise again, dying with cries of agony" in order "to make the awful sufferings of India real to . . . God's children in America," Fuller suggested that something was wrong with this method of encouraging almsgiving.[80]

In part, his ambivalence stemmed from anxiety about the spiritual state of American evangelicals who apparently required such sensational photographs to shock them out of their indifference toward the suffering of others. Surrounded by plenty and abundance, Fuller charged, most Americans had become captives of their own comfort, capable of ignoring the "cries of agony . . . of the perishing millions of India." Rather than giving even "the price of a single meal," Fuller declared, "they go on using the money for the transitory things of this world, its pleasures, its follies, its carnal, soul-destroying indulgences, and leave the heathen to starve and die without Christ." Since straightforward facts recounting the severity of India's affliction failed to rouse these selfish and materialistic Americans to extend sympathy to their "fellow beings," Fuller concluded, he and his missionary coworkers would have to resort to sending "terrible and vivid pictures" of "ghastly scenes" that might finally stir evangelicals to action. Appealing to the public's appetite for pictures, in this view, was at best a necessary evil that exposed the sorry condition of spirituality in the United States.[81]

At worst, Fuller and his missionary colleagues suggested, publishing photographs that emphasized the helplessness of India's famine sufferers might work to reinforce the sense of superiority and attitude of disdain that prevented prosperous Americans from recognizing afflicted people as worthy of care and respect. "The sad fact is that the majority of Christians in America do not consider the millions of India worth saving; neither their souls nor their bodies," Fuller wrote. Although sensational pictures of people in pain might succeed in generating pity for the sufferers, they also risked bolstering assumptions about the spiritual, racial, and social disparities that separated "heathen India" from "Christian America." For missionaries struggling to engender empathy for distant sufferers that bridged these differences, the possibility that pictorial humanitarianism might exacerbate feelings of alienation, preeminence, or even antipathy toward India's stricken people was a distressing prospect.[82]

To counteract these potential pitfalls, missionaries like the Fullers underscored the active part aid beneficiaries took in ameliorating the situation. In her letter thanking the *Christian Herald* for sending assistance, for example, Jennie Fuller explained that she and her fellow missionaries were "putting the money you have sent us to the best use" by supplying starving weavers with yarn, paying them to make cloth, and then purchasing their products so they would have the means to buy food. Reverend Robert Hume reported that he was also using relief funds to employ weavers or to hire workers to dig wells, rather than simply providing free handouts. Wherever possible, he wrote, "we set the people to work." During Klopsch's tour of the famine fields, Hume and other members of the interdenominational committee persuaded the publisher to appropriate additional monies from the *Christian Herald*'s relief fund so they could commission their weavers to produce one hundred thousand blankets for the aged and infirm who were unable to work or for orphans in the missionaries' care.[83]

Alongside the pictures of famine's ravages they sent to goad American evangelicals into helping India's sufferers, these missionaries supplied images documenting what they called an "industrial" approach to humanitarian relief. In July 1900, for example, the *Christian Herald* published a photograph of "women weavers waiting to welcome Dr. Klopsch." Although scenes of Indians at work were far less common than the graphic portrayals of "living skeletons" that populated so many pages of popular media during the food shortages of 1897 and 1900, their occasional appearance did disrupt—ever so slightly—the dominant representation of India's starving millions as helpless victims passively waiting for rescue from "Christian America."[84]

Missionaries striving to persuade supporters in the United States to see Indian people—and particularly converts to Christianity—as active partners in the process of fighting famine rather than as powerless petitioners wholly reliant on American charity also emphasized the crucial humanitarian work of local leaders like the well-known reformer Pandita Ramabai. By the time of India's 1897 food crisis, Ramabai had become a celebrated figure among American evangelicals because of her advocacy on behalf of women's rights and her forthright proclamation of Christian faith. Having traveled throughout the United States for several years in the mid-1880s, Ramabai had formed relationships with many prominent Protestant leaders (such as Woman's Christian Temperance Union president Frances Willard) and established networks of supporters who continued to sponsor her when she returned to Bombay in 1889 to found the Sharada Sadan, a school for Hindu widows. As an outspoken convert to Christianity, Ramabai faced strong opposition to this project from many of her countrymen but garnered enthusiastic praise from American benefactors and missionaries who appreciated her forceful critiques of both the caste system and the status of women in Indian society.[85]

When reports of famine in central India reached her in the fall of 1896, Ramabai determined to expand her facilities (now located in Poona) in order to shelter young widows who were in danger of starvation and/or moral degradation in poorhouses or government relief camps. Having experienced the horrors of hunger herself during the great food crisis of 1876—a catastrophe that took the lives of both her parents as well as a sister—Ramabai felt compelled to help as many suffering women and children as she could. By the end of 1897, she had gathered over three hundred girls on a new property in Kedgaon that she named Mukti, or Salvation.[86]

Given Ramabai's reputation among American evangelicals, she had no trouble mobilizing support for her relief effort. In early March 1897, the *Christian Herald* reported that Ramabai had begun to take in famine orphans, and published excerpts from an appeal she had written urging "good Christian people in England and America" to send money to missionaries trying to help the sufferers. By June, Klopsch and his associates had contributed $1,000 from the newspaper's famine fund to Ramabai's work "for the succor of the widows." In July, the *Christian Herald* published a full-page article describing Ramabai's ministry, which included several photographs furnished by Presbyterian missionary Robert Wilder, who strongly endorsed Ramabai's character and testified to the excellent results of her efforts.[87]

Rather than depicting the pitiful sufferings of starving people, these images emphasized the transformative effects of Ramabai's work with Indian women. Before-and-after photographs of "Tara"—a widow who had "enjoyed a year of care and kindness" in Ramabai's home—made the value of this ministry "obvious to the most skeptical," the article claimed. When Ramabai wrote to Klopsch in August to thank the *Christian Herald* for the generous donation to her relief effort, she enclosed a picture showing that the children she had taken in during the recent food crisis were "no longer 'Famine Girls'" but instead looked "quite plump and happy." Several months later, she sent another photograph of several "bright and intelligent" young women who were now thriving and demonstrating a notable "aptitude for learning and a gratitude for her kindness." In these and other communications with American sponsors, Ramabai consistently highlighted the potential and achievements of the widows and orphans she was assisting at her institution. Many of them, she claimed, had "learned to read in an incredibly short time," and would "soon be placed in higher standards," where they would receive training in a variety of professions, such as teaching and skilled nursing. Conversion to Christianity was common, and as a result, quite a few young women were preparing to become missionary assistants. Ramabai's goal was to educate every girl to do some useful work to "exercise an influence for good" in order "to give life and joy to this nation."[88]

Although Ramabai certainly deployed the rhetoric of rescue to describe her ministry among the famine sufferers, she steadfastly refused to portray those struggling to survive as passive victims entirely depen-

SHELTERING INDIA'S STARVING WIDOWS.

An Institution Established by Pandita Ramabai Crowded by Widows and Little Girls—Ramabai's Early Sufferings—Letters from Grateful Missionaries.

EXT to the children, the greatest sufferers by the famine in India have been the widows, whose lot under the most favorable circumstances is always pitiful. Social prejudice is strong against their contracting a second marriage, even when, as very often happens, their deceased husbands were boys of six or seven years old who died before married life began. Formerly widows cast themselves into the fire in which their husbands' bodies were cremated, believing that only in that way could they rejoin them in the next life. So extensive was this practice that in the year 1817, when public opinion was stirred against it, it is on official record that seven hundred widows thus perished in Bengal alone. In 1829 the British authorities prohibited it by statute, thereby causing a howl of opposition from the religious leaders of the people. They persisted, however, and a further statute provided for the trial of any person assisting or conniving at such a sacrifice of life, on the charge of culpable homicide. Since that time the widows have been permitted to live, but their heads are shaven and they remain a burden on the hands of their relatives. In time of famine these dependents were the first to feel the pinch of scarcity. Their lot aroused the sympathy of that noble lady, Pandita Ramabai, who during her education in this country won the respect and cordial affection of many American churches. Her efforts on her return to her native land were directed specially to the alleviation of the suffering of her charges. She clothes and feeds them and gives them a Christian education. The numbers who have applied to her for succor during the past few months have severely tried the good lady's faith, but she has received all the cause, relying on God to supply the means. THE CHRISTIAN HERALD sent her a thousand dollars from its fund, which would do much to relieve her anxieties.

On this page we give a portrait of this brave lady with a picture of her surrounded by ten of her widows. Two faces appear in the vignette. The second, the intelligent lady on the left, wearing a broad scarf, is Ramabai's chief assistant, whose services in the educational branch of her work have been most valuable. With these we give also two pictures of a "Famine widow." Tara by name, the first as she was, almost unclothed, with shaven head and attenuated limbs, so miserable that she almost lamented that her widowhood came after the fire when death by fire would have put a speedy end to her sufferings; the other picture is of the same woman after she had enjoyed a year of Christian care and kindness. Ramabai's work of this kind of transformation and its beneficence is obvious to the most sceptical.

Ramabai was herself a famine child. In the last great famine in 1877 she was a child of her parents who were of high caste. Gradually all their money was spent for food, the famine prices being then, as now, advanced beyond the

reach of the poor. She saw her father die of starvation; then her mother fell with the fever that comes of hunger and died pitifully pleading for only a morsel of bread. Then her elder sister died of the same awful want and Ramabai and her brother wandered through the country seeking work. Finally they reached Calcutta where the brother obtained employment; but the months of cruel suffering to get food for four or five days at a time had undermined his constitution and he too died. Ramabai was left alone, but her beauty and still more the learning, which had won her the coveted title of Sarasvasti, brought her friends who cared for her. Ultimately she married a Bengali gentleman and for about a year and a half she tasted the sweets of domestic happiness. A baby girl came to bless the union, but sorrow seemed reluctant to relax its grip on the devoted woman. After a brief illness her husband died and again Ramabai had to face the world and support herself and child. Through the kindness of friends she was enabled to go to England, where, for a year or two, she supported herself at a college at Cheltenham by teaching Sanscrit. Then she came to America and spent two years in practical work. Her heart was set on giving relief to the widows among her people, and her pathetic story of their lot won the sympathy of Christian people wherever she went. When she returned to India she took with her sufficient funds to establish the home, the name of which, Sharada Sadan (the abode of wisdom), became dear to many a hopeless widow. Chiefly through American gifts Ramabai has been enabled to carry on this home to the present time. Again the country is passing through the horrors of famine, and Ramabai has, with the sympathy born of bitter experience,

TARA, A FAMINE WIDOW, BEFORE RECEPTION.

TARA, AS SHE LEFT RAMABAI'S HOUSE.

held out her sheltering arms to women and girls who are suffering as she suffered. We are sure that our readers will be glad that a portion of their gifts has gone to so good a woman to help her continue and extend her beneficent work.

Writing of her work in the present fam-

ine, Pandita Ramabai says: "It is impossible for the Government officers alone to look after the little children and to protect the virtue of young women and girls. There is a large field of work for me and for you, if only we undertake to do it. Old people and middle-aged persons and delicate women who are unable to break

twelve baskets of stone, and carry it to the appointed place, and who cannot get their wages at the Relief Camps unless they do so much work every day, need our help. The sad sight of aged men and delicate women stretching forth their sore hands and begging you to help them, pouring out their sorrows into your ears, and lamenting over their hard fate, while their tearful eyes look straight into yours to find out if there were a particle of sympathy for them, is altogether too much to bear for a person having a heart of flesh.

"Why do not good Christian people in England and America send money to the missionaries in this country, who are so anxious to help the poor people, and are trying hard to do as much as they can for them, but cannot do more for want of means? The great motherly heart of missionary ladies is yearning for the dying children and other poor of the Central Provinces. Let benevolent people send generous donations to them for feeding and caring for the Lord's little ones. Men can do much, but all godly women must come forward at this time, and care for little children and protect young women whom the Government officials are not able to help and care for. It is woman's work and cannot be left to the officers and their subordinates. My sympathies are excited by the needs of young girl-widows especially, at this time. To let them go to the Relief Camps and Poor Houses, or allow them to wander in the streets and on the highways means their eternal destruction. I humbly request you to pray for me and mine, that we may be made strong in the Lord, and walk by faith and not by sight."

Rev. Robert Wilder, Presbyterian Missionary at Poonah, to whom we are indebted for the photographs of Pandita Ramabai, and her widows, speaks in the highest terms of her character and work. He has personally witnessed her efforts on behalf of her unhappy sisters, and has seen the results. He says that the training she is giving the poor waifs fits them for useful careers, and that many who have heard of Christ through her will become missionaries to their Hindoo sisters whom American and English missionaries could never reach.

At the same time that help was sent to Ramabai, a remittance was sent to Rev.

T. S. Johnson, of Jubulpur, who has been thirty-five years laboring in India under the auspices of the Methodist Episcopal Board. In acknowledging its receipt he says: "In all the thirty-five years of my work here I have never seen anything to compare with the present condition. "We are right in the very worst part of

the famine; the crops in these parts have been almost a failure for four years and great numbers had perished from starvation before it was recognized that we were famine-stricken. In parts of the district the death rate is 626 out of 1,000 for the year, where the average rate is 50 to 1,000 for the year. The distress is beyond description.

"Beside being associated with Relief Committees in general relief work, we are doing what we can to give homes to orphan children. We have provided for several hundred of them; and many hundreds more right around us must be provided for or perish. To provide premises for and to undertake the support of these helpless ones a great financial responsibility must be assumed. Our missionary society is so heavily burdened that it cannot authorize additional expenditure and a great question now facing me—as well as others—is, shall I personally assume this additional responsibility or let the helpless children at my door perish? I have already assumed a great deal and must confess I no not now know what to do. Merciful Father, direct me!"

Bishop Thoburn writes: "I called a large committee of eighteen missionaries in order to get the fullest possible reports and to provide for a wide and careful distribution of the funds. As the famine fluctuates, growing worse in some districts and abating in others, I have called a second meeting for next week in order to revise our basis of distribution and provide for new contingencies which have arisen. The prompt and very generous help sent to India by THE CHRISTIAN HERALD has been fully appreciated, and I need hardly say it has been most timely. The reports received late last night indicate that the number of starving people receiving relief from Government had increased over 150,000 during the week. We are now watching with intense eagerness for reports of the coming rains, which usually begin in Southern Ceylon about this date, and slowly work their way along the Southwestern coast of India. We cannot hope for any abatement of the famine until these rains begin, but after they fully set in we must wait four months until seed can be sown and the various crops grow to maturity and be harvested. You will thus see that at the very least *the situation is still extremely grave.*"

Col. Ishwa Das, of the Salvation Army, writes: "We have received the remittance of $500 and thank you for the same. Our command in North India comprises the North-West Provinces and Oudh, and the Punjab, and, as you are probably aware, they are the parts of India most affected by the present famine. To see the famine at its worst it is necessary to go into the valleys, amongst the agricultural classes. This explains why some newspaper reporters and artists come out to India, visit the large cities and see so little of the famine."

PANDITA RAMABAI AND HER CHIEF HELPER—TEN OF RAMABAI'S WIDOWS.

Pandita Ramabai's relief work with India's widows. From the *Christian Herald,* July 14, 1897, 547. Courtesy of the Christian Herald Association, New York.

dent on foreign aid. When she first heard that conditions in central India were becoming dire in the fall of 1896, for example, Ramabai spoke with her assistants and pupils at the Sharada Sadan to determine how they could help alleviate the affliction. All agreed to live on one meal a day so that Ramabai could make room for more women and girls. As the number seeking shelter continued to swell, the students "willingly cared for the famine sufferers, and nursed them back to life and health." Over the next several years, residents of the newly established Mukti mission worked to make the enterprise self-supporting: digging wells; tending fruit trees and cultivating crops on the farm; establishing an oil mill and a dairy; learning to weave saris and carpets with handlooms; and doing their own cooking, cleaning, and laundry. Although Ramabai continued to appeal for funds from patrons in the United States as well as other nations during the start-up phase, she expressed confidence that the operation would no longer need to rely on charity once its various industries were better established.[89]

With the onslaught of the second great Indian famine in 1900, Ramabai's hopes for independence from Western donors were deferred. As drought and disease ravaged the region around Kedgaon, she and her co-workers again agreed to open Mukti's doors to widows and orphans facing starvation. Knowing she would need money to feed so many new mouths— by late summer, the mission had taken in over a thousand additional residents, bringing the total to more than thirteen hundred—Ramabai reached out to the *Christian Herald* and other contacts throughout the United States.

Her petitions stressed the role former famine sufferers who had come to Mukti in 1897 were now playing in relieving distress during the current calamity. "It rejoices my heart to see some of the girls saved from the last famine going out into the famine districts with my workers to save the lives of their perishing sisters in the present famine," Ramabai wrote. Many of these "noble young women," she reported, were "incessantly working… day and night" to care for the newcomers seeking refuge within the Poona compound. For example, she explained to Klopsch, one of the widows the *Christian Herald* had sponsored in the previous crisis had volunteered to take charge of two blind girls who had recently arrived at the mission. This young woman learned the Braille alphabet so that she could teach the two blind girls how to read. "I was so pleased when I saw her guiding their hands over the page and explaining it to them," Ramabai recounted, "that I had

A famine widow from Pandita Ramabai's Mukti Mission teaching blind girls to read. From the *Christian Herald,* May 2, 1900, 379. Courtesy of the Christian Herald Association, New York.

their portrait taken in the act, thinking that you would like to see what the *Christian Herald* fund did for one of the hundred widows it supported" in 1897. Even as many missionaries were sending home grisly photographs of gaunt figures on the verge of death in an effort to arouse pity and stimulate almsgiving from foreign donors, Ramabai continued to underscore the abilities and accomplishments of Indian women in easing the affliction of their own people.[90]

From Ramabai's perspective, relieving suffering in India—or elsewhere—was a cooperative enterprise that required the active participation of all God's children regardless of race, gender, or nationality. Although she eagerly solicited and happily accepted financial assistance from the *Christian Herald* and other charitable organizations, Ramabai clearly rejected the notion that the United States (or any nation, for that matter) was uniquely qualified to save the world's needy, oppressed, and afflicted people. Americans might have more money than their Indian sisters and brothers, but wealth did not necessarily translate into wisdom about how to evoke empathy for fellow human beings.

Years earlier, Ramabai had observed that while the United States was famous for its affluence and "advancement," "racial discrimination and prejudice, which are most inimical to all progress and civility," continued to cast "a stigma on this so-called respectable, freedom-loving people." Although she believed Americans were moving toward a more just society that reflected the ideals of liberty, equality, and justice enshrined in their founding documents and in the gospel most claimed to profess, Ramabai was not afraid to point out the ongoing hypocrisies she witnessed firsthand in so-called "Christian America." Nor was she willing to accept the idea that wealthy Americans somehow possessed superior insight about how best to carry out humanitarian aid projects in unfamiliar contexts. Throughout her career as an educator, reformer, and relief worker, Ramabai insisted on doing things her own way—regularly chafing against what she considered the presumptuous and patronizing directives of her foreign sponsors.[91]

Although some benefactors withdrew their support when Ramabai refused to comply with their instructions, others recognized they had a lot to learn from this remarkable leader. When the famine of 1900 was at its height, for example, American missionaries struggling to cope with a huge influx of sufferers looked to Ramabai for advice about how to conduct their relief efforts more effectively. "By July we had grown weary," wrote Eunice Wells of the CMA. "Thus far we had no definite organization. We had taken the children in as they came, and cared for them the best we could." At this critical juncture, the CMA sent one of their staff members to Mukti to observe Ramabai's methods, which they promptly put in place at their own station. Ramabai also helped longtime American missionaries Albert and Mary Norton establish an orphanage for famine boys in nearby Dhond, since her institution accepted only widows and girls. Moving forward, the Nortons' Boys Christian Home Mission and Mukti remained closely connected, often meeting for worship, matchmaking, and mutual encouragement. For years after the famine of 1900 abated, Ramabai's mission remained a hub of humanitarian activity, attracting admirers from all over the world who wanted to witness her work with widows and orphans firsthand. Quite a few Western workers were so impressed with Ramabai's vision that they asked to stay on at the Mukti mission as helpers.[92]

As they regained their health and strength, the women and children at Mukti pursued education, developed proficiency in various agricultural and trade industries, and became actively engaged in humanitarian relief efforts both within and beyond India. Several of the young women

Ramabai trained founded their own schools and orphanages. Many more served as evangelists, nurses, and teachers in American and British missions. Some of these women developed relationships with American supporters and traveled to the United States to promote ongoing investment in India. Ramabai's daughter Manoramabai, along with several other girls from the Sharada Sadan, for example, spent several years studying at the Free Methodist Seminary in North Chili, New York.

During their time in the United States, these young women served as spokespersons for Indian women's education as well as fund-raisers for disaster relief. When famine flared in 1900, Manoramabai appealed to donors at the American Ramabai Association annual meeting as well as to participants at the World's Missionary Conference in New York City, speaking to "vast throngs" on behalf of India's sufferers. At this gathering, the *Christian Herald* reported, "she told of the young girls and children rescued by her mother in the last famine, many of them now doing excellent work as missionaries to their own race." Even as they were struggling to survive their own humanitarian crises, Manoramabai explained, the women of the Mukti mission were engaging in efforts to relieve the afflictions of others in both their own country and distant lands. When they heard about the violence Chinese Christians were experiencing as the result of the Boxer Uprising in the summer of 1900, for example, residents of Ramabai's institutions decided once again to forgo meals so they could save money to help their brothers and sisters overseas. "As a result of this sacrifice," one missionary reported, "Ramabai sent $300 to China" through the American Board of Commissioners on Foreign Missions, and this gift was "but a portion" of Mukti's "tithing and self-denial fund." Surely, this author asserted, these Indian women had something to teach "us Christianized Americans" about the "Christ-like, sacrificing spirit" required for effective humanitarian service.[93]

Over the years, the Mukti mission continued to send evangelists, relief agents, and financial contributions to alleviate suffering and spread the gospel in India and around the world. According to one biographer, Ramabai "was able to function as the strongest single pivot and conduit for 'international aid' to Indian women through funds and volunteer workers" from the time she founded her school for girls in 1889 until her death in 1922. Reports of her ongoing accomplishments and those of her pupils and protégés continued to circulate in the *Christian Herald* and other publications during this period, making her one of the most well-known figures in the fields of evangelical missions and humanitarianism. Like Klopsch, she was awarded the Kaisar-i-Hind Medal from the British government for her service to humanity.[94]

Ramabai's story and the work she carried out through her reform and relief efforts highlight the significant role she and her associates played in shaping the meaning and practice of international Christian charity at the turn of the twentieth century. By showcasing the agency and independence she encouraged among India's widows and orphans, Ramabai presented an alternative to the dominant image of the United States as the savior of a benighted and powerless people frequently publicized in the *Christian Herald*. Her willingness to criticize the United States for allowing racial prejudice and discrimination to persist despite the nation's professed commitment to equality enabled her to push back against presumptions of American superiority in the arenas of almsgiving and foreign aid distribution. Finally, through her expertise in the fields of education, social reform, and famine relief, as well as her lifelong commitment to training other Indian women for leadership in these areas, Ramabai influenced an entire generation of American missionaries and aid workers.

Although images like the *Christian Herald*'s "America, the Almoner of the World" obscured Ramabai's contributions to humanitarian relief campaigns in India and elsewhere, accounts of the Mukti mission and its ministries show that the efforts of American evangelicals to lessen affliction on an increasingly global scale involved intensive cooperation, negotiation, and contestation among Christians of diverse racial and national backgrounds. These interactions helped set the stage for ongoing collaborations, as well as conflicts, that would have an enduring impact on the development of evangelical humanitarianism within the United States and around the globe during the early years of the twentieth century and beyond.

5

THE LIMITS OF EVANGELICAL
BENEVOLENCE

In late June 1900, as the famine relief ship *Quito* sailed into Bombay Harbor on an errand of mercy, another U.S. military vessel steamed toward China's north coast on a different kind of mission. Transporting a battalion of American infantrymen stationed in the Philippines, the warship was sent by General Arthur MacArthur Jr. to provide reinforcements to the Eight-Nation Alliance—an international military coalition undertaking what the U.S. government called a "relief expedition" to rescue foreign diplomats, soldiers, and civilians trapped in Beijing's Legation Quarter by the Chinese Imperial Army and members of the Militia United in Righteousness or, as they were called in English, the Boxers.[1]

For the past several months, aggression against foreigners—and particularly Christian missionaries—had been escalating as the Boxer Uprising spread from Shandong province into surrounding regions. Angered by the growing interference of the "Great Powers" in China's economic, political, and religious spheres, the Boxers sought to revive the Qing Dynasty by destroying foreign influences. During the spring of 1900, they stormed the countryside, burning churches and attacking Western missionaries and native Christians. In response to the mounting violence, European and American envoys called for protection. The arrival of a multinational military force in Beijing in early June only exacerbated the volatile situation, prompting the Dowager Empress Cixi to align with the Boxers and declare war against all foreign powers.[2]

Over the next few weeks, as Allied troops fought to free the captives who had taken refuge in the Legation district and suppress the rebellion, a "carnival of riot and massacre" ensued. Throughout the northern provinces, the *Christian Herald* reported, hundreds of missionaries and their families were slaughtered alongside thousands of Chinese converts. Accounts of the horrific torture and execution of Christians at the hands of brutal "Boxer hordes" filled the pages of popular American newspapers well after foreign forces succeeded in breaking the siege of Beijing in mid-August. "Many weeks, perhaps months, must elapse before the complete story of the Christian martyrdoms of China can be fully told," one contributor to the *Christian Herald* wrote in a late-October article detailing a number of "authenticated instances" of atrocities. "In one case," the correspondent declared, "a missionary had his eyes burned out; then a portion of his body was cut off; and finally a red-hot staff was driven through his back." Tales like these dominated coverage of the Boxer Rebellion as the Allied powers and the dowager empress negotiated peace terms, punishment of war criminals, and reparations through the winter of 1901.[3]

Alongside the tragic headlines about missionary sufferings, however, another story about the China Relief Expedition and its aftermath began to emerge in the American press. Soon after Beijing's fall to Allied forces, several popular newspapers began to report on the pervasive looting of the capital city. Throughout the countryside, "brutal outrages" against women were being perpetrated—allegedly by German troops who had arrived too late to participate in the pillage of Beijing and were engaging in "punitive expeditions" that included extrajudicial killings of suspected Boxers "under peculiarly atrocious conditions." While correspondents indicated that American soldiers were ordered to abstain from exacting vengeance through violence or plunder and instead to cooperate in constraining the barbarous behavior of their allies, some reporters portrayed missionaries in a less favorable light. Whereas American commander General Adna Chaffee was working to prevent the ongoing ransacking of Beijing, one *New York Tribune* writer observed, "the missionaries complain because the Sacred City has not been looted. They urge that the royal family and other high Chinese personages who were behind all the trouble should be made to suffer more than those who blindly followed them."[4]

By December, critiques of missionary demands for reparations had become more pointed. On Christmas Eve, the New York *Sun* published a story about the Reverend William Scott Ament, a missionary from the American Board of Commissioners on Foreign Missions (ABCFM) who helped evacuate colleagues under threat from Boxer forces and then participated in the defense of the Legation district during the siege. After the liberation of Beijing, Ament lobbied U.S. officials on behalf of missionary organizations and native Christians who had lost lives and property in the uprising. Insisting that the victims be justly compensated for their suffering, Ament began negotiating claims settlements for Chinese church members with local officials. According to *Sun* correspondent Wilbur Chamberlin, Ament had just returned from a trip to collect reparations. "Everywhere he went," Chamberlin reported, "he compelled the Chinese to pay" and "assessed fines amounting to thirteen times the amount of the indemnity."[5]

Several weeks after the *Sun* article appeared, the *New York Times* published a series of editorials painting an even more unflattering picture of missionary actions and attitudes in China. Not only were leaders like Ament exacting exorbitant sums to repay damages from impoverished peasants, the editors charged, they had actively participated in looting and had even instigated "the promiscuous taking of Chinese lives" in punitive expeditions. When asked by ABCFM officials to justify these accusations, the newspaper editors reiterated their conviction that missionaries in China—including Americans like Ament—"were showing a vindictiveness, in respect to the outrages and the situation which did not exactly comport with the Gospel they professed to be spreading."[6]

This simmering public debate over missionary behavior became even more explosive in February, after nationally renowned humorist Mark Twain published a scathing essay in the *North American Review* criticizing Ament and linking his conduct with a larger condemnation of American imperialism in the Philippines. Twain's "To the Person Sitting in Darkness" made clear that he considered Ament's actions an example of the "hideous and colossal" hypocrisy that characterized American efforts to extort land and resources from vulnerable people under the guise of exporting a supposedly Christian civilization.[7]

For evangelical leaders like Talmage and Klopsch, this controversy over the integrity of the American missionary enterprise and the character of the United States as a Christian nation came at a particularly inconvenient moment. Just as they were celebrating American missionaries' noble work distributing *Christian Herald* readers' generous contributions to India's starving millions with the hope of demonstrating that evangelicals could bolster the nation's reputation as God's chosen instrument for redeeming the world's poor and oppressed, Twain called into question the central premises of their project. Missionaries were not self-sacrificing almsgivers but unscrupulous "thieves and extortioners," Twain wrote. Nor was the United States uniquely qualified to advance the kingdom of Christ and the progress of Western civilization around the globe. American soldiers and political leaders, Twain alleged, had been just as rapacious and greedy in the Philippines as the Germans and Russians had been in China or the British in the Boer War. In fact, some critics charged, the United States was far worse than these other nations. Not only were Americans murdering and exploiting the needy people they had pledged to protect abroad, but they were doing the same thing at home to Asian immigrants, Native Indians, and, especially, African Americans.[8]

Outcries against injustice toward these domestic populations were nothing new at the turn of the century: Ida B. Wells-Barnett, for example, had been protesting the widespread practice of lynching—which affected all these groups—since 1892. By 1900, however, several horrific instances of mob brutality, including the torture and burning alive of African American Sam Hose near Atlanta in April 1899, prompted renewed public attention throughout the United States and Europe to what Wells-Barnett called "our country's national crime." "No American travels abroad without blushing for shame for his country on this subject," she asserted in January 1900.[9]

If the United States hoped to restore its global image, Wells-Barnett contended, its citizens would have to do more than send missionaries and intervene in humanitarian crises overseas. "Our nation has been active and outspoken in its endeavors to right the wrongs of the Armenian Christian, the Russian Jew, the Irish Home Ruler, the native women of India, the Siberian exile, and the Cuban patriot," she declared. "Surely it should be the nation's duty to correct its own evils!" How could a nation "posing as a civilizer of foreign countries" remain "so complacent about the savagery at home," another observer wondered. After another spate of violence resulting in a four-day race riot that claimed the lives of twenty-eight people in New Orleans in July 1900, Wells-Barnett called for an "earnest, active, united endeavor to arouse public sentiment" in order to "put a stop to these demonstrations of American barbarism." "Men and women of America, are you proud of this record which the Anglo-Saxon race has made for itself?" she demanded. "Your silence seems to say that you are. Your silence encourages a continuance of this sort of horror."[10]

In the decade since Klopsch and Talmage took leadership of the *Christian Herald,* the newspaper had remained mute on the subject of lynching. Even after Wells-Barnett's renewed plea for leaders of public opinion to speak out against this "disgrace to civilization," the editors maintained their reticence. Instead, they again turned their attention to the plight of distant strangers—this time the sufferers of a serious food shortage in the very site of recent consternation over the alleged misconduct of American missionaries.[11]

Why did evangelical philanthropists like Klopsch and Talmage choose to sound the alarm in response to foreign disasters like the China famine of 1901 while keeping quiet about what was arguably the most sustained and pressing humanitarian crisis of their era: the increasingly violent and systematic oppression of African Americans, Native communities, and certain classes of foreign immigrants throughout the United States and its "insular" territories? Examining what contributors to the *Christian Herald* did have to say about what they called "the negro question," "the Indian problem," and the rising "tide of immigration" reveals the complex and increasingly fraught relationships among evangelical nationalism, domestic charity, and foreign aid during a critical period in the history of American racial politics and international relations.[12]

RESCUING CHINA, REDEEMING "CHRISTIAN AMERICA"

Soon after the *North American Review* printed Mark Twain's condemnation of American missionary actions in China, the *Christian Herald* published an article describing the devastating famine afflicting up to twenty-four million people in China's northern provinces. Having heard of the "wonderful generosity of the *Christian Herald* to India during the famine in that country," Wu Ting Fang, China's minister of foreign affairs in Washington, DC, appealed to the newspaper for help. Klopsch and Talmage were happy to oblige. On February 20, 1901, they announced that the *Christian Herald* would begin collecting donations. Given the controversy still swirling around the peace negotiations between the Eight-Nation Alliance and the Chinese Empire, however, fund-raising for the campaign got off to a relatively slow start. By mid-April, reports of worsening conditions prompted Talmage to visit Wu Ting Fang to ask whether more aid was needed and if immediate relief measures were feasible. The minister affirmed that famine had spread throughout a vast region where it was raging "in most dreadful form." A week later, Li Hung Chang, China's foremost statesman and principal diplomatic negotiator, cabled Talmage from Beijing to verify that urgent relief was warranted.[13]

Immediately, Talmage and Klopsch took action. Klopsch contacted Secretary of State John Hay and William Rockhill, the U.S. minister in Beijing, to inquire about the best way to send supplies. At Klopsch's request, Rockhill agreed to organize and chair an emergency relief committee consisting mostly of American missionaries who would purchase and distribute aid with funds sent through the *Christian Herald*. Once peace and indemnity terms between China and the Western powers were largely settled in late May, Rockhill and an interdenominational group of five missionaries began work. On June 4, Klopsch cabled the first $20,000 remittance from the relief fund. Over the next few months, the *Christian Herald* reported extensively on the suffering in China's northern provinces and the heroic efforts of American missionaries to alleviate affliction. In addition to collecting donations, the newspaper sent journalist Francis H. Nichols to cover the crisis and report on the distribution work. By the time the famine committee had finished its work in late November, American evangelicals had contributed $128,281 to aid China's starving millions.[14]

Although this amount was only one-fifth of the total donations amassed during the *Christian Herald*'s 1900 India famine relief campaign, the editors proclaimed that the significance of their readers' efforts to relieve suffering in China was on par with, and perhaps more salient than, the work to rescue women and orphans in India. In both places, they contended, "our benevolence . . . has been an object lesson to the Asiatic races," demonstrating to these "two great nations yet to be civilized . . . that Christianity is better than barbarism." These evangelicals also asserted that providing evidence of Christian superiority was particularly urgent in China given the recent allegations of Western military and missionary vindictiveness in the region. Although Talmage and Klopsch conceded that "it may seem inhuman to talk of such a disaster as Presidential or opportune," they could not help but declare that China's appeal for humanitarian aid came at a fitting moment. "At this time, when our devoted missionaries are being so unjustly maligned and misrepresented," they wrote, the *Christian Herald*'s relief campaign enabled American evangelicals to prove that "Christians are kind, merciful and forgiving."[15]

Even as they insisted that the allegations of misbehavior by the missionaries were unwarranted, the editors were willing to give credence to the charges made against German and Russian military forces. During the suppression of the Boxer Uprising, one journalist quoted in the *Christian Herald* wrote, "there were many things done calculated to bring disgrace upon Christianity and upon Christian civilization." Despite the fact that the United States was not responsible for the misdeeds of its allies, still "we had to share in the shame" that redounded on "Christendom" as the result of these atrocities. Providing "prompt and liberal" succor to China's starving sufferers, this author argued, gave the citizens of the United States a chance to differentiate themselves from their European counterparts: "A generously sustained famine fund will show the people of China that the Americans, at least, recognize them as fellow-men, and . . . in spite of our share in the nameless infamies that have been perpetrated by our allies in China, we have no enmity against them." Talmage and

Klopsch heartily agreed: "Is not the famine a Providential opportunity afforded to us to prove to China that we are her friend, though all the world else may be her spoilers?"[16]

If the *Christian Herald*'s China famine relief campaign offered American evangelicals an occasion to redeem the "good name of the United States" in the aftermath of the indemnities controversy and the pillaging of Beijing, Klopsch and Talmage suggested, the outpouring of charity also provided a way of making amends for previous injustices committed against the Chinese by the American government. Although the United States had behaved more nobly than its allies during the suppression of the Boxer Uprising, the nation's actions toward Chinese immigrants over the past twenty-five years, the editors charged, had been reprehensible.[17]

In an editorial urging leniency toward China in the current peace negotiations, Talmage excoriated American officials for having encouraged Chinese laborers to come work in the United States earlier in the nineteenth century and then failing to protect them from rising nativist prejudice and violent abuse. Since their arrival on American shores in the 1860s, Talmage argued, the Chinese had been beaten, slain, and unfairly taxed. "The way from the steamboat wharf to their stopping in the Chinese quarters," Talmage wrote, was "one long scene of blasphemy and bloodshed, and no police." The passage of restrictive legislation, notably the Chinese Exclusion Act of 1882, had added insult to injury. Talmage condemned the maltreatment of the Chinese in no uncertain terms. "In the name of the Almighty God, the Maker of nations, He who hath made of one blood all people, I impeach the United States Government for its perfidy toward the Chinese twenty years ago," he thundered. Now, he suggested elsewhere, it was time for the United States to change course by showing "magnanimity and fair dealing toward the prostrate nation . . . in accord with the principles of Christianity." Through the *Christian Herald*'s famine relief campaign, he implied, American evangelicals would play a preeminent role in restoring trust and friendly relations between the United States and China—paving the way for the advancement of American commercial interests in the East, for more widespread acceptance of the gospel throughout Asia, and ultimately for the commingling of nationalities that would unite all people in "one great nation—one nation on five continents—a grand, homogenous, great-hearted . . . world-encircling, universal Christian nation."[18]

Talmage's vision of a world community forged through evangelical charity was rooted in his conviction that God was working in and through "Christian America" to usher in the millennial kingdom. In this next phase of sacred history, he believed, discord among the world's diverse tribes and nations would dissolve as everyone embraced the gospel message of peace, harmony, and mutual goodwill. Throughout his ministry, Talmage celebrated the many signs of the coming kingdom manifest in the remarkable advances in technology, industry, travel, and communications that were bringing the nations closer together and making it possible for missionaries to take the teachings of Christ to the ends of the earth. As these emissaries carried Christian civilization across borders, he contended, long-standing barriers of racial animosity would crumble, and all humanity would recognize they belonged "to one family" that shared a common destiny. Although Americans did not have a monopoly on this gospel message, Talmage fervently believed that the United States was specially ordained by God to serve as the cradle of Christ's kingdom and the place from which righteousness, justice, and mercy would spread across the globe.[19]

This expectation about "Christian America's" role in God's plan for redeeming and reconciling all tribes and nations profoundly influenced Talmage's perspective on U.S. foreign affairs and domestic policy. Although he initially disapproved of deploying military force in Cuba and the Philippines, for example, Talmage eventually embraced American imperialism as a divinely sanctioned method of extending Christian civilization globally. As peace negotiations continued in China, he praised American diplomats for setting an example for all the European powers by manifesting "a disinterested desire for the rehabilitation of the distracted empire" rather than insisting on retaliatory reparations or pursuing territorial aggrandizement. In so doing, the United States was, Talmage believed, fulfilling its God-given responsibility to spread international goodwill among diverse nations. Through the *Christian Herald's* famine relief campaign, American evangelicals were furthering world peace by cultivating friendship with the Chinese, showing that "liberality and beneficence make no distinction of race or country."[20]

Yet even as Talmage and his colleagues celebrated the ways in which the United States was advancing the Lord's dominion internationally, they remained concerned about aspects of the nation's domestic policy that seemed to be undermining this mission. As Talmage's comments about the mistreatment of Chinese immigrants indicate, he was especially troubled by the rising antipathy toward foreigners that was spreading among American citizens in the latter decades of the nineteenth century. Growing hostility toward newcomers from Asia and elsewhere, he worried, threatened the United States' status as a "refuge for the oppressed and the downtrodden of every clime, where all are welcome, and all may abide in peace and safety."[21]

Throughout his career, Talmage had vigorously promoted the idea that "Christian America" was the place where God would bring together people of "every race, nationality, and religion under the sun" to live in peaceful unity through the process of immigration. In his 1879 sermon "The Democracy of Religion," for example, he laid out biblical and scientific evidence in support of his inclusive vision. According to Acts 17:26, he preached, God "hath made of one blood all nations of men." Recent work in physiology had confirmed this text by demonstrating that human plasma did not differ among people of diverse regions, thus invalidating popular theories of polygenesis that proclaimed "God originally made an Asiatic Adam, and a European Adam, and an African Adam, and an American Adam."[22]

Rather than presuming that distinctions among the world's races resulted from divine decree, Talmage insisted that variations in physiognomy and temperament could be explained by climate. "Much of the difference between an American and a European, between an Asiatic and an African, is atmospheric," he declared. "The lack of the warm sunlight pales the Greenlander. The full dash of the sunlight darkens the negro." If racial divisions were not inherent, Talmage reasoned, nor were they necessarily permanent. When people migrated from one region to another, they eventually adapted to the environment and adopted the habits and dispositions of their new home. As more of the earth's inhabitants moved and intermingled, he prophesied, differences would disappear and all would recognize their kinship as members of "one family" with "the same great mother—God."[23]

No place was better suited to facilitate this process, Talmage contended, than the United States. "Here in America I believe the work is to begin," he wrote. In addition to possessing an invigorating yet soothing atmosphere that would help promote unity among diverse peoples, the United States had enough space to accommodate representatives of every tribe and tongue. During a cross-continental tour in 1894, Talmage celebrated the nation's expansive geography. "Five hundred millions of people will not crowd us," he asserted. "Let the English come.... Let the Irish come. Let the French come. Let the Germans come. Let the Chinese come. Let all nations come. Plenty of room." Rather than worrying about overcrowding, Americans ought to give thanks for foreign immigration as a divinely inspired process making America "the greatest nation of the ages."[24]

The arrival and "commingling here of all nationalities under the blessing of God," Talmage predicted, would not only mitigate distinctions between diverse peoples but would also produce "the most magnificent style of man and woman the world ever saw"—a new Adam and Eve—through intermarriage. If "the cradle of the human race was the Tigro-Euphrates basin," Talmage asserted elsewhere, "the cradle of its regeneration will be this continent." These future Americans would embody the best qualities of every race that contributed to their genealogy: "the wit of one race, the eloquence of another race, the kindness of another, the generosity of another, the aesthetic taste of another, the high moral character of another." "And that," Talmage concluded, "is what is going to make this the mightiest nation on the earth. Intermarriage of nationalities!" Through this new American race, the deserts of the United States would be "Edenized" and the country would become a harbinger of God's peaceable kingdom.[25]

Despite Talmage's confidence in the divine blessings of foreign immigration, he failed to convince many fellow citizens that newcomers arriving on American shores during the latter part of the nineteenth century were anything but a menace to the United States. As economic instability increased, many Americans viewed the influx of laborers from other lands as a growing threat to their livelihoods. Animosities toward Asian immigrant workers had provoked riots in cities along the West Coast in particular, such as the Los Angeles Chinatown massacre of 1871, during which at least twenty Chinese residents were tortured and murdered by a white mob, the 1886 Seattle riots that forcibly expelled over two hundred Chinese residents from the city, and similar incidents in territories throughout the Pacific Northwest.

By the early 1890s, the arrival of massive numbers of southern and eastern Europeans elicited alarm from observers, who feared further dilution of American labor markets and questioned whether these immigrants possessed the proper education, political values, moral virtues, and work habits to become responsible and productive citizens. The fact that many of these recent immigrants were Roman Catholic and had grown up in countries that lacked strong democratic traditions exacerbated anxieties about their assimilation. Some critics charged that the United States needed more stringent legislation to prevent socialists, communists, and anarchists from entering the nation and trying to overthrow the government and capitalist system.[26]

Although Talmage endorsed laws closing the nation's borders to "foreign thieves, pickpockets and anarchists," in an 1891 editorial entitled "The Open Door" he warned that passing more restrictive immigration policies would provoke God's "omnipotent indignation" against the United States. To "build up a wall" against worthy people was to obstruct God's plan for bringing together all tribes and tongues in a common enterprise of ushering in the reign of Christ. Instead, Talmage persistently argued, American evangelicals ought to welcome the newcomers with enthusiasm and devote themselves to helping foreigners learn the habits of industry and the duties of Christian citizenship that made the United States "the best place to live in." From their earliest days at the helm of the *Christian Herald,* Talmage and Klopsch committed themselves to counteracting escalating anti-immigrant sentiment and violence by publishing articles and editorials emphasizing the benefits of embracing people who could contribute to the nation's providential destiny. They also offered readers concrete ways to participate in missionary and philanthropic enterprises dedicated to educating newcomers in the common "moral and intellectual culture" of white, Protestant Christianity that they believed bound the United States together and guaranteed its success.[27]

Throughout the 1890s, the *Christian Herald* urged subscribers to support efforts to train foreign immigrants in the political principles, economic practices, social customs, and religious doctrines the editors saw as essential to the nation's greatness. A few months after Klopsch and Talmage took over at the newspaper, for example, the front page featured sketches of the life and work of Klopsch's father-in-law, the Reverend Stephen Merritt of New York City's Jane Street Methodist Episcopal Church and its associated chapels. Since 1888, Merritt had overseen the work of several religious missions in the city's downtown neighborhoods—an area largely abandoned by most Protestant churches because of the crowding in of tenements predominately populated by immigrants. All around, the *Christian Herald* reported, "are Jews, Romanists, Atheists, Anarchists in embryo, and a population of many nationalities, generally careless about religion and eager to mend the social condition by violent measures." Through both preaching and charitable outreach that included the provision of food, clothing, and medical assistance to the destitute, Merritt and his coworkers encouraged these outsiders to come in to the gospel fold and "adopt . . . the true and only remedy for the sorrows and burdens and miseries of life." In the coming years, Talmage and Klopsch would continue to advertise Merritt's outreach to New York's immigrant population and invite readers to send financial contributions to keep his ministries solvent.[28]

Similar endeavors to evangelize and aid expanding foreign populations in urban centers across the United States also received the *Christian Herald*'s commendation and support. At the height of the West Coast's anti-Chinese outburst in 1885, one contributor to the newspaper recounted, several pastors in Portland, Oregon, had opened a school, a medical dispensary, and a legal assistance society for the city's Chinese residents that improved relations with this community and resulted in several conversions to Christianity. Missionaries in San Francisco had also established organizations to assist Chinatown dwellers in the wake of anti-immigrant violence. Back in New York, the Five Points House of Industry had long been a hub of educational and evangelistic work among the Chinese as well as many other recent immigrant communities in the neighborhoods of Lower Manhattan.[29]

Whereas many Chinese who passed through Five Points had been receptive to the language training and basic "American education" offered there, other immigrant groups were resistant to missionary outreach and schooling in the nation's "moral and intellectual culture." In an article describing the founding of the Forsyth Street Hebrew Christian Mission, the editors asserted that New York's growing Jewish population clustered in the "densely populated lower-East side" remained dangerously isolated in their ethnic enclaves. "Most of these foreigners know little of our language and less of our institutions. . . . They cling to their traditions, and are suspicious of any attempt to separate them from their faith or alienate them from their own people." Because many Jews had long regarded Christianity as "the symbol of oppression for their race," and some had experienced persecution directly, these evangelicals cautioned, they were more susceptible to the overtures of agitators trying to recruit them "to swell the ranks of socialists and anarchists." Given this danger, it was imperative to support the Hebrew mission's efforts to show Christian love and kindness. In particular, Klopsch and Talmage encouraged the *Christian Herald*'s readers to contribute to the establishment of an industrial home that would provide training in various trades, thereby assisting Manhattan's Jews to "make a place for themselves" in American society.[30]

Although they expressed some anxiety about integrating Jewish immigrants who viewed Christianity in a negative light, Klopsch and Talmage remained confident that the newcomers possessed the political motivation and work ethic necessary to become loyal and productive American citizens. They were more worried about Catholics, particularly those arriving from Italy, Mexico, Cuba, or other Spanish-speaking countries. While both Talmage and Klopsch were far less suspicious of Catholics than were many of their contemporaries—rarely citing allegiance to the pope as a disqualification for participation in democratic society—they did suggest that certain Catholic cultures promoted superstition and fanaticism in order to "hold the masses in spiritual and secular bondage." Immigrants from lands dominated by Spanish rule, especially, were likely either to remain enthralled by priests or to have broken away from the restraints of Catholicism's "empty rites and exorbitant demands . . . to lead lives practically without religion."[31]

Indeed, many Spanish-speaking Catholics, one contributor to the *Christian Herald* noted, were "restless, adventurous people, pleasure-seeking, fond of festivities and public amusements, not much devoted to education or literary pursuits." Ensuring that such impious people, as well as their overly devout counterparts, would adopt American Protestant norms of diligence, sobriety, self-improvement, and intellectual independence, the editors implied, was essential for the ongoing stability of the United States and for the continued progress of Christ's dominion. Readers who wished to shore up the prosperity of Christian America, they suggested, could send donations to Caroline and Susan Strong—sisters who had started a mission to educate the children of Spanish-speaking immigrants in Brooklyn and New York.[32]

In addition to making the *Christian Herald* a clearinghouse for contributions to evangelistic and charitable enterprises that helped assimilate the "great variety of races landing at American ports," Talmage and Klopsch founded their own institution to incorporate foreigners into the United States. Following the *Christian Herald*'s campaign to relieve suffering in Lower Manhattan during the economic crisis of 1894, Klopsch applied surplus monies from the food fund to furnishing a property in Nyack-on-the-Hudson, New York, to serve as a fresh-air home for city children. That summer, Mont-Lawn began to welcome young people between the ages of five and twelve in groups of about 120 to a ten-day retreat, serving approximately two to three thousand children over the months of July and August. Guests were selected from the poorest families in New York's worst slums, and "no distinctions were made as to creed or nationality."[33]

During their stay at Mont-Lawn, children enjoyed healthy food and recreation while receiving religious training and instruction in good citizenship. "Every weekday afternoon when the weather permits," the directors explained, "the children will be seated around the flagstaff on the lawn, with the Union flag flying above them, and taught to sing patriotic songs." Each Saturday was "patriotic day," and the Fourth of July was always the highlight of the season, with a great parade, fireworks, and special entertainments. Through a daily regimen of "Christian kindness" and lessons in the values of cleanliness, order, and reverence for American institutions, the missionaries at Mont-Lawn worked to promote "the proper development of the mental, moral, and spiritual side of the thousands of children in the metropolis who must become influences in the political, moral and religious future of our republic."[34]

What made the Mont-Lawn ministry especially compelling, its sponsors argued, was the bringing together of children "representing so many different nationalities, joining in tuneful praise of the great Republic that

SUBSCRIPTION, $1.50 PER ANNUM
Published 52 Times a Year

NEW YORK, JULY 20, 1904
COPYRIGHT 1904 BY LOUIS KLOPSCH

VOL. 27—NO. 29. PRICE 5 CENTS
Offices : Bible House, New York

CHRISTIAN HERALD

DR. KLOPSCH OPENING THE EXERCISES

SEE PAGES 622-623

"The Children's Temple" Corner-Stone Laying at Mont-Lawn

Louis Klopsch at Mont-Lawn on the Fourth of July. From the *Christian Herald,* July 20, 1904, cover. Courtesy of the Christian Herald Association, New York.

has given them shelter." At any one time, the *Christian Herald* reported, youths from at least twelve to fifteen ethnic backgrounds might be counted under one roof, including immigrants from almost every European country (Western, Eastern, and Southern) and Russia as well as a "sprinkling" of Chinese, Cubans, Hebrews, Japanese, and Syrians. During their stay, these diverse young people "all gather together at one family board," one observer noted, learning to live by a common set of rules and in harmony with one another. Mont-Lawn was thus designed to serve as a microcosm for the future United States: a nation that would successfully absorb all tribes and tongues into a shared set of social norms, political values, and moral sensibilities. Through their experiences at this "Children's Paradise," the missionaries hoped, Mont-Lawn's many guests would carry with them the basic habits and orientations necessary to embrace the "glorious destiny of American citizenship which awaits them." "How many mean to make noble American men and women?" Klopsch asked one such group of children during an Independence Day celebration. To his great delight, "every arm flew to its highest point."[35]

Throughout his tenure at the *Christian Herald,* Klopsch remained especially devoted to Mont-Lawn, spending most of the summer there with the children. By sending contributions to support the ongoing operation of the children's home, he and his coworkers argued, the newspaper's subscribers could share in the essential work of "shaping the Christian American citizenship of the future." As the tide of immigration continued to rise over the course of the 1890s, many American evangelicals deemed the task of acclimating foreigners—particularly young people—to the nation's political and social culture increasingly urgent. In cities like New York, newcomers were congregating in packed, already overcrowded neighborhoods. As a result, squalor, disease, and crime were becoming rampant. "Our slums are the worst and most densely populated in the world," one contributor to the *Christian Herald* lamented in an article explaining how the newspaper's fresh air fund sought to aid the thousands of "child-dwellers" being "swallowed up in the vortex without a hand extended to rescue them from our human shambles."[36]

Not only were children suffering and dying of filth and neglect in the tenement districts, they were also becoming a menace to American society because of a lack of education and moral training. Although some were blessed to have "honest, industrious Christian parents," many were "absolute waifs and outcasts" with no one to care for them. "It has got to be a question of stupendous import what is to be done with the destitute children of our streets or the ragamuffins, as society contemptuously calls them," Talmage declared. "These so-called ragamuffins are coming up to be the men and women of this country," he warned, and without proper guidance they would eventually exercise a deleterious influence on American politics and economic life. "The great, hard knotted fist of ruffianism will have more power than the gentle hand of sobriety and intelligence" at the ballot box, and "industry . . . will be unappreciated while multitudes of able-bodied men will wander about in utter idleness, with their hands on their hips, saying: 'The world owes us a living.'" To prevent such an ominous future, Talmage asserted, American evangelicals needed to surround these young people with edifying Christian influences through charitable enterprises like Mont-Lawn that would set them on a more productive path. "We must act upon them or they will act upon us. We must Christianize them or they will heathenize us," he proclaimed. "By the Gospelization of the rising generation let us save this land for civilization and Christianity."[37]

Although evangelizing and educating the children crowding New York City's tenement districts became a major emphasis of the *Christian Herald*'s humanitarian mission during the 1890s, Talmage and Klopsch insisted that immigrant youths were not the only young people who needed social, political, and religious training at this critical juncture in American history. "Whether we study the condition of people in the urban or the rural districts, we find elements which are grounds for apprehension," they observed. In the southwestern territory of the country, for example, there were at least "one million white children . . . without religious privileges." Because this section—which included the states of Missouri, Arkansas, Texas, and Louisiana—was growing rapidly as a result of white settlement, "its influence on the course and destiny of the whole nation will soon be enormous." Given this prospect, the editors argued, offering the neglected children of this "semi-civilized region" the "Christian training that will fit them to become intelligent God-fearing men and women" was "a work of national moment." By partnering with missionaries of the American Sunday School Union (ASSU) to minister among these "little white heathens," *Christian Herald* subscribers could help secure the future prosperity and stability of the United States.[38]

Similar work was necessary among the "Mountain Whites" of the Kentucky, Tennessee, and North Carolina hills. These "strange, uncouth, and only half-civilized people," one ASSU missionary wrote, were mostly descendants of Scotch-Irish settlers who had been driven into the mountains by "the Slave Power" that forced them off their original farming lands. Over the past several decades, this group had become increasingly "isolated from such Gospel privileges as the church, with its educated and consecrated pastor, the Sunday School and weekly prayer meeting, and the religious press." Even exposure to newspapers and basic schooling was limited, leaving many illiterate and susceptible to "moral degradation." Here, too, *Christian Herald* readers had an opportunity—if not a serious obligation—to invest their resources in the project of providing the "elevating and helpful influences" needed to instruct these outsiders in the political, moral, and spiritual duties of American citizenship. In addition to encouraging their subscribers to sponsor missionaries of the ASSU, Klopsch and Talmage publicized the efforts of educational innovators to found schools in these regions. Former Civil War general O. O. Howard, for example, was working to raise support to establish "an institution of learning" at Cumberland Gap, Tennessee, that would "afford thousands in the mountains the opportunities to become godly men and women" and therefore more productive participants in American economic and political life.[39]

By devoting themselves to benevolent enterprises like the Mont-Lawn Children's Home, the ASSU, and schools in the frontier and mountain regions of the country, Klopsch and Talmage argued, American evangelicals could help ensure the United States would remain a strong, prosperous, *Christian* republic. Although they admitted there was ample cause for concern about the country's future, the editors insisted that the myriad dangers threatening the nation could be overcome "by a stratagem of charity." It was true that "the worst form of government on earth is a republican form of government unless the people are intelligent and moral," Talmage wrote. "Without the schoolhouse and the church, free government is a dead failure." Therefore, "if you would have the form of government under which we live benign and perpetual," he counseled, "urge on all educational and evangelizing influences"—especially those that targeted the throngs of neglected children all across the nation, "turning them from vagrancy into useful citizenship."[40]

Ever the optimist, Talmage chided those discouraged by dire predictions about the decline of the United States resulting from rising delinquency and ignorance among the nation's young people. "I have so much faith in the advancement of our race under the Gospel that I suppose the rising generations are to have in their numbers more noble men than their predecessors," he wrote. "They who are now scoffed at as ragamuffins will pass on to be the men of might and the men of God in future years." Nor did Talmage countenance laments about the dilution of American character due to the introduction of too many "foreign elements." To give in to such fears was to lack faith that God was working through evangelical agencies like the *Christian Herald* and the many philanthropies its readers supported to make the United States the birthplace of the millennial kingdom: the gathering point for peoples of all nations to join together in "a doxology that shall roll around the world."[41]

To counteract rising concerns about educating and assimilating the country's youth, the editors of the *Christian Herald* frequently publicized the success of evangelical charities in transforming the nation's waifs and strays into models of propriety. "Many of our children are now servants of the Master whose Gospel of peace and love was first interpreted to them at Mont-Lawn, and the moral tone of whole families and neighborhoods have been changed through their influence," the managers of the children's home reported during its seventh season. The *Christian Herald*'s Sunday School missionaries on the frontier and in the mountains had also been effective in "bringing about a marked improvement in the morals of the scattered communities" through their work with the youth and families of these regions. Through accounts like these, Klopsch and Talmage worked to assure their readers that their contributions to the newspaper's philanthropies were helping to preserve the United States as a Christian nation destined to incorporate the world's diverse peoples in a unified community devoted to peace and prosperity for all.[42]

EVANGELICAL CHARITY IN THE AGE OF JIM CROW

As the numerous success stories published in the *Christian Herald* reveal, this narrative of assimilation proved a powerful force for advancing an evangelical vision of American destiny during a period of escalating anxiety about the nation's future. And for some—like the model children of

Mont-Lawn or the exemplary Sunday school scholars of the western plains and Appalachian mining towns—conforming to the expectations of their evangelical sponsors did offer access to certain social, economic, and cultural benefits. By embracing habits of cleanliness and order, industriousness and sobriety, lawfulness and self-improvement, these young people and their families might increase their chances of receiving material aid from charitable organizations in times of financial crisis or prepare themselves for better job opportunities through agencies like the *Christian Herald*'s employment bureau.

Over time, adopting the prescriptions of evangelical philanthropists like Klopsch and Talmage enabled some immigrants originally deemed indelibly foreign to gain acceptance as worthy American citizens who could actively contribute to the interrelated projects of building a greater republic and ushering in the kingdom of God. As a growing cadre of historians have shown, however, integration was much more challenging for some groups than for others—particularly for those whose "colored" skin made it difficult, if not impossible, to claim the basic human rights that were increasingly associated with whiteness in an era of intensifying racism. Despite ongoing evangelical efforts to show that many Chinese residents throughout the country eagerly embraced offers of education and often complied willingly with missionary training in personal hygiene, moral comportment, and sometimes even Christian faith, for example, prejudice against the "Asiatics" remained strong, and legal barriers to their inclusion became only more firmly fixed during the 1890s.[43]

If evangelical philanthropists like Klopsch and Talmage failed to convince their contemporaries that Chinese immigrants could become productive American citizens through missionary benevolence, similar efforts to demonstrate that Christian charity could also incorporate the country's recalcitrant Indian tribes and expanding African American population proved equally vexing. Unlike the Chinese—relative newcomers to the United States—these groups had been perplexing to white American settlers and citizens for centuries. Although some early evangelicals—like the eighteenth-century English revivalist George Whitefield and his contemporary David Brainerd—insisted on the common humanity and potential spiritual equality of America's enslaved and Native populations, most stressed the stark social and cultural cleavages between these "heathen" and "savage" people and the Protestant colonists whom God had ordained to Christianize and civilize the continent. In theory, conversion could dissolve the divisions and create a unified family of fellow believers. But in practice, faith in Jesus was often not enough to bridge the gap between Euro-American missionaries and their Native or African American converts.[44]

Instead, becoming part of the Christian community almost always required new disciples to abandon all political, social, and cultural practices that seemed to conflict with European civilization and to adopt the values, norms, and behaviors that would make them more like their evangelical missionary mentors. For some, embracing this program was impossible: Most slaves had scant opportunity to transform themselves into neatly dressed, self-sufficient agents of Protestant evangelicalism. For others, like members of communally oriented Native American tribes, espousing the thoroughgoing individualism or agriculturalism that supposedly characterized Christian civilization was undesirable—especially when this meant disavowing their political sovereignty and relinquishing their land to white settlers. Even those who did strive to conform discovered that their efforts rarely led to full acceptance as equal members of the body of Christ. Despite the gospel promise that in Jesus "there is neither Jew nor Greek . . . bond nor free . . . male nor female," deeply rooted assumptions of difference continued to shape relations among Euro-American, African American, and Native American communities throughout the nineteenth century.[45]

If incorporating Native and African American converts within Christian churches proved challenging, absorbing these groups within the developing political and social structures of the United States also became increasingly problematic. As debates over Indian removal policies and the spread of slavery roiled the nation from the 1830s on, white evangelicals struggled to reconcile the inclusive implications of their theology with the escalating demands of building a politically stable, economically prosperous, and socially cohesive country. A few radical leaders drew on Christian teachings to protest the injustices perpetuated against enslaved and Native communities in the name of financial gain and territorial expansion. Others developed biblical arguments in support of bondage, manifest destiny, and emerging racial theories that posited permanent distinctions among peoples that could not be effaced or even mitigated through conversion.

After the Civil War, proponents of scientific racism deployed their increasingly popular ideas to advocate for the disenfranchisement of newly emancipated African American citizens and the ongoing dispossession of Native communities. For some, the failure of Reconstruction and the outbreak of Indian wars lent credence to the notion that African and Native Americans remained unfit for self-government and required the supervision of "superior" white Anglo-Saxons who could (perhaps) help prepare them for fuller integration into the nation's political, economic, and social life. Evangelical missionaries and philanthropists seized the opportunity to participate in the "uplift" of former slaves and the pacification of warlike Indian tribes. Although few of these reformers interpreted their work as an effort to dismantle existing racial hierarchies or promote true political and social equality, most hoped their endeavors to educate and civilize would help unify the nation under the banner of Christ.[46]

By the time Klopsch and Talmage acquired the *Christian Herald* in 1890, efforts to incorporate racial minorities through the practice of evangelical charity were in full swing. From the outset of their tenure at the journal, they expressed enthusiastic support for a variety of benevolent enterprises that aimed to train African and Native Americans for more constructive participation in the nation's economic, civic, and religious spheres. Schools like the Hampton Normal and Industrial Institute, founded in 1872 for "the education of the neglected races," they wrote in an 1890 article, offered proof that "both Indians and negroes can work well at all the mechanical trades and in agriculture." By providing instruction in basic farming methods, handicrafts, and home industries like sewing and cooking, the *Christian Herald* reported, Hampton and similar institutions offered students opportunities to gain an "education adapted to their peculiar condition." Having suffered the deprivations of slavery or savagery for decades, proponents of "industrial education" asserted, these populations needed to acquire both practical skills and proper moral dispositions, not "mere secular learning," in order to "earn an honest livelihood" and make themselves valuable to the broader economy.[47]

That the United States desperately needed the labor of its Indian wards and former bond servants to fulfill its God-given destiny was certain, the *Christian Herald*'s editors declared with confidence. Sequestering Native tribes on separate reservations (many of which, they admitted, were entirely unsuitable) or sending blacks back to Africa, they argued, would be disastrous for the nation's future prosperity. In an 1891 article entitled "The Negro Emigration Question," for example, they praised former U.S. senator Blanche Bruce for encouraging his fellow African Americans to resist campaigns for wholesale relocation to Liberia. Because "the American negro . . . has practically a monopoly of the agricultural labor of the South," they wrote, "any general emigration movement among the colored population would paralyze the industries of at least eight great States."[48]

Several years later, Talmage preached a sermon praising the "industrious black hands of the coal and iron mines of the South," which were achieving for the region "fabulous and unimagined wealth." In the western and northwestern states, another contributor to the *Christian Herald* wrote, "thousands of red men . . . are now farmers and stock-raisers, and large numbers subsist by hunting, fishing and gathering berries for the markets." Thanks to the work of schools like the Hampton Normal and Industrial Institute, where they were "brought under the influence of a progressive and peaceful Christianity," the nation's "wild nomads" were abandoning "their old, roving ways" and "learning the dignity and utility of labor." Many of the younger generation had begun to "dress like the whites" and were gradually adopting their customs and manner of living. Overall, this author concluded, "the outlook among these people—and especially among progressive tribes like the Cherokees and Iroquois—is very promising for industrious citizenship, neat homes, good farms, and self-supporting mechanical skill."[49]

By sponsoring charitable efforts to educate, civilize, and Christianize the nation's African and Native American populations, the *Christian Herald*'s editors confirmed, its evangelical constituents were contributing to the broader project of acclimating these groups to the demands of a growing national economy that required their diligent services in the particular occupational spheres of agriculture, mining, mechanical trades, and other forms of manual labor. Through their cooperation with this program, the nation's black citizens and Indian tribes could earn a stake in the nation's future prosperity and, according to Talmage's prophetic vision, help claim the country, the continent, and ultimately the world for God.[50]

For African and Native Americans suffering the effects of escalating racism in the 1890s, evangelical prescriptions of uplift and assimilation held some appeal. During this period, many southern blacks struggled under oppressive sharecropping arrangements, decreasing access to education of any kind, and increasingly restrictive legislation that effectively excluded them from voting and almost all other forms of civic participation while also barring them from public transportation, meeting places, and health services. Physical violence against African Americans became commonplace, with lynching reaching an all-time high in 1892. At the same time, Native Americans were grappling with the implementation of the Dawes Act of 1887, which authorized the federal government to divide Indian lands throughout much of the West into individual allotments. The forced transition from a communal social structure devastated many Native communities. Numerous families suffered ruinous financial losses at the hands of unscrupulous land speculators; others endured harassment from white settlers and military agents. During the 1890s, Native peoples lost control over nearly half of their territory. Within this context, some African and Native American leaders pursued alliances with agents of evangelical charity like Talmage and Klopsch, hoping that by embracing "opportunities" for assimilation into the nation's labor economy, their people would avoid full-scale destruction at the hands of an increasingly racist and rapacious white society.[51]

Among African Americans, the chief spokesperson for this strategy was Booker T. Washington, principal of the Tuskegee Normal School in Alabama from 1881 until his death in 1915. As a student at the Hampton Institute, Washington had observed firsthand the practical workings of industrial training. After graduating, he was inspired to help found a similar establishment to instruct teachers in the philosophy and practice of racial self-help. Under Washington's leadership, Tuskegee became one of the premier centers of black agricultural, mechanical, and trade education in the United States.[52]

At the 1895 Cotton States and International Exposition in Atlanta, Washington delivered a seminal speech articulating his convictions about the role African American workers could play in "cultivating friendly relations with the Southern white man" by learning to "dignify and glorify common labor." Although he did not foreclose the possibility that blacks could be successful commercially or professionally, Washington asserted that "the masses of us are to live by the production of our hands," and he encouraged his fellow African Americans to embrace this reality in the present political and social climate. "No race that has anything to contribute to the markets of the world is long in any degree ostracized," he assured his black audience. From his white listeners, Washington sought recognition that industrious African American workers had already contributed to the outstanding progress of the South on display at the exposition and asked that employers favor loyal black laborers over foreign immigrants. He promised whites that blacks could continue "interlacing our industrial, commercial, civil and religious lives with yours," while remaining completely separate socially. For the economic and educational advances African Americans had made since emancipation, Washington thanked benefactors from the southern states but especially the northern philanthropists who had supported blacks' struggles to better themselves as workers. By continuing their efforts to expand the material prosperity of the region, he concluded, African Americans would help allay racial animosities and "bring into our beloved South a new heaven and earth."[53]

Washington's belief that blacks could help usher in God's millennial kingdom through their patient and faithful participation in the labor market fit well with Talmage's vision for African and Native American inclusion in the nation's economic future. Given this resonance, Tuskegee received frequent and enthusiastic praise in the pages of the *Christian Herald,* as did similar institutions promoting racial uplift through agricultural, mechanical, and industrial training combined with moral teaching. Throughout the 1890s, Klopsch and Talmage publicized the work of educational pioneers across the South and West, giving special attention to institutions in the nation's "black belt," where "transforming a thriftless, lazy, superstitious and densely ignorant class into industrious workmen and intelligent Christians" was deemed most urgent.[54]

One of their favorite philanthropic ventures along these lines was an experiment conducted by the Industrial Missionary Association of Alabama (IMAA), which had purchased four thousand acres of former plantation land, divided it into twenty-five-acre tracts, and rented out the plots to black farmers under a ten-year lease with a contract to buy. During the rental phase, missionaries would teach tenants improved methods of agriculture and other industries. The Mission Farm also boasted a sawmill, gristmill, cotton gin, blacksmith shop, store, post office, and two railroad stations, along with two churches, three schools, and a night school. By "holding out the stimulus of 'home-getting' as an inducement to economy and faithful industry," the managers of this enterprise wrote, they aimed to inspire the "most isolated, neglected and needy negroes" of the nation to become self-sufficient, independent workers, familiar with modern methods of mechanics and "used to the life that is led in ordinary, civilized communities." *Christian Herald* readers were warmly invited to cooperate in this effort to address one of the most pressing problems confronting "Christian America" by contributing funds to offset the IMAA's outstanding debt.[55]

The *Christian Herald* took an even more direct role in raising money to support the Mayesville Educational and Industrial Institute in South Carolina. Founded by African American educator Emma J. Wilson in 1882, the school aimed to further the "mental and moral advancement" of poor black children. Wilson first operated out of an old ginhouse, but her ambition of offering more training in "useful trades such as shoemaking, carpentering, and blacksmith's work . . . for the boys, and sewing and cooking for the girls" eventually prompted her to seek out patrons among Mayesville's white community and to garner sponsorship from northern philanthropists.[56]

During a fund-raising trip to New York in 1895, Wilson met Klopsch, who became so intrigued by her story that he determined to make Mayesville one of the *Christian Herald*'s signature charities. Over the next several years, Klopsch served as treasurer of the school's building fund and eventually became a trustee. The appeal of Wilson's enterprise, he explained to the newspaper's subscribers, was that "it has in it the best kind of philanthropy inasmuch as it is designed to help the colored race in that section to help themselves." From the outset, Klopsch observed, Wilson understood that her pupils needed more than book knowledge if they were to "enter the field of labor equipped for useful service." By offering both elementary education and practical training, he wrote, Mayesville aimed "to turn out of the Institute boys who will be efficient workmen and girls who by their skill in sewing, cooking and household occupations can render valuable service in the home." Through their contributions to this "benevolent undertaking," Klopsch concluded, the *Christian Herald*'s readers were helping prepare African American young people to contribute more profitably to the nation's expanding economy rather than swelling "the already over-full ranks of unskilled labor." Noting that Booker T. Washington had voiced his support for Wilson's work, Klopsch expressed his hope that evangelical almsgivers would continue to sponsor institutions like Tuskegee and Mayesville, "for in such efforts are the best prospects for a happy solution of the colored problem."[57]

In addition to championing black proponents of industrial education, the editors of the *Christian Herald* celebrated Native Americans who embraced the "opportunity for advancement" available through boarding schools and missionary outreach programs designed to "break down the last barriers of their old savage customs and beliefs" through training in the moral values and work habits of "Christian civilization." Numerous graduates of the Carlisle Industrial Indian School in Pennsylvania, for example, had abandoned "the ignorance and slavish traditions of their ancestors" under the influence of a "progressive and peaceful Christianity." After completing a curriculum that taught them to use a savings bank, keep their own books, and buy their own clothing, the *Christian Herald* reported, many students returned to their communities to serve "as examples and teachers among their dusky kindred." Others, like the Apache physician Dr. Carlos Montezuma and the Omaha journalist Levi Levering, made their way within white communities. Over the course of the 1890s, Klopsch and Talmage claimed, many tribal leaders recognized the benefits of industrial education.[58]

"A SPIRIT OF SEPARATION AND HOSTILITY"

Despite the success of institutions like Carlisle and Hampton in transforming thousands of Native students from "wild and rebellious" savages into "intelligent, law-abiding, industrious" citizens, Klopsch and Talmage admitted that these efforts were not proving robust enough to fully integrate all Indian tribes into the nation's social, political, and economic life. Although many Native communities had "taken most readily to the employments introduced by the whites," some resisted abandoning hunting for farming, communal living for individual land-owning, traditional dress for suits and ties, and tribal government for American citizenship. As white settlers continued to encroach on their territory and government agencies failed to deliver promised provisions, some tribes defended themselves by force—raising anxieties among evangelical missionaries and philanthropists who believed the peaceful incorporation

TINSMITHING   BRICKLAYING   PLASTERING   A NEW ARRIVAL   THE SAME, A YEAR LATER   BAKING   COOKING

UNCLE SAM'S FAMOUS INDIAN SCHOOL

CIVILIZING THE SAVAGE --- TRAINING THE RED BOYS AND GIRLS

THERE is probably no institution on this continent which more strikingly illustrates the advance of civilization and the influence of education than the Indian Industrial School at Carlisle, Pa., which recently celebrated its twenty-second anniversary, and at the same time held its thirteenth graduating exercises. From this school there went forth a band of native American Indians, boys and girls, to become useful citizens and to teach the advantages of education to the youth of the various tribes. The Carlisle School is not an ordinary educational institution. It is a great school because it does a great work—represents the very best in its management, its teaching force, and above all in its high aims for the pupils in its care. It lifts up and inspires the pupils, and the determination to do "my very best" is in the atmosphere. When one knows the general indifference of the average Indian elsewhere, he only then realizes what the Carlisle School, under Colonel Pratt, has done and is doing.

The number of students on roll during the past year was 1,218, representing 76 tribes. In the neighborhood of 700 are placed during the summer, and about 300 stay out all winter attending public schools. The students are allowed to keep their country earnings. In the past year they earned $27,255.52, and saved $15,518.39. Their aggregate earnings in the past eleven years has been $226,255.54.

The training of the Indian in the past has been toward dependence. He has learned to look to the Government for his rations, his cash annuity, or his lease money. The Carlisle School aims to lead the Indians into the national life, by associating them with that life, and by giving them a primary education and a knowledge of some common and practical industry which will be a means of self-support. There are shops at Carlisle where the principal trades are taught to boys and there are two farms for their instruction in agriculture, and suitable rooms and appliances where the girls are taught cooking, sewing, laundry and house-work. But the crowning influence in the accomplishment of the school's purposes is the extensive

INDIAN GIRLS AT RECITATION, CARLISLE

outing system. Information from agencies, where the students have made their homes since leaving Carlisle, indicate that by far the greater number are leading useful lives.

Colonel Pratt, superintendent at Carlisle, served eight years in the U. S. cavalry against the Indians. From that experience grew the idea of the Carlisle Indian School. During the Indian war of 1874-75 he had charge of hundreds of red-skinned prisoners at Fort Sill. Seventy-four of those men were selected and sent in his care to the old Spanish fort in St. Augustine, Fla., in April, 1875. They remained there three years under kindly influences. When they were released, twenty-two of the younger men promptly offered to remain East three years longer, if they could go to school. The Government would not provide the means. Their wants were made known to a few friends of the Indian, and one by one their expenses were provided. Seventeen were sent to Hampton Institute, Virginia. When they arrived at Hampton and Gen. Armstrong discovered their adaptability, he at once asked the Interior Department for forty more Indian boys and girls. Colonel Pratt went to Dakota and brought to Hampton forty-nine young Indians of the Sioux tribe. Dissatisfied with the scope of the effort at Hampton, Colonel Pratt applied to the Government for the Carlisle Barracks and 250 or 300 young Indians, that he might work out in his own way plans which had been growing in his mind during all the years of his Indian contact. His request was granted in 1879. He went to Dakota and brought from the Rosebud and Pine Ridge agencies to Carlisle 82 boys and girls. From Indian Territory he brought 57 Kiowa, Comanche, Cheyenne and Arapahoe children. The school opened November 1, 1879, and has steadily increased in numbers and reached out to the various tribes, until now it has nearly 1,000 students, coming from over 70 different tribes. As a civilizing and refining influence Carlisle certainly must be accorded an important place. It has done much toward solving the Indian problem, by making good, law-abiding, industrious Christian men and women of a people born amid savagery.

INDIANS AS THEY ARRIVED AT THE SCHOOL   COL. PRATT, SUPERINTENDENT   THE SAME INDIANS AFTER TRAINING

The Carlisle Indian Industrial School. From the *Christian Herald,* April 24, 1901, 377. Courtesy of the Christian Herald Association, New York.

of Native peoples and their property was essential to the fulfillment of the United States' God-given destiny.[59]

Talmage expressed these mounting fears in an 1896 editorial calling for revisions to governmental policy relegating Indians to reservations. Over the past several decades, he argued, this approach had contributed to ongoing violence between whites and Native peoples that had cost American taxpayers more than $700 million. Corrupt officials who cheated Indians of necessary supplies were part of the problem, he wrote, but the reservation system also fostered a crippling dependency rather than promoting self-sufficiency. "We have been supporting in idleness a multitude of Indians," who were perfectly capable of engaging in more profitable work, he charged. Since so many of them were refusing to cultivate their land productively, he asserted, they should no longer have a right to occupy these territories. "Let the tribes be broken up and sent through all parts of the United States, and then they will learn to pick up a living like the rest of us," Talmage concluded.[60]

Although he and his associates continued to commend the "civilizing" efforts of evangelical missionaries and educational institutions like Hampton and Carlisle, Talmage suggested that a more systematic approach was needed to bring Native peoples out from isolation and make them more useful contributors to American economic prosperity and political stability. Over the next several years, the *Christian Herald* offered vocal support for legislation that would expand the stipulations of the Dawes Act to those tribes that remained exempt under previous treaty provisions. With the passage of the Curtis Act in 1898, the process of absorbing remaining Indian lands and peoples into the United States by allotment was made mandatory. Through these laws, one contributor to the *Christian Herald* observed, the Indian was finally placed on equal footing with the white man as an American citizen and allowed "to work for his own salvation." Under the allotment system, the outrages that Native people suffered at the hands of unscrupulous agents who robbed them of their land and supplies through the reservation plan would now cease, and a new "era of justice" and "healthy progress . . . for the education and elevation of the Indian races" would ensue.[61]

The turn to legislation as a means of compelling assimilation suggests that by the late 1890s Talmage and his colleagues had begun to concede the limitations of evangelical charity as a mechanism for achieving racial harmony. Since frontier missionaries and boarding school teachers had been unable to prevent ongoing conflict between greedy white settlers and intractable Indians who refused to adapt to "white man's ways," the editors of the *Christian Herald* reasoned, something more than private benevolence was needed to bring about the peaceable kingdom they believed God intended to inaugurate in the American west. Compulsory integration through the government policy of allotment, from this perspective, was the only way to ensure the continued advance of Christ's reign across the continent. Once "the Reds" became "assimilated— absorbed as it were in the great mass of civilized whites," one *Christian Herald* correspondent predicted, race hatred would finally cease and "the 'Indian question' would disappear." As "aboriginal nomads" abandoned the error of their ways and adopted "the customs of the whites," this author asserted, intermarriages, which were already well known on the frontier, would become more common throughout the United States, contributing to a cohesive "Christian America" capable of incorporating even the most hostile tribes and nations within its expanding empire.[62]

Even as they hailed this vision of a society made more stable, productive, and peaceful through racial mixing, the *Christian Herald*'s editors confessed that resistance to integrating nonwhite groups remained strong among certain segments of the population. If some could conceive of a country that included "civilized" Indians on equal and even intimate terms with white citizens, it was also the case that "the prejudice felt by the whites . . . against negroes" precluded the vast majority of white Americans from imagining the United States as a multiracial nation in which blacks could be fully accepted. Despite the efforts of African American educators and their evangelical supporters to equip blacks with skills enabling them to contribute to building a stronger national economy, opposition to "the uplift of colored race" became increasingly virulent throughout the 1890s.[63]

While proponents of Native American assimilation lobbied for legislation that would accelerate the incorporation of Indians and their lands into the body politic, lawmakers throughout the South passed statutes designed to keep blacks segregated from whites in all spheres of political and social life. In May 1896, the U.S. Supreme Court effectively legalized racial discrimination by upholding the constitutionality of regulations that prescribed "separate but equal" accommodations in the

Plessy v. Ferguson case. At the same time, African Americans suspected of violating laws or even of transgressing social boundaries with whites were frequently subjected to vigilante "justice" carried out by lynch mobs.[64]

As the systematic and violent oppression of African Americans spread across the nation during the closing decade of the nineteenth century, the editors of the *Christian Herald* made almost no mention of the challenge rising racism posed to their conviction that the United States was God's chosen instrument for the harmonious reconciliation of the world's diverse peoples. Even when other religious periodicals devoted significant coverage to the horrors of lynching or the legislation that segregated public schools in the South, Klopsch and Talmage had no comment.

During the summer of 1894, for example, *The Outlook*, a weekly magazine edited by Talmage's peer, the Reverend Lyman Abbott of the Plymouth Church in Brooklyn, published a scathing article condemning "the inhuman treatment colored people have received in this country solely on account of their race." In "Our Nation's Shame," Congregationalist minister Amory H. Bradford denounced lynching as "the culmination of a systematic plan for the social isolation of the colored race" in which all white Americans were implicated. In addition to criticizing white southern churches for refusing to associate with their black brothers and sisters in Christ, Bradford rebuked complacent northerners for "discriminations against colored men in almost all the trades." That American Christians consented to segregation and violence against African Americans was a scandal that exposed their hypocrisy in claiming to promote liberty and justice for all within and beyond the United States, Bradford charged. "For many years the American people have imagined that they were giving lessons to the world in what we may call the practice of humanity," he wrote. "Where there has been any glaring injustice in South Africa, in Russia, in Turkey, or elsewhere, our people have been quick to utter their protest."[65]

That so many American Christians were "willing to be quiet" about the "barbarities inflicted by lynch-law on the negroes" in their own nation, Bradford concluded, was "the saddest part of the whole matter." Was it too much to hope, he asked, "that . . . there may rise a feeling of remorse for past inaction, and that a sentiment may be created which will soon bring into our social, ecclesiastical, and political life something a little more like real Christian brotherhood?" If the *Christian Herald*'s continued silence about the ongoing and escalating violence against African Americans was any indication, the answer to Bradford's question was apparently yes: It was too ambitious to expect that American Christians would speak out about racial injustice in order to foster a truly righteous and virtuous society in which all of God's children would live together in fellowship and peace.[66]

If Bradford's plea for American Christians to repent of their complacency and begin to actively reform race relations went largely unheeded, he was probably not surprised. His article identified one of the central issues that prevented so many from publicly protesting the atrocious injustices perpetrated against African Americans: By demanding fair and equal treatment for blacks in church and society, Bradford suggested, whites often exacerbated the rift between North and South that had only recently begun to heal. As a case in point, Bradford asserted that "the chief objection to reunion between the Presbyterians of the North and South is the fact that the Southern Church will not recognize the negro as the Northern Church does." Similarly, when an Episcopal bishop treated "a colored minister like a man and a Christian," he was almost run out of state by his fellow church members.[67]

For evangelical leaders like Talmage, who had spent the decades since the Civil War striving to restore cordial relations across sectional lines, the possibility of imperiling progress toward national unity by decrying discrimination proved too great a risk. Ten years before assuming his position at the *Christian Herald*, Talmage had denounced northern journalists for their "outrageous misrepresentation" of race relations in the former Confederate states. "All this talk about the dragging of the rivers and the lakes of the South to haul ashore negroes murdered and flung in . . . is a falsehood," he declared. Such "slanders" only served to aggravate sectional acrimony rather than promoting cohesion among the United States.[68]

More than a decade later, Talmage was still calling on the North and South to bury old grudges and strive for solidarity in order to avoid "permanent compound fracture." Although by 1892 Talmage was no longer accusing northern correspondents of spreading lies about the lynching of African Americans, he never acknowledged the terrible truth of their reports in the pages of the *Christian Herald*. Not once in his years as editor in chief did Talmage even come close to confessing the nation's complicity in these crimes against what Bradford and others called "our common humanity."[69]

Instead, Talmage and Klopsch perpetuated the myth of American moral superiority. When activists like Bradford and Ida B. Wells-Barnett urged the United States to admit its failings and work to right the wrongs of injustice against its black citizens, these evangelicals continued to insist that "Christian America" was a harbinger of racial progress at home and humanitarian preeminence abroad. As the public outcry against lynching intensified after Wells's successful tour of Great Britain in the summer of 1894, the *Christian Herald*'s contributors refrained from commenting on the controversy. Instead, they chose to profile the charitable efforts of African American ministers such as the Reverend D. J. Jenkins, who had recently opened an orphanage and school for impoverished black children in Charleston, South Carolina, or the ongoing expansion of the industrial education movement through the work of black leaders like Professor J. J. Higgs, who founded a new institution in Waycross, Georgia.[70]

Then, in the spring of 1896, just as the Supreme Court was debating the merits of racial segregation in the *Plessy v. Ferguson* case, the *Christian Herald* invited its readers to participate in a crusade to eradicate slavery and racial oppression in Africa by supporting the work of the Philafrican Liberators' League (PLL). Founded by Héli Chatelain—a Swiss missionary who had worked with famous American Methodist bishop William Taylor in Angola—this organization proposed to establish a string of colonies along the west coast of Africa where emancipated and fugitive slaves could receive protection, education, and industrial training that would "transform them into hard-working, thrifty Christian farmers, mechanics and law-abiding citizens." Lending their support to the PLL gave Klopsch and Talmage a perfect opportunity to promote the effectiveness of evangelical charity in advancing racial justice on the global stage at a moment when similar efforts to foster African American uplift were under increasing attack within the United States.[71]

By sponsoring Chatelain's campaign, Klopsch and Talmage suggested, the *Christian Herald*'s subscribers would help restore faith in their nation's status as the world's leading advocate of liberty and equality for all humanity. Although "under the Treaty of Brussels the great powers decreed the abolition of African slavery," the editors declared, "the evil still exists with the knowledge and tacit permission of the English, French and Portuguese officials in Africa." Since European nations had failed to deliver on their promises to eliminate, or even to diminish, the slave trade, they implied, it was up to the United States to take charge in "one of the leading philanthropic and humanitarian movements of the present day."[72]

To accomplish this mission, they proposed that American evangelicals send funds to Klopsch, who had agreed to serve as treasurer for the PLL; even better, they could volunteer to serve alongside Chatelain as pioneer colonists. "In Darkest Africa," one PLL promoter declared, "countless acres of virgin, yet fertile soil await the arrival of the American farmer, who will transform that wilderness into fruitful fields. . . . Thousands of strong and untutored arms and hands await the American mechanic who will train them in the handicrafts of the more advanced civilization. Thousands of bright and eager, yet undeveloped, intellects await the American teacher who will lead them into the knowledge of the wonderful book-world, of God's great family of nations, of the rights and duties of Christian citizenship."[73]

The fact that many European settlers—such as the Dutch-speaking Boers of the Transvaal and Belgian officials who supervised King Leopold's commercial enterprises in the Congo Free State—were reportedly abusive toward native Africans helped publicists like Klopsch and Talmage make the case for American intervention in the region. "To remain indifferent to this great evil, and inactive in any responsible effort to secure its permanent removal," one of Chatelain's supporters contended, was unthinkable for any Christian nation. Through the colonizing efforts of the PLL, evangelicals could shore up confidence that the United States was best qualified to lead the world in advancing prosperity, industry, education, democracy, and Christianity among the world's most oppressed and benighted peoples.[74]

Despite all the fanfare surrounding Chatelain's new antislavery campaign, enthusiasm for the movement fizzled quickly. Only a handful of missionary-settlers departed for Africa in the summer of 1897. As the "pioneers" faced unexpected obstacles in establishing a colony and securing the freedom of slaves in the surrounding communities, Klopsch and Talmage quietly withdrew their sponsorship. The *Christian Herald* made no mention of the PLL after 1898, with the exception of reprinting one letter from Chatelain explaining that the recruits he had brought to Africa had abandoned him and that the American officers of the league had ceased to support the work.[75]

The dissolution of the PLL in 1901 coincided with rising uncertainty about racial progress and reconciliation among American evangelicals—both black and white. Although contributors to the *Christian Herald* continued to promote industrial education at Tuskegee, Mayesville, and similar institutions, some questioned whether integration was a realistic or desirable goal. Beginning in 1898, a succession of lynchings, starting with the murder in February of African American postmaster Frazier Baker and his two-year-old daughter in Lake City, South Carolina, provoked an outbreak of race hatred that swept across the country. Similar killings occurred in Georgia, Mississippi, Arkansas, and elsewhere. While incidents like these were nothing new, the headlines they garnered rekindled anxiety about rising lawlessness and brutality throughout the nation. Undaunted by outcries against the "disgrace to our civilization," a white mob massacred at least thirty African Americans in Wilmington, North Carolina, following local elections in November. Violence continued unabated throughout 1899. After the brutal torture and execution of Sam Hose near Atlanta, Georgia, in April, African American leaders organized a day of protest against the ongoing campaign to disenfranchise black voters, enforce segregation, and uphold white supremacy throughout the South.[76]

Although a number of white journalists and ministers expressed outrage about Hose's lynching and supported efforts to address racial injustice, many others—including Klopsch and Talmage—stayed silent. Despite direct appeals for reform and intervention, politicians at all levels of government declined to take action. Within this context, belief that the United States was destined to usher in God's millennial kingdom of racial harmony and peace among all peoples became increasingly difficult to sustain.[77]

Although Klopsch and Talmage were loath to admit their hopes for Christian America were faltering, indications that their optimism had begun to waver became apparent after the turn of the twentieth century. In February 1901—as Mark Twain stoked controversy over American missionary vindictiveness toward the Chinese in the wake of the Boxer Rebellion—the *Christian Herald* published an account praising the efforts of Henry McNeal Turner, a bishop in the African Methodist Episcopal Church, to promote large-scale emigration of American blacks to Africa, "the negroes own country." Just ten years after concluding that emigration would be disastrous for the American economy, Klopsch and Talmage now seemed willing to lend support to the back-to-Africa movement.[78]

Maintaining faith that the United States could overcome deepening racial divisions became even more challenging for the *Christian Herald*'s constituents after Talmage died in April 1902. Having come down with influenza over the winter, the usually robust minister took a trip to Mexico to recuperate but became critically ill. When he returned to Washington after six weeks away, he was suffering from "cerebral congestion" and soon slipped into an unconsciousness from which he did not recover. With his passing, American evangelicals lost one of the most enthusiastic and tenacious champions of their efforts to extend influence around the globe through Christian charity. While Klopsch and his associates at the *Christian Herald* remained committed to advancing this vision, they struggled to sustain the consistently sanguine tone that was Talmage's trademark—particularly in dealing with deteriorating race relations.[79]

As violence against African Americans continued unabated after Talmage's death, the editorial staff seemed more willing to consider the possibility that evangelical philanthropy might not offer a sufficient solution for "the colored problem." In December 1905, after more gruesome lynchings—including the burning of Will Cato and Paul Reed in Statesboro, Georgia—that "embarrassed the United States before the world," the *Christian Herald* published a statement from Bishop Turner advocating separation of the "white and colored races." "The so-called Negro problem keeps this nation in a whirlpool of discontent," Turner declared. Rather than wasting resources trying to allay racial hostilities or force integration, he suggested, the American people ought to devote themselves to the "noblest and most important work of . . . racial separation." If subscribers of the *Christian Herald* would provide "a line of steamers between this country and Africa . . . the negroes would leave by the millions," he promised. The result would "be a blessing to both races, and hence to the nation." Although Klopsch and his coworkers did not start a fund-raising campaign on behalf of Turner's emigration movement, their publication of his plea suggests they were finding it increasingly challenging to imagine a harmonious multiracial society in an era of rancorous discord.[80]

Rising doubts about the United States' ability to overcome racial antipathies and foster unity in the early twentieth century also affected evangelical perspectives on the incorporation of Native Americans into the broader political, economic, and cultural spheres. Within a few years of Talmage's passing, problems with the allotment system and the ongoing challenges of transforming Native cultures through educational institutions like the Carlisle School were becoming apparent to a broader public. In November 1904, *Christian Herald* correspondent Kate Upson Clark described recent protests over white settlement of Indian land under the Dawes and Curtis Acts. Despite the hope that this legislation would protect Native peoples from dishonest land brokers, many Indians had been sold plots that proved insufficient for sustainable agriculture and were struggling—failing—to survive. Men who could not make a living farming their land were forced to leave their families to find work on government projects. As a result, one observer complained, "little by little the homes are being deserted and the nomadic life is being resumed." In some parts of what had been "Indian territory," white settlers had diverted water sources away from Native communities, leaving the lands barren. Finally, Clark reported, there had been much debate about boarding schools established for the Indians. Although some philanthropists defended the good work of the institutions, others accused them of "snatching" young children from their parents at too young an age, comparing the process to the "'round up' of cattle on a great ranch." All of these developments indicated that the process of assimilating Native Americans was proving much more difficult on multiple fronts than Talmage and his colleagues had anticipated. While Klopsch and his coworkers at the *Christian Herald* did not give up hope, they did worry that attempts to "civilize the Indian" were exacerbating rather than allaying the "spirit . . . of separation and hostility to the rule of the white man" that they hoped evangelical charity would help overcome.[81]

If many Native and African Americans found the United States inhospitable in the early twentieth century, the immigrant communities Talmage had fervently welcomed also faced growing antagonism from white evangelicals. In August 1903, for example, the *Christian Herald* published an opinion piece warning that the nation's ability to assimilate newcomers was about to be put to a severe test. "So long as the immigrants came from Great Britain, Germany, and Scandinavia," the editors declared, "the task, though arduous, was not hopeless." Whereas these previous applicants for American citizenship had possessed a basic education and hailed from countries with a political and social structure similar to that of the United States, the majority of recent arrivals from southern and eastern Europe were "of a much lower intellectual caliber" and "unaccustomed to self-government." Rather than strengthening the American economy and national character, therefore, these newcomers threatened the country's prosperity and stability. "The time has come," Klopsch and his colleagues contended, for Congress to pass legislation refusing entry to immigrants "who, by racial instinct or by mental obstusements, or by illiteracy, increase the numbers of the dangerous classes."[82]

Gone was Talmage's confidence that commingling nationalities would produce a more robust American citizen who would absorb the best characteristics of all the world's diverse peoples—a new Adam who would make the United States the birthplace of God's millennial kingdom. "Thirty years ago, this nation was enriched by Anglo-Saxon corpuscles" injected "into the national blood and temperament," one *Christian Herald* contributor explained, but with the new immigration "there is a grave menace where formerly there was only great beauty." Now, the "racial *mélange*" was "diluting," rather than augmenting, "the national characteristics with so much devitalized blood"—passing on traits that would propagate a harmful social and moral influence and ultimately undermine the United States' destiny.[83]

Not all of the *Christian Herald*'s constituents were so negative about the prospects for integrating non–Anglo Saxon newcomers into American society. As calls for immigration restriction escalated in 1905, the newspaper published several articles by famous journalist, reformer, and philanthropist Jacob Riis advocating a continuation of more open policies. Sounding a lot like Talmage, Riis urged American evangelicals to remain confident that Christian charitable efforts could enable immigrants of all nations "to become more democratic." By instilling habits of industry, hygiene, patriotism, and brotherly love, he argued, evangelical

CHRISTIAN HERALD

COPYRIGHT 1903 BY LOUIS KLOPSCH

SUBSCRIPTION, $1.50 PER ANNUM
Published 52 Times a Year

NEW YORK, MAY 6, 1903

VOL. 26—NO. 18. PRICE 5 CENTS
Offices: Bible House, New York

PHOTOGRAPHED SPECIALLY FOR THE CHRISTIAN HERALD

The Tidal Wave of Immigration = Scenes at Ellis Island, New York Harbor

1. A crowd of newly-arrived immigrants buying tickets on the railroad floor.   2. At the Register's desk.   3. On the way to the Immigrant "Clearing-House."   4. Dinner-time—the women sit at table, the men pass in line.   5, 6, 7. Scandinavian types.   8. Detained immigrants, mostly Italians.   9. Excluded ones, to be returned.   SEE PAGE 387

"The Tidal Wave of Immigration." From the *Christian Herald,* May 6, 1903, cover.

Courtesy of the Christian Herald Association, New York.

benevolent institutions like Mont-Lawn—of which he was an avid supporter—could help "make a people fit for the great destiny which we must believe the Almighty has marked out for the great American republic." Rather than shutting the door against "the Jew, the Italian, the Bohemian, the Hungarian," Riis wrote, the United States ought to welcome "the races to which objection is made now-a-days as material for citizenship every bit as good as that which is to the manner born." All of these diverse groups, if brought together in brotherhood, he maintained, could "help build our common country and make it great.... Only so can the Kingdom come on earth."[84]

But there was one group Riis, despite his inclusive vision, could not imagine incorporating into the American nation. "I draw the line at the Asiatic," he declared. Riis insisted that his prejudice against Asians was not based on appearance but on intractable and insurmountable cultural incompatibilities. "The warp of his mind," he wrote, "is not mine. I do not understand him.... We don't mix, and mixing is essential if we are to make of our immigrant mortar to build a nation with that which will endure." Even the best efforts of evangelical philanthropists, Riis implied, could not overcome the barriers that kept these foreigners from becoming familiar to their American benefactors and trustworthy contributors to the national project.[85]

Questions about which groups of racial outsiders could help create a stronger, more durable "Christian America" continued to vex evangelicals in the early years of the twentieth century. With the loss of Talmage as a guiding light, many contributors to the *Christian Herald* struggled to see how charity could meld people of every clime, culture, and color into a unified community. Ongoing injustices against Native Americans, alongside intensifying anti-immigrant sentiment and recurrent race riots targeting African Americans and Asians, further clouded hopes of achieving harmony.

As evangelicals became increasingly divided about how to deal with these escalating difficulties, leaders like Klopsch—who had worked so hard to foster cohesiveness among this constituency—needed to devise new ways to keep the group from fracturing. Even as he and his colleagues continued to support benevolent enterprises for the uplift and integration of American Indians, blacks, and new immigrants into white

"Christian America," they also began to channel resources toward campaigns to secure the nation's evangelical identity against several other perceived threats to its integrity, such as the expanding "menace" of Mormonism and the rising influence of secularism in public schools, the political sphere, and even the field of philanthropy. By rallying the *Christian Herald*'s readers to crusade against these "grave dangers," Klopsch and his coworkers once again diverted attention from the seemingly insoluble dilemmas of racial discrimination and violence plaguing the United States. In order for evangelicals to maintain their position as arbiters of American culture, shapers of the nation's destiny, and premier providers of humanitarian aid at home and abroad, liberty and justice for all would have to wait.

6

TO SAFEGUARD CHRISTIAN AMERICA

The years following Talmage's death in April 1902 marked a period of transition for the *Christian Herald*. As Klopsch and his colleagues mourned the loss of their famous figurehead and charted a new course for the newspaper without Talmage at the helm, they found solace in the fact that their chief competitor among humanitarian organizations was also facing leadership challenges. Shortly after winning her long-fought battle for congressional recognition of the American Red Cross (ARC), Clara Barton came under intense scrutiny from critics who questioned her management and accounting practices. Along with the prestige the Charter of June 1900 conferred on the ARC as "the official voluntary relief organization of the United States" came greater congressional oversight. New annual reporting requirements quickly exposed

Barton's erratic record keeping and the precarious state of the ARC's finances. When a group of ARC board members pushed for more professionalism in the organization's policies, Barton chafed at the perceived attacks on her authority, further exacerbating the perception that she was temperamentally unqualified to lead an organization charged with representing the United States on the global stage.[1]

By January 1903, the dispute between Barton and her detractors had become public, with many of the nation's leading newspapers taking sides. Some defended Barton as a victim of unfair accusations from ungracious upstarts. Others supported her opponents, especially the outspoken former ARC Executive Committee member Mabel Boardman, who was leading the charge for organizational reform. Although Klopsch had raised many of the same complaints about Barton's inefficient, unsystematic, and authoritarian approach, he refrained from commenting on the Red Cross controversy in the *Christian Herald*. Perhaps he and his colleagues hoped the escalating turmoil within the ARC would result in the agency's demise or demotion, creating a renewed opportunity for the *Christian Herald* to assert preeminence as the nation's premier provider of charitable relief both at home and abroad.[2]

Maintaining the primacy of evangelical almsgiving, however, was becoming increasingly challenging given intensifying debate about the role religion should play in the nation's foreign policy, social reform efforts, political institutions, and public life. Within each of these arenas, Klopsch and his associates grappled with calls for a less sectarian, more scientific, increasingly professional approach to the challenges of modern society. As the United States sought to establish its influence as a global power, strengthen a growing economy without exacerbating the conflict between capital and labor, and integrate a diversifying population that continued to swell as a result of immigration, some critics argued that evangelical organizations like the *Christian Herald* were no longer equipped to serve as the nation's principal agents of humanitarian aid.

Drawing on more than a decade of experience in foreign disaster relief and domestic charity, Klopsch and his colleagues fought to remain at the forefront of these fields. By continuing to compete (and sometimes to cooperate) with the ARC, the *Christian Herald* sought to demonstrate that its volunteer, grassroots, explicitly spiritual methods of aiding distant sufferers remained compelling among a significant portion of the American population. When proponents of scientific philanthropy attacked the Bowery Mission's breadline as an outmoded and counterproductive means of addressing poverty, unemployment, and homelessness within the United States, Klopsch and his coworkers vigorously defended the ministry's "Christlike" effort. Meeting the immediate needs of those struggling to survive in an increasingly exploitative capitalist system, while striving to remedy the causes of such widespread privation, they argued, was a spiritual obligation and an essential step toward creating a more just, humane, and godly economic order in an era of inequality.

As they worked to counter the corrosive effects of greed and selfishness in American life through Christian benevolence and the pursuit of social reform, Klopsch and his associates became increasingly concerned about additional threats to America's religious integrity. To preserve the *Christian Herald*'s position within the spheres of domestic charity and international humanitarianism, the newspaper's editors concluded, they needed to fend off the immorality and irreligion invading the nation's political institutions and public culture. Through campaigns to combat the presence of Mormons in the federal government, to defend the celebration of Christmas in New York City's schools, and to reinstate the motto "In God We Trust" on U.S. currency, these evangelicals sought to safeguard "Christian America" from spiritual dissolution and rising secularism.

These forays into the domain of direct political action represented a departure for the *Christian Herald,* signaling a shift rooted in anxiety about the future of American evangelicalism in a diversifying society. As Klopsch and his constituents experienced some success with these initiatives, they redoubled their efforts to show that the *Christian Herald*'s relief campaigns and charitable ministries remained essential to the United States' humanitarian mission even—and perhaps especially—when the nation's international relations, economic structures, political culture, social ethics, and religious identity were rapidly changing.

"FIRST IN THE FIELD OF A GOOD WORK FOR HUMANITY"

In January 1903, as the debate between Clara Barton and Mabel Boardman over ARC leadership unfolded in the sensational press, Klopsch and his associates were publicizing the travails of "famine-swept Finland." By early February, they were reporting that suffering had spread to almost all the Scandinavian countries, intensifying the need for contributions to the *Christian Herald*'s Northland (Finnish) famine fund. Over the next few months, subscribers donated $132,681, most of which Klopsch forwarded to a committee made up primarily of Lutheran pastors. In March, he traveled with journalist Gilson Willets to inspect the distribution of aid.[3]

During the journey, Klopsch confirmed that relief agents in Helsingfors and Stockholm were working closely with local Christian communities to disburse supplies quickly and efficiently so that every dollar contributed went directly to the afflicted. He was also granted an audience with the king and queen of Sweden, who expressed their thanks to the people of America. On his way home, Klopsch spent time with King Christian of Denmark, Queen Alexandra of England, and King Christian's daughter, the Dowager Empress of Russia—all of whom praised the generosity of *Christian Herald* readers during this and earlier famines. Back in the United States, Klopsch was overwhelmed with gratitude from Scandinavian immigrants and from prominent government officials such as Cabinet Secretary George B. Cortelyou, Norwegian Minister Sigurd Ibsen, and American Ambassador to Sweden William W. Thomas. "When we reflect that these grand benefactions are not the gifts of millionaires but . . . all come from the little savings of the one million Americans who read the *Christian Herald* of New York," Thomas wrote, "it seems to me that these noble gifts constitute an act of Christian benevolence which both in kind and amount are perhaps without a parallel in history."[4]

Through this successful crusade, Klopsch concluded as he drew the campaign to a close, the *Christian Herald*'s evangelical almsgivers demonstrated their proficiency in fund-raising, commitment to responsible accounting and distribution methods, and unparalleled ability to augment the United States' reputation as the world's most compassionate and generous Christian nation. Meanwhile, the ARC was increasingly mired in scandal. As Klopsch turned his attention to alleviating suffering in the flood-stricken states of Kansas and Missouri during the summer of 1903 and then to war-torn Macedonia in the fall, Barton and Boardman were still engaged in a bitter battle for control of the ARC, which had done little over the past few years to relieve hardship at home or abroad. In the spring of 1904, at Boardman's urging, Congress opened an investigation into the ARC's internal affairs. The ensuing inquiry, which confirmed complaints about financial irregularities, embarrassed the organization and led ultimately to Barton's resignation on May 14. With the *Christian Herald*'s primary rival facing public disgrace, the future of evangelical humanitarianism looked bright.[5]

Whatever satisfaction Klopsch may have derived from the downfall of his longtime nemesis proved short-lived, however. For if Barton had been a formidable adversary bent on securing supremacy for the ARC over all other organizations, her successor was equally intent on dominating the fields of foreign and domestic aid. After successfully deposing Barton, Boardman moved quickly to solidify the ARC's relationship with the federal government. In December 1904, she submitted a new charter for the ARC that placed the agency under the direct supervision of the War Department and gave the president of the United States power to appoint six out of eighteen members of the organization's central committee. Over the course of 1905, Boardman cultivated support for the reorganized ARC among a host of federal officials, including War Secretary William Howard Taft, who agreed to serve as president. Although Taft's position was largely honorary, he embraced the role with enthusiasm, using his influence to increase the ARC's stature among fellow government agents and the broader public.[6]

The implications of the ARC's closer connections with the federal government became clear to Klopsch and his coworkers early in 1906 as the *Christian Herald* commenced a campaign to assist famine sufferers in Japan. For the past several weeks, the editors wrote in mid-January, missionaries and other observers had been sending letters describing the devastation in northern Japan, where almost a million people were facing starvation. In response to urgent requests, Klopsch agreed to open a relief fund, sent a missionary representative to investigate conditions in the field, inquired about the possibility of sending a food-laden steamer, and organized local committees in Tokyo to oversee the distribution of aid. Several weeks into the *Christian Herald*'s fund-raising operation, however, President Theodore Roosevelt issued an appeal asking the American people to send donations for Japan's starving people through either their local ARC chapter or the organization's treasurer in Washington, DC. All monies received, the president explained, would be forwarded to the Japanese Red Cross (JRC), which would allocate aid under the direction of the Japanese government.[7]

Roosevelt's appeal struck a blow to Klopsch's ongoing efforts to position the *Christian Herald* as the nation's foremost humanitarian aid organization. For the first time, the president of the United States had designated the ARC as the government's preferred agency for both the collection and delivery of relief funds. Not one to back down easily, Klopsch came up with a strategy he hoped would enable the *Christian Herald* to continue playing a prominent role in international almsgiving. He began by urging subscribers to keep sending gifts for Japan to the *Christian Herald*. At the same time, he agreed to forward the bulk of the contributions to the JRC for distribution after having obtained guarantees from the organization that donations from the *Christian Herald* would be used "immediately and exclusively in supplying food to the neediest in those districts where the suffering is the keenest" and "not one *sen* of this money will be spent in administration." Klopsch also insisted that missionaries be allowed to cooperate in the work wherever possible, and he continued to send funds to missionaries stationed beyond the JRC's reach.[8]

This approach allowed Klopsch to claim that the *Christian Herald* was complying with Roosevelt's appeal for aid while seeming to bypass the ARC. In reality, the funds Klopsch forwarded to the JRC did pass through the ARC treasurer's office by way of the State Department, but the *Christian Herald*'s editors obscured that detail in their coverage of the relief effort. Instead, they emphasized the disproportionate success of the *Christian Herald*'s fund-raising campaign: by the end of March, the ARC had collected approximately $20,000 for the Japanese sufferers, whereas their own subscribers had donated $85,500. This disparity, Klopsch and his associates suggested, demonstrated that the American people preferred to send relief through an explicitly Christian humanitarian organization with a proven track record of financial transparency, integrity, and effectiveness.[9]

As collections poured in, even President Roosevelt acknowledged the *Christian Herald*'s "very real service to humanity and to the cause of international good will" in a telegram thanking Klopsch for his work on behalf of Japan's starving people. With this commendation, Klopsch contended, Roosevelt recognized that thousands of American citizens from across the nation had responded to his appeal by selecting the *Christian Herald*, rather than the ARC, as their "chosen channel of benevolence." The president's encouraging message, Klopsch claimed, proved that Roosevelt appreciated the real motive underlying the newspaper's relief work: to provide the world with evidence that "Christianity is a living, vital, helpful religion which inspires its followers with a love for their fellow-men." The purpose of humanitarianism, from this perspective, was not only to alleviate suffering and promote international harmony, but to spread the gospel around the globe. Only an evangelical relief agency could accomplish these interrelated tasks, Klopsch argued.[10]

By the time the *Christian Herald* closed its Japan famine fund, the newspaper had raised $241,882. Of this amount, Klopsch forwarded $200,000 to the JRC and sent the remainder to American missionaries stationed in the northern provinces. By comparison, the ARC had collected a total of $65,866. These tallies confirmed that the *Christian Herald* remained "first in the field of foreign relief," Klopsch declared. Over the next year, he received several accolades from Japanese officials extolling him for the service he and his constituents had extended to the starving sufferers. The most prestigious award was the Order of the Rising Sun, conferred in the name of the emperor of Japan. With these honors from high-ranking government agents, Klopsch emerged triumphant in his struggle to prove that the *Christian Herald* was vastly more popular than the ARC and far better equipped to serve as the nation's primary instrument for the collection and delivery of international aid.[11]

But even as Klopsch and his colleagues were celebrating victory in the first battle with the reorganized ARC, Boardman and her staff were readying themselves for another fight. The next showdown between the two relief agencies began just as the *Christian Herald* was drawing its Japan campaign to a close. Early in the morning of Wednesday, April 18, 1906, a massive earthquake struck San Francisco. Within moments, hundreds of buildings collapsed and much of the downtown lay in ruins. Victims were buried in rubble or trapped by fires that spread across the city, consuming entire blocks and forcing thousands to flee.[12]

When news of the disaster reached the East Coast on Wednesday afternoon, both Klopsch and Boardman sprang into action. Klopsch immediately telegraphed an offer of help to San Francisco's mayor Eugene

Schmitz, but by the time he sent the message, all the wires were down and communication with the city was completely cut off. After receiving no response from Schmitz, Klopsch reached out to the Reverend Frank De Witt Talmage—son of the *Christian Herald*'s late editor—who was pastoring a church in Los Angeles. Talmage agreed to travel to San Francisco on Klopsch's behalf. When he arrived several days later, however, he found that the relief work was already in the hands of the ARC.[13]

Because of the ARC's official connections with the federal government, Boardman had been able to secure a meeting with President Roosevelt the day after the earthquake to discuss how the agency ought to respond to the disaster. Roosevelt gave Boardman and her staff his full support and on Thursday, April 20, issued a proclamation announcing that a specially appointed Red Cross agent would be taking charge of the San Francisco relief effort. "In order that this work be well-systematized, and in order that the contributions . . . may be wisely administered," Roosevelt wrote, "I appeal to the people of the United States . . . to express their sympathy and render their aid by contributions to the American Red Cross treasurer." Just as he had several months earlier, the president once again publicly endorsed the ARC as the national organization best equipped to undertake relief work.[14]

This time, Boardman was determined to capitalize on her organization's favored status. When the ARC's special agent, Dr. Edward Devine, arrived in San Francisco, he moved speedily to establish relations with city officials, local businessmen, and U.S. military officers who had been working to help survivors and bring order to chaos. With the support of these groups, the ARC assumed control of relief depots throughout the city where food, clothing, and other supplies were distributed. Once these measures were in place, there was little room for other agencies to step in to assist victims—a fact Frank Talmage reported to Klopsch after surveying the situation. That Congress had voted to appropriate $1 million in aid also made additional fund-raising redundant, especially since the American public seemed to be complying with Roosevelt's request that contributions be sent to the ARC.[15]

Realizing that he and the *Christian Herald* had been effectively shut out of the relief effort, Klopsch conceded defeat. In early May, he forwarded $5,000 to the secretary of the ARC, along with a letter commending the organization for "promptly seizing the opportunity presented by this appalling calamity." The agency's success in San Francisco, he wrote, "renders any other organized charitable effort in the same field wholly unnecessary." A week after sending the missive, Klopsch explained to readers why the *Christian Herald* would not be opening a campaign to collect donations for disaster relief. "The quick action of the national government and the organization of efficient local committees made separate action on the part of this paper unnecessary, and, in consequence, it has joined forces with those already at work," he wrote. In practice, the purported partnership between the *Christian Herald* and the ARC proved weak and short-lived. Although Klopsch pledged to pass along any contributions received to the ARC, he did not report forwarding any monies after the initial $5,000 remittance to the rival organization. Nor did he and his editorial staff grant much subsequent coverage to the San Francisco calamity once it became clear the *Christian Herald* would not play a significant part in raising funds or distributing aid for the stricken city.[16]

The ARC's apparent success in San Francisco boosted confidence in the organization among government leaders. Despite some legitimate complaints about red tape that delayed disbursement of supplies and privileged some groups over others, the ARC mostly garnered praise from local officials and national media outlets for its relief and fund-raising efforts. With receipts topping $3 million and a new staff of professional aid workers with extensive backgrounds in charity administration, the agency seemed to have established itself as a clear leader in the field of humanitarian assistance. When reports reached the United States of a severe famine threatening over fifteen million people in China's central provinces in November 1906, therefore, it made sense for the president to charge the ARC with responsibility for responding to the emergency. On December 23, Roosevelt published a proclamation calling on American citizens to send contributions to the ARC, which would oversee the purchase of appropriate food supplies and work with the U.S. government to transport them by steamer to Shanghai.[17]

Much to Roosevelt's dismay, however, the response to his appeal was less robust than expected. Although the ARC did ship three hundred tons of donated flour to U.S. Consul-General James Rodgers in mid-January 1907, Rodgers made clear that what the Chinese famine relief committees working in Shanghai and Zhenjiang really needed was money. As of February 1, Rodgers reported, the ARC had forwarded only $15,000; of that amount, fully two-thirds had been furnished by the *Christian Herald*. Immediately upon receiving word of Roosevelt's plea for China, Klopsch had cabled $5,000 to the State Department. By assuring that this donation was the first contribution received from any source, Klopsch could boast that "our readers have once more the unique distinction of being first in the field of a good work for humanity." After hearing from Rodgers and other missionary correspondents that suffering in China was becoming more severe while cash resources remained scarce, Klopsch relayed a second $5,000 on January 28.[18]

When it became apparent the ARC simply could not match the fundraising capabilities of the *Christian Herald*, Roosevelt reached out to Klopsch for help. In early February, Secretary of State Elihu Root wrote to Klopsch expressing support for the *Christian Herald*'s relief efforts on behalf of the president. The envelope contained two checks for $100 each, one from Root and the other from Roosevelt himself. Klopsch was ecstatic. Up to this point, he and his associates had refrained from launching a full-fledged campaign on behalf of China's famine sufferers; now that the *Christian Herald* had the stamp of approval from the nation's foremost government officials, the call to service was clear. "The *Christian Herald* has once more been chosen as the channel of America's benevolence," he rejoiced. "The President and Secretary of State have officially approved the popular choice." Therefore, "we invite every reader . . . to unite with us in this Christlike work of rescue, and to send in a mite to help save China. The fund is now open."[19]

Over the next several weeks, Klopsch and his colleagues pulled out all the stops to show that the *Christian Herald* and its evangelical almoners were worthy of the president's approval. In response to Root's letter, Klopsch cabled an additional $25,000 to the State Department—clearly outshining the ARC, which had yet to forward any cash beyond its initial $5,000. He also promised to send even greater contributions over the next several months until May, when the harvests were expected to improve the situation in China. In exchange for this offering, Klopsch asked for assurances that all monies donated through the *Christian Herald* would be distributed by missionaries in the famine area, even if the funds first passed through the ARC or the relief committees in Shanghai and Zhenjiang.

Given the *Christian Herald*'s long-standing connections with evangelical workers throughout China, this approach offered the editors greater control over the disbursement of supplies than the ARC had achieved working with U.S. Consul Rodgers, who had limited time and far less experience in humanitarian aid delivery than American missionaries in the field.[20]

In addition to guaranteeing that money forwarded through the *Christian Herald* would place food directly into the hands of starving Chinese families rather than being wasted on administrative expenses, employing missionaries as distribution agents enabled Klopsch and his coworkers to stress the spiritual dimensions of the humanitarian crusade. "Let every gift be sent with a prayer," the editors urged. "Let it have a higher object than the fighting back of famine; let it be a gift consecrated to the advancement of Christ's kingdom in that heathen land, where we, as almoners for Jesus' sake, may give to these suffering people an object lesson of practical Christian helpfulness." In this aid campaign, as in previous efforts, Klopsch confirmed, the idea of spreading the gospel and furthering the reign of Christ across the globe through the practice of international charity resonated with his evangelical subscribers.[21]

Contributions for China's famine victims came flowing in as soon as Klopsch announced the relief fund was open. As gifts swelled the *Christian Herald*'s coffers, Klopsch proposed to supplement the large outlays of cash he was forwarding to the missionaries—over $100,000 by mid-March—with a cargo of grain that could help sustain the sufferers until the next harvest. Now that the newspaper had raised so much money, he reasoned, sending a steamer full of food made more sense. On March 20, Klopsch received a telegram from the State Department indicating that the government had agreed to provide an army vessel to transport five thousand tons of supplies to China. Over the next several weeks, the *Christian Herald* amassed so much flour that the government had to charter a second ship to accommodate all the donations. Together, the *Buford* and the *Logan* carried over $150,000 worth of foodstuffs—more than sixteen times the amount of grain the ARC had sent to Shanghai several months before.[22]

Before the *Buford* sailed out of San Francisco Harbor on April 30, a large crowd assembled to bid farewell and Godspeed to the famine ship. That so many supporters turned out for the send-off showed "the strong hold this great international charity has obtained upon the hearts and sympathies of the public," the *Christian Herald* reported. Attendees included prominent officials such as the Honorable James Gillett, governor of California; important civic leaders like Benjamin Wheeler, president of the University of California; ministers from a wide range of denominations; and the regimental band of the U.S. Army's 22nd Infantry Division.[23]

The Reverend Frank Talmage, who presided over the government-sanctioned worship service, praised the relief effort as a mission of mercy that was not only saving thousands of lives but bolstering American influence in maintaining world peace. Talmage also lauded Klopsch's leadership in this and other humanitarian campaigns, calling him one of the nation's "most potent . . . men driving us ahead in solving the problems of international difficulties." In his remarks, Governor Gillett declared that the *Buford*'s cargo offered "evidence . . . of the fact that we belong to a Christian land" called to expand into "every market of the world" not only through trade but through charity. Popular journals covering the event affirmed this interpretation of the *Buford*'s mission, applauding the *Christian Herald*'s China famine campaign as a "union of effective missionary work, relief, and international amity" and dubbing Klopsch "the King of Emergency Benevolences." Always one to revel in accolades, Klopsch accepted these tributes on behalf of the many subscribers who sent donations. He stressed, once more, the "seal of official approval" conferred by the secretary of state, secretary of war, and president of the United States on the "humanitarian work of the readers of this journal . . . as an enterprise which merits the cordial support of the American people."[24]

Klopsch's public magnanimity, however, masked a private frustration that the *Christian Herald* was still sharing responsibility for the relief effort with the ARC. As the *Buford* was preparing to sail, Klopsch wrote to Charles Hurd, a field agent of the New York State Red Cross Branch, complaining that the ARC had not given the *Christian Herald* the credit it deserved and taking issue with the ARC's failure to emphasize the evangelical motivations of the humanitarian mission. Hurd passed along Klopsch's grievances to Boardman. Within several days, the disgruntled publicist received a letter from war secretary and ARC president William Taft expressing "the thanks and deep appreciation of the Society for . . .

the great sum raised by the *Christian Herald,* and the bountiful cargo of the 'Buford' provided by it" (which Klopsch promptly reprinted in the newspaper). The ARC also granted Klopsch greater recognition in its next few bulletins for his role in procuring monetary and food donations, praising "the remarkable work" of the *Christian Herald* and the munificence of its readers for sending a total of $400,000 to save Chinese famine sufferers. Then in July, Boardman offered an olive branch by contributing an article to the *Christian Herald* in which she told of having acknowledged the great generosity of the newspaper's readers at the recent International Red Cross Conference in London.[25]

These conciliatory gestures mollified Klopsch enough for him to consider pursuing a more productive partnership with Boardman and the ARC. In the spring of 1908, he even agreed to help the ARC with marketing for its membership drive. Later that year, at the ARC's annual meeting, Klopsch was recognized alongside philanthropist Olivia Sage as an honorary member of the agency. In 1909, the ARC and the *Christian Herald* would find ways to work together in collecting and distributing relief for earthquake victims in Italy. Despite developing more cordial relations, however, Klopsch and Boardman continued to promote very different practices and philosophies of humanitarian aid through their respective organizations.[26]

Relying on proven tactics for stirring up sympathy among the *Christian Herald's* subscribers, for example, Klopsch used sentimental narratives and heartrending images to solicit gifts. He boasted that most contributions to the newspaper's relief campaigns came from individuals who scrimped and saved to send their mites to suffering strangers. Until the San Francisco earthquake, mass fund-raising had never been a strength of the ARC, and the agency continued to struggle to build a grassroots constituency in subsequent years. To compensate, Boardman cultivated relationships with wealthy donors and organizations such as the newly established Russell Sage Foundation, aligning the ARC with the priorities, demands, and ambitions of an emerging class of elite, influential philanthropists intent on making humanitarian relief more scientific and professional.[27]

The support of affluent patrons and charitable foundations was necessary in part to finance the ARC's expanding staff of salaried aid workers. Unlike Klopsch, who preferred to partner with missionaries, pastors, and local relief groups to ensure efficiency and cost-effectiveness, Boardman invested in developing a sizable infrastructure for administering disaster assistance on a large scale both at home and abroad. Among her earliest recruits were Edward T. Devine and Ernest Bicknell, both leading lights of the organized charity movement. Effective relief operations, these men argued, could not be carried out by ad hoc volunteer committees, but instead required the expertise of trained social-science professionals. Under their leadership, the ARC would hire personnel to research best practices in philanthropy, plan ahead for emergency preparedness, develop more sophisticated financial accounting systems, and implement all these techniques when disaster struck.[28]

The ARC's associations with prominent donors, its embrace of professionalized philanthropy, and its formal relationship with the federal government helped the organization gain recognition and prestige during the first decade of the twentieth century. Its nonsectarian outlook also appealed to some citizens and policymakers who questioned the wisdom of entrusting the nation's humanitarian relief efforts to explicitly evangelical agencies. Internationally, missionaries were coming under fire for meddling in foreign affairs to the detriment of the United States' reputation and diplomatic goals. Rather than helping promote friendly relations with non-Christian nations, some detractors charged, American missionaries often exacerbated tensions with host governments, making it more difficult to conduct trade and negotiations or even—in cases like the Boxer Rebellion—provoking a crisis that required military intervention. For critics, the possibility of channeling American aid through the ARC—a secular agency already part of a successful international Red Cross movement—proved appealing.[29]

Klopsch and his colleagues fought back against suggestions that missionary almsgivers were to blame for any "international complications." Over the next few years, however, as the United States became more religiously heterogeneous through ongoing immigration, proponents of nonsectarian aid that was offered "in the name of humanity" rather than on behalf of "Christian America" gained more ground. Although the majority of the Americans remained dedicated to the ideal of a Protestant nation, a growing number began to view an ostensibly neutral organization like the ARC as a better conduit for collecting contributions and distributing disaster assistance in the service of an increasingly diverse United States.[30]

By strengthening official ties with the government, securing financial backing from wealthy benefactors and philanthropic trusts, hiring professionals committed to scientific charity, and emphasizing the benefits of a nonsectarian model of humanitarian assistance, Boardman successfully positioned the ARC as the agency best equipped to carry out U.S. relief efforts at home and abroad. Although Klopsch kept the *Christian Herald* at the forefront of many humanitarian campaigns by working alongside the ARC, his commitment to a grassroots, volunteer, and unapologetically evangelical approach to foreign aid ultimately diminished his organization's stature. As federalization, the creation of large philanthropic foundations, the professionalization of social work, and the secularization of charity continued to transform global humanitarian relief, these increasingly influential developments also put pressure on the *Christian Herald*'s efforts to alleviate affliction at the local level. During this period of intensifying change, even the "signature charities" so central to the *Christian Herald*'s long-term mission came under increasing scrutiny.

POVERTY AND CHARITY IN THE EARLY
TWENTIETH CENTURY

As the flour-laden *Buford* steamed toward famine-stricken China in May 1907, Klopsch and his New York colleagues were about to be confronted with a humanitarian crisis much closer to home. Over the past several months, the stock market had been sliding precipitously amid rumors that President Roosevelt was planning legislation to regulate abuses in the railroad industry. As a result, industrial production slowed, fueling rising unemployment. At the same time, increasingly tight lending practices pushed interest rates higher—making it more difficult for manufacturers and ordinary laborers to access much-needed credit. By summer's end, stock prices had declined almost 25 percent since the beginning of the year. The ongoing volatility in both the economy and the financial sector contributed to a run on banks in October, sending several major brokerage firms and trust companies into bankruptcy.

Although intervention from financier J. P. Morgan, working together with fellow bankers and federal officials, helped quell the immediate crisis, the Panic of 1907 devastated many of the nation's workers. The *Christian Herald* reported in early January 1908 that in New York City alone, 160,000 men were seeking employment—most of them skilled laborers. With so many wage earners out of work, many more—"probably not short of half a million mouths"—were suffering from hunger and perhaps even starvation. "Society is thus face to face with the problem of poverty in acute form," the editors wrote. The desire of most of the unemployed to work made the situation all the more shameful—especially when some among the wealthy classes continued their conspicuous consumption without any concern for the destitute on their doorsteps.[31]

Klopsch and his associates urged American evangelicals to respond to the crisis in several ways. "Christ intended us to work toward this object of bringing the kingdom of God to the earth, this kingdom of love and brotherhood," they declared. That so little progress had been made toward this goal was a "disgrace to a civilized community" and a signal that the church must advocate with renewed urgency for more just and equitable social conditions. In addition to striving for longer-term reforms to remedy growing economic disparities, rampant unemployment, and rising poverty, Klopsch implored readers to support charitable organizations like the *Christian Herald*'s own Bowery Mission, which was striving to meet the immediate needs of those affected by the recent downturn. "In view of the severe winter and the widespread suffering," he wrote in early February, the *Christian Herald* had opened a temporary "Night Refuge . . . to afford shelter to homeless and destitute men and boys until the hardest part of the winter is past." In addition, the Bowery Mission had doubled the capacity of its breadline so that it was now feeding 2,000 unemployed workers a day. Even with this expansion, the *New York Times* reported several weeks later, the supply of rolls and coffee at the Bowery Mission was exhausted before all those waiting outside could be fed, and scores went away hungry.[32]

As the Bowery Mission and similar institutions struggled to meet the needs of growing crowds seeking relief from biting hunger and bitter cold, they suddenly found their efforts under attack from critics who blamed them for offering free food to the down-and-out in the first place. Led by Edward T. Devine, the general secretary of the New York Charity

Bowery Mission breadline, January 1908. Courtesy of the Library of Congress.

Organization Society (COS) who had supervised the ARC's relief operations following the San Francisco earthquake, the detractors charged that breadlines and similar almsgiving perpetuated poverty by assisting "the criminal, the vicious, and the unemployable classes" who sought to avoid honest work. In a scathing article published in the March 7 issue of *Charities and the Commons,* Devine called breadlines a "shocking disgrace" that attracted "tramps, panhandlers, and vagrants" to the city, where they knew they could receive daily sustenance. All these "disorderly persons," Devine wrote, had been offered help from the COS, which would supply not only meals and lodging but transportation home, "woodyard work, or whatever other relief, on a full knowledge of the facts, was found to be appropriate." Unwilling to subject themselves to inquiries by COS's investigators, he complained, these "thieves, pickpockets . . . loafers, runaway boys," and "dissolute drunkards" remained content to "live from the proceeds of mendicancy" provided through the Bowery Mission and similar institutions.[33]

Rather than allowing this cycle of delinquency to persist, Devine argued, those concerned about the poor ought to discontinue "indiscriminate doles" and instead advocate for "better police methods, the establishment of a state farm and industrial colony, with voluntary and compulsory departments, and the prompt and adequate relief of *genuine* distress by competent and experienced experts." The editors of the *New York Times* agreed, reporting that Devine was "wholly right" in his assessment of the breadline as "a hopeless and much worse than useless example of an anachronistic charity" that catered mostly to "plain bums." The "indiscriminate methods" employed at the Bowery Mission, they wrote in another article, represented an archaic practice that ought to be abandoned in favor of the modern, scientific, systematic approaches Devine and his professional colleagues promoted.[34]

Although Devine's condemnation echoed long-standing criticisms of indiscriminate almsgiving, his complaints about the breadline were heightened by anxiety over escalating unemployment, poverty, and income inequality. By the first decade of the twentieth century, the enormity of the nation's intensifying economic challenges convinced many observers that comprehensive strategies for solving these problems were essential to U.S. political stability and financial prosperity. As an influential spokesperson for the superiority of scientific philanthropy who had played a prominent role in systematizing the ARC's processes, Devine made a persuasive case in favor of permanently closing charitable agencies that aided and abetted undeserving paupers.[35]

From their first forays into poor relief in the early 1890s, Klopsch and his associates had contended with concern about their methods for relieving suffering among the hungry and homeless of New York City. Although they agreed that systematic investigation could improve efficiency in many aid operations, they also insisted that some situations called for a more direct approach. Forcing aid applicants to submit to investigation during an acute crisis, they contended, would cause delays in the delivery of sorely needed services, thereby exacerbating, rather than alleviating, affliction.[36]

Over the years, Klopsch and his colleagues continued to distinguish disasters that demanded a rapid response from relief campaigns they could conduct with greater deliberation. When critics complained about the breadline's indiscriminate charity during the winter of 1908,

Klopsch and his Bowery Mission coworkers insisted that the present circumstances—rampant unemployment, unrelentingly cold weather, and severe and widespread hunger—were "anomalous" and warranted a generous outpouring of sympathy without worrying about whether the thousands of men who waited hours for a cup of coffee and morsel of bread were really "worthy" of receiving this modest "midnight meal."[37]

Most of the unfortunate souls, Klopsch argued, were not the "petty criminals, worthless vagabonds, loafers, tramps, and 'unemployables'" observers such as Devine made them out to be. "It would be hard to find anything farther from the actual fact," he complained in an editorial published several weeks after Devine's essay appeared. Soon after expanding the breadline's capacity, Klopsch reported, the Bowery Mission's superintendent had polled the nearly 1,600 men standing in the queue one night. He found that seventy-seven were too old or sick to work, and twenty-five admitted to having no occupation. The rest—more than 94 percent—were formerly employed in a variety of trades and professions that had been hard hit by the depression.[38]

Rather than demonizing these sufferers or refusing to feed them, Klopsch explained, the Bowery Mission sought to fulfill their urgent need for sustenance and shelter while helping them secure paid work through the organization's Free Labor Bureau, an agency founded three years earlier during a similar economic recession. During the most recent crisis, the bureau had registered at least two thousand job seekers and succeeded in matching 760 of these "earnest, sober, and reliable men" with reputable employers by early spring. The promising results showed that the Bowery Mission's "simple, elementary way of relieving hunger" could lead to more permanent and productive change.[39]

Having worked closely with New York's destitute since assuming charge of the Bowery Mission thirteen years earlier, Klopsch rejected the claim that "what has been crudely termed 'indiscriminate charity'" caused or perpetuated poverty. "What 'pauperizes the people' is not the helping hand they occasionally get at a pinch from their sympathetic brothers and sisters," he fumed, "but low sweatshop wages, exorbitant rents, high prices for food caused by cornering the necessities of life, labor strikes, panics, wholesale enforced idleness, privation and sickness. For how much or how little of this the poor themselves are responsible any fair-minded person can judge." Rather than blaming the needy for their penury or condemning Christian charities for striving to relieve suffering in a straightforward—rather than scientific—fashion, Klopsch argued, "professional philanthropists" like Devine ought to recognize that the "real root of the problem" of ongoing poverty lay in structural inequalities that plagued American society. Although he agreed with Devine that the COS proposal for founding labor colonies might offer some relief for the working poor, Klopsch contended that such measures "would hardly affect general conditions." Only a full-scale reform of the nation's unjust economic system could ultimately eliminate poverty.[40]

To accomplish this transformation, Klopsch and his associates called on Christians of all denominations to apply "the teachings of Jesus to the commercial and mercantile life of the world." By advocating for more equitable labor laws, fair housing policies, and an expansion of public works projects that could reduce unemployment, American evangelicals could help create a more just society based on "the principle of universal brotherhood" laid down by Christ. For several years, the *Christian Herald* had encouraged readers to embrace the program of "Christian Socialism" put forward by the Reverend Charles Sheldon. Although Talmage and Klopsch had disagreed with Sheldon's critique of American imperialism, the famous author of *In His Steps* remained a regular contributor to the *Christian Herald* during the early twentieth century. From November 1904 through March 1905, the newspaper published Sheldon's *The Heart of the World,* a serial novel about a minister who strove to reconcile rifts between union workers and local factory owners by advocating for "a new and different order of social life" based on "the teaching of the Golden Rule and the Sermon on the Mount."[41]

Aware that many of his contemporaries conflated socialism with anarchy and communism, Sheldon sought to defend Christian Socialism as a clear expression of economic theories plainly stated in the Bible. Properly understood, he contended, scripture supported a social revolution that would substitute cooperation for competition in commercial enterprises; institute "common ownership of . . . common needs" such as transportation facilities, heating and electric utilities, water and food sources, and health care while allowing for "private ownership of articles of consumption"; and introduce a more equitable distribution of wealth. All of these changes reflected "the logic of Christian teaching as applied to the commerce of men" and therefore ought to be espoused by all those who desired to see the kingdom of God in everyday life. What set Christian Socialism apart from other economic or labor reform movements, Sheldon asserted, was the religious foundation on which "true progress towards an ideal social condition" depended. "Making laws or trying to establish legislative rules to govern society, will not, in itself be enough to bring about an ideal social order among men," he maintained. Revolutionary transformation required "the essential factor of love," which could break down hatred of one class for another, root out racial prejudice, and replace selfish greed with generosity toward the poor and oppressed.[42]

Sheldon's expansive vision for remaking society according to biblical principles inspired many American evangelicals to participate in campaigns to ameliorate the structural conditions that perpetuated poverty and exploitation. Sheldon himself was especially supportive of the temperance movement and actively promoted the work of leaders like Frances Willard of the Woman's Christian Temperance Union (WCTU), who also publicly endorsed Christian Socialism. Klopsch and his associates agreed that "the liquor business" was a major cause of human greed, misery, crime, and poverty and commended efforts to reduce the problem.[43]

The *Christian Herald* also actively crusaded to expose "the evil child-labor system." Beginning in the summer of 1902, the newspaper investigated "the enslavement and debasement" of children in the mines of Pennsylvania, the mills of New Jersey, and the factories of New York. The outrage this series of articles evoked, the editors claimed, led to widespread demand for remedial legislation and eventually to the passage of new child labor laws in New York State in October 1903. The following year, the *Christian Herald* castigated officials for failing to enforce these regulations. The paper called on its readers to remain vigilant in their efforts to eradicate the sin of child slavery, which was spreading from the sweatshops of Massachusetts to the manufacturing states of the South.[44]

Klopsch and his staff writers continued to call attention to the "national evil of child labor" over the next several years. By January 1906, the editors were petitioning Congress to enact federal legislation to stop the continuing "massacre of the innocents," having concluded that leaving this matter to the states had produced only sporadic reform. When the Judiciary Committee of the House of Representatives determined that

THE CHRISTIAN HERALD

AN ILLUSTRATED FAMILY MAGAZINE

MOTHER AND CHILDREN IN A CANNING FACTORY   THREE LITTLE CHILD SLAVES   LIKE GANGS OF TINY SLAVES, THEY STAND AND WORK

THE LITTLE SLAVES OF TOIL

A MOVEMENT TO COUNTERACT THE EVILS OF CHILD LABOR IN NEW YORK

MANY thousands of New York children of tender years are engaged illegally in various forms of labor at the present time. They are robbed of their childhood, stunted in growth, deprived of educational opportunities and ruined in health and, too often, in morals also.

The New York Child Labor Committee, represented by Mr. Mornay Williams, Dr. Ernest J. Lederle and Mr. Robert Hunter, had a hearing before the Governor-elect, for the purpose of protesting against the re-appointment of the present Labor Commissioner, on the ground that his inefficiency was such as almost to render useless the present laws for the protection of children. They presented photographs of children five, six and seven years of age working in the factories of the State. The chairman of the delegation said that there were hundreds of children under the legal age working in all portions of the State, and the Bureau of Labor was making very little effort to enforce the law. In 1902, children were found employed in violation of the law in 2,607 factories, but only five firms employing these children illegally were prosecuted.

A special inquiry was made by the Child-Labor Committee into conditions prevailing in one of the important industries up-State. In one factory a child of four years was found at work; in another, a child of five; in another, one of six, who worked until nine in the evening. In one factory alone, the man in charge of the shed estimated the children under fourteen to number three hundred—all working in violation of law. In the busy season they worked until two and three o'clock in the morning. The Chairman of the Committee said he and his associates were surprised to find these evils in New York State, and it had begun to believe that the conditions were little better than those said to exist in the South. They urged upon the Governor-elect the importance of the enforcement of the laws. The trades-unions are, without exception, in favor of the abolition of child labor.

Reports made to the Child Labor Committee by its special agents, contain some startling revelations. In a factory at Syracuse, N. Y., the assistant foreman said that "wee little ones" (and he made a motion with his hand to about the height of his knee), had been at work, and said with glee that their little hands were just

right. They very seldom saw an inspector. At another factory, elsewhere, mothers and children sat in long rows at work. A few were Italians, but most were Americans of good village or farm stock. One woman said she and her children worked from 9 A.M., to 9 P.M., daily, except Saturday. Another group included a mother and her children, whose ages were as follows: "Elsie Pearl, four years' old; Earl, three years' old in February." The woman said: "I am so sorry Will isn't here.

BABY TOILERS IN A NEW YORK STATE FACTORY

He is seven, but he gets tired. I left him home sick." At another factory, the foreman said, in answer to a question about the length of time the children worked: "Yes, they stay as long as their mothers, from 9 A. M. to 9 P. M. It is all the same. Fine lot, aren't they? That little one of three, there, can't do much to count. Inspectors? Yes, they're awful strict. Well, they have been twice, but they dassen't say nothing about this place. They dassen't say a word."

In still another factory there were found ten boys under fourteen, working in a packing room. One little lad of five years said: "I work in the factory. Ain't doing nothin' much to-day. Made fifty cents yesterday." Another boy of this group was aged six. At another place there were a number of small girls not over eleven or twelve years' old. They go to the factory at seven o'clock in the morning. One boy of twelve had worked for three years in the factory. He can scarcely write his name, and is unable to read or to do simple sums. This year only three boys out of ten of his playmates have gone back to school, and it is the same with the girls. This boy's story is a typical one.

At still another place the visitors found three boys and three girls hardly over twelve years' old, but the foreman said that during the summer they employed children seven and eight years' old, with their parents. He said, "Of course they must have their children with them in order to keep the law." The hours are from seven in the morning till nine or ten at night, as a rule, but the factory runs till twelve, and is sometimes open until three A.M. It also was in operation two Sundays this summer. Ten hours is the usual period of work, but variations up to fifteen are quite frequent. Wages vary from five cents for the small boys, to seven cents for the women and girls.

Chairman Hunter, of the Child Labor Committee, writing to THE CHRISTIAN HERALD concerning these little slaves of toil, says:

"We have got our laws, but they are not enforced. These laws are, as you know, as vital to the welfare of the State as are the tenement-house laws. They protect the workers in the factories. Both the labor laws and the tenement-house laws are sanitary ones, aiming in all cases, I believe, to protect the health, the life and limbs of people employed in all industries. It is lamentable that this work should be considered unimportant, and that any person who may happen to be a successful politician is considered fit to do this important service for the community. The efforts of our Committee are now bent toward the one end of obtaining a person fully equipped and capable to bring to this work ability, fearlessness, energy and honest purpose."

"The Little Slaves of Toil." From the *Christian Herald,* December 28, 1904, 1155.

Courtesy of the Christian Herald Association, New York.

the federal government did not possess the constitutional authority to pass a national child labor law in early 1907, the *Christian Herald* railed against craven politicians who chose to defend states' rights rather than champion the cause of "the millions of American children of tender age now wearing out their lives in factories and on coal-breakers." Despite complaints from critics who accused them of contributing to national hysteria by publishing exaggerated statistics about child labor, the editors refused to relent in their struggle to "safeguard the natural rights of a very considerable proportion of the children of the republic" through federal legislation.[45]

Almost ten years elapsed before Congress passed a national child labor law in 1916 (which the Supreme Court quickly deemed unconstitutional). Although the protracted progress on this and many other issues may have frustrated Klopsch and his fellow evangelical reformers, they remained convinced that patience and perseverance were essential traits of the true Christian socialist. "The growth of the Kingdom of God in the world," Sheldon had explained, was certain but "slow moving" and could not be brought about "by force or legislation in a day." Permanent social change, he asserted, was best accomplished through persistent, peaceful persuasion. Although the achievement of a more just social order "may be to our human impatience unreasonably delayed," he remarked, "in the end righteousness shall prevail, and the Brotherhood shall be established on earth as it is in heaven." Following Sheldon's lead, the editors of the *Christian Herald* affirmed that the "best type of socialist" was not a "riot breeder but one who, seeing present evils, wisely plans to remedy them by peaceful means of education, frank, intelligent discussion and suitable legislation." God would "make all things right in his own good time," they declared.[46]

This conviction that righting society's many wrongs was a painstaking process requiring persistence and the adoption of a long-term perspective profoundly shaped Klopsch's beliefs about the proper conduct of Christian charity. Since abolishing the liquor traffic, reforming labor laws, and eliminating other root causes of poverty might take many years, Christians simply could not cut off aid to the homeless and hungry in the interim. Even as they worked toward more permanent solutions for the problems that caused unemployment, privation, and pauperism, he explained, American evangelicals "hold it to be a duty to share their abundance with 'their brothers in need.'" Taking aim at Devine's proposal to restrict relief only to those who passed COS inspection, Klopsch declared that allowing any man or woman to starve would be "a crime against God and nature." Proponents of scientific philanthropy ought to remember that Jesus fed the multitudes indiscriminately, without asking questions, "under conditions which might have rendered him liable to the charge by the Pharisees of 'pauperizing the people.'" His ministry offered a model for contemporary relief operations, like the Bowery Mission's breadline, that sought to meet immediate need regardless of "the circumstances that may have produced such a condition."[47]

Although Klopsch's spirited defense of the Bowery Mission's breadline failed to convince skeptics like Devine, his rationale for generous and unrestricted almsgiving resonated with the many American evangelicals who continued to send their mites to support the midnight meal. Like the donations the *Christian Herald* collected during its emergency humanitarian relief campaigns, gifts for the Bowery Mission came from numerous small contributors all over the United States, some of whom were "poor men, themselves redeemed in the mission." The fact that the charity was "supported by Christian workers of limited means from all denominations" who gave unostentatiously and often anonymously set the organization apart from agencies that relied on a few wealthy donors to bankroll their endowments, frequently with great fanfare.[48]

The trend toward "mammoth beneficences" and the establishment of large philanthropic foundations around the turn of the twentieth century was the subject of frequent comment in the pages of the *Christian Herald*. While the editors praised "financial princes" such as Andrew Carnegie, William E. Dodge, and John D. Rockefeller for their generous bequests to colleges, libraries, and other institutions designed to "uplift the masses," Klopsch and his associates also questioned whether poor people would truly benefit from these benevolent organizations. "Ought there not to be some other forms of administration of these colossal fortunes," they asked, that would more directly "ameliorate and assuage the conditions of all the creatures of toil who are practically the creators of these fortunes?" Rather than amassing riches and then donating from deep pockets to agencies that might—or might not—help the destitute to better themselves, these evangelicals suggested, "captains of industry" ought to pay higher wages and expand employment opportunities.[49]

Charles Sheldon echoed this argument in *The Heart of the World*. After lamenting the "personal acquisition of large fortunes" in contemporary American society, Sheldon lambasted wealthy philanthropists for attempting to ease their consciences by contributing a portion of their proceeds—gained at the expense of underpaid workers and inflated product prices—"to some college or university or missionary society" and then taking credit for the endowment without recognizing the employees whose labor had built their fortunes in the first place. Furthermore, Sheldon observed, most magnates "lived all their lives selfishly" in "idle luxury," without lifting a finger or donating a cent to relieve the suffering of the poor.[50]

Contributors to the *Christian Herald* regularly reiterated Sheldon's condemnation of greedy capitalists who ignored the plight of impoverished workers. An editorial published in January 1905, while Sheldon's serial story was running, derided the extravagance of New York City millionaires who feasted on "delicate exotics in rich profusion" on plates of gold while "within a few blocks the long breadlines were waiting, anxiously and wearily, for their loaves of bread." The complete disregard among the affluent for the hungry men who waited outside the Bowery Mission, not to mention the hundred thousand people unemployed throughout the metropolis, reflected "an indifference to suffering worthy only of an animal." Such inhumanity was "a disgrace to a civilized community," the editors proclaimed a few years later in an article decrying ongoing callousness toward those struggling to survive the perils of joblessness and destitution during the terrible winter of 1908.[51]

Given their deep disappointment in the nation's millionaire class, Klopsch and his coworkers became even more convinced that only grassroots evangelical charity could save the nation from economic decline and moral depravity. Large philanthropic trusts such as the Russell Sage Foundation and massive gifts to educational institutions from the likes of Carnegie and Rockefeller were certainly commendable, but they simply could not ensure the future prosperity or integrity of Christian America. Even when millionaires contributed to explicitly religious causes, some contributors to the *Christian Herald* questioned whether donations from industrial magnates who accumulated their fortunes through "oppression and spoliation of the people" could really help create a more just society, let alone usher in the kingdom of God.[52]

John D. Rockefeller's March 1905 bequest of $100,000 to the American Board of Commissioners on Foreign Missions (ABCFM), for example, stirred up a controversy that had been simmering for the past decade over whether Christian organizations ought to accept "tainted money ... gained by nefarious methods." Congregational minister and well-known social reformer Washington Gladden had originally raised this question in an 1895 article condemning the "cool brutality" by which the nation's multimillionaires had built up their fortunes. He cautioned churches not to take funds from such "iniquitous sources" lest they defile themselves and compromise their freedom to preach against unjust business practices and consequent social wrongs. When Rockefeller presented the ABCFM with his sizeable gift ten years later, Gladden again spoke out in protest. "The people of the United States have a tremendous battle on their hands with the corporate greed which has intrenched [sic] itself," he declared. "And now on the eve of this battle they are asked to accept a great gift of money from a man who more completely than any other represents the system they have been summoned to fight. We do not want this money."[53]

Although Klopsch and his editorial staff refrained from openly disparaging Rockefeller—whom many defended as a person of piety—they did agree with Gladden's overall message. "Money from an impure source, or which was amassed unrighteously, carries with it no blessing, but the reverse," they wrote. "Christ's kingdom is not of this world, and it is not to be advanced in this age by gifts from an evil source." Turning the argument of scientific philanthropists on its head, the evangelicals insisted that "indiscriminate acceptance" of "vulgar, tainted tribute"—not unrestricted almsgiving to the poor and outcast—posed the greatest threat to the practice of responsible Christian charity. During this era of "ill-gotten gains," they argued, the nation needed more than ever the benevolent donations of ordinary evangelical givers like the poor widow who offered her mite out of "purity of motive, intrinsic generosity, and spiritual value."[54]

The anxiety Klopsch and his associates expressed about the corrupting effects of greed and materialism within the field of philanthropy reflected their mounting apprehension about the spiritual state of American society at the dawn of the twentieth century. While they continued to praise God for blessing the United States and making it a beacon of prosperity for the entire world, they also warned that Christian America was increasingly under siege from forces that threatened the country's integrity. "Because as a nation we are so rich, we are disposed to congratulate ourselves and to ignore the gigantic evils that are leavening society," one contributor proclaimed. "It is true the gifts to colleges, libraries, and Christian institutions were never so large as now; that religion is outwardly honored, and that we call ourselves a Christian nation. But there are enough blots beneath the decorous exterior to arouse concern." Alongside "our worship of wealth" and "our indifference to the suffering of the poor," this author charged, "the appalling immorality prevailing in our great cities, the scepticism and open infidelity . . . everywhere are ominous signs of national corruption."[55]

Although none of these perils were unprecedented, all seemed more menacing given intensifying class conflict, escalating immigration, rising racial tensions, and growing religious diversity. As charity became an increasingly uncertain indicator of true Christian character, evangelical leaders like Klopsch began to explore alternative strategies for coping with the various ills plaguing American society. By the time the controversy over Rockefeller's "tainted money" erupted in the spring of 1905, Klopsch and his coworkers had decided to enlist the "great united army" of *Christian Herald* subscribers in several campaigns to defend the United States against the forces of ungodliness.

Unlike the *Christian Herald*'s previous crusades to feed the hungry, clothe the naked, and succor the suffering, the battles to ensure that the nation remained Christian amid the mounting pressures of sin, secularism, and spiritual multiplicity emphasized the mobilization of public opinion rather than the collection of financial contributions. The first of these fights rallied American evangelicals to "make war on Mormonism." This so-called church, the editors charged, was really "a political power disguised under the cloak of religion." Echoing critics like the Reverend Josiah Strong, who condemned Mormonism as one of the principal perils endangering Protestant America in his influential text *Our Country* (1885), contributors to the *Christian Herald* denounced the church hierarchy as a despotic and un-American system bent on destroying the "well-being of our Republican institutions." They also decried the practice of polygamy as a "noxious relic of barbarism which should be rooted out of the soil of our civilized and progressive land."[56]

Articles accusing Mormons of treason and national debasement appeared regularly in the *Christian Herald* from the mid-1890s on, but the editors increased their invective against the movement after Brigham H. Roberts, a high-ranking church leader with three wives, was elected to the U.S. House of Representatives in November 1898. Over the next twelve months, Klopsch and his associates urged American evangelicals to join the national crusade calling for Roberts's expulsion from Congress. While churches and religious organizations across the country adopted resolutions opposing the admission of "an avowed polygamist, who is breaking the laws of God and of the land" to the U.S. legislature, publisher William Randolph Hearst played a leading role in rousing public protest through his sensational newspaper, the *New York Journal.* By December 1899, the *Christian Herald* reported, the *Journal* had collected nearly seven million signatures from citizens in every state demanding Roberts's dismissal. Soon after Hearst submitted the massive list of names to the House of Representatives, Congress voted to ban the Mormon member from retaining his seat.[57]

Having seen how Hearst harnessed the power of the press to garner publicity and engage in direct political action, Klopsch determined not to be outdone by his secular rival the next time a Mormon was elected to national office. When Reed Smoot, one of the church's twelve apostles, was chosen in 1903 to represent Utah in the Senate, the *Christian Herald* immediately called for his removal. Over the next several months, the newspaper celebrated the inauguration of a new anti-Mormon crusade led primarily by women's groups across the nation. As a congressional investigation against Smoot proceeded, Klopsch and his associates encouraged their constituents to send letters to their representatives in Washington urging them not only to unseat the senator but also to pass a constitutional amendment prohibiting plural marriage and requiring elected officials to take an oath forswearing allegiance to any organization—such as the Mormon hierarchy—that "defies and endeavors to subvert the laws of the United States."[58]

By June 1905, with the Smoot inquiry still underway, Klopsch decided it was time for the *Christian Herald* to enter the battle to overthrow the "evil Mormon power" more directly. Throughout the remainder of the year, the newspaper distributed copies of a memorial petitioning Congress to immediately remove Smoot from his place in the Senate. By January 1906, the newspaper had collected eighty volumes of signatures from a million women throughout the United States.[59]

Although Klopsch and his colleagues had every expectation of success as they sent off their petition to the Senate Committee on Privileges and Elections, they quickly found themselves on the defensive against opposing forces that launched an effective counterattack. By characterizing the women's memorial as "a war on religion—a crusade against creed," critics of the *Christian Herald*'s campaign to unseat Smoot cast doubt on the constitutionality of the entire enterprise. As proceedings dragged on over the course of the spring, Smoot's allies alleged that his detractors sought to disqualify him for political office solely because of his Mormon faith—a clear infringement on his religious liberty. Although the Senate committee voted in June to expel Smoot, the matter was tabled for several months while legislators debated whether the ruling violated his First Amendment rights.[60]

Klopsch and his staff staunchly defended the signatories of the women's memorial against accusations that they attempted "to influence the Senate to a decision based on popular prejudice" against Mormonism. The petition, they claimed, contained no intimation that Smoot should be removed because of his religion. The case against the senator rested instead on the fact that he remained "*a sworn apostle of the Mormon hierarchy,* under vows and pledges that are antagonistic in form and expression to our national government and institutions, and that as such Apostle, *he is the defender and apologist of polygamy,* which is expressly prohibited by statute." Whatever the merits of this argument—which Congress had been deliberating for nearly four years—the charge against Smoot ultimately failed to carry. When the full Senate finally voted on his case in February 1907, they resolved that he was entitled to retain his position.[61]

THE CHRISTIAN HERALD

A WEEKLY ILLUSTRATED MAGAZINE FOR THE HOME

NEW YORK, JANUARY 31, 1906

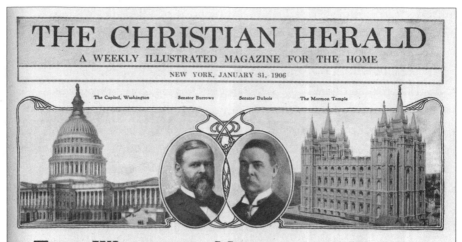

The Capitol, Washington   Senator Burrows   Senator Dubois   The Mormon Temple

THE WOMEN'S MEMORIAL READY

Their Signatures Protesting Against the Mormon Apostle in the Senate Fill Eighty Large Volumes

GLAD would have been the hearts of the American women who have worked earnestly and patriotically to gather the names of their sisters for the memorial to the United States Senate against the Mormon Apostle, Reed Smoot, if they could have seen the imposing array made by the eighty volumes of signatures, as they stood in the offices of THE CHRISTIAN HERALD, ready for shipment to Washington. Bound in green and crimson, and bearing on their backs the names of the States from which the petitions came, they reached 6½ feet toward the ceiling, and extended 5½ along the wall.

With no political axes to grind, with no selfish desire for personal preferment, the women were able to present their case against the polygamous Mormon hierarchy with far greater confidence of success than if it had been made an affair of parties, and not a question of loyalty to our common country and to American ideals. It has been a woman's campaign, and when the results are placed before the Senators they cannot fail to be convincing.

Every State is well represented in the signatures, New York and Pennsylvania standing first in numbers. 43,396 women of New York State, at the latest count, entered their signed protest against the retention of the Mormon Senator. Hundreds of members of the Women's Christian Temperance Union have signed the petition, and have been instrumental in gaining signatures outside their own organization. Hundreds of letters written by the women of the Empire State, show that they are heart and soul in favor of the Anti-Mormon movement, and have followed it with their prayers.

The wives, mothers, sisters, and daughters of Pennsylvania have rallied around the banner raised by the Federation of American Women, and 36,630 of them have signed, pleading with the Senate to remove the representative of the Mormon hierarchy.

All the States are represented in proportion to population except Utah, and a few others that are under strong Mormon influence, and where the women, even those who do not belong to the church of Brigham Young, dare not speak against the Mormon senator, or express their honest opinions, as by so doing their husbands and fathers would be ruined in business. A few hundreds were brave enough to sign the Memorial, but the signatures made a pitiful showing in comparison to

The Great Memorial of the Women of America to the U. S. Senate

These eighty large volumes (each measuring 10½ x 13½ inches and 3 inches thick), are filled with signatures, demanding the expulsion of the Mormon Senator

that they have been personally cognizant of the workings of the hierarchy, having lived in or near Mormon settlements. Every woman in the town of Laton, Calif., signed the Memorial. New Jersey sent nearly 11,000 signatures, the result of splendid efforts by self-appointed workers.

the great avalanche of signatures from other States.

California sent over 12,000 names, one lady, Mrs. Dudore, of San Diego, forwarding 500. Many correspondents from this State say that they have been personally cognizant of the workings of the hierarchy, having lived in or near Mormon settlements. Every woman in the town of Laton, Calif., signed the Memorial. New Jersey sent nearly 11,000 signatures, the result of splendid did efforts by self-appointed workers. The women of Colorado are among the most earnest in their appeal. A letter says: "I believe I would be in great danger if my name was known. I have lived among the Mormons, and know whereof I speak." With this letter came a long list of protestors. Delaware made a goodly list, and from the women of Wilmington comes the words: "We sincerely hope that not only may Reed Smoot be expelled from the Senate, but that the Mormon apostles may never again have an opportunity to be represented in that body."

The women of Florida, cities and towns, have worked valiantly, with the result that many signatures have been gathered. The popular sentiment of the women of Georgia, is shown by the signed petitions sent from Savannah and other cities. "Every true Georgian is in arms against Reed Smoot," writes one correspondent from that State.

Over seventeen thousand women of Illinois, led by some of the largest women's organizations in the State, make written protest against the Mormon Apostle. The Chicago Woman's Club unanimously endorsed the petition.

Over 22,000 signatures came from Ohio. Thousands of signatures and hundreds of letters from Indiana, voice the women's prayer that "God will hasten the day when the women of our sister State (Utah) enjoy the liberty they should possess. The women of Indian Territory bitterly oppose the retention of Senator Smoot, and have signed the memorial in large numbers.

Fifteen thousand names came from Kansas, Mrs. N. A. Roxencrantz, of Emporia, leading with the largest individual list of 544, which includes nearly all the women of that place. Kansas women's clubs are splendidly represented, and the petition was signed by a few Mormon women, who dared thus to place themselves on record.

Kentucky sends a long list of signatures.

CONTINUED ON PAGE 95

83

The "Women's Memorial" to unseat Mormon Senator Reed Smoot of Utah. From the *Christian Herald,* January 31, 1906, 83. Courtesy of the Christian Herald Association, New York.

Smoot's victory was a major blow to Klopsch's campaign to secure the nation's evangelical identity in the face of mounting anxiety about the future of Christian America. The Senate's decision was particularly troubling for participants in the anti-Mormon crusade because it confirmed that expediency could prevail over moral argument in politics. Vigorous activism by a million American women fighting to preserve "the Christian ideals of home" and to protect the federal government from "disloyal" lawmakers simply had not been enough to sway the outcome of the investigation, signaling a loss of evangelical influence within the halls of American power. The petitioners' "implicit confidence in the wisdom and patriotism of the Senate," Klopsch lamented, had been misplaced. As a result, the *Christian Herald*'s first foray into organized political action was a failure.[62]

Concern about the U.S. government's commitment to Christian morality resurfaced several months after the Smoot case was resolved, when President Theodore Roosevelt commissioned a new design for American coins that did not include the national motto "In God We Trust." The departure from a practice in place since the Civil War provoked a public outcry. Klopsch and his associates immediately urged American evangelicals to participate in the national protest by sending their views to the *Christian Herald* for publication. Because "public opinion is one of the most potent agencies of which civilization knows," they declared, the controversy offered "an opportunity for every one to aid in the general enlightenment on this question, which involves so much more than the motto itself." Indeed, Klopsch explained elsewhere, "this fight for the motto is really part of the greater battle that has been waging for some time past, for the purpose of establishing . . . the fundamental truth that ours is a Christian nation; that this government was founded on the principles of the Christian religion." By participating in the *Christian Herald*'s letter-writing campaign, American evangelicals could persuade Congress to reaffirm these commitments and thus help "to make a part of the nation's history."[63]

As Klopsch's comments implied, the movement to restore the motto took place in the context of a much broader contest over American religious identity. Most recently, for example, conflicts over the recitation of the Lord's Prayer and the celebration of Christmas in public schools had provoked animosity between Jewish communities and Protestant majorities in New York City. The trouble began in the fall of 1906, when a rabbi lodged a complaint with the Board of Education alleging that Jewish children were compelled to take part in Christian practices "contrary to their religious teachings." Several months later, the *Christian Herald* reported, "a certain portion of the Hebrew population of New York" launched an "extraordinary crusade . . . against the observance of Christmas in the public schools."[64]

Although Klopsch and his associates initially thought these efforts would amount to no more than "a tempest in a teapot," they soon discovered that the storm would not be so easily contained. By December 1907, just as their own campaign to restore the motto was picking up steam, the editors lamented a decision by public school authorities to remove any mention of Christ in connection with the holiday festivals in order to avoid antagonizing Jewish "prejudices." This policy provoked so much outrage among the city's Christian population that the school board quickly rescinded the ruling. "This disclaimer by the Board came none too soon," the *Christian Herald* declared, for the "feeling of rancor and bitterness . . . excited by the recent controversy" had "threatened to develop into a religious and racial antagonism of a character abhorrent to the spirit of our generous American civilization." The resulting truce between Jews and Gentiles would only hold, however, if the Hebrews ceased their "absurd and intolerant requests" and showed greater appreciation for American "hospitality." To prevent the emergence of anti-Semitism, Jews would need to acknowledge that "they have come to a land that is everywhere recognized as Christian" and yield "to the inclinations of their more numerous fellows."[65]

Despite the confidence with which Klopsch and his colleagues declared the United States a Christian nation, a growing number of Americans—not only Jewish immigrants—disagreed with this assertion. The response of several *Christian Herald* readers to the elimination of the motto confirmed the troubling development. "I think the President's action conforms to the spirit of modern times. The trend of thought is away from the State mixing in religious affairs," wrote Newell B. Thatcher of Medina, New York. "I believe in a complete separation of religion and politics." Other reactions were even stronger indicators of the drift toward secularism among some segments of the population. The fact that "the atheists, the sceptics, and the enemies of religion generally" were celebrating the motto's removal and pointing "to its absence as proof... that our people are no longer followers of the faith held by the founders of this Republic," Klopsch declared, ought to spur American evangelicals to "proclaim anew... our national faith in God."[66]

Many *Christian Herald* readers complied enthusiastically with Klopsch's request. Although the newspaper received a few missives from subscribers expressing support for eliminating the motto, the overwhelming majority of correspondents—approximately 96 percent, according to Klopsch—demanded its immediate restoration. "It is everywhere apparent in these letters, that the great Christian heart of the nation has been deeply wounded by the effacement of the acknowledgment of God upon our coinage," he wrote. By mid-January 1908, the *Christian Herald* had received too many communications to publish, so Klopsch decided to forward the results of the newspaper's "plebiscite" to Kentucky congressman Ollie M. James, who had introduced a bill to reinstate "In God We Trust" on American money. James and several of his colleagues used the mass of letters to garner support for their legislation and published many of them in *The Congressional Record*, where they became part of official government proceedings.[67]

When the House of Representatives voted almost unanimously (259 to 5) in mid-March in favor of bringing back the motto, Klopsch and his associates rejoiced that the nation's elected officials had yielded "to the universal demand from men and women of every religious denomination." After the Senate approved the bill in May, the editors declared a great triumph for "loyal, patriotic, God-fearing Americans everywhere." The legislature had restored not only the motto, they proclaimed, but faith that the federal government supported keeping America Christian. That the *Christian Herald* had played such an important part in influencing the outcome was also cause for celebration. "We are sincerely thankful to have been once more the chosen channel through which public opinion has expressed itself so effectually on a great question which deeply touched the religious feelings of the American people," the editors asserted.[68]

Victory in the campaign to reinstate the motto came at a particularly auspicious moment for the *Christian Herald*. While Klopsch and his colleagues were leading the charge to restore "In God We Trust" on American coinage, they were also fighting to defend their organization against attacks from proponents of scientific philanthropy, such as Edward Devine. Devine's diatribe against the breadline appeared just a few days before the House of Representatives voted to bring back the motto. As the controversy over indiscriminate almsgiving escalated during the spring of 1908, Klopsch and his coworkers strove to galvanize support for their evangelical agenda from Christians across the United States and among the country's congressional leaders. The Senate's final authorization of the bill to restore the motto gave the *Christian Herald* staff renewed confidence in their capacity to ward off the corrosive effects of secularism, skepticism, and sin in the arenas of national governance, domestic charity, and even international humanitarian aid.

Over the next several months, Klopsch and his associates sought to capitalize on their recent political success by working to consolidate evangelical influence in each of these spheres. By initiating an aggressive subscription drive to increase the *Christian Herald*'s circulation, they sought to ensure that the publication would remain "a potent factor in our national life" and extend the reach of evangelical charity through its benevolent enterprises both at home and abroad. As the newspaper's readership expanded, Klopsch and his colleagues urged the new constituents to join the ongoing fight against the many foes threatening to undermine "Christian America." During the election season in the fall of 1908, for example, the editors reminded subscribers of "their opportunity to line up with the forces of righteousness and good government in opposition to the enemies of public morals in many of our States and municipalities." Although they refrained, as always, from recommending particular candidates or aligning with a specific party, Klopsch and his associates implored evangelicals to vote for leaders who would preserve "good, honest, decent government conducted on Christian principles." Given their recent triumph in the battle to restore the motto, the editors implied, the *Christian Herald*'s readers could be certain they possessed the power to turn the tide in many other political contests against corruption and ungodliness. In a letter congratulating President-Elect William Howard Taft on his victory in November, Klopsch suggested that "the *Christian Herald* family," as "the largest Christian constituency in America," was a force to be reckoned with in the nation's political affairs.[69]

Since Taft's election was controversial among American evangelicals—many of whom had vigorously backed Democratic nominee William Jennings Bryan for religious reasons—Klopsch hoped his declaration of support would carry weight with the incoming chief executive. Throughout the campaign, Taft had come under attack for his Unitarian faith, particularly among midwestern evangelicals who accused him of being an infidel. Those who preferred Bryan's devout Presbyterianism characterized the contest between the two candidates as a struggle between the forces of irreligious heathenism working to undermine "Christian America" and the defenders of true orthodoxy striving to save civilization from its foes.[70]

By contrast, the *Christian Herald* editors praised both contenders as "men of high ability, sound principles, and unquestioned patriotism" and concluded that national honor and the material interests of the people would be safe whichever way the election went. Never once during the campaign did the newspaper publish a word about Taft's religious convictions. When Taft won the election in a landslide, Klopsch immediately commended the new president on his victory, pledging to pray for God's blessing on his administration. Several weeks later, the *Christian Herald* publicized Taft's recent address to the Women's Foreign Missionary Society, praising the nation's new leader for his defense of overseas missionaries against accusations of diplomatic interference. Given Taft's support for evangelical efforts to extend Christian civilization around the globe, Klopsch encouraged his constituents to see the president-elect as a worthy ally in their humanitarian work abroad.[71]

Although Klopsch's endorsement of a politician whom many evangelicals deemed an enemy of Christian America may have struck some of his constituents as ill-considered, his decision to curry favor with Taft made good strategic sense in light of the publisher's ambitions to keep evangelicals at the forefront of international humanitarianism and domestic charity. As the honorary president of the ARC since 1905, Taft had been an enthusiastic proponent of Mabel Boardman's attempts to professionalize the relief industry and strengthen ties between her organization and the federal government. At the same time, Taft had been willing to concede that the ARC remained reliant on the fund-raising capacities of private, grassroots agencies such as the *Christian Herald* during times of crisis. Just eighteen months prior to his election, in fact, Taft had acknowledged the indispensable part the *Christian Herald* played in collecting donations for the ARC's China relief campaign. By throwing his support behind Taft at a time when so many evangelicals maligned him, Klopsch endeavored to establish a partnership with the incoming president that would ensure an ongoing role for the *Christian Herald*'s aid enterprises under the new administration.

THE ECLIPSE OF EVANGELICAL AID

When a devastating earthquake struck southern Italy in late December 1908, Klopsch seized the opportunity to discern whether his overtures to Taft would advance the cause of evangelical humanitarianism. Although Roosevelt remained in office during the catastrophe and its aftermath, Taft exercised considerable influence throughout the relief campaign as the head of the ARC. Within twenty-four hours of receiving news of the destruction, Klopsch cabled Taft that he had forwarded $20,000 for Italian sufferers through the State Department. When he heard several days later that the ARC needed an additional $30,000 to send a relief ship, Klopsch immediately fronted the money. Mabel Boardman responded without delay, expressing great appreciation for the "prompt action of the *Christian Herald*" in advancing the necessary funds. "It is most timely and a generosity for which the Red Cross feels especially grateful to Dr. Klopsch and the generous givers of the *Christian Herald*," she wrote.[72]

Government leaders working with the ARC to aid Italy also voiced their gratitude. "President Roosevelt, the Department of State, and the National Red Cross appreciate most fully the Wonderful generosity of the *Christian Herald* and the advancement of this thirty thousand dollars," declared Assistant Secretary of State Robert Bacon. "Dr. Klopsch and the *Christian Herald* have again proven benefactors of world-wide fame. . . . There is no other organization that can point to such a record of giving." In fact, federal officials seemed relieved to rely on private agencies like the *Christian Herald* rather than assuming full responsibility for appropriating funds or collecting donations through the ARC. At a benefit for the Italian sufferers, for example, Vice President Charles Fairbanks asserted that the government had done much to relieve the misery but could not be expected to do everything. Every man who could afford it, he stated, "ought to give something toward the cause." Alongside commendations from other political leaders, Klopsch and his associates took Fairbanks's comments as a signal that the *Christian Herald* remained a valued partner in the nation's international humanitarian work.[73]

Throughout the Italian earthquake campaign, the *Christian Herald* stressed the essential role its constituents were playing in advancing the United States' reputation for aiding nations in distress. Although the ARC and the State Department had taken charge of distributing supplies on the ground, the funds Klopsch had forwarded so soon after the disaster ensured that American evangelicals were, through their money, "among the first on the field to succor the injured after the earthquake— certainly the first from any land outside Italy." This prompt response attracted attention from Italy's highest officials, including the prime minister as well as the king and queen. Each of these prominent figures thanked Klopsch and the *Christian Herald* personally, expressing appreciation for American generosity and praising the United States for "outdistancing all others in sympathy."[74]

When Klopsch visited Europe after the conclusion of the relief effort, he was invited for a private audience with the king, Victor Emmanuel III, in Rome. During this interview, Klopsch later wrote, the monarch asked him how he managed to raise such vast amounts of money for international charity. "Do the millionaires of your country give you large sums?" With pride, Klopsch explained that "the money was generally from people in moderate circumstances, who give as God has given them and in His name. . . . The average contribution is $2.75." Religiously inspired almsgiving from ordinary Americans, rather than large-scale scientific philanthropy from wealthy industrialists, Klopsch told the king, remained the driving force of the U.S. foreign aid enterprise.[75]

But even as Klopsch claimed that *Christian Herald* contributors led the charge to assist Italy's sufferers as they had in so many previous relief campaigns, there were signs that evangelical dominance in the field of international humanitarianism was waning. Whereas the *Christian Herald* had far outstripped the ARC in prior fund-raising efforts for foreign disasters, this time local Red Cross societies collected significantly more money than did Klopsch's organization. By the time the *Christian Herald* closed its Italian earthquake fund, donations from subscribers totaled $71,806. During the same period, the ARC amassed almost $1 million from branches across the country.[76]

The ARC's success was due in part to a more coordinated fund-raising effort among the agency's leaders. Recognizing that "a large portion of the public does not realize the significance of the Red Cross" and that many potential donors were puzzled by multiple claims on their attention, the secretary of the New York State chapter, for example, requested that both Governor Charles Hughes and the mayor of New York City identify the ARC as the proper depository for contributions. Both officials complied; as a result, monies donated by churches, Sunday schools, civic associations, and women's clubs—some of which might previously have been sent to the *Christian Herald*—were now collected via the ARC, the "recognized channel for relief."[77]

The ARC's leaders insisted that the agency's efforts to increase collections through popular awareness were never intended to crowd out other charitable organizations like the *Christian Herald*. "The desire," ARC officials explained, "was not, of course, to limit the generosity or to discourage the independent collection of funds, but . . . to procure a public, uniform and central accounting." The ARC continued to acknowledge prominently in its records monies received from the *Christian Herald*, and Mabel Boardman signaled her appreciation for Klopsch's ongoing partnership by paying him a visit at Mont-Lawn in the summer of 1909, helping the "Children's Paradise" to acquire "a national fame" through her patronage.[78]

Despite these attempts to assure Klopsch that the ARC valued the *Christian Herald*'s participation in the agency's disaster relief campaigns, Klopsch sensed that he and his organization were steadily losing ground in their fight to remain at the forefront of the nation's foreign aid enterprise. If American evangelicals were to a retain a leadership position in international humanitarianism, they would need to find ways to work not only alongside but also around, or even above and beyond, the ARC. In late August 1909, after torrential floods devastated the area around Monterey, Mexico, Klopsch saw an opportunity to try a different approach. Although the ARC immediately sent $1,000 to U.S. Consul-General Philip Hanna for the relief of survivors, the donation depleted the organization's emergency fund. An appeal to the American public

CHRISTIAN HERALD

COPYRIGHT, 1909, BY LOUIS KLOPSCH

SUBSCRIPTION, $1.50 PER ANNUM
PUBLISHED 52 TIMES A YEAR

NEW YORK, October 13, 1909

VOL. 32—NO. 41. PRICE 5 CENTS
OFFICES: BIBLE HOUSE, NEW YORK

See page 845

Flood Sufferers Applying for Relief at the U. S. Consulate, Monterey, Mexico

"Flood Sufferers Applying for Relief at the U.S. Consulate, Monterey, Mexico."
From the *Christian Herald,* October 13, 1909, cover. Courtesy of the Christian
Herald Association, New York.

was slow to produce contributions, leaving Hanna helpless to aid the thousands of sufferers—mostly Mexicans but some U.S. citizens as well—who came to him seeking food and shelter.[79]

When Klopsch heard that the ARC was faltering in its fund-raising efforts, he telegraphed the State Department asking what was being done for the afflicted. He also reached out to Hanna directly to find out how the *Christian Herald* could best assist the relief effort. Klopsch learned that Hanna had solicited food contributions from farmers in Texas, New Mexico, and Arizona and had also negotiated for the free transport of duty-free relief supplies through the Wells Fargo Express Company. What he most needed now was help procuring clothing and bedding for the destitute families struggling to survive the cold autumn rains. With this information in hand, Klopsch decided that rather than forwarding money through the ARC, he would send the needed supplies straight to Hanna. By the end of September, he had shipped five thousand heavy blankets to Monterey. Several weeks later, he dispatched fifteen thousand more coverlets along with one hundred sewing machines bearing the inscription: "From American Friends through the Christian Herald."[80]

By marking the sewing machines with this message, Klopsch stressed what he saw as the unique contribution of evangelical almsgivers to the international humanitarian campaign. Through their sympathy and material aid, he asserted, the *Christian Herald*'s constituents had an opportunity to strengthen the bonds between Mexico and the United States when tensions among government officials, business leaders, and citizens of the neighboring nations had been on the rise. In the Nuevo León region where the disaster had taken place, Klopsch explained, some Mexicans had begun to resent the United States, "the people thinking, perhaps, that we were getting too strong a footing" in their territory. In a place where anti-American sentiment had been increasing, he suggested, a nongovernmental aid agency like the *Christian Herald* might prove more effective in winning back the trust of local people who harbored suspicions of state-sponsored enterprises.[81]

When Cayetano Romero, consul-general of Mexico in New York City, telephoned Klopsch to thank him for relieving suffering in Monterey, the proprietor quickly congratulated his constituents for the constructive role they were playing in U.S. foreign policy. "American contributions and kindness are doing more for good international relations than many treaties of commerce and peace," Klopsch claimed. "It is a kind of diplomacy which needs no government commission and in which all can take part." As reports of "eager joy" among recipients of the *Christian Herald*'s contributions reached the editorial office, Klopsch surmised that "this 'blanket business' may become the largest factor in the cementing of American and Mexican friendship in the future. It will keep that friendship warm. More eloquent than words, more convincing than fine diplomatic phrases are kind actions that spring from generous impulses," he wrote.[82]

By finding a niche for the *Christian Herald* in the Monterey flood relief campaign, Klopsch hoped to strengthen his case for the ongoing importance of grassroots evangelical humanitarianism. Having private organizations engaged in international aid was essential not only at times when afflicted nations viewed the U.S. government with suspicion but also to keep the American people actively involved in giving. By assuming responsibility for disaster relief, Klopsch suggested, federal officials inadvertently discouraged individual citizens from seeing themselves as vital participants in the nation's efforts to alleviate distress. When they believed that assistance would come from another source, Klopsch argued, individuals were less apt to give out of their own pockets.[83]

Perhaps this was why the public's response to the ARC's appeal for the Mexican flood sufferers was so meager, Klopsch suggested. Since the *Christian Herald* insisted that almsgiving was a spiritual obligation all faithful believers were required to fulfill, its relief campaigns could continue to stimulate engagement among a broad segment of the American population despite the government's increasing involvement in foreign aid. Every evangelical, Klopsch contended, had a sacred duty to help those in distress. There was never an excuse not to donate "be it in ever so small a measure."[84]

When the *Christian Herald* closed the books on its Mexican relief campaign, the newspaper had collected $8,350 to purchase blankets, sewing machines, and some foodstuffs for survivors of the flood. The ARC spent a similar amount in Monterey but had raised less than half of the money disbursed, resulting in a deficit of $4,750 that had to be covered through a transfer from the general emergency fund. Rather than conceding that they would always need help from private organizations like the *Christian Herald*, ARC officers decided after Mexico that it was time to put their agency on a more stable financial footing.[85]

In November 1909, Taft announced the formation of an endowment fund committee to ensure adequate income so the ARC could always be prepared to carry out relief operations instead of depending on donations through frequent public appeals. "It seems to be necessary in some way or other to fill the American eye and to fill the American ear before you can arouse them to contributions," he complained. When a crisis such as the earthquake in Italy evoked compassion among a broad segment of the population, Taft continued, the ARC succeeded in raising ample funds in a short time. But other calamites—like the catastrophic flood in Monterey—failed to generate sufficient money to meet the need. As "the authorized official organization of the United States for volunteer aid in time of war or great disaster," Taft concluded, the ARC should no longer "be forced to wait" for adequate funding before beginning relief work. Nor should the agency be left with a shortfall at the conclusion of any operation.[86]

Furthermore, although the ARC would continue to welcome contributions from private individuals and charitable organizations during times of crisis, the agency would strongly discourage donors from sending money or supplies directly to government officials such as Consul-General Hanna. "In the past the State Department has been frequently called upon to forward through the foreign service sums for the relief of suffering in foreign countries," explained Secretary of State Philander Knox. Moving forward, he wrote, the department would discontinue this practice "to avoid complications and to avail of a centralized, appropriate, and highly efficient channel" for collecting and distributing international aid.[87]

Contrary to Klopsch's hopes at the start of Taft's term, the new president worked diligently during his first year in office to broaden the ARC's usefulness and to consolidate the agency's status as the nation's only officially recognized organization "chartered and sanctioned by an act of Congress . . . for the sole purpose of relieving the sufferings caused by war or by calamities in times of peace." Although he and his fellow government officials expressed appreciation for the *Christian Herald*'s contributions to aid efforts, the president made clear that Klopsch and his evangelical humanitarians would be subordinate to the ARC in the field of foreign assistance.[88]

Never one to acknowledge a setback, Klopsch continued to commend his constituents for their valuable service in the international arena. "Through the unprecedented generosity of its readers, without regard to color, creed or nationality, the *Christian Herald* has established for our country the proud distinction of being the Almoner to Nations in Distress," Klopsch wrote to subscribers in late November. "Even in a greater degree than intelligent statesmanship," he claimed, the "grand and glorious work carried on by readers of the *Christian Herald* . . . has aided in the development of fraternal relations between our own and other lands." With such a remarkable record to inspire them, Klopsch declared, American evangelicals could have confidence that they would remain an influence for good through their future humanitarian endeavors both at home and abroad.[89]

Several weeks after he published this missive, Klopsch wrote another letter—this one addressed to the president of the United States. When he heard that Taft was scheduled to speak to a gathering honoring Methodist missionaries at New York City's Carnegie Hall on Monday, December 13, Klopsch implored the nation's chief executive to visit the Bowery Mission after his first engagement ended. If he could not convince the president to accept the *Christian Herald* as a full partner in the United States' official foreign relief campaigns, perhaps Klopsch could win Taft's approval of evangelical charity within the domestic arena. Given the heightened criticism the breadline had endured from proponents of scientific philanthropy over the past eighteen months, an endorsement from the man who led both the nation and the ARC would, Klopsch hoped, bolster the cause of the *Christian Herald*'s ministry to the poor and homeless of New York City. Since the Bowery Mission had recently moved to a new building, the timing for a visit from Taft would be perfect.[90]

Through the persuasion of the Reverend John Wesley Hill, who was both a personal friend of the president and a faithful supporter of the Bowery Mission, Taft was convinced to accept Klopsch's invitation. Despite a torrential downpour that made travel difficult, Taft arrived at the Mission just before eleven o'clock on Monday night, while the "usual Gospel service was in progress." After a rousing round of applause from

Christian Herald

$1.50 A YEAR — 5c. A COPY
PUBLISHED 52 TIMES A YEAR

COPYRIGHT, 1909, BY LOUIS KLOPSCH

NEW YORK, October 27, 1909

VOLUME 32 — NUMBER 43
OFFICES: BIBLE HOUSE, NEW YORK

THE
BOWERY MISSION

See Page 893

New Home of the Bowery Mission, 227 Bowery, New York, to be Dedicated Nov. 7 to 14, 1909

The new Bowery Mission. From the *Christian Herald,* October 27, 1909, cover.

Courtesy of the Christian Herald Association, New York.

the six hundred "down-and-out" men who filled the auditorium, Taft rose to address the crowd. During his remarks, the president acknowledged the "enormous energy and tremendous power for good which Dr. Klopsch exercises through the *Christian Herald* in raising hundreds of thousands of dollars to relieve human suffering wherever it may be in the world." Taft also expressed his admiration for the Bowery Mission's efforts to "help men over hard places; help over the time when things seem desperate and when it seems as if the Lord and everybody else have turned against you." "I am glad to come here and to testify by my presence here my sympathy with the great work which Dr. Klopsch is doing," he declared.[91]

The president's unqualified praise for the *Christian Herald*'s international humanitarian campaigns as well as for the Bowery Mission's labors among the unemployed and destitute of Lower Manhattan was precisely what Klopsch had been hoping for. Taft's interaction with the "submerged, the friendless, the hopeless, the down-and-out" made headlines in newspapers across the nation, publicizing the ministries of evangelical charity from one end of the country to the other. The popular *New York World* proclaimed that "President Taft never did a better hour's work than when, hoarse with a heavy cold, he braved the deluge on Monday night to speak to the men in the Bowery Mission." The *News* of Columbus, Ohio, called the chief executive's excursion into the Lower East Side a "proper recognition of one of the greatest religious works in the city" and of "the many humanitarian enterprises undertaken and carried forward by that remarkable paper, the *Christian Herald* and its remarkable proprietor, Dr. Louis Klopsch." Accolades like these, Klopsch suggested, reflected widespread support for evangelical almsgiving among the American people. Taft's visit, he hoped, "might give a new stimulus to philanthropy" at a time when many of the nation's citizens continued to grapple with questions about how to address the problems of increasing poverty, inequality, and suffering both within the United States and around the world.[92]

Certainly, the president's affirmation of the *Christian Herald*'s efforts to alleviate affliction was a "crowning event" in the newspaper's history and a fitting way to celebrate Klopsch's acquisition of the publication twenty years earlier. As Klopsch prepared to lead his "great united army" of subscribers—a force that had grown to 400,000 by January 1910—into a new decade of humanitarian service, he rejoiced that the *Christian Herald* occupied "a commanding position . . . in all of the varied worthy enterprises and undertakings, at home and abroad," for which the journal had become so well known. With "the largest audience of any religious publication on the globe," he asserted, this popular evangelical paper was better situated than ever before to "bring comfort to the comfortless and relieve distress the world over." Buoyed by the president's praise, which eclipsed any apparent setbacks he had suffered over the past several months, Klopsch invited "the cordial cooperation and the prayers of all our friends, new and old, in carrying forward the great mission of the *Christian Herald* in the service of Christ and humanity." "With such aid, great things have been accomplished in the past," he declared. "Let us trust, under God's blessing, the future may be even brighter in noble achievement than all the years that have gone."[93]

7

A SHIFTING LANDSCAPE

On a blustery Wednesday morning in March 1910, a crowd gathered outside the Metropolitan Temple on Seventh Avenue and Fourteenth Street in New York City. When the doors opened shortly after ten o'clock, throngs of people streamed into the sanctuary, quickly filling every seat on the main floor and in the galleries and packing all the passageways but the central aisle. The hundreds who could not find standing room in the building stayed outside, where they hoped to glimpse Louis Klopsch's casket as the bearers carried it into the church. "It was a remarkable funeral, worthy of the man," the *Christian Herald* reported. From all across the city, the surrounding suburbs, and many distant points, friends had come to pay tribute to their "beloved leader in many Christian enterprises." During the memorial, ministers of every denomination stood alongside military officers, municipal officials, a large delegation of editors and publishers, and members of Klopsch's staff who joined together to remember their departed chief.[1]

The service was special not only because of the multitude who came to offer sympathy, one observer commented, but also because the mourners hailed from such diverse backgrounds: "One could note the mingling of the rich and the poor, the prosperous businessmen and humble workers; the men of the Bowery" and the "250 children of the tenements" who were invited to sing hymns in memory of their benefactor. "It was a gathering such as is rarely seen anywhere, and all were drawn by a common impulse to show their respect, honor and love for one whose life had been freely spent for others."[2]

Those who could not attend sent messages expressing their sorrow. Hundreds of missives poured in to the *Christian Herald* offices as news of Klopsch's passing spread. Ordinary subscribers from all parts of the country wrote to share their remembrances, while a slew of prominent religious leaders, foreign diplomats, and fellow humanitarians such as Mabel Boardman of the American Red Cross (ARC) telegraphed their regrets. Even the president of the United States cabled his condolences, sending from the White House a "superb floral wreath of large proportions, which was laid upon the casket."[3]

Klopsch's untimely death at the age of fifty-eight came as a shock to the global community of *Christian Herald* readers. Although he suffered from chronic gastritis, Klopsch had always been a person of enormous energy who never allowed physical ailments to impede his work. Just a few months before his passing, he had proclaimed that the future of evangelical humanitarianism was looking brighter than ever. In an editorial celebrating the *Christian Herald*'s expanding constituency and many accomplishments in the fields of foreign aid and domestic philanthropy, he urged subscribers to embrace the "vast possibilities and equally great responsibilities . . . in the service of Christ and humanity" that lay ahead. When his stomach troubles became more acute in February 1910, therefore, few among his friends and family worried that he would fail to recover. Even after he was rushed to the hospital on Tuesday, March 1, for emergency surgery to remove an abdominal obstruction, most assumed the indomitable Klopsch would soon return to full strength. At first he "rallied a little," the *New York Times* reported, but within a few days, he took a turn for the worse. On Monday, March 7, at one o'clock in the morning, Klopsch passed away.[4]

Just hours after his death, admirers began to commemorate Klopsch's career of worldwide charity. Early Monday afternoon, a large audience of businessmen—"bankers, brokers, clerks, merchants, importers, and men of all sorts of callings known to the downtown district"—assembled for an open-air service on the corner of Wall Street and Nassau Street to pay tribute to his memory. The Reverend William Wilkinson of Trinity Church, who spoke at the gathering, celebrated Klopsch's great success in making the *Christian Herald* "a mighty power for good" through its campaigns to relieve suffering resulting from "pestilence, famine, earthquake, great fire, and flood." Unlike other humanitarians who strove to alleviate distress far afield but neglected suffering at home, Wilkinson proclaimed, Klopsch fought for equitable labor laws, pleaded for proper housing, and worked to give every American citizen—no matter how derelict or downtrodden—"a fair, open, just opportunity of living in good conditions." Before dismissing the crowd, Wilkinson charged his congregation to reflect on Klopsch's example and carry forward his good work on behalf of the poor, the oppressed, and the afflicted throughout the United States and around the globe.[5]

In the coming days, numerous eulogists would echo Wilkinson's commendations and his calls for continuing the *Christian Herald*'s commitment to assuaging suffering and combating injustice. Presbyterian minister Wilbur F. Crafts praised Klopsch for prompting expressions of sympathy that surpassed "all arbitrary boundaries among men—all national and denominational and social and race boundaries" and for striving to assist "every man who needs help for body or soul . . . counting the whole world one neighborhood and one brotherhood." Through the *Christian Herald*'s far-reaching humanitarian campaigns, another colleague wrote, Klopsch had created a medium through which people of all nations were "drawn together in mutual sympathy and helpfulness" as they worked for "the alleviation of human suffering and the advancement of the Cross of Christ." Surely, the family of *Christian Herald* readers had "imbibed something of his enthusiasm" and would continue to advance his ambition of making their newspaper not only the most widely circulated of religious journals but also "the greatest power for good in the whole world."[6]

Although many of Klopsch's associates expressed confidence that the *Christian Herald*'s activities and the charities he organized would remain "as a lasting memorial to his labors in the cause of Christ and humanity," some observers seemed less optimistic about the future of evangelical almsgiving in the wake of his passing. Klopsch had not designated a successor, and all acknowledged his would be a difficult act to follow. "I have been wondering who can take up the work he has left," one reader admitted. "Who can take his place?" another queried.[7]

At first, Klopsch's eldest son expressed his intention to step in as editor in chief, but Louis Jr. had never shown much interest in the *Christian Herald* and had in fact demurred when his father had offered him an apprenticeship at the newspaper several years earlier. When it became clear that the heir apparent was not well suited to assuming his father's mantle of leadership, the journal's advertising manager, Otto Koenig, took over as president and treasurer, keeping long-time staff member George Sandison in his role as managing editor. Both of these men had worked alongside Klopsch for years in the *Christian Herald*'s publishing headquarters as well as on the boards of the Bowery Mission, the Mont-Lawn Children's Home, and several of the newspaper's other charities. Neither, however, possessed the panache of their predecessor, whose name they kept on the newspaper's masthead for marketing purposes for almost two years after his death. Although Koenig and Sandison "faithfully followed the principles laid down by Dr. Klopsch" and even raised about $133,000 for famine relief in China during the winter of 1911–1912, they struggled to keep the *Christian Herald* at the forefront of the nation's humanitarian mission amid a host of pressures that were reshaping the meaning and practice of evangelical charity.[8]

During the early twentieth century, a number of theological forces and social dynamics transformed the field of philanthropy. As debates among Protestant modernists, fundamentalists, and pentecostals threatened consensus about almsgiving as a marker of evangelical identity, the establishment of large foundations by wealthy families like the Carnegies and the Rockefellers diminished the *Christian Herald*'s capacity to compete as one of the nation's premier humanitarian aid agencies. Although the newspaper's direct role in international relief and domestic philanthropy declined as a result of these developments, several of the publication's benevolent enterprises endured over the course of the twentieth century. The staying power of the Bowery Mission and Mont-Lawn shows the durability of evangelical charity despite major shifts in the religious and political landscape.

In the years before Klopsch's death, tensions within the evangelical coalition he had formed through the *Christian Herald* began to divide the movement. Although accusations of heresy against Protestant clergymen who embraced biblical criticism or Darwin's theory of evolution became increasingly common over the course of the 1890s, the *Christian Herald* downplayed these controversies as side issues detracting from the goal of cultivating unity through evangelical philanthropy. During Talmage's lifetime, the editorial staff was relatively successful in keeping the focus on ecumenical efforts to alleviate affliction rather than on divisive theological debates. After 1902, however, the disputes became more difficult to ignore—especially when mounting anxieties about racial discord, growing religious diversity due to immigration, and the expanding influences of skepticism and secularism were fueling evangelical fears about the decline of "Christian America."[9]

Within this context, Klopsch and his associates began to pay more attention to doctrinal trends they worried would further erode evangelical authority within American culture. In April 1903, for example, the *Christian Herald* published an editorial lamenting "the modern tendency to a loose theology, and a grave departure from recognized standards of religious belief" among prominent clergymen such as Dr. Heber Newton, pastor of Stanford University's Memorial Church. By naming Newton as a purveyor of a pernicious pantheism whose "perversion of sacred truths" deserved "to be condemned from every pulpit," the newspaper departed from its long-standing policies of refraining from personal attacks against fellow Christians and maintaining impartiality in theological quarrels. A year later, in April 1904, the *Christian Herald*'s editors reiterated their concerns about the "fast-and-loose orthodoxy" of preachers who were abandoning essential doctrines such as "the miracles . . . the Divinity of Jesus, the Atonement and even the personality of

God himself." "It is time to call a halt in the tendency to too great a tolerance toward such offenders," the editorial proclaimed. "Vital error, once detected, should be vigorously dealt with."[10]

Even as Klopsch and his colleagues became more prosecutorial, they still assumed that the common objective of alleviating suffering from famine and other calamities would create solidarity among believers of diverse theological positions. In a 1905 editorial, they reminded readers that the *Christian Herald* had "demonstrated by the enterprises of benevolence and relief it has inaugurated, that Christians of all denominations" could unite "without distinction of creed, to feed the starving, to relieve the destitute, and to succor the widow and fatherless." This proven success, they argued, ought to inspire confidence that American evangelicals would continue to find common ground through the newspaper's charitable ventures as well as through new ecumenical organizations such as the recently formed Federal Council of Churches.[11]

With each passing year, however, maintaining harmony through humanitarianism became more challenging as proponents of divergent theological positions advanced opposing agendas. By 1908, debates among differing Protestant factions began to focus directly on whether charity ought to play a central role in evangelical practice. Because advocates of the "new theology" envisioned a more "advanced" form of Christianity, for example, they often recommended that conventional approaches to spreading the gospel through preaching be abandoned in favor of modern methods that replaced proselytizing with educational or economic development projects and stressed the essential unity of all the world's religions.[12]

Although Klopsch and his colleagues had always argued that providing material assistance to needy people across the globe was an integral part of the missionary enterprise, they rejected the idea that humanitarian aid could ever take the place of traditional evangelism. When a group of University of Chicago professors published a series of articles attacking "jungle preaching" and proposing that "biological and electrical laboratory work" offered a more effective mode of making connections with people of other faiths, the *Christian Herald* responded with a scathing editorial lambasting the "Chicago fulmination" and defending the "time-honored" practice of "preaching the simple Gospel to the heathen."[13]

At first, the *Christian Herald*'s spirited rejoinder to the new theology resonated with readers who had for many years embraced the message that providing for the physical needs of suffering people was essential to proselytizing. But as the furor over theological modernism intensified, some evangelicals struggled to hold together the long-standing synthesis between caring for bodies and converting souls. As prominent modernist spokespeople continued to proclaim the primacy of ethics over doctrine, and philanthropy over preaching, champions of traditional orthodoxy felt increasingly compelled to stress the importance of "the plain old Gospel." Although a few ministers, such as Christian and Missionary Alliance (CMA) founder A. B. Simpson, had been arguing for years that "humanitarian schemes, social reforms, worthy charities, educational institutions," and similar efforts were not essential to salvation or to the evangelization of the world, after the turn of the century many more evangelical leaders expressed doubts about the effectiveness of benevolent enterprises as a strategy for spreading the gospel.[14]

Some ministers even began to question whether philanthropic endeavors were more a hindrance than a help to the spiritual work of the church. In a book entitled *Evangelism: Old and New* (1905), the Reverend A. C. Dixon—a longtime supporter of the *Christian Herald*'s relief campaigns—observed that all the energy evangelicals had invested in "ministering to the bodies of people" over the past twenty-five years had been largely futile if measured in terms of drawing souls to Christ. As a means to the end of making converts, he contended, humanitarian work was "often a dismal failure." Based on these assessments, Dixon recommended that evangelicals refocus their efforts on preaching "the doctrine of the atonement and individual conversion" rather than continuing to waste resources on charitable activities such as "buying clothes and food, sending children to the country for fresh air, ministering to the sick and paying rent." Over the next several years, Dixon became increasingly involved in the emerging fundamentalist movement that sought to defend classic Protestant theology against modernist attempts to reduce the Christian faith to "moral culture and humanitarian activity." As the initial editor of a collection of ninety essays entitled *The Fundamentals: A Testimony of Truth*—the first volume of which appeared in February 1910, just a few weeks before Klopsch's passing—Dixon commissioned contributions that reaffirmed traditional doctrines such as the Virgin Birth, criticized the "fallacies of the Higher Criticism," and urged American Protestants to prioritize "personal evangelism" over "humanitarian, educational and socialistic matters."[15]

Fundamentalist complaints that philanthropy distracted from the "earnest work for the salvation of souls" had a profound effect on evangelical missions at home and abroad during the early twentieth century. For decades, both denominational agencies and benevolent organizations like the YMCA, the Salvation Army, and the *Christian Herald* had encouraged missionaries to provide medical care, academic instruction, and industrial training for potential converts throughout the United States and around the world. Recognizing that local populations were often eager to access these resources, missionaries and their supporters believed that offering services could open "the hearts of the natives to the Gospel."[16]

In foreign fields like Armenia, India, and China, where violence and natural disaster had left thousands destitute and homeless, caring for survivors had become an essential component of the missionary enterprise. With the help of the *Christian Herald*'s "adoption" campaigns, missionaries had established orphanages, medical clinics, schools, and industrial training centers in all these regions—as well as in the U.S. colonies of Puerto Rico, Guam, and the Philippines. When fundamentalists like Dixon raised doubts about the effectiveness of these institutions in converting the "heathen" to Christ, however, some evangelical agencies began to shift resources away from humanitarian enterprises. In 1908, for example, A. B. Simpson announced that the CMA was reducing its orphanage and industrial missions in India in favor of "emphasizing more and more the evangelistic and aggressive lines of missionary work among the adult masses." Even as he acknowledged that caring for needy children in the wake of the devastating famines had accomplished great things, Simpson insisted it was time for the CMA to focus on preaching the gospel rather than continuing humanitarian work.[17]

Although the *Christian Herald* remained committed to the orphans subscribers had pledged to support following the food shortages in India at the turn of the century, Klopsch and his associates began to emphasize the primacy of preaching in response to critiques of educational and industrial missions from colleagues like Dixon and Simpson. Alongside the newspaper's ongoing campaigns to care for famine sufferers in Japan (1906) and China (1907), Klopsch announced a new venture enabling readers to sponsor a "trained Christian native—preacher, teacher, evangelist, Bible woman" to serve as their substitutes in spreading the gospel among local communities across the globe. Although Klopsch continued to raise support for disaster relief and educational institutions during the last several years of his life, his willingness to allocate significant resources to more conventional missionary work suggests that fundamentalists were gaining ground in reorienting evangelical priorities away from humanitarian endeavors.[18]

These changes in the philosophy and practice of foreign missions caused consternation among many of the *Christian Herald*'s overseas partners. American missionaries who had benefited from the newspaper's ongoing sponsorship of their educational, medical, and industrial efforts worried about declining enthusiasm for these forms of evangelical outreach. Local leaders like Pandita Ramabai, who had always depended on financial backing from Western donors to keep their institutions afloat, feared that a loss of funding would undermine the credibility of Christian organizations—especially among skeptics who had been suspicious of foreign motives from the beginning. How would Ramabai explain to the girls in the Mukti Mission—or to her Hindu critics—that the American Christians who had promised to nurture both body and soul would no longer provide for their physical well-being? Surely such an outcome would cast Christianity in a terrible light and further stymie efforts to spread the gospel through evangelism alone.[19]

As anxieties about the long-term viability of overseas missionary institutions increased tensions between foreign workers and American funders, another transnational debate threatened to disrupt the evangelical solidarity Klopsch was striving to maintain through the *Christian Herald*'s humanitarian campaigns. In May 1906, the newspaper published an account of a remarkable revival that had begun in Wales in 1904. After spreading to India, where Welsh missionaries were working among the Khasi hill people of Assam, it eventually reached Ramabai's Mukti Mission in June 1905, when several young women experienced "a wonderful visitation of the Holy Spirit." During the following months, prayer meetings took place at all hours, hundreds experienced conviction of sin and repentance followed by an "infilling of the Spirit and great joy," and many new converts were baptized.[20]

CHRISTIAN HERALD

COPYRIGHT 1906 BY LOUIS KLOPSCH

SUBSCRIPTION, $1.50 PER ANNUM
PUBLISHED 52 TIMES A YEAR

NEW YORK, MAY 16, 1906

VOL. 29—NO. 20. PRICE 5 CENTS
OFFICES: BIBLE HOUSE, NEW YORK

PHOTOGRAPHED FOR THE CHRISTIAN HERALD

SEE PAGE 436

A Widow of Pandita Ramabai's Mission Preaching the Gospel to Villagers of India

A widow of Pandita Ramabai's mission preaching during India's pentecostal revival. From the *Christian Herald,* May 16, 1906, cover. Courtesy of the Christian Herald Association, New York.

These features of the Indian revival were all fairly conventional, but there were other aspects of the "outpouring of the Holy Ghost in Pentecostal power" that engendered controversy. "In Assam and India," one chronicler observed, the revivals were "accompanied with manifestations of the Holy Spirit," which included dramatic emotional and bodily responses such as "trembling under the power of conviction, loud crying in prayer, . . . sudden falling on the ground, writhing, being twisted and violently thrown down, . . . shouting, dancing, and losing strength as under an 'exceeding weight of glory.'" Some participants even became unconscious, while others were "convulsed" by burning and tingling sensations. Although Ramabai and her associates defended the "strange ways" as the mysterious work of a sovereign God, detractors countered that such displays of religious excitement were the result of fanaticism or perhaps even possession by an evil spirit.[21]

As news of the revivals in Wales and India spread around the world, many more communities began to experience the "baptism of the Holy Ghost with fire." Churches and missionary centers in Korea, Australia, China, Latin America, Europe, and the United States reported similar outpourings of God's spirit, all marked by intense ecstatic experiences. Although many evangelicals expressed hope that these revivals represented the long-awaited global awakening they had been praying for, critics continued to question their legitimacy and decry the dangers of mistaking "hysterical manifestations for divine power."[22]

The dispute between proponents and detractors became even more rancorous when some American revival leaders began to argue that one particular experience—speaking in tongues—was a necessary evidence of Holy Spirit baptism. According to this view, those who failed to receive "the gift of tongues" had not been blessed with the fullness of God's sanctifying presence. By early 1907, this debate was fueling conflict among numerous evangelical communities. Organizations such as the CMA, with which the *Christian Herald* had close ties both at home and abroad, were torn apart over the issue. Eventually, supporters of the "evidentiary tongues" position broke with the CMA and other denominations that disagreed with this doctrine to form new organizations such as the Assemblies of God.[23]

In the midst of the controversy, the *Christian Herald* tried to maintain a middle ground in hopes of preserving evangelical unity. "Far be it from us to decry any manifestation of the Holy Spirit," the editors wrote in April 1907. Although they hesitated to criticize the revival, Klopsch and his colleagues simultaneously stressed the need for care when assessing recent claims about prophesying and speaking in tongues. Because "the human mind is treacherous and the possibility of self-deception is unlimited and the contagion of excitement is very great," they counseled, "caution is imperative, lest the subjects of the movement suffer harm and do harm to others, by bringing religion into ridicule." Rather than denouncing the revivals too hastily or embracing them uncritically, Klopsch and his associates urged readers to wait and see whether the "strange ecstasy" produced Christian love and "consecration to service" among participants.[24]

Several months later, however, the editors had become increasingly concerned that the pentecostal movement had sown dissension and discord, instead of generating peace and harmony, among evangelical communities across the globe. Although they still refrained from condemning the revivals altogether, Klopsch and his coworkers warned readers that the expanding movement was "full of grave dangers." By granting "undue prominence" to dramatic spiritual displays such as "prostrations or visible, audible manifestations," they suggested, some proponents of pentecostal revivals were creating a division between those who spoke in tongues and others who had not yet been baptized with the Holy Spirit.[25]

Not only did the stress on ecstatic experiences give rise to "a censorious spirit and to a vainglorious idea of superiority" among those who participated in the revivals, they argued, but the focus on subjectivity also fostered a self-indulgent spirituality that prioritized the individual over the community. Most often, the editors observed, those who spoke in tongues during worship services uttered "a torrent of words, incomprehensible and unintelligible to the hearers." Because these proclamations were rarely interpreted, it was impossible for the congregation to receive inspiration from them. "No one is benefited by hearing shrieks and ravings which have no intelligible meaning. It is not so that God speaks to men," the editors declared. Since "God is not the author of confusion, but of edification," they concluded, the *Christian Herald*'s readers had every reason to remain wary of the pentecostal movement and to resist its pernicious effects on evangelical charity.[26]

Despite criticisms from the *Christian Herald* and other evangelical organizations, however, pentecostalism continued to expand exponentially during the early years of the twentieth century (and indeed throughout the coming decades). As participants in the revivals withdrew from churches that rejected ecstatic spirituality or beliefs about the necessity of speaking in tongues, they established new denominations, missionary organizations, and publications through which they pursued their distinctive goals. In many cases, these agencies raised funds for missionaries who felt called to spread the pentecostal message to the ends of the earth. Given their conviction that the revivals were a sign of Christ's imminent return, many participants in the movement insisted that aggressive preaching was the primary responsibility of the spirit-filled evangelist. At the same time, some influential pentecostals such as Pandita Ramabai had always stressed the importance of meeting both the physical and spiritual needs of potential converts. As a result, periodicals such as Ramabai's *Mukti Prayer Bell,* the *Latter Rain Evangel* (published by a prominent pentecostal church in Chicago), *Triumphs of Faith,* and the *Pentecostal Evangel* (the official organ of the Assemblies of God) also collected money for humanitarian relief during times of disaster. Although none of these publications rivaled the *Christian Herald* in circulation or influence, they did contribute to fracturing the evangelical coalition Klopsch had worked so hard to build, drawing subscribers and resources away from his enterprise.

FOUNDATION PHILANTHROPY AND THE FATE OF EVANGELICAL CHARITY

By the time of Klopsch's passing in 1910, frictions among modernists, fundamentalists, and pentecostals had created rifts in the evangelical community that would only widen in the coming years. Maintaining the *Christian Herald*'s place as a preeminent provider of international humanitarianism and domestic charity became increasingly difficult as a result. In addition to contending with internal tensions that destabilized evangelical solidarity, Koenig and Sandison faced external challenges to the newspaper's position as one of the nation's foremost aid agencies, especially from proponents of organized philanthropy committed to creating large-scale, professional relief and development organizations.

Just days before Klopsch's death, for example, a bill to incorporate the Rockefeller Foundation was brought before the U.S. Senate. According to the proposed legislation, the objective of this philanthropic corporation was "to promote the well-being and to advance the civilization of the United States and its Territories and possessions and of foreign lands in the acquisition and dissemination of knowledge; in the prevention and relief of suffering; and in the promotion of any and all of the elements of human progress." By devoting their colossal fortune to this enterprise, the Rockefellers aimed to create "the largest, richest foundation in the world . . . national and international in scope—America's first global foundation." Although Congress declined to approve the bill because of concerns the proposal represented "an indefinite scheme for perpetuating vast wealth," the Rockefellers eventually gained a charter for their charity through the New York State legislature in May 1913. During the first year, the Rockefellers transferred $100 million to the trust (approximately $2.5 billion in 2017); in 1919, they added another $82.8 million ($1.17 billion in 2017). By the 1920s, several historians of the organization have noted, "the Rockefeller Foundation had become the largest philanthropic enterprise in the world."[27]

Despite efforts to carry forward Klopsch's ambition "to make the *Christian Herald* not merely the most widely circulated of religious journals but the greatest power for good in the whole world," Koenig and Sandison could not compete with charitable organizations established by multimillionaires like the Rockefellers, Andrew Carnegie (whose foundation received congressional approval in 1911), and Olivia Sage. When they heard about Rockefeller's proposal to donate his massive fortune to a family trust, the editors admitted this was likely to become "the greatest scheme of philanthropy ever known in human history." Although the *Christian Herald* continued soliciting funds for humanitarian relief both at home and abroad, the amounts collected paled in comparison to the hundreds of millions that poured into charitable foundations from wealthy donors. By 1928, for example, Sandison proudly reported that the *Christian Herald* had raised and distributed $8 million for the needy in all parts of the world since Klopsch's first campaign to assist starving Russians in the winter of 1891–1892. The Rockefeller Foundation's annual report for 1928, by contrast, showed that receipts and disbursements for just the previous twelve months totaled more than $28 million and that the general fund closed the year with a balance of over $150 million.[28]

With such vast financial resources at their disposal, the officers of large philanthropic corporations profoundly influenced both foreign aid and domestic charity in the years following Klopsch's death. As early as 1914, for example, the recently incorporated Rockefeller Foundation began to support ARC leaders' ongoing bid to become the United States' only official international relief agency. With the outbreak of World War I, several of the foundation's trustees joined State Department officials in urging the ARC to help civilians across the European continent who were suffering as a result of hostilities. Although Mabel Boardman and her associates agreed that the ARC ought to take charge of all the nation's overseas aid enterprises, they initially limited the organization's work to attending wounded soldiers. Until the ARC could attract more members, employ more staff, and raise more money, the agency would have to leave the assistance of noncombatants to other humanitarian organizations.[29]

Taking advantage of this situation, Koenig and Sandison opened the *Christian Herald* Relief Fund for the Widows and Orphans of the War in Europe on September 16, 1914. By the time they closed the campaign in 1920, subscribers had contributed $446,391. Meanwhile, however, government officials and private philanthropists continued to implore the ARC to take charge of the civilian aid effort. To facilitate this outcome, President Woodrow Wilson worked with the ARC Executive Council to reorganize the agency's leadership and expand its membership. In October 1915, Wilson asked his former rival William Taft to resume the position of ARC chairman (a role Taft had relinquished upon Wilson's election). Taft agreed and immediately devoted himself to bolstering public support for the ARC's work among noncombatants in Europe.[30]

Over the next several years, and especially after the United States officially entered the conflict, Taft's efforts paid off: The ARC's membership grew from 22,500 in 1915 to over twenty million by 1920. During this period, the agency collected more than $400 million for its war-time relief initiatives through intensive fund-raising campaigns, as well as from wealthy donors such as financier J. P. Morgan, who contributed $100,000 to the ARC's endowment, and the Rockefeller Foundation, which gave over $8 million. With these resources, the organization employed more than 12,700 professional staff members in twenty-five countries who put in place a vast infrastructure for providing assistance to soldiers and civilians. These staggering figures show that the ARC had finally and definitively succeeded in eclipsing all other organizations—including the *Christian Herald*—as the nation's most popular, recognized, and well-endowed foreign aid agency.[31]

Within ten years of Klopsch's death, evangelical almsgivers were forced to concede leadership of the U.S. overseas humanitarian mission to the organization that had embraced and benefited from the federalization of foreign aid, the corporatization of philanthropy, the professionalization of relief work, and the secularization of charity. This combination of conditions, historians of the ARC have argued, made the agency well suited to "effectively serve and symbolize the American commitment to alleviating civilian suffering abroad" from World War I onward. Although the *Christian Herald* conducted one final relief campaign to assist famine victims in China during the winter of 1920–1921, the editors subsequently focused most of their attention on supporting the newspaper's domestic philanthropies and preserving "the vitality of America's religious life."[32]

According to a 1928 retrospective celebrating the publication's history, the *Christian Herald*'s signature charities—including the Mayesville Educational and Industrial Institute, the Mont-Lawn Children's Home, and the Bowery Mission—continued to flourish after Klopsch's passing, despite ongoing criticism from proponents of scientific philanthropy and professionalized social work. In fact, Sandison reported in the *Christian Herald*'s anniversary issue, contributions to these institutions had increased significantly since Klopsch's death. Between 1910 and 1928, for example, donations to the children's home averaged $43,407 per year, whereas during Klopsch's lifetime subscribers gave about $17,319 annually.[33]

In the coming years, Sandison indicated, the *Christian Herald* would carry on these benevolent enterprises while emphasizing the important mission of offering readers "spiritual guidance and inspiration for meeting their everyday problems." Although he looked back with great pride on the *Christian Herald*'s past and particularly on the publication's unparalleled record of charity to the needy in many lands, Sandison suggested a new leadership team—editor in chief Dr. Daniel A. Poling (minister of the Marble Collegiate Church in Manhattan) and president J. C. Penney (the department store magnate)—would be taking the periodical in a different direction. Certainly, the many international humanitarian enterprises conducted during and after Klopsch's tenure as proprietor "represent an important and dramatic phase of the magazine's activities," Sandison concluded, "but after all they were only a part of the *Christian Herald*'s ministry, which reached into hundreds of thousands of homes." Moving forward, Poling and Penney would concentrate primarily on the domestic arena, aiming to "make the magazine more than ever before a powerful constructive force in the religious life of America" by publishing articles designed "to diffuse the principles and teachings of the Christian religion."[34]

This more narrowly focused vision served the *Christian Herald* well over the next several decades. After Poling and Penney took charge, the journal's circulation expanded significantly, reaching nearly a half million subscribers in the mid-twentieth century. Despite continued bickering among the fundamentalist, modernist, and pentecostal factions of the evangelical movement, the *Christian Herald* was able to maintain a solid market share among American Protestants well into the 1960s. By the time Poling retired from his editorial post in 1965, historian Martin Marty observed, the *Christian Herald* had become "the most successful 'mass' magazine in Protestant independent circles." During its peak decades from the 1930s through the early 1960s, another scholar of evangelical media has noted, the *Christian Herald* "was frequently mentioned in the same company with other mass audience general magazines like *Life*."[35]

Although Poling and his associates gave thanks for the *Christian Herald*'s expanding influence and its ongoing support of domestic charities, they sometimes sounded wistful when reflecting on Klopsch's accomplishments in the realm of foreign relief. Although subscribers continued to sponsor an orphanage in Fuzhou, China, through at least the mid-twentieth century, the periodical's international stature had declined substantially since Klopsch's passing. "During his proprietorship the *Christian Herald* became the most influential religious journal in the world," Poling wrote in 1938. "Coincident with his passing," he continued, "came the twilight of personal journalism all over this country. Publications which were dependent upon the popularity of some great editor were doomed to slow death, unless they found some formula which of itself was popular. Hence great changes took place in the character and content of all publications." For the *Christian Herald*, these adjustments involved abandoning Klopsch's crusade to make the periodical "a medium through which the woes of mankind could be given voice and so be rectified" by evangelical almsgivers.[36]

Without their "modern knight of mercy" leading the charge to liberate the captives, promote freedom from oppression, and ameliorate misery across the globe, Klopsch's successors soon gave up the fight to maintain the *Christian Herald*'s position as a leading provider of foreign assistance. Although this strategy made sense given ongoing evangelical wrangling over the value of charitable enterprises in Christian outreach as well as the determination of government agencies and corporate philanthropies to dominate overseas relief and development, Poling and his colleagues seemed to regret relinquishing the field of international aid to competing organizations. As the prestige and influence of agencies like the ARC and the Rockefeller Foundation grew, their successes cast the *Christian Herald*'s significant contributions to the history of global humanitarianism further into the shadows.

By the late 1960s, changes in both the publishing industry and the non-profit sector had begun to erode the *Christian Herald*'s ability to alleviate affliction in the United States. Increasing competition from other religious periodicals and philanthropic organizations caused a decline in advertising revenues, circulation, and donations to the *Christian Herald*'s charities. The financial pressures became even more acute during the 1970s and 1980s, causing hardship at the Bowery Mission and the children's home, which had moved from Nyack to the Pocono Mountains in 1963. In an attempt to salvage the two institutions, the directors of the Christian Herald Association (CHA) ceased publication of the periodical in 1992 and directed their energies to the organization's core mission of ministering to the homeless, the hungry, and at-risk youth in New York City.[37]

With new leadership in place after 1994, the CHA solicited funding from thousands of individuals, dozens of philanthropic foundations, several large corporations, and two government agencies. These resources enabled the organization to renovate facilities at the Bowery Mission, transform and expand the children's ministry to include year-round services, open new residential programs for substance abuse recovery, and provide free medical services and employment training for its clients and community. By 2015, the CHA had become "one of New York's most respected and effective charities," with more than one hundred employees, thousands of volunteers, and $15 million in combined revenue.[38]

The successful revival of the Christian Herald Association at the turn of the twenty-first century reveals the resiliency of evangelical almsgiving from Klopsch's time to our own day. Despite fierce competition from bigger and better-resourced relief agencies, forceful criticisms from proponents of scientific philanthropy, and fractious dissension among their own constituents about the purpose and proper practice of aiding the afflicted, several of the *Christian Herald*'s signature charities have survived for over one hundred and twenty years. During Klopsch's funeral services, many of his admirers prophesied that the "great works that he inaugurated" would thrive for years to come. "The deep impression he made on his own generation," his biographer wrote, "rendered it certain that his influence would continue and endure." Although Klopsch's remarkable career as a "twentieth century captain of philanthropy" has been largely overlooked, his forays into the fields of international relief and domestic charity have profoundly shaped the landscape of American almsgiving both at home and abroad in the decades since his death.[39]

EPILOGUE

On a glorious summer day in July 2017, I sat across from Reverend Jason Storbakken, the director of Chapel and Compassionate Care at the Bowery Mission. Sunlight streamed into Jason's second-story office through stained-glass windows depicting the parable of the prodigal son. Downstairs, residents and guests of the Mission were coming in off the street for the midday meal. As Jason and I discussed our mutual interest in the *Christian Herald*'s history, he shared stories about former superintendents whose photographs hung on the walls and showed me his collection of first-edition volumes from the Christian Herald library—including a copy of *Life-work of Louis Klopsch: Romance of a Modern Knight of Mercy*. Knowing that I was finishing a book about Klopsch's humanitarian enterprises, Jason asked me what I thought of the man. What was he like as a person? Could I say anything about his character?

Before I could respond, a disturbance broke out in the chapel. While Jason went down to see what was happening, I considered how I would answer his questions. Over the course of my research, I had received many similar queries. Almost everyone with whom I discussed this project wanted to hear my opinion about Klopsch and Talmage. Were these men as trustworthy as they claimed, or were their critics right to suggest their financial dealings be subjected to greater scrutiny? Did their relief campaigns reflect sincere concern for suffering people, or were the sensational media events motivated by a desire for fame and fortune? How should we assess the fact that they seemed to abandon their cosmopolitan ethics or pacifist principles as soon as the tide of public opinion shifted in another direction? Was Talmage really innocent of "falsehood and deceit," or was he always a mountebank with something to hide? Did Klopsch truly transform from a duplicitous convert to a "modern knight of mercy," or did he remain a hustler with a talent for telling tall tales?

Some of my conversation partners—like Jason—framed their inquiries in a more open-ended fashion: asking for insight, rather than seeking a verdict. But others pushed me to take a stand: Were the evangelical almsgivers at the helm of the *Christian Herald* saints or sinners? Do these men deserve admiration for the tremendous good they accomplished or condemnation for having overlooked, hidden, or even caused terrible harm? To these interlocutors, I can say only that I believe history has more than two sides and that the people who live it are far more complex than such simple dualisms allow.

Rather than passing judgment on the past or its protagonists, my aim has been to present Klopsch, Talmage, and their many coworkers not as altruistic heroes, nor as unscrupulous villains, but as human beings whose experiences, achievements, and failures offer opportunities to reflect on the enduring challenges of alleviating affliction, combating poverty, and creating a more just global society. At the Bowery Mission, these goals remain at the forefront of the organization's daily programs, outreach operations, and plans for the future. How does the *Christian Herald*'s history continue to shape these efforts? Do the sensibilities about suffering and the practices of helping that the publication promoted during its heyday still hold sway among evangelical almsgivers?

What lasting influences have Klopsch, Talmage, and their associates had on the fields of domestic philanthropy and international aid? And what are the implications of their legacy for the ethics and practice of Christian charity in the present? These are questions I hope *Holy Humanitarians* can help answer.

THE *CHRISTIAN HERALD*'S ENDURING INFLUENCE

As I waited for Jason to return, I watched as hungry men and women came through the doors of the Bowery Mission. Within minutes, the lunchroom was full. Volunteers who had spent the last few hours preparing food moved quickly to serve the crowd. Some of the guests would ask to take a shower after eating; others would stay the night in the shelter or come back on Wednesday evening for free medical care.

Klopsch's legacy—with all of its ambiguities—continues among the women and men who strive to provide "holistic recovery" and "life transformation for hurting people in New York City" through "simple act[s] of kindness." Like their predecessor, many of the Bowery Mission's staff have dedicated themselves to serving others after having experienced adversity themselves. Some have struggled with drug and alcohol addiction, others have spent time in prison, and most can tell stories of dramatic personal transformation through encounters with Jesus Christ.[1]

Beyond the Bowery Mission and Kids with a Promise (the new name of the Christian Herald Association's children's charities), many contemporary evangelicals are carrying forward Klopsch's humanitarian mission through myriad efforts to alleviate distress on a global scale. Although the *Christian Herald* effectively withdrew from the arena of international aid after World War I, a new generation of evangelicals reengaged in overseas disaster relief during and after World War II. In 1944, the National Association of Evangelicals established a commission to send food and clothing to survivors in battle-torn Europe. Renamed World Relief in 1950, this organization was the first of several evangelical agencies founded to alleviate suffering in the aftermath of global conflict.[2]

Over the next several decades, World Relief, Compassion International, and especially World Vision—the largest Christian humanitarian organization in the world by the turn of the twenty-first century—increased in size and scope. The growth of these and other religious philanthropies was driven in part by federal policies that encouraged charitable giving and channeled government resources to nonprofit organizations through grants and contracts. During the 1950s and 1960s, changes in the tax code and government spending practices fueled an exponential expansion of new charities and humanitarian agencies striving to alleviate affliction. Scholars have estimated that over 90 percent of today's nonprofits were founded during the second half of the twentieth century.[3]

Some of the best known philanthropies established after World War II are large private foundations created by wealthy donors: the Pew Charitable Trusts and the Bill and Melinda Gates Foundation, for example. Although these prominent organizations (along with older ones like the Carnegie, Rockefeller, and Ford Foundations) have frequently been the primary focus of both public and academic conversations about philanthropy, they comprise only a fraction of the charitable agencies at work since the mid-twentieth century. Statistics indicate that there were approximately 100,000 private foundations registered with the federal government in 2016, compared with almost 1.2 million public nonprofits.[4]

As scholars such as David King have recently shown, thousands of these public charities are grassroots agencies, and nearly 40 percent are faith-based organizations with a spiritual basis to their mission. Indeed, King contends, religious charities like the Salvation Army and evangelical humanitarian agencies such as World Vision (found in 1950) and Samaritan's Purse (established in 1972) "are among the largest NGOs in the country with billion dollar budgets." All of these aid organizations (like most public nonprofits) receive federal funding for their social service, relief, and development work through the White House Office of Faith-Based and Neighborhood Partnerships, USAID, and other government channels. The bulk of their support, however, comes from ordinary citizens who donate money, purchase items at charity auctions, and volunteer countless hours serving at soup kitchens, packing disaster relief kits, or tending the sick on medical mission trips. Despite the perceived dominance of professionalized secular foundations or government agencies in the fields of domestic philanthropy and global aid, the kind of popular evangelical charity Klopsch and his colleagues promoted through the *Christian Herald* remains a powerful force in contemporary American society.[5]

Over the past one hundred years, the *Christian Herald*'s influence on humanitarianism has extended well beyond the arena of religious relief organizations. The groundbreaking visual technologies, narrative strategies, and fund-raising tactics Klopsch employed to inspire sympathy for distant sufferers, for example, became standard practices in the twentieth-century aid industry. A number of competing evangelical journals had already begun to employ some of these approaches before Klopsch's passing. With the spread of pentecostalism, new periodicals like the *Latter Rain Evangel* also adopted the now-familiar methods to arouse compassion for strangers in distress during times of draught, famine, flood, and war.[6]

Even state-sponsored agencies such as the American Red Cross (ARC) began to embrace the innovative journalistic and photographic techniques that the *Christian Herald* first made popular. Just a few years after Klopsch's death, the ARC hired an agent to transform its quarterly bulletin into "an interesting, instructive, attractively illustrated humanitarian publication." During World War I, the *American National Red Cross Magazine* included graphic accounts of civilian suffering in Europe and more images of the conditions of misery than ever before. By the close of the conflict, ARC leaders were convinced that describing and depicting the afflictions of distant strangers was a most effective strategy for fund-raising and membership recruitment—just as Klopsch and his colleagues at the *Christian Herald* had shown several decades earlier. "The magazine is one of the most powerful agencies in forwarding the objects for which the American Red Cross stands," one prominent official wrote in 1919.[7]

Scholars such as Kevin Rozario have confirmed that the ARC's deliberate efforts to dramatize suffering through "sensational tales and spectacular images" played a pivotal role in the rapid and successful expansion of the agency during the second decade of the twentieth century. More broadly, Rozario has argued, the widespread circulation of stories and displays of misery in media such as the *American Red Cross Magazine* helped make modern philanthropy a mass phenomenon in those years. It was precisely through marketing the "appeal of the appalling," he contends, that humanitarianism became entrenched as an ideal and as a practice within American culture.[8]

By pioneering "pictorial humanitarianism" during the disasters of the 1890s, the *Christian Herald* built what Rozario has called "the social and emotional scaffolding" of the twentieth-century charity industry. Klopsch's relentless rhetorical and visual campaign to make "Christian America" the "Almoner to Nations in Distress" also had a lasting effect on humanitarian sentiments and habits in the decades following his death. Through their insistence that the United States was divinely ordained and therefore uniquely qualified to uplift the downtrodden, unshackle the oppressed, and become the world's "most generous benefactor in times of famine, plague, flood and earthquake," Klopsch and his colleagues fostered an enduring faith in the myth of American exceptionalism.[9]

The *Christian Herald*'s June 1901 cover illustration "America, the Almoner of the World" depicted the United States as a noble, magnanimous savior who alone possessed the power and resources to aid suffering people around the globe. Within a few years, the ARC had begun to incorporate strikingly similar images into its ostensibly secular publications. The drawing on the cover of the ARC *Bulletin* for July 1910, for example, bears a remarkable resemblance to the *Christian Herald*'s iconic figure from June 1901: a regal woman with outstretched arms offers shelter to both soldiers and victims of natural disaster. Depictions of the ARC as "Protector in War and Peace" (1909), as a "Protecting Angel" (1918), and perhaps most famously as "the Greatest Mother in the World" (1918)—an image reminiscent of Michelangelo's *Pietà*—became increasingly popular during World War I when the ARC was working to consolidate its status as the country's only official relief agency. Illustrations like these, several scholars have argued, conveyed not only the message that the ARC was *the* aid organization to which all patriotic citizens should contribute but also that the United States had both a duty and the capacity to save the world's suffering people through humanitarian intervention in foreign conflicts.[10]

These assumptions about the nation's responsibility to help distant strangers continued to influence American foreign policy throughout the twentieth and twenty-first centuries. From World War I to the Iraq War and beyond, the United States' development as a global power has often been premised on belief in the country's special obligation and singular ability to aid the afflicted and advance the rights of humanity. While critics—including some evangelicals—have questioned the ethics of empire and intervention, many Americans have embraced the image of the United States as a nation specially commissioned by God to rescue and protect the world's oppressed and needy people. Even those who have expressed reservations about characterizing military invasion as a form of

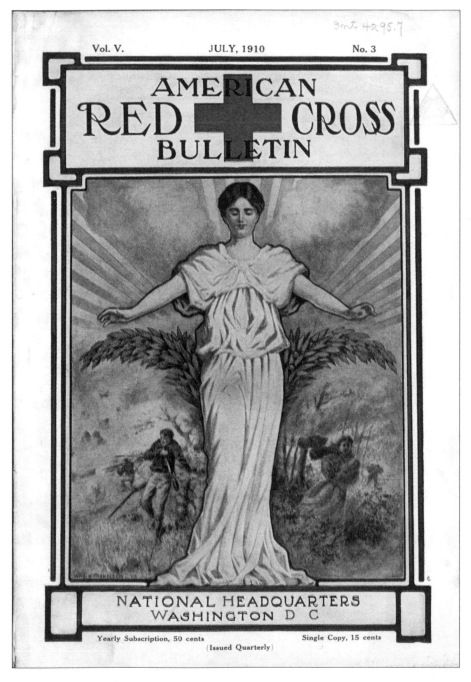

9mt 4295.7

Vol. V.   JULY, 1910   No. 3

AMERICAN RED ✚ CROSS BULLETIN

NATIONAL HEADQUARTERS
WASHINGTON D C

Yearly Subscription, 50 cents   Single Copy, 15 cents
(Issued Quarterly)

American Red Cross Bulletin cover, July 1910. Courtesy of Widener Library,
Harvard University.

humanitarian mission, or who have worried about the entanglement of almsgiving with American imperialism, have occasionally commended decisions to deploy the armed forces to provide disaster assistance both within and beyond the nation's borders. This support for the U.S. military's emergency relief activities stems in part from the broader conviction—championed by the *Christian Herald* and furthered by the ARC and other charitable organizations—that aiding sufferers is the best and most benevolent means of advancing American ideals, interests, and influence at home and abroad.[11]

Certainly not all Americans have embraced the idea that the United States is an exceptionally philanthropic nation duty-bound to alleviate distress within and beyond its borders. Even so, the proliferation of charitable agencies over the past half-century suggests that many Americans believe aiding the afflicted is a moral imperative. "Our entire society upholds the wonderful value that helping others is a big part of the American character," one observer recently declared. According to polling data, "more than 90 percent of Americans believe that it is 'important to be personally involved in supporting a cause we believe in' in their communities and in the world at large."[12]

As these statistics show, and as scholars such as Rosemary Corbett have confirmed, Protestants are not the only ones promoting public service as a "way of life for all Americans." Over the course of the twentieth century, Corbett has argued, religious minorities—Jews, Catholics, and most recently Muslims—have attempted to "demonstrate their Americanness through community and social service endeavors and disaster relief." By conforming to dominant cultural norms of charitable giving, volunteerism, and humanitarian engagement disseminated by Protestants like Klopsch and his colleagues at the *Christian Herald,* marginalized groups have endeavored to showcase their "patriotism, moderation, and community-mindedness" and thereby "gain acceptance in the United States."[13]

Creating a common ethic of service among Americans of all religious, racial, and economic backgrounds has resulted in an outpouring of financial donations, a plethora of philanthropic organizations, and ongoing crusades to liberate the oppressed and succor the suffering both at home and around the globe. By 2011—just over one hundred years after Klopsch's passing—his dream that the United States would be recognized as the most generous nation in the world had come true. Since that year, the World Giving Index has consistently reported that Americans have the highest rate of charitable contributions as a percentage of gross domestic product. Through their monetary gifts and active participation in humanitarian relief efforts, Americans from Klopsch's era to our own time have saved millions of disaster victims from starvation, disease, and death; rescued hundreds of thousands of war orphans and refugees; and provided medical care and education in the world's poorest communities. These benevolent enterprises have offered people of all faiths and no faith opportunities to live out their moral and ethical convictions about the duty to help suffering strangers— whether those tenets come from the Bible, the Torah, the Quran, or other philosophical frameworks.[14]

THE ETHICAL AMBIGUITIES OF AMERICAN AID

While the statistics highlight the impressive accomplishments of American humanitarians in aiding the afflicted, they also risk masking the downside of charitable activity. The story of the *Christian Herald*'s aid enterprises has shown that benevolence has not always been benign, despite the best of intentions. Critics of the "compassion industry"—following in the footsteps of Charles Sheldon, Marcus Fuller, Mark Twain, Ida B. Wells-Barnett, and even Louis Klopsch and Thomas De Witt Talmage themselves in some cases—have consistently called attention to the mixed motivations that drive philanthropic endeavors, to the ways relief efforts can obscure or exacerbate deeper structural injustices, and to the many instances in which even the most altruistic actions have produced distressingly harmful consequences, however inadvertent.

As numerous observers have noted, for example, humanitarian interventions to alleviate suffering in other nations have often made matters worse. By providing assistance to foreign governments in times of emergency, some analysts contend, well-meaning philanthropists have frequently enabled leaders to ignore the underlying causes of affliction. Klopsch and Talmage faced this reproach when they sent relief to famine-stricken Russia. Opponents charged that coming to the rescue of starving peasants allowed the tsar to maintain the regressive land and economic policies that perpetuated poverty and oppression in his domains.[15]

Complaints that aid agencies have provided cover for despotic rulers trying to evade political reform have resurfaced regularly since 1892: Alex de Waal's *Famine Crimes: Politics and the Disaster Relief Industry in Africa* (1997) is one of the most trenchant examples. Michael Ignatieff has similarly asserted that "humanitarian assistance allows the West the illusion that it is doing something," while leaving in place the dynamics of inequality that "more serious political engagement" could address. When philanthropy becomes a "substitute for politics, a sop for hopeful publics," these scholars have argued, relief efforts can have damaging effects among the communities they are designed to help: propping up authoritarian governments, fueling corruption and exploitation, and impeding lasting structural change.[16]

Detractors have also alleged that many so-called humanitarian missions have been implicated in imperialist schemes to advance economic, territorial, and political interests. At the turn of the twentieth century, Charles Sheldon and Mark Twain, along with many of their contemporaries, condemned attempts to characterize the invasion of the Philippines as an expression of Christian charity. Ever since, critics have decried similar efforts to describe empire building as a form of philanthropy.

Particularly since the end of the Cold War, several historians have contended, the United States and other powerful nations have disguised neocolonial ambitions by appearing to defend victims of oppression in order to justify armed intervention in conflicts ranging from Somalia and Kosovo to Afghanistan and Iraq. According to scholars such as Conor Foley and Mahmoud Mamdani, the United States found enthusiastic collaborators among humanitarian nongovernmental organizations (NGOs), many of which abandoned their tradition of neutrality by calling for military action and "even collaborating in invasions and occupations." The history of NGOs' complicity with American imperialism has given both scholars and practitioners of international relief and development pause as they assess the catastrophes that U.S.-backed interventions have wrought around the world.[17]

Angst about the entanglement of humanitarian assistance with American empire has also prompted some philanthropists to reflect critically about the complex and often deeply problematic relationships between charitable organizations and their beneficiaries. As a result, many have acknowledged the damaging effects of what industry insider Peter Buffett dubbed "philanthropic colonialism": the widely shared tendency among Western aid agents to assume that they can "save the day" by "transplanting what worked in one setting directly into another with little regard for culture, geography, or societal norms." This paternalistic approach has resulted not only in ineffective attempts to alleviate distress but also in the destruction of local communities and ways of life in the process of trying to "make a difference."[18]

Although Klopsch and his coworkers were not nearly as concerned about cultural imperialism as their twentieth- and twenty-first-century successors have been, they did believe that relief efforts were best conducted through partnerships with missionaries and indigenous leaders like Pandita Ramabai. The ARC model of sending professional aid workers to distribute supplies in foreign nations where they were unlikely to understand the language, political dynamics, or local conditions, Klopsch argued, was expensive and inefficient. If recent investigations of how the ARC spent 25 percent of the money donated to help survivors after the 2010 Haiti earthquake—almost $125 million—on its internal overhead costs are any indication, Klopsch's concerns have proven prescient.[19]

Over the past several decades, humanitarian agencies like the ARC have also come under scrutiny for employing marketing techniques that reinforce social hierarchies rather than reduce the economic, cultural, or emotional distance between donors and recipients. Although the heart-rending appeals and graphic images of suffering that the *Christian Herald* pioneered have succeeded in generating financial support for countless relief enterprises since the late nineteenth century, they have accomplished this goal, some critics have argued, at the expense of exoticizing distant others, fetishizing affliction, and perpetuating "a set of power relations where the 'victim' is a passive recipient of aid from the heroic aid organization." Pictures of bodies in pain, political scientist Denis Kennedy has shown, often present their subjects as "powerless, helpless" objects "defined not by agency or ability but rather by vulnerability and deficiency." Rather than eliciting empathy (a form of engagement involving identification with one's fellows), these representations risk promoting pity (a response that entails "the feeling of difference" and perhaps even "antipathy" or "appalling disgust"). By working to constitute or maintain disparities between privileged and poor communities, human-itarian marketing campaigns have eroded a sense of shared humanity and responsibility for the common good, foreclosing alternative possi-bilities for cooperation, collaboration, and—in the case of faith-based philanthropies—creating a broader spiritual fellowship that transcends social, economic, ethnic, and national boundaries.[20]

In their enthusiasm for alleviating affliction, aid workers from Klopsch's time to our own have often been oblivious to this darker side of humanitarian imagery. Occasionally, a missionary like Marcus Fuller has bemoaned the moral and political hazards of photographing famine victims. Even less frequently, a reformer such as Pandita Ramabai has advanced an alternative iconography emphasizing mutuality, partner-ship, and equality among sufferers and their benefactors. For most of the twentieth century, however, the sensational appeals popularized by the *Christian Herald* remained dominant.[21]

In the 1980s, images of starving Ethiopians provoked criticism and widespread calls to replace representations of passive victims with pic-tures highlighting the participation, empowerment, and resilience of aid recipients in the process of relief and development. Since that time, some humanitarian agencies have experimented with marketing strategies that shift toward "positive" messaging. Even so, debates about the ethics of representation remain fraught. In the judgment of sociologist Sanna Nis-sinen, controversies over the politics of photography may even distract from what is really at stake for contemporary humanitarian organizations. "Altering representations," Nissinen has argued, "is less complex than combating issues of social inequality, structural violence, and inequality in the distribution of wealth."[22]

How to tackle these more entrenched problems has challenged phi-lanthropists in every era, and the issue has arguably become even more vexing since Klopsch's death in 1910. In fact, some scholars have main-tained that the expansion of the nonprofit sector in the United States over the past century (and particularly since World War II) has exacer-bated, rather than mitigated, the economic and social disparities that many benevolent organizations strive to address. According to Peter Dobkin Hall, changes in tax policies since the 1940s have encouraged charitable giving while allowing for the accumulation and concentration of assets among the richest Americans, resulting in unprecedented wealth and income inequality. The remarkable growth of American philanthropy has therefore come at the expense of the dispossessed and disenfranchised and has forestalled efforts to create a more just society through policies that reduce economic disparity and promote a more equitable distribution of resources.[23]

The dynamics of structural inequality that have intensified in the United States over the past half-century are spread well beyond American borders. As economist Thomas Piketty has demonstrated, wealth and income disparity have been accelerating in developed countries across the world since the mid-1970s. During this period, he and others have argued, policies favoring "patrimonial capitalism"—the preservation of inherited wealth among an increasingly powerful elite class—have resulted in a pattern of asset concentration and income divergence that promises to continue unabated unless governments intervene to reform the global tax system. Meanwhile, by most measures, the gap between rich and poor countries has also grown over the past fifty years.[24]

While billionaire philanthropists have asserted that charity can play a productive role in reducing dynastic wealth and alleviating global inequality, their opponents have countered that humanitarian aid has abetted and aggravated the very problems it purports to resolve. Critics of the "charitable-industrial complex"—another term coined by Peter Buffett—contend that this "massive business" is designed to enable affluent donors to ease their guilty consciences about continued asset accumulation without actually challenging the economic structures that produce poverty and inequality. "The rich sleep better at night, while others get just enough to keep the pot from boiling over," Buffett wrote in a 2013 opinion piece for the *New York Times.* "Nearly every time someone feels better by doing good, on the other side of the world (or street), someone else is further locked into a system that will not allow the true flourishing of his or her nature or the opportunity to live a joyful and fulfilled life."[25]

Buffett's denunciation of the contemporary aid industry and its wealthy patrons echoes criticisms that Klopsch and his associates at the *Christian Herald* leveled against the millionaire benefactors of their own era. Although these evangelical almoners appreciated the generosity of business tycoons like Carnegie and Rockefeller, they worried that the foundation model of philanthropy maintained the unjust labor practices that allowed for the amassing of great fortunes in the first place. They also feared that the rise of scientific charity conducted by professional aid agents would increase condescension toward the poor, diminish sympathy for the destitute, or even discourage grassroots engagement with the downtrodden altogether.

Many of the anxieties that troubled Klopsch and his colleagues have continued to agitate subsequent generations of evangelical humanitarians. At the Christian Herald Association, Klopsch's successors wrestle with some of the same questions he and Talmage raised in their newspaper over a century ago: Does charity create dependency? Who should philanthropists help? Is it better to meet the immediate needs of the hungry and homeless or to invest in efforts to ameliorate the root causes of poverty? How can cash-strapped organizations with limited resources do both? When should relief operations recruit volunteers rather than relying on trained social workers? Why are so many people indifferent to the suffering of others? How can charitable agencies encourage empathy for the afflicted without reinforcing racial, social, economic, and national hierarchies?

Given the ongoing uncertainties about how best to alleviate distress in an increasingly global world, some Christian activists have expressed unease about the ethics and consequences of their charitable engagements. To what extent, they wonder, are their attempts to help needy and oppressed people of all nations toxic rather than transformative for both themselves and those they seek to serve? Given all the difficulties and destructive dynamics that distort efforts to aid the afflicted, should followers of Jesus (and, we might ask, anyone who wants to alleviate distress) simply stop volunteering at soup kitchens, sending money to hurricane survivors, supporting humanitarian interventions, or working for philanthropic agencies like the ARC, World Vision, or the Bowery Mission?[26]

Most of the Christians I encountered over the course of my research on evangelical almsgiving would likely see such drastic disengagement as both morally wrong and spiritually damaging. Obeying biblical injunctions to "give to the poor" (Matthew 19:21) and "look after widows and orphans in their distress" (James 1:27) is an essential aspect of Christian practice that no committed believer ought to abandon. In my conversations with the extraordinary women and men who have dedicated themselves to assuaging suffering in Lower Manhattan, post-Katrina New Orleans, Nepal, Nigeria, and numerous other places across the globe, I have found that many have been eager to consider how they and their organizations can extend compassion in ways that avoid the dangers that detractors of the humanitarian aid industry have identified. What would it take, they have asked, to disentangle their efforts to love both neighbors and strangers from social forces, political agendas, and cultural prejudices that do not reflect the grace of Christ? Are there better strategies for acting justly, loving mercy, and walking humbly with God (Micah 6:8)?

These were some of the issues Jason and I were discussing before he was called away. Neither of us presumed to have answers to these questions, but I hope this book offers insights for further dialogue and reflection. By telling the largely forgotten story of Louis Klopsch and his media campaign to make "Christian America" the "Almoner of the World," I have endeavored to make visible the theological principles, economic assumptions, racial biases, nationalist aspirations, gendered suppositions, and religious convictions that have shaped the meaning, practice, and trajectory of evangelical charity in the United States over the course of the twentieth century. Highlighting how these factors have influenced the development of humanitarianism provides crucial historical perspective that can help put contemporary philanthropic efforts into a broader context.

To be sure, this is a cautionary tale. At the same time, the many accounts of personal transformation and persevering commitment to addressing the root causes of poverty, hunger, and homelessness that participants in the Bowery Mission shared during my visits indicate that Klopsch's life story might offer hope and inspiration for all those still striving to relieve affliction, challenge injustice, and make a better world.

When I finally went to check on Jason, I found him comforting a woman who had come into the Mission in severe distress. Watching their interaction, I was reminded of a passage from Klopsch's biography:

> I never saw him refuse an appeal for help or turn a deaf ear
> to the voice of trouble.... He was constantly taking upon
> himself the burdens of other men. He was, indeed, very
> human, but he was also very true and genuine.... He gave and

forgave and helped and loved and did as he would be done by. Mainly he preached with bread, he prayed with human kindness. . . . His happiness was in mitigated pain.

This tribute could describe many of my friends at the Bowery Mission. Whatever we might surmise about Klopsch's character, his works do follow him.[27]

ABBREVIATIONS

NOTES

ACKNOWLEDGMENTS

INDEX

ABBREVIATIONS

ISR	International Socialist Review
JAH	Journal of American History
JH	Journalism History
JHA	Journal of Humanitarian Assistance
JHI	Journal of the History of Ideas
JTS	Journal of Transnational Studies
LT	Living Truths
MR	Material Religion: A Journal of Art, Objects, and Beliefs
NAR	North American Review
NYDT	New York Daily Tribune
NYH	New York Herald
NYHST	New York History
NYS	New York Sun
NYT	New York Times
NYTR	New York Tribune
PHR	Pacific Historical Review
PP	Pittsburgh Press
RAAC	Religion and American Culture: A Journal of Interpretation
RAL	Research in African Literatures
SFCH	San Francisco Chronicle
SFCL	San Francisco Call
SSR	Social Service Review
TDC	Topeka Daily Capital
TOF	Triumphs of Faith
WP	Washington Post
WSG	Washington Sunday Globe
WT	Washington Times

INTRODUCTION

1. "Police Intelligence," *NYH,* August 12, 1866, 5; and "Alleged Embezzlement and Forgery by a Boy," *NYH,* January 21, 1867, 7.
2. "Police Intelligence," 5; and "Alleged Embezzlement," 7.
3. "Police Intelligence," 5; and "Alleged Embezzlement," 7.
4. On Klopsch's criminal record, see "Essex Market Police Court: A Life Insurance Swindle," *NYH,* January 6, 1875, 11; "A Swindling Insurance Agent," *NYT,* January 7, 1875, 10; "Louis Klopsch," Inmate Admission Registers, 1865–1971, vol. 12 (January 1875): 120, Sing Sing Correctional Facility Institutional Records, NYSA; and Registers of Commitments to Prisons, 1842–1908, vol. 6 (January 1875): n.p., Records of the Governor's Office, NYSA.
5. "Dr. Klopsch Laid at Rest," *CH,* March 23, 1910, 275–277, 299–300; "Our Departed Chief," *CH,* March 16, 1910, 256; "The Whole World Loved Him," *CH,* March 30, 1910, 321, 328; "Starving India's Pitiful Cry for Bread," *CH,* April 4, 1900, 286; "Louis Klopsch, Almoner," *Outlook,* March 19, 1910, 94; "Dr. Klopsch Laid at Rest," *NYT,* March 10, 1910, 9; and Charles M. Pepper, *Life-work of Louis Klopsch: Romance of a Modern Knight of Mercy* (New York: Christian Herald Association, 1910), 327.
6. "Seven Fruitful Years," *CH,* December 1, 1897, 912; "Dr. Klopsch Laid at Rest," 275–277, 299–300; "Good Works Remembered," *CH,* April 27, 1900, 415; "Dr. Klopsch's Life in Outline," *CH,* March 16, 1910, 256; and Pepper, *Life-work,* ix, 104, 215–217, 341, 380, 358–394.
7. Pepper, *Life-work,* 392.
8. "About the Bowery Mission," Bowery Mission, http://www.bowery.org/about-us; and "Faith-Based," Bowery Mission, http://www.bowery.org/about-us/faith-based.

9. The most thorough discussion of the *Christian Herald*'s humanitarian work may be found in Merle Curti's *American Philanthropy Abroad: A History* (New Brunswick, NJ: Rutgers University Press, 1963). Other studies that mention Klopsch and his associates include Julia Irwin, *Making the World Safe: The American Red Cross and a Nation's Humanitarian Awakening* (New York: Oxford University Press, 2013); Marian Moser Jones, *The American Red Cross from Clara Barton to the New Deal* (Baltimore, MD: Johns Hopkins University Press, 2013); Norris Magnuson, *Salvation in the Slums: Evangelical Social Work, 1865–1920* (Eugene, OR: Wipf and Stock, 1977); George M. Marsden, *Fundamentalism and American Culture: The Shaping of Twentieth-Century Evangelicalism, 1870–1925* (New York: Oxford University Press, 1980); Keith Pomakoy, *Helping Humanity: American Policy and Genocide Rescue* (Lanham, MD: Lexington Books, 2011); Roger G. Robins, *A. J. Tomlinson: Plainfolk Modernist* (New York: Oxford University Press, 2004); Ian Tyrrell, *Reforming the World: The Creation of America's Moral Empire* (Princeton, NJ: Princeton University Press, 2010); and Ann Marie Wilson, "Taking Liberties Abroad: Americans and International Humanitarian Advocacy, 1821–1914" (PhD diss., Harvard University, 2010).

10. Important works in this vein include Foster Rhea Dulles, *The American Red Cross: A History* (New York: Harper, 1950); Irwin, *Making the World Safe;* Jones, *American Red Cross;* and Inderjeet Parmar, *Foundations of the American Century: The Ford, Carnegie, and Rockefeller Foundations in the Rise of American Power* (New York: Columbia University Press, 2015).

11. The literature on the histories of philanthropy, evangelical charity, and humanitarianism in the United States is well developed and too extensive to cite comprehensively. While some scholars have differentiated among these terms, especially as their meanings changed over time, Klopsch and his associates used them interchangeably. Works that chart a shift from religious charity to scientific philanthropy, professional social work, and / or secular humanitarianism include Elizabeth N. Agnew, *From Charity to Social Work: Mary E. Richmond and the Creation of an American Profession* (Urbana: University of Illinois Press, 2004); Michael Barnett, *Empire of Humanity: A History of Humanitarianism* (Ithaca, NY: Cornell University Press, 2011); Jeremy Beer, *The Philanthropic Revolution: An Alternative History of American Charity* (Philadelphia: University of Pennsylvania Press, 2015); Robert Bremner, *American Philanthropy,* 2nd ed. (Chicago: University of Chicago Press, 1988); Peter Dobkin Hall, *Inventing the Nonprofit Sector and Other Essays on Philanthropy, Voluntarism, and Nonprofit Organizations* (Baltimore, MD: Johns Hopkins University Press, 2001); Lawrence J. Friedman and Mark McGarvie, eds., *Charity, Philanthropy and Civility in American History* (Cambridge: Cambridge University Press, 2003); and Brent Ruswick,

Almost Worthy: The Poor, Paupers, and the Science of Charity in America, 1877–1917 (Bloomington: Indiana University Press, 2013).

12. Studies that focus primarily on elites include Bremner, *American Philanthropy;* James Kloppenberg, *Uncertain Victory: Social Democracy and Progressivism in European and American Thought, 1870–1920* (New York: Oxford University Press, 1988); and many others. Curti's *American Philanthropy Abroad* and Tyrrell's *Reforming the World* are exceptions to this trend.

13. For an incisive analysis on this last point, see Susan M. Ryan, *The Grammar of Good Intentions: Race and the Antebellum Culture of Benevolence* (Ithaca, NY: Cornell University Press, 2003).

14. Pepper, *Life-work,* 2.

15. "The Sing Sing Camp Meeting," *NYT,* August 11, 1885; and "Children's Day at Sing Sing," *NYT,* August 12, 1887. Klopsch's prison records show that he identified as a Presbyterian when committed to Sing Sing.

16. Pepper, *Life-work,* 359, 6; and Louis A. Banks, *T. DeWitt Talmage: His Life and Work* (London: O. W. Binkerd, 1902), 66, 67. For more on Talmage's life and ministry, including his denominational background (from Dutch Reformed to Presbyterian to "undenominational"), consult Ferenc M. Szasz, "T. DeWitt Talmage: Spiritual Tycoon of the Gilded Age," *Presbyterian History* 59, no. 1 (1981): 18–32; and Reid Starkey Thomas, "Thomas De Witt Talmage in Perspective" (PhD diss., Emory University, 1974).

17. "Mr. Talmage to Be Tried," *NYT,* March 11, 1879, 1; "Sensation vs. Stagnation: Talmage for the Plaintiff," *NYT,* January 20, 1879: 8; and Pepper, *Life-work,* 321, 6.

18. Pepper, *Life-work,* 7–8. See also "Our History," Bowery Mission, http://www.bowery.org/about-us/history/#1890s.

19. Pepper, *Life-work,* 9, 10; and "Publisher's Notice," *CH,* February 26, 1890, 136. Circulation figures are drawn from *American Newspaper Directory* (New York: Geo. P. Rowell, 1902), 655–661. The *Union Signal* (WCTU), by comparison, had 47,000 subscribers in 1900.

20. For this statistic, see Stephen Board, "Moving the World with Magazines: A Survey of Evangelical Periodicals," in *American Evangelicals and the Mass Media: Perspectives on the Relationship between American Evangelicals and the Mass Media,* ed. Quentin James Schultze (Grand Rapids, MI: Zondervan, 1990), 128; and Martin Marty, "The Protestant Press," in *The Religious Press in America,* ed. Martin Marty, John G. Deedy, David Wolf Silverman, and Robert Lekachman (New York: Holt, Rinehart, and Winston, 1963), 12.

21. W. N. Hartshorn and Louis Klopsch, *Glimpses of Bible Lands: The Cruise of the Eight Hundred to and through Palestine* (New York: Christian Herald Association, 1905), 379.

22. Scholarly debates about how to define "evangelicalism" as it applies to any historical period, including the late nineteenth century, are complicated

and ongoing. The fourfold definition I employ here was first proposed by historian David Bebbington to describe evangelicalism in Britain from the late eighteenth century and has since been adopted by many scholars of nineteenth-century American Protestantism. One goal of this study is to analyze how this category was being constructed and contested through popular media and the practice of humanitarianism. For discussions of the "Bebbington quadrilateral" and the problem of definition in general, see Linford D. Fisher, "Evangelicals and Unevangelicals: The Contested History of a Word, 1500–1950," *RAAC* 26, no. 2 (Summer 2016): 184–226; and Mark Noll, David Bebbington, and George Rawlyk, eds., Introduction, in *Evangelicalism: Comparative Studies of Popular Protestantism in North America, the British Isles, and Beyond, 1700–1990* (New York: Oxford University Press, 1994).

23. T. DeWitt Talmage, "A Greeting to All," *CH*, February 26, 1890, 136; Pepper, *Life-work*, 370; and "Dr. Klopsch Laid at Rest," 275–277. Useful histories of the evangelical "united front" and the pressures that challenged this coalition after 1870 include David Bebbington, *The Dominance of Evangelicalism: The Age of Spurgeon and Moody* (Downers Grove, IL: InterVarsity Press, 2005); Charles I. Foster, *An Errand of Mercy: The Evangelical United Front, 1790–1837* (Chapel Hill: University of North Carolina Press, 1960); William R. Hutchison, *The Modernist Impulse in American Protestantism* (Durham, NC: Duke University Press, 1992); Marsden, *Fundamentalism and American Culture*; George Marsden, *Understanding Fundamentalism and Evangelicalism* (Grand Rapids, MI: Eerdmans, 1991); Mark A. Noll, *American Evangelical Christianity: An Introduction* (Malden, MA: Blackwell, 2001); Jean Miller Schmidt, *Souls or the Social Order: The Two-Party System in American Protestantism* (Brooklyn, NY: Carlson, 1991); and Ferenc M. Szasz, *The Divided Mind of Protestant America, 1880–1930* (University of Alabama Press, 1982).

24. This figure comes from Pepper, *Life-work*, 357, and is reiterated by numerous contemporary news reports. The 2017 value of contributions was calculated using the Consumer Price Index.

25. On this point, see Curti, *American Philanthropy*, 216–219.

26. For Klopsch's many connections with American political figures and foreign leaders, see Pepper, *Life-work*. Talmage describes his interactions with these presidents and other prominent government officials in his autobiography, Thomas De Witt Talmage, *T. De Witt Talmage as I Knew Him* (New York: E. P. Dutton, 1912).

27. On Klopsch's relationships with business leaders, missionary organizations, Christian benevolent societies, and humanitarian agencies, see Pepper, *Life-work*.

28. Pepper, *Life-work*, 323.

29. For context on evangelical millennialism in this era, see especially James H. Moorhead, *World without End: Mainstream American Protestant Visions of the Last Things, 1880–1925* (Bloomington: Indiana University Press, 1999).

30. For an example of anti-Muslim rhetoric, see, for example, "Armenia's Heroine Home Again," *CH,* September 30, 1896, 711.

1. A RELIGIOUS PAPER THOROUGHLY HUMANITARIAN

1. Thomas De Witt Talmage, "Ministers and Their Slanderers," *CH,* January 16, 1879, 196–198.

2. Thomas De Witt Talmage, "What the Cities Teach," *CH,* January 30, 1879, 228–229; and Charles M. Pepper, *Life-work of Louis Klopsch: Romance of a Modern Knight of Mercy* (New York: Christian Herald Association, 1910), 359.

3. Robert H. Bremner, *From the Depths: The Discovery of Poverty in the United States* (New York: New York University Press, 1956), offers a useful overview of this history.

4. For an example of Talmage's views, see "A Brooklyn Pastorate," *CH,* April 26, 1893, 274–275. Talmage's evolving ideas about poverty reflected the trend toward "social Christianity" in the late nineteenth century. See Paul T. Phillips, *A Kingdom on Earth: Anglo-American Social Christianity, 1880–1940* (University Park: Pennsylvania State University Press, 1996).

5. Pepper, *Life-work,* 6–7, 343; and Louis A. Banks, *T. DeWitt Talmage: His Life and Work* (London: O. W. Binkerd, 1902), 66–67.

6. Pepper, *Life-work,* 8–10.

7. Talmage, "Ministers and Their Slanderers," 196–198.

8. Pepper, *Life-work,* 323.

9. David G. McCullough, *The Johnstown Flood* (New York: Simon and Schuster, 1987).

10. "The Johnstown Disaster," *CH,* June 19, 1889, 386–387; Thomas De Witt Talmage, *T. De Witt Talmage as I Knew Him* (New York: E. P. Dutton, 1912), 228–229; and "Miss Clara Barton," *CH,* June 19, 1889, 396. Marian Moser Jones, *The American Red Cross from Clara Barton to the New Deal* (Baltimore: Johns Hopkins University Press, 2013), 47–52, describes the relief effort of the ARC.

11. "Newspaper Influence," *CH,* September 13, 1893, 598. For postmillennialism, see James H. Moorhead, *World without End: Mainstream American Protestant Visions of the Last Things, 1880–1925* (Bloomington: Indiana University Press, 1999).

12. "A Life of Christian Service Ended," *CH,* May 27, 1908, 435; "George H. Sandison," in *American Statesmen,* ed. Thomas W. Herringshaw (Chicago: American Publisher's Association, 1907), 476; "Death of Sandison," *CH,*

December 1934, 25; and "The Christian Herald for 1896," *CH,* December 4, 1895, 815.

13. Ted Curtis Smythe, *The Gilded Age Press, 1865–1900* (Westport, CT: Praeger, 2003), 123; "The Secular Newspaper," *CH,* February 3, 1892, 70; "Newspaper Influence," 598; and "Newspaper Reading," *CH,* September 20, 1893, 614. On "new journalism," see also W. Joseph Campbell, "1897: American Journalism's Exceptional Year," *JH* 29, no. 4 (Winter 2004), 190–200; W. Joseph Campbell, *The Year That Defined American Journalism: 1897 and the Clash of Paradigms* (New York: Routledge, 2006); and David R. Spencer, *The Yellow Journalism: The Press and America's Emergence as a World Power* (Evanston, IL: Northwestern University Press, 2007).

14. "A Greeting to All," *CH,* February 26, 1890, 136; "Religious Newspapers," *CH,* June 18, 1890, 392; "The Christian Herald," *CMA,* November 3, 1897, 460; Editorial, *CH,* May 18, 1892, 310; "Secular Newspaper," 70; "Forward," *CH,* June 4, 1890, 360; and Pepper, *Life-work,* 328, 322.

15. Pepper, *Life-work,* 8.

16. Talmage, "A Greeting to All," 136; and "Important Session of the Brooklyn Presbytery," *NYT,* February 4, 1879, 5. Talmage discusses his financial critics in his autobiography, *Talmage as I Knew Him,* 246–248.

17. Talmage, *Talmage as I Knew Him,* 231; and "Publisher's Notice," *CH,* February 26, 1890, 136.

18. "Two Deaths," *Outlook,* April 19, 1902, 945–946; *WT,* April 26, 1902, 6; and *WSG,* April 27 1902, 4.

19. Charles H. H. Cottrell to Stephen Barton, March 22, 1898, Red Cross File, 1863–1957; American National Red Cross, 1878–1957; Relief Operations; Spanish-American War; Klopsch, Louis, 1898, undated; CB. "Dr Louis Klopsch: Inquiry to Be Made as to Charity Funds Which He Collected," *CN,* April 21, 1910; "Dr. Louis Klopsch Left $643,239 Net," *NYT,* August 1, 1916, 9; "Muckraking the Dead," *DFP,* April 23, 1910, 4; and "Exploiter of Talmage Died Rich," *BDE,* August 1, 1916, 6.

20. Pepper, *Life-work,* 364.

21. "Famine in Russia," *CH,* August 19, 1891, 519; "Forty Millions Starving," *CH,* February 3, 1892, 71; "Russia's Starving Millions," *CH,* February 10, 1892, 89; and "Russia's Cry for Bread," *CH,* March 23, 1892, 177, 181.

22. "Russia's Cry for Bread," 177, 181; "God Speed the 'Conemaugh,'" *CH,* April 27, 1892, 257; and Pepper, *Life-work,* 16–17.

23. "We Hear Russia's Groan," *CH,* April 13, 1892, 230; "Making It a Million," *CH,* April 27, 1892, 264; "Blessing the 'Leo's' Cargo," *CH,* June 15, 1892, 369; "Russia Greets the 'Leo,'" *CH,* July 27, 1892, 467; and Pepper, *Life-work,* 11–27.

24. "Closing the Relief Fund," *CH,* May 25, 1892, 326; "Last Week of the Russian Fund," *CH,* May 25, 1892, 328; and Pepper, *Life-work,* 24–25. On the

Northwestern Miller's contributions, see Merle Curti, *American Philanthropy Abroad* (New Brunswick, NJ: Rutgers University Press, 1963), 112–113.

25. "Russia's Starving Millions," 89; "Russia's Cry for Bread," 177, 181; and "Our Russian Fund," *CH*, May 4, 1892, 278.

26. Studies of the emergence of humanitarianism sentiment include Norman Fiering, "Irresistible Compassion: An Aspect of Eighteenth Century Sympathy and Humanitarianism," *JHI* (April 1976): 195–218; Karen Halttunen, "Humanitarianism and the Pornography of Pain in Anglo-American Culture," *AHR* 100, no. 2 (1995): 303–334; Thomas L. Haskell, "Capitalism and the Origins of the Humanitarian Sensibility, Part I," *AHR* 90, no. 2 (1985): 339–361; Lynn Hunt, *Inventing Human Rights: A History* (New York: W. W. Norton, 2007); Thomas Laqueur, "Bodies, Details, and the Humanitarian Narrative," in *The New Cultural History,* ed. Lynn Hunt (Berkeley: University of California Press, 1989): 176–204; and Daniel Wickberg, "What Is the History of Sensibilities? On Cultural Histories, Old and New," *AHR* (June 2007): 661–684.

27. On the role of images in antislavery literature, see especially Elizabeth B. Clark, "'The Sacred Rights of the Weak': Pain, Sympathy, and the Culture of Individual Rights in Antebellum America," *JAH* 82, no. 2 (September 1995): 463–493; and Radiclani Clytus, "'Keep It before the People': The Pictorialization of American Abolitionism," in *Early African American Print Culture in Theory and Practice,* ed. Lara Langer Cohen and Jordan Alexander Stein (Philadelphia: University of Pennsylvania Press, 2012), 290–317.

28. Pepper, *Life-work,* 4.

29. "Russia's Cry Heard!," *CH,* April 13, 1892, 225, 229; "Blessing the Meal," *CH,* April 20, 1892, 249; and "God Speed the 'Conemaugh,'" 257, 265.

30. "Russia's Cry for Bread," 177, 181; "Russia's Cry Heard!," 225 229; and "Blessing the 'Leo's' Cargo," 369.

31. Charles O. Burgess, "The Newspaper as Charity Worker," *NYHST* (July 1962): 249–268; and Curti, *American Philanthropy,* 88–98.

32. Curti, *American Philanthropy,* 93, 89; and Burgess, "Newspaper as Charity Worker," 249–268.

33. "Russia's Cry Heard!," 229.

34. William C. Edgar, quoted in Curti, *American Philanthropy,* 101; "We Hear Russia's Groan," 230; and "God Speed the 'Conemaugh,'" 257.

35. "God Speed the 'Conemaugh,'" 265; and "Ready to Ship the Flour," *CH,* June 1, 1892, 344.

36. "Our Russian Fund," 278; and "Blessing the Meal," 249.

37. "Our Russian Fund," 278; "Making It a Million," 264; "Blessing the Meal," 249; "God Speed the 'Conemaugh,'" 257; and "The Fund Is Now $20,000," *CH,* May 11, 1892, 296.

38. "Russia's Cry for Bread," 177, 181; "The Russian Address of Thanks," *CH*, August 31, 1892, 549; and "Russia Was Grateful," *CH*, August 3, 1892, 481.

39. "Russia's Cry Heard!," 225, 229; "Russia's Cry for Bread," 177, 181; and "Ready to Ship the Flour," 344.

40. "Russia's Gratitude," *CH*, August 24, 1892, 534.

41. "The Famine Cloud Lifted," *CH*, August 24, 1892, 529–531; "Russia's Cry Heard!," 225, 229; and "Ready to Ship the Flour," 344.

42. "To the Rescue of the Veterans," *CH*, May 25, 1892, 321, 325.

43. Ibid.; and "Grateful Veterans," *CH*, February 8, 1893, 85.

44. "The Panic in Wall Street," *CH*, August 9, 1893, 519; and "Wall Street," *CH*, August 16, 1893, 534.

45. "The Berlin Labor Conference," *CH*, April 16, 1890, 242–243.

46. Thomas De Witt Talmage, "The Old Fight to Be Settled," *CH*, May 21, 1890, 322–323; and Thomas De Witt Talmage, "Crooked Things," *CH*, September 24, 1890, 610–611.

47. Andrew Carnegie, "Wealth," *NAR* 148, no. 391 (June 1889): 653–665.

48. Carnegie, "Wealth," 653–665; and Andrew Carnegie, "The Best Fields for Philanthropy," *NAR* 149, no. 397 (December 1889): 682–699.

49. Carnegie, "Best Fields for Philanthropy," 683; and "Andrew Carnegie," *CH*, March 12, 1890, cover and 162–163.

50. "Poor, Yet Making Many Rich," *CH*, January 3, 1894, 1, 13.

51. "Jane Street M. E. Church: Its Mission and Its Pastor," *CH*, May 14, 1890, cover and 308–309.

52. "The Friend of the Homeless," *CH*, January 24, 1894, 49, 53; and "The Travelers' Club," *CH*, January 11, 1893, 17, 26.

53. "Friend of the Homeless," 49, 53; and "The Travelers' Club," *CH*, December 5, 1894, 771.

54. "A Temple of Helpfulness," *CH*, March 22, 1893, 193. On the rise of scientific charity, see Elizabeth N. Agnew, *From Charity to Social Work: Mary E. Richmond and the Creation of an American Profession* (Urbana: University of Illinois Press, 2004); Robert Bremner, *American Philanthropy*, 2nd ed. (Chicago: University of Chicago Press, 1988); Lawrence J. Friedman and Mark McGarvie, eds., *Charity, Philanthropy and Civility in American History* (Cambridge: Cambridge University Press, 2003); Charles L. Mowat, *The Charity Organization Society, 1869–1913: Its Ideas and Work* (London: Methuen, 1961); Brent Ruswick, *Almost Worthy: The Poor, Paupers, and the Science of Charity in America, 1877–1917* (Bloomington: Indiana University Press, 2013); and Frank D. Watson, *The Charity Organization Movement in the United States* (New York: Macmillan, 1922).

55. Carnegie, "Wealth," 653–665; and Carnegie, "Best Fields for Philanthropy," 682–699.

56. "To Raise the Fallen," *CH,* August 5, 1891, 490; and "Thanksgiving with 'God's Poor,'" *CH,* November 23, 1892, 745.

57. "Feeding the Hungry Hundreds," *CH,* December 6, 1893, 803.

58. "A Bread and Beef Charity," *CH,* January 10, 1894, 19; and "Help All You Can," *CH,* January 24, 1894, 54.

59. "The Travelers' Club," 771.

60. J. B. Hawthorne, "The Army of the Unemployed," *CH,* June 13, 1894, 392.

61. "A Bread and Beef Charity," 19; and "Friend of the Homeless," 53.

62. "Helping 'The Lord's Poor,'" *CH,* February 7, 1894, 85; and "Our 'Food Fund's' Mission," *CH,* February 14, 1894, 102.

63. Pepper, *Life-work,* 365, 9; and "A Greeting to All," 136.

64. Lyman Abbott, "The Duty of Charity," *CH,* February 14, 1894, 110.

65. "An Opportunity for All," *CH,* April 18, 1894, 246.

66. "Dr. Talmage's Decoration-Day Sermon," *CH,* June 3, 1891, 388. Helpful studies on the ongoing struggles for national unity include Edward Blum, *Reforging the White Republic: Race, Religion and American Nationalism,* updated ed. (Baton Rouge: Louisiana State Press, 2015); David W. Blight, *Race and Reunion: The Civil War in American Memory* (Cambridge, MA: Belknap Press of Harvard University Press, 2003); and Nina Silber, *Romance of Reunion: Northerners and the South, 1865–1900* (Chapel Hill: University of North Carolina Press, 1993).

67. "The People's Palace in Jersey City," *CH,* April 22, 1891, 252; "Mr. Wanamaker's Mission," *CH,* September 24, 1890, 612; and "A Hive of Busy Workers," *CH,* March 16, 1898, 219. For a helpful history of urban Christianity in this period, see Matthew Bowman, *The Urban Pulpit: New York City and the Fate of Liberal Evangelicalism* (New York: Oxford University Press, 2014).

68. Jane Addams, "The Subjective Value of a Social Settlement," *The Forum* (November 1892), http://nrs.harvard.edu/urn-3:FHCL:777422; and "Settlement Homes," *CH,* May 22, 1895, cover and 327.

69. "Social Salvation," *CH,* November 19, 1890, 741.

70. For example, "Many Good Causes Helped," *CH,* November 7, 1894, 707.

71. "Jubilee and Conflagration," *CH,* May 23, 1894, 322; and "Second Day of the Jubilee," *CH,* May 23, 1894, 323.

72. Circulation figures from *American Newspaper Directory* (New York: Geo. P. Rowell, 1894), 537, 1110. "A Word about Ourselves," *CH,* December 5, 1894, 771.

73. "A Truly Happy Hundred," *CH,* June 27, 1894, 401; and Pepper, *Life-work,* 290–291.

74. Pepper, *Life-work,* 260–261; "A Beacon Light to the Lost," *CH,* April 3, 1895, 217; and "They Bless the Bowery Mission," *CH,* January 1, 1896, 10.

75. "A Beacon Light to the Lost," 217.

1. "Constantinople's Day of Terror," *CH,* October 31, 1894, 696; and "Thousands Homeless and Helpless," *CH,* September 12, 1894, 581.

2. "Miles upon Miles of Ruins," *CH,* October 24, 1894, 677; and "To Aid the Earthquake Victims," *CH,* September 19 1894, 597.

3. "Thousands Homeless," 581; "An Appeal to Christian America from Turkish Relief Committee," *CH,* September 26, 1894, 613–614; and "Constantinople's Cry Heard," *CH,* October 3, 1894, 625, 629.

4. "Constantinople's Cry Heard," 625, 629; and "An Appeal to Christian America," 613–614.

5. Charles M. Pepper, *Life-work of Louis Klopsch: Romance of a Modern Knight of Mercy* (New York: Christian Herald Association, 1910), 395; and "An Appeal to Christian America," 613–614. On international relief efforts during the nineteenth century, see Merle Curti, *American Philanthropy Abroad* (New Brunswick, NJ: Rutgers University Press, 1963).

6. For histories of these events and American responses to them, see Richard Hovanissian, "The Armenian Question in the Ottoman Empire, 1876–1914," in *Armenian People from Ancient to Modern Times,* vol. 2, ed. Richard Hovanissian (New York: St. Martin's Press, 1997); Arman J. Kirakossian, ed., *The Armenian Massacres, 1894–1896: U.S. Media Testimony* (Detroit, MI: Wayne State University Press, 2004); Jeremy Salt, *Imperialism, Evangelism and the Ottoman Armenians 1878–1896* (London: Frank Cass, 1993); and Ann Wilson, "In the Name of God, Civilization and Humanity: The United States and the Armenian Massacres of the 1890s," *Le Mouvement Social* no. 227 (April–June, 2009): 27–44.

7. "Armenia's Black Christmas," *CH,* December 25, 1895, 887; and "Gave His Life for Christ," *CH,* November 27, 1895, 785.

8. "Armenia's Reign of Terror," *CH,* November 13, 1895, 750; "The Blight of the World: Ottoman Despotism," *CH,* May 6, 1896, 363; "Armenia's Only Hope," *CH,* May 20, 1896, 389, 395; "Greeting to the Exiles," *CH,* November 4, 1896, 817; and "To Aid the Earthquake Victims," 597.

9. For fund-raising figures, see Curti, *American Philanthropy,* 125; and Pepper, *Life-work,* 49.

10. On the "collective culture of humanitarianism," see Ian Tyrrell, *Reforming the World: The Creation of America's Moral Empire* (Princeton, NJ: Princeton University Press, 2010), 98.

11. "An Appeal to Christian America," 613; and "Thousands Homeless," 581.

12. "Solomon's Splendor," *CH,* April 25, 1894, 271; and "Armenia's Reign of Terror," 750.

13. On Orientalism, see Edward W. Said, *Orientalism,* 25th anniversary ed. (New York: Vintage Books, 2003); and Timothy Marr, *The Cultural Roots of*

American Islamicism (New York: Cambridge University Press, 2006). For an example of this rhetoric, see W. E. Gladstone's *Bulgarian Horrors and the Question of the East* (London, 1876), 10–11.

14. "An Appeal to Christian America," 613; "To Aid the Earthquake Victims," 597; and "Stanboul's Desolate Homes," *CH,* October 10, 1894, 643.

15. "Many Good Causes Helped," *CH,* November 7, 1894, 707; and "An Appeal to Christian America," 613.

16. "The Relief Committee's Appeal," *CH,* September 26, 1894, 613; "Many Good Causes Helped," 707; "An Appeal to Christian America," 613; and "Stanboul's Desolate Homes," 643.

17. "An Appeal to Christian America," 613.

18. "To Aid the Earthquake Victims," 597; "Thousands Homeless," 581; and "Our Mail Bag," *CH,* September 26, 1894, 614.

19. "Our Mail Bag," 614; and A. B. Simpson, "Established," *CMA,* September 22, 1893, 179–182. For relevant background on premillennialism, consult Ernest R. Sandeen, *The Roots of Fundamentalism: British and American Millennarianism, 1800–1930* (Chicago: University of Chicago Press, 1970); Matthew Avery Sutton, *American Apocalypse: A History of Modern Evangelicalism* (Cambridge, MA: Harvard University Press, 2014); and Timothy P. Weber, *Living in the Shadow of the Second Coming: American Premillennialism, 1875–1982* (Chicago: University of Chicago Press, 1987).

20. "The Pulse of the World," *CH,* March 10, 1897, 188.

21. Thomas De Witt Talmage, "A Greeting to All," *CH,* February 26, 1890, 136; and "Russia's Peasants," *CH,* September 7, 1892, 565.

22. "Parliament of Religion," *CH,* October 11, 1893, 661; and "A Congress of Religions," *CH,* September 6, 1893, 577, 591. On "sympathy" at the World's Parliament, see Leigh Eric Schmidt, "Cosmopolitan Piety: Sympathy, Comparative Religions, and Nineteenth-Century Liberalism," in *Practicing Protestants: Histories of Christian Life in America, 1630–1965,* ed. Laurie F. Maffly-Kipp, Leigh E. Schmidt, and Mark Valeri (Baltimore: Johns Hopkins University Press, 2006), 199–221; and Richard H. Seager, *The World's Parliament of Religion: The East / West Encounter, Chicago 1893* (Bloomington: Indiana University Press, 2009).

23. Thomas de Witt Talmage, "The Democracy of Religion," *CH,* October 9, 1879, 804; "Cultivate Sympathy," *CH,* December 2, 1896, 902; and Thomas de Witt Talmage, "Sympathy for the Fallen," in "Twelfth Anniversary," *CH,* May 26, 1881, 325. Scholarship on the racial theories that shaped Talmage's views includes Derek Chang, *Citizens of a Christian Nation: Evangelical Missions and the Problem of Race in the Nineteenth Century* (Philadelphia: University of Pennsylvania Press, 2010); George M. Frederickson, *The Black Image in the White Mind: The Debate on Afro-American Character and Destiny, 1817–1914* (Middletown, CT: Wesleyan University Press, 1987); and Ralph E.

Luker, *The Social Gospel in Black and White: American Racial Reform, 1885–1912* (Chapel Hill: University of North Carolina Press, 1991).

24. "A Congress of Religions," 591; and "A Word about Ourselves," *CH,* December 5, 1894, 771.

25. "Miles upon Miles," 677.

26. "Our Mail Bag," *CH,* December 19, 1894, 818.

27. "How the Armenians Suffer," *CH,* October 23, 1895, 689; "Armenia Plunged in Sorrow," *CH,* December 4, 1895, 824; and "Armenia's Black Christmas," 887.

28. "The Armenian Outrages," *CH,* October 30, 1895, 712; Thomas De Witt Talmage, "Points of the Compass," *CH,* January 23, 1895, 50–51; and "Women of Armenia," *CH,* April 24, 1895, 265.

29. "To Aid Stricken Armenia," *CH,* October 16, 1895, 673; and "More Armenians Massacred," *CH,* November 6, 1895, 730.

30. "Armenian Outrages," 712; "More Armenians Massacred," 730; "Blight of the World," 363; and "The Sultan's Fanaticism," *CH,* January 22, 1896, 76.

31. Thomas De Witt Talmage, "The Cry of Armenia," *CH,* January 15, 1895, 42–43.

32. Ibid., 42–43. On U.S. foreign policy debates about intervention in Armenia, see Andrew Preston, *Sword of the Spirit, Shield of Faith: Religion in American War and Diplomacy* (New York: Knopf, 2012); and Karine V. Walther, *Sacred Interests: The United States and the Islamic World, 1821–1921* (Chapel Hill: University of North Carolina Press, 2015).

33. "Fighting Famine in Armenia," *CH,* February 26, 1896, 166; "Hunger's Death-Roll in Armenia," *CH,* October 9, 1895, 649–653; "All Christendom Stirred," *CH,* September 11, 1895, 589; "Mr. Howard's Perilous Journey," *CH,* November 27, 1895, 787; and "Armenia's Cry for Help," *CH,* October 2, 1895, 633, 637.

34. "Armenia's Cry for Help," 633, 637; and "Let All Help Armenia," *CH,* December 25, 1895, 884.

35. "How the Armenians Suffer," 689; "Women of Armenia," 265; Margaret E. Sangster, "Mrs. Sangster on Armenia," *CH,* January 15, 1896, 45; "Armenia Plunged in Sorrow," 824; and "A Broadside on Public Affairs," *CH,* March 31, 1897, 256.

36. "Sent with Prayer and Blessing," *CH,* October 30, 1895, 709; and "To Aid Stricken Armenia," 673.

37. "Armenia's Black Christmas," 887.

38. "All Now Helping Armenia," *CH,* December 18, 1895, 862.

39. Ibid., 862; "Armenia's Cry for Help," 633, 637; and William Willard Howard, "Has God Forgotten Eden?" *CH,* January 29, 1896, 87.

40. "One Godly Woman's Work," *CH,* September 18, 1895, 601, 603; "Ten Relief Stations Now Open," *CH,* January 22, 1896, 67; and "Our Mail Bag," *CH,* January 1, 1896, 8.

41. "All Now Helping Armenia," 862.

42. "Armenia's Reign of Terror," 750.

43. Henry Dwight, quoted in Judson Smith to George Frisbie Hoar, November 29, 1895, ABC 1.1 Vol. 179, ABCFM; and Henry Dwight to Louis Klopsch, in "Busy Relief Work at Van," *CH,* January 1, 1896, 6.

44. Judson Smith to Louis Klopsch, December 6, 1895, ABC 1.1 Vol. 179, ABCFM. Clara Barton to Louis Klopsch, December 22, 1895, enclosed in Louis Klopsch to Judson Smith, December 23, 1895, ABC 10, ABCFM (in this letter, Barton refers to two inquiries from Klopsch dated December 16 and 20, 1895). Louis Klopsch to Clara Barton, January 10, 1896, Red Cross File, 1863–1957; American National Red Cross, 1878–1957; Relief operations; Armenia and Turkey; Correspondence, 1895–1902, undated; CB [hereafter: Armenia Correspondence, CB]. Louis Klopsch to Clara Barton, January 15, 1896, Armenia Correspondence, CB.

45. Barton to Klopsch, December 22, 1895, enclosed in Klopsch to Smith, December 23, 1895, ABCFM. On the ARC's difficulties in Russia, see Marian Moser Jones, *The American Red Cross from Clara Barton to the New Deal* (Baltimore: Johns Hopkins University Press, 2013), 66–68.

46. Clara Barton to Louis Klopsch, December 14, 1895, Letterbooks, 187–1911; 1895, June-1898, Dec.; CB. Barton to Klopsch, December 22, 1895, enclosed in Klopsch to Smith, December 23, 1895, ABCFM.

47. Louis Klopsch to Judson Smith, December 31, 1895, ABC 10 Vol. 89, ABCFM; Howard, "Has God Forgotten Eden?," 87; and "Ten Relief Stations Now Open," 67.

48. Clara Barton to Stephen Barton, n.d., Armenia Correspondence, CB.

49. Ann Marie Wilson, "Taking Liberties Abroad: Americans and International Humanitarian Advocacy, 1821–1914" (PhD diss., Harvard University, 2010), 218–219.

50. "Closing the Relief Fund," *CH,* April 15, 1896, 307; and Clara Barton, *The Red Cross: A History of This Remarkable International Movement in the Interest of Humanity* (Washington, DC: American National Red Cross, 1898), 289.

51. "Armenia's Only Hope," 389, 395; "At Freedom's Gate," *CH,* August 26, 1896, 625, 629; and "Greeting to the Exiles," 817.

52. "Our Armenian Colonists," *CH,* March 27, 1896, 409; and "Greeting to the Exiles," 817.

53. "Shall the Armenians Come to America?," *CH,* October 14, 1896, 755; "Home for the Armenians," *CH,* October 21, 1896, 783; and "Armenian Exiles Welcomed," *CH,* October 21, 1896, 808.

54. "Armenian Aid," *CH,* December 8, 1896, 937; "Dr. Kimball Voices Armenia's Gratitude," *CH,* October 14, 1896, 756; and "Miss Frances E. Willard Thanks Our Readers," *CH,* November 25, 1896, 880.

1. "Armenian Aid," *CH,* December 9, 1896, 937; "Miss Frances E. Willard Thanks Our Readers," *CH,* November 25, 1896, 880; "Look Back," *CH,* December 2, 1896, 902; and "The Christian Herald for 1897," *CH,* December 2, 1896, 905.

2. "Our Congress and Struggling Cuba," *CH,* January 6, 1897, 3; "Cuba's Struggle," *CH,* February 12, 1896, 129; "American Hearts with Cuba," *CH,* December 30, 1896, 991; and "Cuba's Hope Undimmed," *CH,* June 23, 1897, 495.

3. "American Hearts with Cuba," 991; "Cuba's Hope Undimmed," 495; and "Our Congress and Struggling Cuba," 3. For the broader history of the Cuban War of Independence (1895–1898), see John Lawrence Tone, *War and Genocide in Cuba 1895–1898* (Chapel Hill: University of North Carolina, 2006).

4. "American Hearts with Cuba," 991.

5. "Our Mail Bag," *CH,* December 18, 1895, 864; "A Broadside on Public Affairs," *CH,* March 31, 1897, 256; and "Cuba's War for Freedom," *CH,* July 3, 1895, 425. This chapter builds on the work of scholars who have analyzed the constitutive connections between religion, humanitarianism, and American foreign policy in the Spanish-American War and the ensuing conflicts in the Philippines and other former Spanish colonies, especially: Edward Blum, *Reforging the White Republic: Race, Religion and American Nationalism* (Baton Rouge: Louisiana State University Press, 2005), chapter 7; Susan K. Harris, *God's Arbiters: Americans and the Philippines, 1898–1902* (New York: Oxford University Press, 2011); Matthew McCullough, *The Cross of War: Christian Nationalism and U.S. Expansion in the Spanish American War* (Madison: University of Wisconsin Press, 2014); and Keith Pomakoy, *Helping Humanity: American Policy and Genocide Rescue* (New York: Lexington Books, 2011), chapter 3.

6. "Religious Journalism," *CH,* December 1, 1897, 908; and Louis Klopsch, "Seven Fruitful Years," *CH,* December 1, 1897, 912.

7. For Sherman's December press release: *FRUS* (Washington, DC: U.S. Government Printing Office, 1898), 514. "Let All Help Poor Cuba Now," *CH,* January 12, 1898, 23.

8. *Messages of the President . . . on the Relations of the United States to Spain* (Washington, DC: U.S. Government Printing Office, 1898). On the establishment of the CCRC, see *FRUS* (Washington, DC: U.S. Government Printing Office, 1901), 655–656; and *Report of the Central Cuban Relief Committee,* part 3 (1898), 9–12; see also Marian Moser Jones, *The American Red Cross from Clara Barton to the New Deal* (Baltimore: Johns Hopkins University Press, 2013), 84–86.

9. "A Call to Service," *CH,* January 19, 1898, 48.

10. Klopsch, "Seven Fruitful Years," 912.

11. Thomas De Witt Talmage, "Alleviations of War," *CH*, May 18, 1898, 428–429.

12. "Face to Face with Our Destiny," *CH*, May 25, 1898, 448; and "America's New Responsibility," *CH*, October 19, 1898, 808.

13. Subscriptions rose approximately 40 percent from 1897 to 1899. Although circulation decreased somewhat after the official close of the Philippine War (and Talmage's death) in 1902, the paper retained a significant portion (approximately 13 percent) of the new subscribers added during these crucial years of American imperialism. *American Newspaper Directory* (New York: Geo. P. Rowell, 1902), 655–661.

14. "Cuba Needs Our Help," *CH*, January 5, 1898, 5.

15. "Cuba's Struggle," 129; "Let All Help Poor Cuba Now," 23; and "A Call to Service," 48.

16. Klopsch, "Seven Fruitful Years," 912.

17. Ibid.; and "Let All Help Poor Cuba Now," 23.

18. "A Call to Service," 48; "Dying Cuba!," *CH*, February 23, 1891, 148; "Look Back," 902; and "Let All Help Poor Cuba Now," 23. For the history of American exceptionalism that Talmage expresses here, see especially: Conrad Cherry, ed., *God's New Israel: Religious Interpretations of American Destiny* (Chapel Hill: University of North Carolina Press, 1998); Robert Handy, *A Christian America: Protestant Hopes and Historical Realities,* 2nd ed. (New York: Oxford University Press, 1984); Martin Marty, *Righteous Empire: The Protestant Experience in America* (New York: Dial Books, 1970); and Ernest Lee Tuveson, *Redeemer Nation: The Idea of America's Millennial Role* (Chicago: University of Chicago Press, 1968).

19. "Our War with Spain Begun," *CH*, May 4, 1898, 390–391; and "Hawaii and Cuba," *CH*, July 7, 1897, 532.

20. "A Call to Service," 48.

21. "Contributions to Aid Starving Cuba," *CH*, February 9, 1898, 105; "Cuba's Story Told at Last!," *CH*, February 9, 1898, 104–105; and "Face to Face with Our Destiny," 448.

22. On the press response to the sinking of the *Maine,* see W. Joseph Campbell, *Yellow Journalism: Puncturing the Myths, Defining the Legacies* (Westport, CT: Praeger, 2001); and David R. Spencer, *The Yellow Journalism: The Press and America's Emergence as a World Power* (Evanston, IL: Northwestern University Press, 2007).

23. "Spain Sends a Warship," *CH*, March 2, 1898, 175.

24. "Waiting for the Verdict," *CH*, March 9, 1898, 201; "War's Barbarities," *CH*, March 9, 1898, 200; and "The Dead War Steamer," *CH*, March 9, 1898, 200.

25. "War's Barbarities," 200; and "Our Work in Cuba," *CH*, March 2, 1898, 174.

26. "Dying Cuba!," 148.

27. Talmage's move to Washington was prompted by the destruction of the third Brooklyn Tabernacle, which burned to the ground May 13, 1894—just one day before he was scheduled to depart on a world tour. Although Klopsch promised to raise money to rebuild the church debt-free, Talmage ultimately decided to move on, perhaps amid insinuations (reported by the *New York Times* but never investigated) that the Tabernacle was "set on fire, not accidentally, but purposefully." One "feature of the fire, and a curious one," according to a *Times* journalist, "was that it burned the church out of debt. The amount of insurance on the building and the value of the site are sufficient to cancel all the obligations of the congregation." See: "Third Tabernacle Burned," *NYT,* May 14, 1894, 1; and "Was the Fire Incendiary? No Electric Wires Were Near the Tabernacle Organ," *NYT,* May 15, 1894, 9.

28. "Food Cargoes for Starving Cuba," *CH,* January 26, 1898, 63; "Cuba's Story Told at Last!," 104–105; and "Cuba's Appeal Not in Vain," *CH,* February 2, 1898, 87.

29. "Fighting Back Famine in Cuba," *CH,* March 30, 1898, 274.

30. "Our Mail Bag," *CH,* March 9, 1898, 194; "Our Mail Bag," *CH,* March 23, 1898, 242; and "Our Mail Bag," *CH,* February 16, 1898, 122.

31. "Klopsch Arrives in Cuba," *CH,* March 9, 1898, 194.

32. "Fighting Back Famine in Cuba," 274–275; "Our Life-Saving Mission in Cuba," *CH,* March 23, 1898, 250; "Back from Scenes of Suffering," *CH,* April 13, 1898, 313–322; and "Food Cargoes for Starving Cuba," 226.

33. Redfield Proctor, "Condition of Cuba under Spanish Misrule," reprinted in *The American-Spanish War: A History by the War Leaders* (New York: Chas. Haskell, 1899), 541–553; and "Sympathy for Cuba," *CH,* March 23, 1898, 259.

34. "Food Cargoes for Starving Cuba," 226; and "Fighting Back Famine in Cuba," 274–275.

35. "Food Cargoes for Starving Cuba," 226; "Fighting Back Famine in Cuba," 274–275; and "Food Train Speeding across Cuba," *CH,* April 6, 1898, 298–299.

36. "Food Train Speeding across Cuba," 299.

37. Ibid.; "A Correction from Dr. Klopsch," *NYTR,* April 5, 1898, 4.

38. "Klopsch's Plea for Spain," *NYS,* April 3, 1898, 1. See also "The President Wins," *WT,* April 3, 1898, 2; "Sure of Freedom," *CT,* April 4, 1898, 2; and "M'Kinley [*sic*] Now Working on His Message," *SFCH,* April 3, 1898, 1.

39. "Klopsch's Plea for Spain," 1; and "Says General Lee Favors Autonomy: Dr. Klopsch Makes Some Startling Statements," *BDE,* April 3, 1898, 1.

40. "McKinley Is for Peace," *NYS,* April 3, 1898, 1; "Cubans and an Armistice," *NYT,* April 5, 1898, 4; and "Says General Lee Favors Autonomy," 1, 8.

41. "Says General Lee Favors Autonomy," 1, 8; and "An Apology for Spain," *NYS*, April 5, 1898, 6.

42. "Dr. Klopsch's Statement," *BDE*, April 4, 1898, 3; and "A Correction from Dr. Klopsch," 4.

43. Thomas De Witt Talmage, "War or Peace?," *CH*, April 13, 1898, 320.

44. On Klopsch's travel to Cuba and the conflict it caused with Barton, see Red Cross File, 1863–1957; American National Red Cross, 1878–1957; Relief Operations; Spanish-American War; Klopsch, Louis, 1898, undated; CB [hereafter: Klopsch folder, CB]. On this point, see also Marian Moser Jones, *The American Red Cross from Clara Barton to the New Deal* (Baltimore, MD: Johns Hopkins University Press, 2013), 85–89; Merle Curti, *American Philanthropy Abroad: A History* (New Brunswick, NJ: Rutgers University Press, 1963), 201–204; and Ian Tyrrell, *Reforming the World: The Creation of America's Moral Empire* (Princeton, NJ: Princeton University Press, 2010), 116–117.

45. "Fighting Back Famine in Cuba," 274–275; Charles H. H. Cottrell to Stephen Barton, March 15, 1898, Klopsch Folder, CB.

46. "Says Miss Barton Will Be Upheld: Question of Authority: Mr. Klopsch Thought His Publication Was in Charge of the Relief Work," *NYH*, March 25, 1898, n.p., in Scrapbooks, 1835–1930; 1898, Spanish-American War; CB [hereafter Scrapbooks, CB]. "Fighting Back Famine in Cuba," 274–275; "Fighting Over the Relief Work," *PP*, March 25, 1898, 4; and "Red Cross Gives Up Cuban Work," *NYH*, March 24, 1898, n.p., in Scrapbooks, CB.

47. "Miss Barton Indignant," *NYTR*, March 25, 1898, 4; and "Food Train Speeding across Cuba," 299.

48. "Fighting Back Famine in Cuba," 274–275.

49. Ibid.; Cottrell to Barton, March 15, 1898, Klopsch Folder, CB.

50. "Let All Help Poor Cuba Now," 23; and Clara Barton Diary, January 1, 1898, CB.

51. Louis Klopsch to Clara Barton, January 31, 1898, Red Cross File, 1863–1957; American National Red Cross, 1878–1957; Relief operations; Spanish-American War; Correspondence; General; 1897, Jan.-1898, Mar. 1897; CB [hereafter: Spanish-American War Correspondence, CB]. Stephen Barton to Clara Barton, February 18, 1898, Klopsch Folder, CB; and Louis Klopsch to Clara Barton, February 8, 1898, Klopsch Folder, CB.

52. Stephen Barton to Louis Klopsch, February 4, 1898, Spanish-American War Correspondence, CB; and Stephen Barton to Charles H. H. Cottrell, February 25, 1898, Spanish-American War Correspondence, CB.

53. Charles H. H. Cottrell to Stephen Barton, March 15, 1898, Klopsch Folder, CB; and Stephen Barton to John D. Long, March 2, 1898, Spanish-American War Correspondence, CB.

54. "Says Miss Barton Will Be Upheld," n.p.

55. Charles H. H. Cottrell to Stephen Barton, March 14, 1898, Klopsch Folder, CB; Charles H. H. Cottrell to Stephen Barton, March 15, 1898, Klopsch Folder, CB; and Charles H. H. Cottrell to Stephen Barton, March 16, 1898, Klopsch Folder, CB.

56. Stephen Barton to Clara Barton, March 19, 1898, Klopsch Folder, CB; Stephen Barton to Charles H. H. Cottrell, March 20, 1898, Klopsch Folder, CB; and Stephen Barton to Fitzhugh Lee, March 20, 1898, Spanish-American War Correspondence, CB.

57. Louis Klopsch to Stephen Barton, March 21, 1898, Klopsch Folder, CB; and "Friction over Cuban Relief Work," n.d, n.p., Scrapbooks, CB.

58. Charles H. H. Cottrell to Stephen Barton, March 22, 1898, Klopsch Folder, CB.

59. Fitzhugh Lee, quoted in "Work of Relief in Cuba," *BDE*, March 25, 1898, 5; Fitzhugh Lee to Stephen Barton, March 26, 1898, Spanish-American War Correspondence, CB; "Food Train Speeding across Cuba," 298–299; Fitzhugh Lee quoted in "General Lee on Relief Work," *NYT*, March 26, 1898, 3; Charles H. H. Cottrell to Stephen Barton, March 27, 1898, Klopsch Folder, CB; and Charles H. H. Cottrell to Stephen Barton, March 22, 1898, Klopsch Folder, CB.

60. "Miss Barton Indignant," 4; "Miss Barton Makes a Denial," *NYT*, March 25, 1898, 2; "Cuban Relief Committee: Miss Barton Says She Knows Nothing about the Reported Difference with Klopsch," *NYT*, March 30, 1898, 3; "Miss Barton Makes Denial," *NYH*, March 25, 1898, Scrapbooks, CB; and "Fighting over the Relief Work," *PP*, March 25, 1898, 4.

61. "Relief Work in Cuba," *NYS*, April 3, 1898, 4; "Dr K.'s Statement," *BDE*, April 4, 1898, 3; and "Food Train Speeding across Cuba," 299.

62. "Food Train Speeding across Cuba," 298–299.

63. "Quarrel Is Impending," *NYH*, March 26, 1898, n.p., Scrapbooks, CB; James Gordon Bennett, "Klopsch and the Red Cross," *SFCL*, March 26, 1898, 2; "Says Miss Barton Will Be Upheld," n.p.; and "Friction over Cuban Relief Work," n.p.

64. "Quarrel Is Impending," n.p.; and Charles H. H. Cottrell to Stephen Barton, March 27, 1898, Klopsch Folder, CB.

65. Stephen Barton to Clara Barton, March 25, 1898, Spanish-American War Correspondence, CB; "Miss Barton Will Return," *NYT*, April 1, 1898, 2; and Stephen Barton to Clara Barton, March 28, 1898, Klopsch Folder, CB.

66. "Clara Barton's Summons," *NYT*, April 5, 1898, 4; and Charles H. H. Cottrell to Stephen Barton, March 27 and 29, 1898, Klopsch Folder, CB.

67. Stephen Barton to Clara Barton, April 8, 1898, Klopsch Folder, CB. On Klopsch's resignation, see Charles Schieren to Louis Klopsch, May 18, 1898, Klopsch Folder, CB; and *Report of the Central Cuban Relief Committee, New York City, to the Secretary of State, Washington, DC*, June 15, 1898, 21.

68. William McKinley, "Message to the Congress of the United States," U.S. Department of State, *FRUS* (Washington, DC), 1898, 750–760.

69. Talmage, "War or Peace?," 320.

70. "A Righteous War," *CH,* May 4, 1898, 392.

71. "Face to Face with Our Destiny," 448; Talmage, "Alleviations of War," 428–429; "Our War with Spain Begun," 390–391; "Humanity in the War," *CH,* July 20, 1898, 590; "A Righteous War," 392; "What Next after War?," *CH,* August 3, 1898, 624; "Indemnity Not Revengeful," *CH,* August 17, 1898, 656; "Good Samaritan among Nations," *CH,* August 3, 1898, 624; and "Our Mail Bag," *CH,* September 14, 1898, 714. McCullough's *The Cross of War* analyzes similar rhetoric in American religious publications but does not mention the *Christian Herald.*

72. "A Righteous War," 392; "Our Mail Bag," *CH,* June 1, 1898, 468; Talmage, "Alleviations of War," 428–429; and "Indemnity Not Revengeful," 656.

73. "End of the War at Hand," *CH,* August 10, 1898, 638; "America's New Responsibility," 808; Talmage, "Alleviations of War," 428–429; "Face to Face with Our Destiny," 448; and "A Righteous War," 392.

74. Talmage, "Alleviations of War," 428–429; "Shall We Love Our Enemies?," *CH,* July 13, 1898, 576; and "What Next after War?," 624.

75. Thomas De Witt Talmage, "Cradle of the Twentieth Century," *CH,* November 30, 1898, 924.

76. Thomas De Witt Talmage, "The Makers of the Republic," *CH,* May 25, 1898, 452.

77. "Scenes in Our New Colonial Possessions in the Philippines," *CH,* May 18, 1898, 43; and "The Philippines Problem," *CH,* January 25, 1899, 61.

78. "Our Opportunity in the Pacific," *CH,* September 17, 1898, 704; and "Allied for Righteousness," *CH,* February 1, 1899, 91.

79. "Our Mail Bag," *CH,* June 8, 1898, 482; and "Our Mail Bag," *CH,* August 17, 1898, 650. With the exception of Edward J. Blum, "God's Imperialism: Mark Twain and the Religious War between Imperialists and Anti-imperialists," *JTS* 1, no. 1 (2009), few scholars focus on religion in the anti-imperialist movement. See, for example, Robert L. Beisner, *Twelve against Empire: The Anti-imperialists, 1898–1909* (New York: McGraw Hill, 1968); Michael P. Cullinane, *Liberty and American Anti-imperialism, 1898–1909* (New York: Palgrave, 2012); George P. Marks, *The Black Press Views American Imperialism (1898–1900)* (New York: Arno Press, 1971); Daniel Schirmer, *Republic or Empire: American Resistance to the Philippine War* (Cambridge, MA: Schenkman, 1972); Ian Tyrrell and Jay Sexton, eds., *Empire's Twin: U.S. Anti-imperialism from the Founding Era to the Age of Terrorism* (Ithaca, NY: Cornell University Press, 2015); and Richard E. Welch Jr., *Response to Imperialism: The United States and the Philippine-American War, 1899–1902* (Chapel Hill: University of North Carolina Press, 1979).

80. "End of the War at Hand," 638; and "Too Big a Question," *CH*, November 2, 1898, 848.

81. "What Next?," *CH*, April 5, 1899, 260; and Thomas De Witt Talmage, "Expansion," *CH*, June 7, 1899, 436–437.

82. Talmage, "Expansion," 436–437.

83. "Scenes in Our New Colonial Possessions," 431; "America's New Responsibility," 808; "Let All Help Porto Rico!," *CH*, August 23, 1899, 646; and "Famine Follows Flood in Cyclone-Swept Porto Rico," *CH*, August 23, 1899, 644–645.

84. Margaret Sangster, "Our Friends in Luzon," *CH*, February 14, 1900, 132; and Margaret Sangster, "The Gospel in Our New Colonies," *CH*, April 26, 1899, 325. On the affective dimensions of American imperialism, see Amy Kaplan, "Manifest Domesticity," 70, no. 3 *AL* (1998): 581–606.

85. "To Our Subscribers," *CH*, July 5, 1899, 530; and Charles M. Pepper, *Life-work of Louis Klopsch: Romance of a Modern Knight of Mercy* (New York: Christian Herald Association, 1910), 324–325.

86. "The Future of the Philippines," *CH*, October 18, 1899, 792; and Talmage, "Expansion," 436.

87. "Our Mail Bag," *CH*, February 22, 1899, 134.

88. "Scenes from the Seat of War in the Philippines," *CH*, March 29, 1999, 242–243; "The Philippines Problem," 61; "The Filipino Napoleon," *CH*, April 5, 1899, 270; and "The Second Battle of Manila," *CH*, February 15, 1899, 121.

89. "Imperialism of Christianity," *CH*, December 4, 1901, 1034; "Scenes from the Seat of War in the Philippines," 242–243; and "The Philippines Problem," 61.

90. "Imperialism of Christianity," 1034.

91. "Our Mail Bag," *CH*, August 10, 1898, 634.

92. "A Broadside on Public Affairs," 256.

4. ALMONER OF THE WORLD

1. "An Appeal from India," *CH*, November 22, 1899, 899; J. M. Thoburn, "Another Cry from Far-Off India," *CH*, December 13, 1899, 968; and "Hunger in India," *CH*, December 20, 1899, 989.

2. Charles M. Pepper, *Life-work of Louis Klopsch: Romance of a Modern Knight of Mercy* (New York: Christian Herald Association, 1910), 53–67; Thoburn, "Another Cry from Far-Off India," 968; "India's Piteous Appeal," *CH*, January 19, 1900, 36; and "Starving India's Pitiful Cry for Bread," *CH*, April 4, 1900, 286. For statistics on the 1896–1897 India famine, see Nibedita Shankar Ray-Bennett, "Indian Famine (1896–1902)," in *Encyclopedia of Disaster Relief*, ed. Matthew Stadler and K. Bradley Penuel (Thousand Oaks, CA:

Sage, 2011), 340–341. In this chapter, I retain the spelling and place names indicated in the primary sources.

3. Pepper, *Life-work,* 68–88; "India's Piteous Appeal," 36; and "$5,000 More for Starving India," *CH,* January 17, 1900, 52.

4. "A Relief Ship for Starving India," *CH,* March 7, 1900, 185; "Pioneer of the Famine Fleet," *CH,* April 18, 1900, 329; "The Whole Nation Helping India," *CH,* May 2, 1900, 379; and "Our Famine Ship on the Ocean," *CH,* May 16, 1900, 413, 417.

5. "Blessing the Famine Ship's Cargo," *CH,* May 23, 1900, 434–435, 445; and Pepper, *Life-work,* esp. 68–74.

6. Pepper, *Life-work,* 88, 89–104, 351. See also Merle Curti, *American Philanthropy Abroad: A History* (New Brunswick, NJ: Rutgers University Press, 1963), 133–136; and Ian Tyrrell, *Reforming the World: The Creation of America's Moral Empire* (Princeton, NJ: Princeton University Press, 2010), 111–115. Present value of contributions calculated using the Consumer Price Index.

7. On the ARC's difficulties in Cuba, consult Marian Moser Jones, *The American Red Cross from Clara Barton to the New Deal* (Baltimore: Johns Hopkins University Press, 2013), 89–93.

8. Richard E. Welch Jr., "American Atrocities in the Philippines: The Indictment and the Response," *PHR* 43, no. 2 (1974): 233–253; D. H. Smith, "American Atrocities in the Philippines: Some New Evidence," *PHR* 55, no. 2 (1974): 281–283; and Paul Kramer, *The Blood of Government: Race, Empire, the United States and the Philippines* (Chapel Hill: University of North Carolina Press, 2006), 145–151.

9. "Feeding India's Famishing Millions," *CH,* May 9, 1900, 389, 398; and "Corn for Starving India," *CH,* April 14, 1897, 294.

10. The literature on race, gender, and U.S. imperialism is extensive; studies that have shaped my thinking include Gail Bederman, *Manliness and Civilization: A Cultural History of Gender and Race in the United States, 1880–1917* (Chicago: University of Chicago Press, 1995); Kristen Hoganson, *Fighting for American Manhood* (New Haven, CT: Yale University Press, 1998); Amy Kaplan, "Manifest Domesticity," *AL* 70, no. 3 (1998): 581–606; Kramer, *Blood of Government;* Gretchen Murphy, *Shadowing the White Man's Burden: U.S. Imperialism and the Problem of the Color Line* (New York: New York University Press, 2010); Tyrrell, *Reforming the World;* and Rubin Frances Weston, *Racism in U.S. Imperialism: The Influence of Racial Assumptions on American Foreign Policy, 1893–1946* (Columbia: University of South Carolina Press, 1972).

11. "Famine-Stricken India," *CH,* January 13, 1897, 25. On the visual culture of abolition, see Elizabeth B. Clark, "'The Sacred Rights of the Weak': Pain, Sympathy, and the Culture of Individual Rights in Antebellum America," *JAH* 82, no. 2 (September 1995): 463–493; and Radiclani Clytus, "'Keep

It before the People': The Pictorialization of American Abolitionism," in *Early African American Print Culture in Theory and Practice,* ed. Lara Langer Cohen and Jordan Alexander Stein (Philadelphia: University of Pennsylvania Press, 2012), 290–317.

12. Mrs. Marcus B. (Jennie) Fuller, *The Wrongs of Indian Womanhood* (New York: Fleming H. Revell, 1900), dedication. On the role of images in the production of imperialism, see Heather Curtis, "Depicting Distant Suffering: Evangelicals and the Politics of Pictorial Humanitarianism in the Age of American Empire," *MR* 8, no. 2 (2012): 153–182; Mary Louise Pratt, *Imperial Eyes: Travel Writing and Transculturation,* 2nd ed. (London: Routledge, 2008); Molly Rogers, *Delia's Tears: Race, Science and Photography in Nineteenth-Century America* (New Haven, CT: Yale University Press, 2010); James R. Ryan, *Picturing Empire: Photography and the Visualization of the British Empire* (Chicago: University of Chicago Press, 1997); and Laura Wexler, *Tender Violence: Domestic Visions in an Age of U.S. Imperialism* (Chapel Hill: University of North Carolina Press, 2000).

13. Pepper, *Life-work,* 9.

14. "India's Twin Horrors," *CH,* February 3, 1897, 83.

15. *Soldier's Letters: Being Materials for the History of a War of Criminal Aggression* (Boston: Anti-imperialist League, 1899), 15. On the reaction from the *NYT,* see Robert Mann, *Wartime Dissent in America: A History and Anthology* (New York: Palgrave Macmillan, 2010), 63.

16. "Our Mail Bag," *CH,* November 22, 1899, 894; "The Philippines," *CMA,* October 21, 1899, 328; and "Our Mail Bag," *CH,* November 15, 1899, 874.

17. On Sheldon, see Paul S. Boyer, "In His Steps: A Reappraisal," *AQ* 23, no. 1 (1971): 60–78; Billie Barnes Jensen, "A Social Gospel Experiment in Newspaper Reform: Charles Sheldon and the *Topeka Daily Capital,*" *CHSCC* 33, no. 1 (March 1964): 74–83; Timothy Miller, *Following in His Steps: A Biography of Charles M. Sheldon* (Knoxville: University of Tennessee Press, 1988); and Gary Scott Smith, "Charles M. Sheldon's *In His Steps* in the Context of Religion and Culture in Late Nineteenth Century America," *FH* 22, no. 2 (Summer 1990): 47–69. Despite his strong stance against the Philippine War, Sheldon is rarely mentioned in studies of the anti-imperialist movement.

18. "The War Spirit," *TDC,* March 13, 1900, 1; Charles M. Sheldon, "The Topeka Capital This Week," *TDC,* March 13, 1900, 2; Charles M. Sheldon, "The Soldier's Worst Enemy: The End of the Canteen Farce," *TDC,* March 13, 1900, 2; and "The Philippines: What Justice Brewer Would Do with Them," *TDC,* March 13, 1900, 5.

19. "The Philippines: What Justice Brewer Would Do with Them," 5; "Our Colonial Trade," *TDC,* March 14, 1900, 5; "Is This Your Boasted Christian Civilization?" *TDC,* March 16, 1900, 1; "Against War," *TDC,* March 16, 1900, 1;

"For the Sake of Humanity, Draw the Curtain on This Act," *TDC*, March 14, 1900, 1; and "The War Spirit," 1.

20. "Starving India," *TDC*, March 13, 1900, 1

21. "Must They Starve? While Standard Oil Company Makes Millions," *TDC*, March 16, 1900, 1.

22. "Pastor Sheldon's Editorial Experience," *CH*, March 21, 1900, 230; "An Interesting Experiment," *CH*, January 31, 1900, 89; and "What Will Mr. Sheldon Do?" *CH*, February 7, 1900, 103.

23. "The Fund Grows," *TDC*, March 17, 1900, 3.

24. On the 1897 Interdenominational Missionary Committee, see "These All Helped Stricken India," *CH*, June 23, 1897, 502; and "India's Grateful People," *CH*, October 6, 1897, 747.

25. "A Bitter Cry for Food," *CH*, January 3, 1900, 15; and "Saving India's Starving Millions," *CH*, May 30, 1900, 458.

26. "All Help to Fill the Famine Ship," *CH*, April 25, 1900, 354; and "Our Famine Ship on the Ocean," 413, 417.

27. See, for example, "The Christian Herald India Famine Relief Supplement," *CH*, April 4, 1900, 280–283. This pattern continues in the April 25, May 8, May 16, June 6, and June 13 issues.

28. "Our Famine Ship on the Ocean," 413, 417. See also Curti, *American Philanthropy*, on the multiple constituencies involved in aiding India.

29. "How One Pastor Helped India," *CH*, March 31, 1897, 251; and "The Christian Herald India Famine Supplement," *CH*, April 21, 1897, 317–320.

30. "Starving India's Pitiful Cry for Bread," *TDC*, March 14, 1900, 8; "Our Mail Bag," *CH*, May 9, 1900, 390; and "Facts about the Famine," *CMA*, March 17, 1900, 174.

31. "Our Mail Bag," 390; "Corn for Starving India," 294; and "To Fill the Famine Relief Ships," *CH*, May 12, 1897, 386–387.

32. "America, the Almoner of the World," *CH*, June 26, 1901, cover; "Still in the Throes of Famine," *CH*, April 7, 1897, 274–275; and "Now Fill the Corn Ships," *CH*, April 14, 1897, 296.

33. "Pioneer of the Famine Fleet," 329; and "Friends of India," *CH*, April 25, 1900, 352.

34. "Our Famine Ship on the Ocean," 413, 417; "In the Final Throes of the Famine," *CH*, June 20, 1900, 517; "India Welcomes Our Relief Ship," *CH*, July 11, 1900, 569, 578; and "The Whole Nation Helping India," 379.

35. Jones, *American Red Cross*, 93; "All Help to Fill the Famine Ship," 354; and "Starving India's Pitiful Cry for Bread," 286. On Barton's efforts to secure a congressional charter for the ARC, see Jones, *American Red Cross*, 93–94, and Julia Irwin, *Making the World Safe: The American Red Cross and a Nation's Humanitarian Awakening* (New York: Oxford University Press, 2013), 27.

36. Alvey A. Adee, quoted in "India's Viceroy Invites American Help," *CH*, April 4, 1900, 279.

37. "Feeding India's Famishing Millions," 398; and "Blessing the Famine Ship's Cargo," 433–434.

38. "Feeding India's Famishing Millions," 398; and "Our Famine Ship on the Ocean," 413, 417.

39. "Feeding India's Famishing Millions," 389.

40. On Barton's discomfort with fund-raising and accounting, see Irwin, *Making the World Safe*, 28–29; and Jones, *American Red Cross*, 99–102.

41. Pepper, *Life-work*, 328–330.

42. "To Feed Starving India," *CH*, February 17, 1897, 127; "A Bitter Cry for Food," 15; "The Pioneer of the Famine Fleet," 329; and "$5,000 More for Starving India," 52.

43. "$5,000 More for Starving India," 52; "India's Starving Millions," *CH*, January 20, 1897, 45; "$20,000 More for India," *CH*, March 17, 1897, 210; "Our Corn Ship in India," *CH*, September 29, 1897, 721, 723; and "Blessing the Famine Ship's Cargo," 445.

44. "India's Great Famine Nearing the Crisis," *CH*, June 13, 1900, 501.

45. "India," *CH*, April 7, 1897, 276; Thomas De Witt Talmage, "Hunger in India," *CH*, May 5, 1897, 264–265; and "$20,000 More for India," 210.

46. "In the Final Throes of the Famine," 517; and "Blessing the Famine Ship's Cargo," 433, 445.

47. "Blessing the Famine Ship's Cargo," 433, 445.

48. "India Welcomes Our Relief Ship," *CH*, July 11, 1900, 569; A. B. Simpson, "The Grounds of Missionary Obligation," *CMA*, October 27, 1897, 416–418; and A. J. Gordon, "Foreign Missions," Supplement to *CMA*, October 9 and 16, 1891, 14–15. On Simpson's views and the growing debate about humanitarian missions, see William R. Hutchison, *Errand to the World: American Protestant Thought and Foreign Missions* (Chicago: University of Chicago Press, 1987); Dana Robert, *American Women in Mission: A Social History of Their Thought and Practice* (Macon, GA: Mercer University Press, 1996); and Jean Miller Schmidt, *Souls or the Social Order: The Two-Party System in American Protestantism* (Brooklyn, NY: Carlson, 1991).

49. For example, see "Editorials," *CMA*, May 5, 1897, 516; "Editorials," *CMA*, August 18, 1897, 180; "The Situation in India," *CMA*, May 26, 1900, 348; and "The India Famine," *CMA*, June 16, 1900, 402.

50. "Hunger in India," 989; and Talmage, "Hunger in India," 364–365.

51. "Corn for India Pouring In," *CH*, May 5, 1897, 367; and "Correspondence," *CMA*, March 3, 1900, 142.

52. "Still in the Throes of Famine," 274; "For Starving India," *CH*, March 24, 1897, 225; "To Fill the Famine Relief Ships," 386–387; and "India's Perishing Millions," *CH*, March 21, 1900, 229.

53. "India's Perishing Millions," 229; "For Starving India," 225, 237–240; "Hunger in India," 989; "India's Piteous Appeal," 36; "Corn for Starving India," 294; and "India's Fight with Famine," *CH*, June 9, 1897, 461.

54. Thomas De Witt Talmage, "Sympathy for the Fallen," in "Twelfth Anniversary," *CH*, May 26, 1881, 325; Thomas De Witt Talmage, "The Democracy of Religion," *CH*, October 9, 1879, 804; "Cultivate Sympathy," *CH*, December 2, 1896, 902; "Thousands Homeless and Helpless," *CH*, September 12, 1894, 581; "A Congress of Religions," *CH*, September 6, 1893, 577; and "Parliament of Religion," *CH*, October 11, 1893, 661.

55. Talmage, "Hunger in India," 364–365.

56. "Questions and Answers," *CH*, May 2, 1900, 370. For helpful context on these views, see Jennifer Snow, *Protestant Missionaries, Asian Immigrants, and Ideologies of Race in America, 1850–1924* (New York: Routledge, 2007).

57. "Starving India's Pitiful Cry for Bread," 286; "Effects of the Famine," *CMA*, January 19, 1901, 40; and "Universal Brotherhood," *CH*, March 31, 1897, 261.

58. "Blessing the Famine Ship's Cargo," 433–435; and "Famine Stricken India," *CH*, January 13, 1897, 25.

59. "An Easter Offering of $25,000 for India," *CH*, April 11, 1900, 299.

60. "Blessing the Famine Ship's Cargo," 434; "$5,000 More for Starving India," 52; "The Christian Herald India Famine Supplement," 320; "Starving India's Pitiful Cry for Bread," 286; and "Feeding Christ's Lambs in Stricken India," *CH*, September 5, 1900, 731.

61. "India and the Gospel," *CH*, August 19, 1896, 613; and "Mission Work in India," *CH*, July 30, 1890, cover and 484.

62. "Introduction of the Gospel into India," *CMA*, July 1886, 9–19; and "India's Starving Millions," 45.

63. "Zenana Missions," *CMA*, July 1886, 25–27; and Fuller, *Wrongs of Indian Womanhood*. On evangelical concern for women in "heathen lands," see especially Joan Jacobs Brumberg, "Zenanas and Girlless Villages: The Ethnology of American Evangelical Women, 1870–1910," *JAH* 69, no. 2 (1982): 347–371; and Tyrrell, *Reforming the World*.

64. "Mission Work in India," 484; and "Christ's Work in Ceylon," *CH*, March 9, 1892, 149.

65. "Famine Relief Work," *CH*, April 25, 1900, 352; "Corn for Starving India," 294; and "Starving India's Pitiful Cry for Bread," 286.

66. "Corn for Starving India," 294; "All Help to Fill the Famine Ship," 354; Louis Klopsch, "My Tour through Famine-Stricken India," *CH*, August 15, 1900, 672–673; "Blessing the Famine Ship's Cargo," 435; and "Our Mail Bag," *CH*, March 28, 1900, 250.

67. "Saving the Children in India," *CH*, September 22, 1897, 710; letter from Grace E. Wilder in "A Bitter Cry for Food," 15; "An Easter Offering of

$25,000 for India," 299; and "Thousands in India Saved from Starving," *CH,* June 6, 1900, 480.

68. "Thousands in India Saved from Starving," 480; "India's Orphan Children Plead for Help," *CH,* September 19, 1900, 772; "Saving India's Starving Millions," 458; and "What Christian America Is Doing for India," *CH,* December 5, 1900, 993.

69. Pepper, *Life-work,* 89–104; "Miscellaneous Questions," *CH,* March 28, 1900, 250; "Our Orphan Roll of Honor," *CH,* August 8, 1900, 652; and "India's Orphan Children Plead for Help," 772.

70. John Bancroft Devins, "Our Famine Orphans Visited," *CH,* July 6, 1904, 582; Louis Klopsch, "A Personal Letter from Dr. Klopsch," *CH,* August 19, 1903, 698; and "What Christian America Is Doing for India," 993. The *Christian Herald*'s campaign reflects a broader imperial effort to "civilize" nonwhite children through Christian conversion. On this point, see Kaplan, "Manifest Domesticity," 581–606; Shurlee Swain, "Brighter Britain: Images of Empire in the International Child Rescue Movement, 1859–1915," in *Empires of Religion* (New York: Palgrave, 2008), 161–176; and Katherine Bullard, *Civilizing the Child: Discourses of Race, Nation and Child Welfare in America* (Lanham, MD: Lexington Books, 2013).

71. "What Christian America Is Doing for India," 993; "Have You Adopted an India Famine Waif?" *CH,* October 31, 1900, 893; and Thomas De Witt Talmage, "Expansion," *CH,* June 7, 1899, 436.

72. "Starving India's Pitiful Cry for Bread," 286; "Have You Adopted an India Famine Waif?" 893; and "The Whole Nation Helping India," 379.

73. "India's Bitter Cry," *CH,* March 3, 1897, 167. For analysis of the *Christian Herald*'s pioneering role in pictorial humanitarianism in comparison to other publications, see Curtis, "Depicting Distant Suffering."

74. Thomas De Witt Talmage, "Pictures Good and Bad," *CH,* June 21, 1899, 492–493.

75. "India Famine Scenes," *CMA,* June 9, 1900, 378; Louis Klopsch, "My Tour through Famine-Stricken India," *CH,* July 25, 1900, 610–611; Louis Klopsch, "My Tour through Famine-Stricken India," *CH,* August 1, 1900, 633–634; Louis Klopsch, "My Tour through Famine-Stricken India," August 15, 1900, 672–673; Louis Klopsch, "My Tour through Famine-Stricken India," *CH,* August 29, 1900, 706–707; and "Thousands in India Saved from Starving," 480.

76. "Feeding India's Famishing Millions," 398.

77. J. M. Thoburn, "Bishop Thoburn Pleads for India's Orphans," *CH,* September 5, 1900, 722; "India's Bitter Cry," 167; and "Corn for India Pouring In," 367.

78. "America, the Almoner of the World," cover.

79. R. D. Bannister, "Needy Khandesh," *CMA*, June 23, 1900, 412–413; and Jennie Fuller, "Suffering India," *TOF* (January 1900): 18.

80. Marcus B. Fuller, "Famine's Ravages," *CMA*, May 12, 1900, 303–304.

81. Fuller, "Famine's Ravages," 303–304; see also M[ark] B. Fuller, "Famine Prospects in Gujerat," *CMA*, November 25, 1899, 407, 419; and "Editorial," *CMA*, June 18, 1897, 588.

82. Fuller, "Famine's Ravages," 303–304.

83. "The Pioneer of the Famine Fleet," 329; "All Help to Fill the Famine Ship," 354; and "India's Great Famine Nearing the Crisis," 501.

84. "India Appeals: Cable Relief, Quick," *CH*, July 18, 1900, 593.

85. Among the many scholarly biographies and analyses of Ramabai's life, the most useful include Padma Anagol, *The Emergence of Feminism in India, 1850–1920* (Aldershot, England: Ashgate, 2005); Edith Blumhofer, "Consuming Fire: Pandita Ramabai and the Global Pentecostal Impulse," in *Interpreting Contemporary Christianity: Global Processes and Local Identities,* ed. Ogbu Kalu and Alaine Low (Grand Rapids, MI: Eerdmans, 2008), 207–237; and " 'From India's Coral Strand': Pandita Ramabai and U.S. Support for Foreign Missions," in *The Foreign Missionary Enterprise at Home: Explorations in North American Cultural History,* ed. Daniel H. Bays and Grant Wacker (Tuscaloosa: University of Alabama Press, 2003), 152–170; Antoinette Burton, *At the Heart of Empire: Indians and the Colonial Encounter in Late-Victorian Britain* (Berkeley: University of California Press, 1998); Uma Chakravarti, *Rewriting History: The Life and Times of Pandita Ramabai* (New Delhi: Kali for Women in Association with the Book Review Literary Trust, 1998); Kumari Jayawardena, *The White Woman's Other Burden: Western Women and South Asia during British Colonial Rule* (New York: Routledge, 1995); Meera Kosambi, *Pandita Ramabai's Feminist and Christian Conversions* (Bombay: Research Centre for Women's Studies, S.N.D.T. Women's University, 1995); and Gauri Viswanathan, *Outside the Fold: Conversion, Modernity and Belief* (Princeton, NJ: Princeton University Press, 1989).

86. For one account of this history, see Meera Kosambi, introduction to *Pandita Ramabai through Her Own Words: Selected Works,* ed. and trans. Meera Kosambi (New York: Oxford University Press, 2000), 3–13.

87. "Still in the Throes of Famine," 274; "Our Indian Famine Fund," *CH*, June 2, 1897, 447; and "Sheltering India's Starving Widows," *CH*, July 14, 1897, 547.

88. "Sheltering India's Starving Widows," 547; "Rescuing Child Widows in India," *CH*, September 1, 1897, 662; "Saving the Children in India," 710; "India's Widows Sheltered," *CH*, March 2, 1898, 188; "Pandita Ramabai's Report," in *Report of the Third Annual Meeting of the American Ramabai Association Held March 18, 1901* (Boston: American Ramabai Association, 1901):

30–31; and Pandita Ramabai, "To the Friends of Mukti School and Mission," in *Pandita Ramabai through Her Own Words: Selected Works,* ed. and trans. Meera Kosambi (New York: Oxford University Press, 2000), 262.

89. Helen S. Dyer, *Pandita Ramabai: Her Vision, Her Mission, Her Triumph of Faith* (London: Pickering and Inglis, 1923), 72. For an account of self-supporting work at Mukti, see *Report of the First Annual Meeting of the Ramabai Association* (Boston: American Ramabai Association, 1899), 17–18, 26–28.

90. "Work in India," *TOF,* September 1900, 203; and "The Whole Nation Helping India," 379.

91. Pandita Ramabai, *The Peoples of the United States* (1889), trans. and ed. Meera Kosambi (Bloomington: Indiana University Press, 2003), 114–118; see also Robert Frykenberg, ed., *Pandita Ramabai's America: Conditions of Life in the United States* (Grand Rapids, MI: Eerdmans, 2003), 141–147.

92. Eunice Wells, "Orphanage Work in India," *LT* (November 1905): 685; Ramabai was especially influential among independent faith missionaries, Methodists, and workers affiliated with the CMA. On her connection with the Nortons and other Western missionaries, see Dyer, *Pandita Ramabai,* esp. 66, 72, 130–131.

93. "World's Missionary Conference: Appeal for India," *CH,* May 9, 1900, 395; Sadie Cody, "The Work and the Workers," *TOF,* February 1913, 29–31; and "How Indian Widows Give," *CMA,* March 2, 1901, 125.

94. Kosambi, introduction to *Pandita Ramabai,* 13.

5. THE LIMITS OF EVANGELICAL BENEVOLENCE

1. Brigadier General A. S. Daggett, *American in the China Relief Expedition* (Kansas City, MO: Hudson-Kimberly, 1903).

2. On the Boxer Rebellion, see Robert A. Bickers and R. G. Tiedemann, eds., *The Boxers, China, and the World* (Lanham, MD: Rowman and Littlefield, 2007); Diana Preston, *The Boxer Rebellion: The Dramatic Story of China's War on Foreigners That Shook the World in the Summer of 1900* (New York: Walker, 2000); David Silbey, *The Boxer Rebellion and the Great Game in China* (New York: Hill and Wang, 2012); and Larry C. Thompson, *William Scott Ament and the Boxer Rebellion: Heroism, Hubris, and the Ideal Missionary* (Jefferson, NC: McFarland, 2009).

3. "China's Carnival of Riot and Massacre," *CH,* June 27, 1900, 531; "Missionaries Cruelly Slain," *CH,* October 31, 1900, 897; and "China a Prey to Anarchy," *CH,* July 4, 1900, 551.

4. "The Looting of Peking Justifiable," *NYT,* March 17, 1901, 25; and "Pillage in the Capital—Looting at Peking Continued," *NYT,* September 15, 1900, 1.

5. "Meet Peace Envoys To-day," *NYS,* December 24, 1900, 1.

6. "Loot and Indemnity in China," *NYT,* January 26, 1907, 8; and "Our Missionaries in China," *NYT,* February 7, 1901, 8.

7. Mark Twain, "To the Person Sitting in Darkness," *NAR* 172 (February 1901), 161–176.

8. Twain, "To the Person Sitting in Darkness," 161–176; and Mark Twain, "To My Missionary Critics," *NAR* 172 (April 1901), 520–534.

9. Ida B. Wells-Barnett, "Lynch Law in America," *Arena* 23, no. 1 (January 1900): 15–24; see also *Southern Horrors and Other Writings: The Anti-Lynching Campaign of Ida B. Wells, 1892–1900,* 2nd ed., ed. Jacqueline Jones Royster (Boston: Bedford / St. Martin's, 2016). For Wells-Barnett's long-standing anti-lynching campaign and critique of American humanitarianism, consult James W. Davidson, *"They Say": Ida B. Wells and the Reconstruction of Race* (New York: Oxford University Press, 2009); Gary Dorrien, *The New Abolition: W. E. B. DuBois and the Black Social Gospel* (New Haven, CT: Yale University Press, 2015); Kristina DuRocher, *Ida B. Wells: Social Reformer and Activist* (New York: Routledge, 2017); Patricia Schechter, *Ida B. Wells-Barnett and American Reform, 1880–1930* (Chapel Hill: University of North Carolina Press, 2001); Sarah L. Silkey, *Black Woman Reformer: Ida B. Wells, Lynching, and Transatlantic Activism* (Athens: University of Georgia Press, 2015); Ian Tyrrell, *Reforming the World: The Creation of America's Moral Empire* (Princeton, NJ: Princeton University Press, 2012), chap. 8; and Ann Marie Wilson, "Taking Liberties Abroad, Americans and the International Humanitarian Advocacy, 1821–1914" (PhD diss., Harvard University, 2010), chap. 5.

10. Wells-Barnett, "Lynch Law in America," 15–24; and Ida B. Wells-Barnett, *Mob Rule in New Orleans* (Chicago, 1900).

11. Wells-Barnett, *Mob Rule in New Orleans.*

12. For the term "evangelical nationalism" I am indebted to Derek Chang, *Citizens of a Christian Nation: Evangelical Missions and the Problem of Race in the Nineteenth Century* (Philadelphia: University of Pennsylvania Press, 2010), 7–8; see also Matthew McCullough, *Cross of War: Christian Nationalism and U.S. Expansion in the Spanish-American War* (Madison: University of Wisconsin Press, 2014).

13. "Minister Wu Tells of China's Great Famine," *CH,* February 20, 1901, 159; "China's New Calamity," *CH,* May 1, 1901, 406; "Li Hung Chang Appeals to the US," *CH,* May 8, 1901, 425–426; and "Li Hung Chang Appeals to US for Help," *CH,* May 15, 1901, 454.

14. "Horrors of China's Famine," *CH,* May 15, 1901, 451; "Famine-Stricken China's Cry Heard," *CH,* May 19, 1901, 488; "China's Famine Still Spreading," *CH,* June 5, 1901, 511; "First $20,000 for Starving China," *CH,* June 12, 1901, 533; Francis H. Nichols, "A Relief Journey across China," *CH,* November 27, 1901, 995, 1011; and Charles M. Pepper, *Life-work of Louis*

Klopsch: Romance of a Modern Knight of Mercy (New York: Christian Herald Association, 1910), 181.

15. "China's New Calamity," 406; "A Cry for Bread," *CH*, June 19, 1901, 552; "The Famine in China," *CH*, May 15, 1901, 450; and "Li Hung Chang Appeals to the US for Help," 454.

16. "The Famine in China," 450; and "Earl Li's Appeal," *CH*, May 8, 1901, 428.

17. "The Famine in China," 450.

18. "Dealing with China," *CH*, May 29, 1901, 492; and "American Diplomacy Triumphant," *CH*, April 1, 1901, 356.

19. "The Democracy of Religion," *CH*, April 25, 1894, 262. For context on Talmage's millennial views, see James Moorhead, *World without End: Mainstream American Protestant Visions of the Last Things, 1880–1925* (Bloomington: Indiana University Press, 1999).

20. "American Diplomacy Triumphant," 356; Wu Ting Fang, "Earl Li Cables China's Thanks," *CH*, June 19, 1901, 552; and "International Friendships," *CH*, March 26, 1902, 260.

21. "A Cosmopolitan Resort," *CH*, May 5, 1897, 69.

22. "At Freedom's Gate," *CH*, August 28, 1896, 625; and Thomas De Witt Talmage, "The Democracy of Religion," *CH*, October 8, 1879, 804.

23. Talmage, "The Democracy of Religion," 804; and "The Democracy of Religion," 262. Scholarship on the racial theories that shaped Talmage's views includes Edward J. Blum, *Reforging the White Republic: Race, Religion, and American Nationalism, 1865–1898* (Baton Rouge: Louisiana State University Press, 2005); Chang, *Citizens of a Christian Nation;* George M. Frederickson, *Black Image in the White Mind: The Debate on Afro-American Character and Destiny, 1817–1914* (New York: Harper and Row, 1971); and Ralph Luker, *The Social Gospel in Black and White: American Racial Reform, 1885–1912* (Chapel Hill: University of North Carolina Press, 1991).

24. "Freedom of Worship," *CH*, June 12, 1895, 378; "The Great and Growing West," *CH*, June 13, 1894, 374; and Thomas De Witt Talmage, "Before They Adjourn," *CH*, May 13, 1896, 374–375.

25. Thomas De Witt Talmage, "America for God," *CH*, March 11, 1896, 203; "Freedom of Worship," 378; "America for God," *CH*, September 4, 1895, 574; and Talmage, "Before They Adjourn," 375. Helpful studies of changing views about immigration, racial amalgamation, and American exceptionalism include Chang, *Citizens of a Christian Nation;* Reginald Horsman, *Race and Manifest Destiny: The Origins of American Racial Anglo-Saxonism* (Cambridge, MA: Harvard University Press, 1981); Matthew Frye Jacobson, *Whiteness of a Different Color: European Immigrants and the Alchemy of Race* (Cambridge, MA: Harvard University Press, 1998) and *Barbarian Virtues: The United States Encounters Foreign Peoples at Home and Abroad, 1876–1917* (New York: Hill and Wang, 2000); Jason E. Pierce, ed., *Making the White Man's West: Whiteness and the*

Creation of the American West (Boulder: University Press of Colorado, 2016); Jennifer C. Snow, *Protestant Missionaries, Asian Immigrants, and Ideologies of Race in America, 1850–1924* (New York: Taylor and Francis, 2007); and Frank Van Nuys, *Americanizing the West: Race, Immigrants and Citizenship, 1890–1930* (Lawrence: Kansas University Press, 2002).

26. For this history, see especially John Higham, *Strangers in the Land: Patterns of American Nativism 1860–1925* (New Brunswick, NJ: Rutgers University Press, 1955).

27. "The Open Door," *CH*, July 15, 1891, 438; and Talmage, "Before They Adjourn," 374–375.

28. "Portrait of the Life of Stephen Merritt," *CH*, May 14, 1890, 305, 308–309.

29. "Chinese Brought to Christ," *CH*, March 20, 1895, 181; "A School in 'Chinatown,'" *CH*, November 27, 1895, 789; and "Forty Thousand Children Saved!," *CH*, June 19, 1895, 389, 391.

30. Talmage, "Before They Adjourn," 374–375; and "A Jew Teaching of Christ," *CH*, June 27, 1894, 405.

31. "Alien Children Led to Christ," *CH*, June 6, 1894, 353, 355.

32. Ibid.

33. "Across the Seas to Freedom," *CH*, April 7, 1897, 271; and Pepper, *Life-work*, 290.

34. "A Children's Paradise," *CH*, June 13, 1894, 383; "Little Waifs from Hot Ally," *CH*, July 8, 1896, 510; and "Tenement Child-Life in New York," *CH*, June 28, 1899, 512–513.

35. "A Children's Paradise," 383; "Three Great Christian Charities," *CH*, June 7, 1899, 443–456; "What a Stranger Saw at Mont-Lawn," *CH*, September 8, 1909, 376; and Pepper, *Life-work*, 303.

36. "Our Little Folk at Mont-Lawn," *CH*, August 10, 1898, 646; and "Tenement House Children," *CH*, July 24, 1895, 477.

37. "Tenement House Children," 477; "Save the Children," *CH*, April 4, 1894, 214; "Children of the Streets," *CH*, August 12, 1896, 600; and "Children of the Street," *CH*, June 10, 1891, 360. Mont-Lawn was part of the broader "child-saving" movement: Katherine Bullard, *Civilizing the Child: Discourses of Race, Nation and Child Welfare in America* (Lanham, MD: Lexington Books, 2013); and Thomas E. Jordan, *Victorian Child-Savers and Their Culture* (Lewiston, NY: E. Mellen Press, 1998).

38. "A Cry for Sunday Schools," *CH*, May 6, 1891, 276–277; "Training Child Waifs and Strays," *CH*, April 15, 1896, 305; and "Our Little White Heathens," *CH*, November 16, 1892, 741. Helpful histories on efforts to assimilate whites to a national Protestant culture include Nathaniel Deutsch, *Inventing America's Worst Family: Eugenics, Islam, and the Rise and Fall of the Tribe of Ishmael* (Berkeley: University of California Press, 2009); and Daniel Lee, "A Great Racial Commission: Religion and the Construction

of White America," in *Race, Nation and Religion in the Americas,* ed. Henry Gold-
schmidt and Elizabeth McAlister (New York: Oxford University Press,
2004), 85–110.

39. "Among the Mountain Whites," *CH,* December 9, 1896, 927; and "Lincoln
Memorial University," *CH,* February 22, 1899, 137.

40. "Save the Boys," *CH,* September 11, 1895, 590; and "Continental Republic," *CH,* March 27, 1895, 198.

41. "Save the Children," 214; and "Continental Republic," 198.

42. "'Little Twelve Thousand,'" *CH,* September 12, 1900, 754; and "Gospel
among the Ranchman," *CH,* June 3, 1896, 425, 430.

43. On this point, see, for example, Chang, *Citizens of a Christian Nation;* Jacobson, *Whiteness of a Different Color;* and Snow, *Protestant Missionaries, Asian
Immigrants.* See also Sarah Gualtieri, *Between Arab and White: Race and Ethnicity in the Early Syrian American Diaspora* (Berkeley: University of California Press, 2009).

44. Chang, *Citizens of a Christian Nation.*

45. The literature on missions to African Americans and Native Americans
is vast. On the complexities of "conversion" and difference, see especially
Chang, *Citizens of a Christian Nation;* and Linford D. Fisher, *The Indian Great
Awakening: Religion and the Shaping of Native Cultures in Early America* (New
York: Oxford University Press, 2012).

46. For this history of missions, see Blum, *Reforging the White Republic;* Chang,
Citizens of a Christian Nation; Margaret D. Jacobs, *White Mother to a Dark Race:
Settler Colonialism, Maternalism, and the Removal of Indigenous Children in the
American West and Australia, 1880–1940* (Lincoln: University of Nebraska
Press, 2009); and Peggy Pascoe, *Relations of Rescue: The Search for Female
Authority in the American West, 1874–1939* (New York: Oxford University
Press, 1990).

47. "Current Events," *CH,* May 28, 1890, 345; and "A Self-Helping Institu-
tion," *CH,* February 22, 1893, 121. Histories of industrial education in-
clude David W. Adams, *Education for Extinction: American Indians and the
Boarding School Experience, 1875–1928* (Lawrence: University of Kansas Press,
1995); James Anderson, *The Education of Blacks in the South, 1860–1935* (Chapel
Hill: University of North Carolina Press, 1988); John Demos, *The Heathen
School: A Story of Hope and Betrayal in the Age of the Early Republic* (New York:
Knopf, 2014); Robert F. Engs, *Educating the Disenfranchised: Samuel Chapman
Armstrong and Hampton Institute, 1839–1893* (Knoxville: University of Ten-
nessee Press, 1999); Jacobs, *White Mother;* Donald F. Lindsey, *Indians at
Hampton, 1877–1923* (Urbana: University of Illinois Press, 1995); and Francis
Prucha, *The Churches and the Indian Schools, 1888–1912* (Bloomington: In-
diana University Press, 1979).

48. "The Negro Emigration Question," *CH,* August 26, 1891, 535.

49. Talmage, "Before They Adjourn," 374–375; and "Our Indian Wards at Home," *CH*, October 31, 1894, 699.

50. "The Sioux Indian Troubles," *CH*, December 31, 1890, 837; and "The Negro Emigration Question," 535. Histories that put the *Christian Herald*'s approach into historical context include Christine Bolt, *American Indian Policy and American Reform: Case Studies of the Campaign to Assimilate the American Indians* (Boston: Allen and Unwin, 1987); Brian Dipple, *The Vanishing American: White Attitudes and U.S. Indian Policy* (Lawrence: University of Kansas Press, 1982); Frederick E. Hoxie, *A Final Promise: A Campaign to Assimilate the Indians, 1880–1920,* Bixon Books ed. (Lincoln: University of Nebraska Press, 2001); Robert H. Keller, *American Protestantism and United States Indian Policy* (Lincoln: University of Nebraska Press, 1983); Francis Paul Prucha, *American Indian Policy in Crisis: Christian Reformers and the Indian, 1865–1900* (Norman: University of Oklahoma Press, 1976); and *The Great Father: The United States Government and the American Indians* (Lincoln: University of Nebraska Press, 1995).

51. Edward Ayers, *Promise of the New South: Life after Reconstruction,* 15th ann. ed. (New York: Oxford University Press, 2007); Philip Dray, *At the Hands of Persons Unknown: The Lynching of Black America* (New York: Random House, 2002); Grace E. Hale, *Making Whiteness: The Culture of Segregation in the South, 1890–1940* (New York: Pantheon, 1998); Robert Haws, ed., *The Age of Segregation: Race Relations in the South,* 1890–1945 (Jackson: University of Mississippi Press, 1978); Michael J. Pfeifer, *Rough Justice: Lynching and American Society, 1874–1974* (Urbana-Champaign: University of Illinois Press, 2006); Janet McDonnell, *The Dispossession of the American Indian* (Bloomington: University of Indiana Press, 1991); Michael Perman, *Struggle for Mastery: Disenfranchisement in the South, 1888–1908* (Chapel Hill: University of North Carolina Press, 2001); Amy Louise Wood, *Lynching and Spectacle: Witnessing Racial Violence in America, 1890–1940* (Chapel Hill: University of North Carolina Press, 2009); Van C. Woodward and William McFeely, *The Strange Career of Jim Crow,* comm. ed. (New York: Oxford University Press, 2002); and Richard Wormser, *The Rise and Fall of Jim Crow* (New York: St. Martin's Press, 2003).

52. Scholars have written extensively on Booker T. Washington. Recent works that assess his legacy include Michael Scott Bieze and Marybeth Gasman, eds., *Booker T. Washington Rediscovered* (Baltimore: Johns Hopkins University Press, 2012); and Raymond Smock, *Booker T. Washington: Black Leadership in the Age of Jim Crow* (Chicago: Ivan R. Dee, 2009).

53. Booker T. Washington, "Atlanta Exposition Address, September 18, 1895," in *The Booker T. Washington Papers,* ed. Louis R. Harlan et al., vol. 3 (Urbana: University of Illinois Press, 1974), 584–587.

54. "Missions in the 'Black Belt,'" *CH*, April 4, 1894, 218.

55. Ibid.; "A Successful Industrial Work," *CH*, May 27, 1896, 421; and "On a 'Black Belt' Mission Farm," *CH*, March 8, 1893, 165.

56. "Christ-Like Work," *CH*, May 20, 1896, 394; Carolyn Wilson Mbajekwe, "The Difficult Task: Fundraising for Small Southern Black Industrial Schools: The Case of Emma Jane Wilson and the Mayesville Educational and Industrial Institute, 1900–1915," *AEH* 30 (2003): 7–16; and Dorothy Hynes Datiri, "'Saving Grace': Educating African American Children through Industrial Education in Mayesville," *Carologue* (Fall 2013): 20–24.

57. "Christ-Like Work," 394; "Starting Them in Life," *CH*, June 23, 1897, 497; "A Joyful Celebration," *CH*, November 9, 1898, 863; "A Self-Helping Enterprise," *CH*, January 28, 1903, 70; and "Starting Them in Life," 497.

58. "The Cheyenne Rising," *CH*, June 16, 1897, 475; "Our Indian Wards at Home," 699; "The Red Man and the Gospel," *CH*, September 2, 1897, 47; and "Civilizing the Apaches," *CH*, September 2, 1896, 643.

59. "Red Man and the Gospel," 47; and "Our Indian Wards at Home," 699.

60. "The Indians," *CH*, January 15, 1897, 48.

61. "Champions of the Indian," *CH*, November 20, 1901, 976.

62. "To Civilize the Indian," *CH*, March 12, 1902, 221; E. R. Johnstone, "Are We Doing Our Best for the Indians," *CH*, January 27, 1904, 70; and "A New Indian Question," *CH*, January 27, 1904, 72.

63. Johnstone, "Are We Doing Our Best for the Indians," 70; and "An Uplift for the Negro," *CH*, March 13, 1893, 177.

64. Williamjames Hull Hoffer, *Plessy v. Ferguson: Race and Inequality in Jim Crow America* (Lawrence: University Press of Kansas, 2012); and Charles A. Lofgren, *The Plessy Case: A Legal-Historical Interpretation* (New York: Oxford University Press, 1987).

65. Amory H. Bradford, "Our Nation's Shame," *Outlook* 49, no. 25 (June 23, 1894), 1143. The *Outlook* published articles on lynching throughout the 1890s, as did other publications like the *Century Illustrated Monthly*: "Shall We Burn Criminals?" *Outlook* 48, no. 16 (October 14, 1893), 663; "Lynchings in the South," *Outlook* 50, no. 8 (August 25, 1894), 298; "Southern Protests against Lynching," *CIM* (January 1898), 476; "The Lynching Atrocities," *Outlook* 61, no. 13 (April 1, 1899), 711; "A Return to Savagery," *Outlook*, 61, no. 17 (April 29, 1899), 945–946; and "Worse Than Lynching," *Outlook*, 62, no. 1 (May 6, 1899), 8.

66. Bradford, "Our Nation's Shame," 1143.

67. Ibid.

68. Thomas de Witt Talmage, "Mistakes about the South Corrected," *CH*, April 22, 1880, 260–261.

69. Thomas de Witt Talmage, "Before Election Sermon," *CH*, November 9, 1892, 710; and Bradford, "Our Nation's Shame," 1143. On the priority of

national reunion, see especially Blum, *Reforging the White Republic;* David W. Blight, *Race and Reunion: The Civil War in American Memory* (Cambridge, MA: Harvard University Press, 2001); and Nina Silber, *Romance of Reunion: Northerners and the South, 1865–1900* (Chapel Hill: University of North Carolina Press, 1993).

70. "Reclaiming Negro Children," *CH,* December 19, 1894, 827; and "Educating Southern Negroes," *CH,* August 28, 1895, 565.

71. "Liberating African Slaves," *CH,* February 26, 1896, 165. On Chatelain and the PLL, see David Birmingham, *Empire in Africa: Angola and Its Neighbors* (Athens: University of Ohio Press, 2006), especially chaps. 3 and 4; Alida Chatelain, *Héli Chatelain: L'Ami de L'Angola, Fondateur de la Mission philafricaine* (Lausanne: Secrétariat de la Mission Philafricaine, 1918); Héli Chatelain, *The Open Sore of the World: Africa's Internal Slave Trade and a Practical Plan for Its Extinction* (New York: Philafrican Liberators' Leage, 1896); and Gerald Moser, "Héli Chatelain: Pioneer of a National Language and Literature for Angola," *RAL* 14, no. 4 (Winter 1983): 516–537.

72. "Life in Sunny Angola," *CH,* January 29, 1896, 85; and "Freeing African Slaves," *CH,* April 8, 1896, 285.

73. "Sympathy for the Slaves," *CH,* April 29, 1896, 343.

74. Ibid.

75. "Heli Chatelain's Pioneer Band," *CH,* December 8, 1897, 947; and "Preaching to an African King," *CH,* September 1, 1905, 98.

76. Wells, "Lynch Law in America," 15–24. For this history, see Dray, *At the Hands of Persons Unknown;* Luker, *Social Gospel in Black and White;* Pfeifer, *Rough Justice;* Wood, *Lynching and Spectacle.*

77. "A Return to Savagery," *Outlook,* 61, no. 17 (April 29, 1899), 945–946; and "Worse Than Lynching," *Outlook,* 62, no. 1 (May 6, 1899), 8.

78. "An Afro-American Movement," *CH,* February 13, 1901, 148.

79. "His Glorious Life-Work Ended," *CH,* April 23, 1902, 350–352.

80. Luker, *Social Gospel in Black and White,* 235; and Bishop H. M. Turner, "Separate the White and Colored Races," *CH,* December 27, 1905, 1113.

81. Kate Upson Clark, "Indian Problems at Mohonk," *CH,* November 9, 1904, 962; and "To Civilize the Indian," 221.

82. "The New Immigrants," *CH,* August 12, 1903, 672.

83. "Children from Many Lands," *CH,* May 11, 1904, 415.

84. Jacob A. Riis, "The Golden Rule in Poverty Row," *CH,* September 27, 1905, 795, 297; and Jacob A. Riis, "The Gateway of All Nations," *CH,* October 11, 1905, 843, 850.

85. Riis, "The Gateway of All Nations," 843, 850. For more on Riis's views, see Tom Buk-Swienty, *The Other Half: Jacob Riis and the World of Immigrant America* (New York: W. W. Norton, 2008); James B. Lane, *Jacob A. Riis and the American City* (Port Washington, NY: Kennikat Press, 1974); and Lane,

"Jacob A. Riis and Scientific Philanthropy during the Progressive Era," *SSR* 47, no. 1 (March 1973): 32–48.

6. TO SAFEGUARD CHRISTIAN AMERICA

1. Julia F. Irwin, *Making the World Safe: The American Red Cross and a Nation's Humanitarian Awakening* (New York: Oxford University Press, 2013), 27; see also Marian Moser Jones, *American Red Cross: From Clara Barton to the New Deal* (Baltimore: Johns Hopkins University Press, 2013), 94.

2. "Trouble in the Red Cross," *NYTR*, January 30, 1903, 2; "Trouble in the Red Cross," *NYS*, January 30, 1903, 5; "Miss Barton's Reply," *NYDT*, February 2, 1903, 2; "The Trouble in the Red Cross," *NYDT*, February 5, 1903, 9; "Rejoinder of Clara Barton," *NYS*, April 10, 1903, 2; Irwin, *Making the World Safe*, 28–29; and Jones, *American Red Cross*, 104–108.

3. "Finland Swept by Famine," *CH*, January 7, 1903, 3, 14; "The Famine in Finland," *CH*, January 7, 1903, 8; "In the Heart of the Famine Land," *CH*, March 11, 1903, 207; and Charles M. Pepper, *Life-work of Louis Klopsch: Romance of a Modern Knight of Mercy* (New York: Christian Herald Association, 1910), 126, 357.

4. "It Is a Four-Fold Famine," *CH*, February 4, 1903, 94; "Sweden's Monarch Grateful," *CH*, April 8, 1903, 294; Pepper, *Life-work*, 143; and "The Northland Grateful for Our Benevolence," *CH*, September 2, 1903, 734.

5. "The Great Western Floods," *CH*, June 17, 1903, 511; "A Pastor's Experience on the Flood," *CH*, July 15, 1903, 593; "Macedonia's Struggle for Freedom," *CH*, September 16, 1903, 770–771; "A Cry from Macedonia," *CH*, October 21, 1903, 884; Pepper, *Life-work*, 150–160, 249–225; Irwin, *Making the World Safe*, 28–29; and Jones, *American Red Cross*, 104–112.

6. Irwin, *Making the World Safe*, 30; and Jones, *American Red Cross*, 112–115.

7. "Japan in Famine's Grasp," *CH*, January 31, 1906, 87; "Japan Needs Our Aid," *CH*, January 31, 1906, 88; "Fighting Back Famine in Japan," *CH*, February 7, 1906, 111; "Japan's Famine Appeal Is Heard," *CH*, February 14, 1906, 137; and Pepper, *Life-work*, 204–210. For Roosevelt's appeal, see "President Aids Japanese," *NYT*, February 14, 1906, 4.

8. "The Calamity in Japan," *CH*, February 28, 1906, 180; "First $10,000 for Starving Japan," *CH*, February 28, 1906, 183; "Hundreds Now Dying of Famine," *CH*, March 7, 1906, 202; "The Red Cross in Japan: A Great Army of Helpers Who Are Co-operating with Our Missionaries in the Famine Field," *CH*, March 7, 1906, 203; and "Rushing More Aid to Japan," *CH*, March 21, 1906, 250.

9. For the fund pathways, see Acting Secretary of State Robert Bacon to Chargé Wilson, February 15, 1906, *FRUS*, part 2 (Washington, DC: Government Printing Office, 1909), 1000; "Scenes in the Land of Famine," *CH*,

March 14, 2006, 223, 225; and "The Madness of Hunger," *CH,* March 28, 1906, 276. For an accounting of funds donated by the *Christian Herald* and the ARC, see *FRUS,* 1000; and *ARCB* 2, no. 2 (April 1906): 6.

10. "The President and the Famine Fund," *CH,* April 4, 1906, 299; and "An Ambassadorial Meeting," *CH,* May 16, 1906, 436.

11. Pepper, *Life-work,* 212, 216; "Closing Japanese Relief Work," *CH,* May 2, 1906, 396; *ARCB* 1, no. 3 (July 1906): 3–6; and "Japanese Famine Relief Fund," *ARCB* 2, no. 1 (January 1907): 12.

12. "Earthquake and Flame Lay San Francisco Low," *CH,* May 2, 1906, 398–400; Pepper, *Life-work,* 252–253; Keith Pomakoy, *Helping Humanity: American Policy and Genocide Rescue* (Lanham, MD: Lexington Books, 2011); and Andrea R. Davies, *Saving San Francisco: Relief and Recovery after the 1906 Disaster* (Philadelphia: Temple University Press, 2012).

13. "The New San Francisco," *CH,* May 9, 1906, 414.

14. "President Asks Nation to Aid Stricken People," *WP,* April 20, 1906, 2. See also Irwin, *Making the World Safe,* 31–32; and Jones, *American Red Cross,* 117–118.

15. Jones, *American Red Cross,* 118–121; and "California Relief Fund Receipts," *ARCB* 2, no. 1 (January 1907): 13.

16. "The Red Cross and the Earthquake," *CH,* May 2, 1906, 396; and "The New San Francisco," 414.

17. Jones, *American Red Cross,* 132–135; and "Appeal by the President," *NYT,* December 24, 1906, 1.

18. "Chinese Famine Relief," *ARCB* 2, no. 2 (April 1907): 7, 18; "Loading Our China Relief Ship," *CH,* April 10, 1907, 322; "The Chinese Famine," *CH,* January 9, 1907, 28; and "Contributions to the Chinese Famine Fund," *CH,* February 6, 1907, 102.

19. "The President and the Chinese Famine," *CH,* February 13, 1907, 126; and "China's Calamity," *CH,* February 20, 1907, 152.

20. "All Eager to Help Stricken China," *CH,* February 20, 1907, 155; "Chinese Famine Relief," *ARCB* 2, no. 2 (April 1907): 18; "Dying of Hunger in China," *CH,* January 30, 1907, 96; and "All Eager to Help Stricken China," 155.

21. "The Call to Service," *CH,* February 13, 1907, 132.

22. "A Famine Relief Ship for China," *CH,* April 3, 1907, 299; "Famine Grows Worse—$50,000 More Cabled," *CH,* April 3, 1907, 299; and "What Famine-Hunger Means," *CH,* May 22, 1907, 470.

23. "God Speed the Gallant 'Buford,'" *CH,* May 15, 1907, 446, 454; and Pepper, *Life-work,* 191–192.

24. "God Speed the Gallant 'Buford,'" 446; "King of Emergency Benevolences," *CH,* April 17, 1907, 350; and "Let Us Fill the Famine Ship," *CH,* April 3, 1907, 304.

25. Irwin, *Making the World Safe*, 43, 220; Louis Klopsch, paraphrased in Charles Hurd to Mabel Boardman, April 11, 1907, Box 61, RCNA1; "Secretary Taft's Appreciation," *CH*, May 8, 1907, 420; "Chinese Famine Relief," *ARCB* 2, no. 3 (July 1907): 5; "The Chinese Famine," *ARCB* 2, no. 4 (October 1907): 66–68; and Mabel T. Boardman, "The Red Cross Conference," *CH*, July 24, 1907, 643.

26. "The New Propaganda," *ARCB* 3, no. 3 (July 1907), 37; "Fourth Annual Meeting of the Red Cross," *ARCB* 4, no. 1 (January 1909), 44; and "Report of the Chairman," *ARCB* 5, no. 1 (January 1910): 10.

27. On the ARC's relationship with affluent philanthropists and foundations, see Irwin, *Making the World Safe*, 32–34; and Jones, *American Red Cross*, 137, 141–144.

28. On the ARC's staffing practices, see Irwin, *Making the World Safe*, 32–34; and Jones, *American Red Cross*, 118–120, 135–138.

29. On critiques of missionaries in foreign affairs, see Chapter 5; and on the appeal of a more "secular" approach to aid, see Irwin, *Making the World Safe*, 43–44, 92.

30. "Secretary Taft and the Missionaries," *CH*, May 6, 1908, 386; "Judge Taft on Foreign Missions," *CH*, November 25, 1908, 928; "Roosevelt Commends Missions," *CH*, February 3, 1909, 89; and "President Taft and Africa," *CH*, December 29, 1909, 1126.

31. "How the Panic was Fought," *CH*, November 6, 1907, 951, 958; and "The Problem of Poverty," *CH*, January 22, 1908, 64.

32. "The Problem of Poverty," 64; and "Shelter for the Homeless Poor," *CH*, February 19, 1908, 152. See also "The Bread Line at Close Range," *NYT*, February 16, 1908, 1.

33. Edward T. Devine, "The Breadline," *CAC* 19, no. 23 (March 7, 1908): 1655–1656.

34. Devine, "The Bread Line," 1655–1656; "A 'Charity' That Does Harm," *NYT*, March 9, 1908, 6; "The 'Bread Line,'" *NYT*, May 31, 1908, 8; "1,000 in Bread Line," *NYT*, June 8, 1908, 3; and "Says Tramps Fill the 'Bread Line,'" *NYT*, June 9, 1908, 7.

35. On the longer history and changing dynamics of the organized charity movement, see Robert H. Bremner, *American Philanthropy* (Chicago: University of Chicago Press, 1960); Elizabeth N. Agnew, *From Charity to Social Work: Mary E. Richmond and the Creation of an American Profession* (Champaign: University of Illinois Press, 2004); Lawrence J. Friedman and Mark D. McGarvie, eds., *Charity, Philanthropy, and Civility in American History* (New York: Cambridge University Press, 2002); Charles Loch Mowat, *The Charity Organization Society, 1869–1913: Its Ideas and Work* (London: Methuen, 1961); Brent Ruswick, *Almost Worthy: The Poor, the Paupers, and the Science of Charity in America, 1877–1917* (Bloomington: Indiana University Press, 2013); and

Frank Dekker Watson, *The Charity Organization Movement in the United States: A Study of American Philanthropy* (New York: Macmillan, 1922).

36. "A Bread and Beef Charity," *CH*, January 10, 1894, 19. See Chapter 1.

37. "The Poor in Our Cities," *CH*, March 25, 1908, 248; and "Governors and the Unemployed," *CH*, April 1, 1908, 263, 266.

38. "Governors and the Unemployed," 266.

39. "Governors and the Unemployed," 266; "The Bowery Mission Free Labor Bureau," *CH*, May 6, 1908, 378; and "The Poor in Our Cities," 248.

40. "The Poor in Our Cities," 248.

41. Charles M. Sheldon, "Christian Socialism," *CH*, December 21, 1904, 1136; Thomas de Witt Talmage, "Universal Brotherhood," *CH*, June 12, 1907, 524–525; Charles M. Sheldon, "The Heart of the World," serial novel, *CH*, November 23, 1904, 1020–1022; November 30, 1904, 1050–1051; December 7, 1904, 1084–1085; December 14, 1904, 1114–1115; December 21, 1904, 1140–1141; December 28, 1904, 1166–1167; January 4, 1905, 12–13; January 11, 1905, 38–40; January 18, 1905, 58–59; January 25, 1905, 78–79; February 1, 1905, 100–101; February 8, 1905, 128–130; February 15, 1905, 150–151; February 22, 1905, 174–175; March 1, 1905, 198–199; and March 8, 1905, 220–221. On Sheldon and his place within the Social Gospel movement, see Paul S. Boyer, "In His Steps: A Reappraisal," *AQ* 23, no. 1 (1971): 60–78; Billie Barnes Jensen, "A Social Gospel Experiment in Newspaper Reform: Charles M. Sheldon and the Topeka Daily Capital," *CHSCC* 33 (1964): 74–83; Timothy Miller, *Following in His Steps: A Biography of Charles M. Sheldon* (Knoxville: University of Tennessee Press, 1987); and Gary Scott Smith, "Charles M. Sheldon's *In His Steps* in the Context of Religion and Culture in Late Nineteenth Century America," *FH* 22, no. 2 (Summer 1990): 47–69.

42. Sheldon, "The Heart of the World," December 28, 1904, 1166–1167; Sheldon, "Christian Socialism," 1136; and Sheldon, "The Heart of the World," January 25, 1905, 78–79.

43. Sheldon, "The Heart of the World," January 4, 1905, 13. Helpful histories on social Christianity in this period include Paul A. Carter, *The Decline and Revival of the Social Gospel: Social and Political Liberalism in American Protestant Churches, 1920–1940* (Hamden, CT: Archon Books, 1971); Susan Curtis, *A Consuming Faith: The Social Gospel and Modern American Culture* (Baltimore: Johns Hopkins University Press, 1991); Gary J. Dorrien, *The Soul in Society: The Making and Renewal of Social Christianity* (Minneapolis: Fortress Press, 1995); Robert T. Handy, ed., *Social Gospel in America, 1870–1920* (Oxford: Oxford University Press, 1966); Charles Howard Hopkins, *Rise of the Social Gospel in American Protestantism, 1865–1915* (New Haven, CT: Yale University Press, 1940); Norris Magnuson, *Salvation in the Slums, Evangelical Social Work, 1865–1920* (Eugene, OR: Wipf and Stock, 1977); Paul T. Phillips,

A Kingdom on Earth: Anglo-American Social Christianity, 1880–1940 (University Park: Pennsylvania State University Press, 1996); and Gary Scott Smith, *The Search for Social Salvation: Social Christianity and America, 1880–1925* (Lanham, MD: Lexington Books, 2000).

44. "The Evil Child-Labor System," *CH,* December 28, 1904, 1164; Frank H. Nichols, "Child Slavery at the Mines," *CH,* August 13, 1902, 667–668; Frank H. Nichols, "New Jersey's Child Toilers," *CH,* September 3, 1902, 719; and "New Child Labor Laws," *CH,* October 14, 1903, 860.

45. "Congress and the Children," *CH,* January 24, 1906, 68; "America's Little White Slaves," *CH,* February 14, 1906, 133, 135; "Child Labor Laws Needed," *CH,* November 21, 1906, 980; "Congress and the Children," *CH,* February 20, 1907, 152; and "Unprotected Childhood," *CH,* February 10, 1909, 112.

46. Sheldon, "The Heart of the World," January 11, 1905, 38–39; and "Preaching Discontent," *CH,* July 22, 1908, 588.

47. "The Poor in Our Cities," 248; and "Concerning Charity," *CH,* August 26, 1908, 668.

48. Pepper, *Life-work,* 267.

49. "Mammoth Beneficence," *CH,* February 19, 1908, 144; and "Uplifting the Masses," *CH,* February 12, 1902, 136.

50. Sheldon, "The Heart of the World," January 4, 1905, 12–13; and Sheldon, "The Heart of the World," December 14, 1904, 1114–1115.

51. "Social Contracts," *CH,* January 23, 1905, 76; and "The Problem of Poverty," 64.

52. "Both Sides of the $100,000 Controversy," *CH,* April 12, 1905, 331.

53. Washington Gladden, "Tainted Money," *Outlook,* November 30, 1895, 886–887; Washington Gladden, "Tainted Money," *Independent,* April 6, 1905, 410–411; "Good and Bad Gifts," *CH,* September 20, 1905, 780; and "Both Sides of the $100,000 Controversy," 331.

54. "Good and Bad Gifts," 780.

55. "Our National Bondage," *CH,* October 30, 1901, 922.

56. "Women Make War on Mormonism," *CH,* June 21, 1905, 538; "To Wipe Out Polygamy," *CH,* March 22, 1905, 260; and "Mormons and Congress," *CH,* January 11, 1899, 24.

57. "To Bar Out the Polygamist," *CH,* February 8, 1899, 103; "Roberts Not Admitted," *CH,* December 20, 1899, 993; and "A Bugle-Blast against Polygamy," January 25, 1899, 53 and 55. On Hearst's role in this campaign, see Ben H. Procter, *William Randolph Hearst: The Early Years, 1863–1910* (New York: Oxford University Press, 1998), 145–146.

58. "Smoot, the Mormon," *CH,* February 4, 1903, 96; "The New Anti-Mormon Crusade," *CH,* June 24, 1903, 536; "How to Deal with Mormonism," *CH,* January 4, 1905, 10; and "The Anti-Mormon Campaign," *CH,* February 7,

1906, 125. On the campaign against Smoot, see Kathleen Flake, *The Politics of American Religious Identity: The Seating of Senator Reed Smoot, Mormon Apostle* (Chapel Hill: University of North Carolina Press, 2004).

59. "Women Make War on Mormonism," 538; "The Woman's Memorial," June 21, 1905, 540; and "The Women's Memorial Ready," *CH,* January 31, 1906, 83.

60. "The Woman's Memorial," 540.

61. "Senate and Mr. Smoot," *CH,* June 13, 1906, 520; and "Smoot Triumphant," *CH,* March 6, 1907, 204.

62. "Women Make War on Mormonism," 538; and "Smoot Triumphant," 204.

63. "The Motto on the Coinage," *CH,* December 4, 1907, 1040; and "Will Congress Restore the Motto?," *CH,* January 29, 1908, 84.

64. "The Ungracious Protest," *CH,* October 31, 1806, 910; and "The Hebrew Crusade," *CH,* January 23, 1907, 68. On this controversy, see Naomi Wiener Cohen, *Jews in Christian America: The Pursuit of Religious Equality* (New York: Oxford University Press, 1992).

65. "The Hebrew Crusade," 68; "Revising Christmas Festivities," *CH,* December 4, 1907, 1040; "Christianity in the Schools," *CH,* December 11, 1907, 1072; and "The Ungracious Protest," 910.

66. "Let Congress Restore the Motto," *CH,* December 25, 1907, 1125; and "Will Congress Restore the Motto?," 84.

67. "Want the Motto Restored," *CH,* January 1, 1908, 16; "The People and the Motto," *CH,* January 1, 1908, 8; and "Will Congress Restore the Motto?," 84.

68. "The Fight for the Motto Won," *CH,* May 27, 1908, 434; and "The Motto to Go Back," *CH,* May 27, 1908, 436.

69. Louis Klopsch, "Please Regard This as a Personal Letter," *CH,* November 24, 1909, 993; "Moral Aspects of the Election," *CH,* October 28, 1908, 848; and Louis Klopsch, "A Congratulatory Message," *CH,* November 18, 1908, 912.

70. See, for example, "Comments on Taft's Religious Views," *HR* 56 (1908): 417–419.

71. "At Denver," *CH,* July 22, 1908, 588; Klopsch, "A Congratulatory Message," 912; and "Judge Taft on Foreign Missions," 928.

72. "$20,000 for the Relief of Italian Earthquake Sufferers," *CH,* January 6, 1909, 8; "The Red Cross Hard at Work," *CH,* January 20, 1909, 42; and Boardman, quoted in "An Additional Contribution for Italy," *CH,* January 13, 1909, 22.

73. "An Additional Contribution for Italy," 22; "The Christian Herald's Aid Welcome," *CH,* January 20, 1909, 42; and Pepper, *Life-work,* 223–224.

74. "Queen Helen Sends Thanks," *CH,* February 24, 1909, 156; and "All Italy Plunged in Sorrow," *CH,* January 20, 1909, 46.

75. Klopsch, "An Audience with Italy's King," *CH*, May 26, 1909, 451, 453; and Pepper, *Life-work*, 237–241.

76. Pepper, *Life-work*, 233; and *ARCB* 4, no. 2 (April 1909): 64–65.

77. "How New York Raised Funds for Italy," *ARCB* 4, no. 2 (April 1909): 67–69.

78. Ibid., 68; "Turko-Armenian Relief," *ARCB* 4, no. 4 (October 1909), 44; and "Many Noted Guests Visit Mont-Lawn," *CH*, August 25, 1909, 694.

79. "The Monterey Flood, August, 1909," *ARCB* 5, no. 1 (January 1910), 11.

80. "Mexico's Appeal for Help," *CH*, September 29, 1909, 798, 805; "More Help Sent to Monterey," *CH*, October 13, 1909, 845; "5,000 Blankets for Monterey," *CH*, October 20, 1909, 864; "Consul-General Sends Thanks," *CH*, November 10, 1909, 936; and "20,000 Blankets for Mexico's Sufferers," *CH*, November 10, 1909, 940.

81. "Relief Work in Monterey," *CH*, September 22, 1909, 772.

82. Ibid.; "'In the Blanket Business,'" *CH*, November 10, 1909, 936; and Pepper, *Life-work*, 256–259.

83. "A National Duty," *CH*, September 29, 1909, 796.

84. Ibid.

85. Pepper, *Life-work*, 356; and "Financial Statement of the American Red Cross for the Fiscal Year Ended December 31, 1909," *ARCB* 5, no. 1 (January 1910): 14–15.

86. "Address of President Taft," *ARCB* 5, no. 1 (January 1910), 8–9; and "American Red Cross Endowment," *ARCB* 5, no. 1 (January 1910): 61–62.

87. Philander Knox to Diplomatic and Consular Offices, November 1, 1909, quoted in *ARCB* 5, no. 1 (January 1910): 60.

88. William H. Taft to the Governors of the States and Territories, June 4, 1909, quoted in *ARCB* 4, no. 3 (July 1909): 58.

89. Klopsch, "Please Regard This as a Personal Letter," 993.

90. "President Taft at the Bowery Mission," *CH*, December 22, 1909, 1099.

91. John G. Hallimond, "What the Bowery Says of Mr. Taft," *CH*, January 10, 1910, 11; and "President Taft at the Bowery Mission," 1099.

92. "The President and the Bowery," *CH*, December 29, 1909, 1124; "His Inspirational Message," *CH*, January 12, 1910, 29; and "Best Thing Mr. Taft Has Ever Done," *CH*, January 12, 1910, 26.

93. "Our Enlarged Family Circle," *CH*, January 26, 1910, 72; and Louis Klopsch, "Dr. Klopsch Greets Our New Readers," *CH*, January 26, 1910, 72.

7. A SHIFTING LANDSCAPE

1. "Dr. Klopsch Laid at Rest," *CH*, March 23, 1910, 275–277, 299–300; and Charles M. Pepper, *Life-work of Louis Klopsch: Romance of a Modern Knight of Mercy* (New York: Christian Herald Association, 1910), 366–379.

2. "Dr. Klopsch Laid at Rest," 275–277, 299–300; and Pepper, *Life-work,* 367.

3. "Dr. Klopsch Laid at Rest," 275–277, 299–300.

4. "Our Enlarged Family Circle," *CH,* January 26, 1910, 72; "Dr. Klopsch Dying after an Operation," *NYT,* March 7, 1910, 9; and "He Always Planned for Others," *CH,* March 23, 1910, 284.

5. "He Always Planned for Others," 284.

6. "Dr. Klopsch Laid at Rest," 275–300; "Dr. Klopsch's Vision," *CH,* December 14, 1910, 1184; and "Holiday Greetings," *CH,* November 30, 1910, 1119.

7. Louis Klopsch Jr., "To Our Readers," *CH,* March 23, 1910, 280; and "His Great Life-Work Must Go On," *CH,* April 13, 1910, 373.

8. Klopsch Jr., "To Our Readers," 280; and George H. Sandison, "The Story of the Christian Herald," *CH,* October 27, 1928, 1119–1120.

9. On the rise of theological modernism, see William R. Hutchison, *The Modernist Impulse in American Protestantism* (Durham, NC: Duke University Press, 1992); and George M. Marsden, *Fundamentalism and American Culture: The Shaping of Twentieth-Century Evangelicalism, 1870–1925* (New York: Oxford University Press, 1980).

10. "A Christless Religion," *CH,* April 8, 1903, 296; and "Trial for Heresy," *CH,* April 20, 1904, 352.

11. "Christian Union," *CH,* November 15, 1905, 956.

12. "Christianity's Center," *CH,* October 16, 1907, 884; and "Another Attack on the Bible," *CH,* August 19, 1908, 652.

13. "Another Attack on the Bible," 652.

14. Ibid.; and A. B. Simpson, "But God," *CMA,* July 28, 1893, 56–57.

15. A. C. Dixon, *Evangelism Old and New* (New York: American Tract Society, 1905); 39, 41, 49; and *The Fundamentals: A Testimony to the Truth* (Chicago: Testimony Pub. Co. 1910–1915), especially L. W. Munhall, "The Doctrines That Must Be Emphasized in Successful Evangelism," vol. 12, 131.

16. Editorial, *CMA,* February 28, 1903, 118; and "Annual Report of the Superintendent and Board of Managers, C. and M. A.," *CMA,* May 19, 1900, 322. For fundamentalism's effects on missionary work, see Joel Carpenter and William Shenk, eds., *Earthen Vessels: American Evangelicals and Foreign Missions, 1880–1980* (Grand Rapids, MI: Eerdmans, 1990); William R. Hutchison, *Errand to the World: American Protestant Thought and Foreign Missions* (Chicago: University of Chicago Press, 1987); and Dana Robert, *American Women in Mission: A Social History of Their Thought and Practice* (Macon, GA: Mercer University Press, 1996).

17. Simpson, quoted in *Alliance Missions in India, 1892–1972,* vol. 1, comp. William F. Smalley (n.p., n.d.), 85. See also *Annual Report of the Christian and Missionary Alliance, Adopted at the Annual Meeting of the Society, May 24, 1910, Nyack, NY,* 9.

18. "Native Missionaries," *CH*, February 19, 1908, 144. See also "The New Idea in Missions," *CH*, January 23, 1907, 68; and "Substitutes in the Field," *CH*, February 6, 1907, 108.

19. For an expression of this anxiety, see *Annual Report of the CMA, 1910*, 9.

20. "India Too Has a Revival," *CH*, May 16, 1906, 434; and Minnie Abrams, *Baptism of the Holy Ghost and Fire*, 2nd ed. (Pune, India: Pandita Ramabai Mukti Mission, 1906), 3.

21. Abrams, *Baptism of the Holy Ghost and Fire*, 4, 39–42. For a history of the pentecostal revivals, see especially Allan Anderson, *Spreading Fires: The Missionary Nature of Early Pentecostalism* (Maryknoll, NY: Orbis Books, 2007) and *To the Ends of the Earth: Pentecostalism and the Transformation of World Christianity* (New York: Oxford University Press, 2013); Edith Blumhofer, *Restoring the Faith: The Assemblies of God, Pentecostalism, and American Culture* (Urbana: University of Illinois Press, 1993); and Grant Wacker, *Heaven Below: Early Pentecostalism and American Culture* (Cambridge, MA: Harvard University Press, 2001).

22. "A Strange Movement," *CH*, April 3, 1907, 304.

23. "Speaking in Unknown Tongues," *CH*, August 28, 1907, 746. On this controversy, see Blumhofer, *Restoring the Faith;* Wacker, *Heaven Below;* and Heather D. Curtis, "A Sane Gospel: Radical Evangelicals, Psychology, and Pentecostal Revival in the Early Twentieth Century," *RAAC* 21, no. 2 (Summer 2011): 195–226.

24. "A Strange Movement," 304.

25. "Speaking in Unknown Tongues," 746.

26. Ibid.; "Unknown Tongues," *CH*, August 7, 1907, 688.

27. Eric John Abrahamson, *Democracy and Philanthropy: The Rockefeller Foundation and the American Experiment* (New York: Rockefeller Foundation, 2013), 24; Robert H. Bremner, *American Philanthropy* 2nd ed. (Chicago: University of Chicago Press, 1988), 118; and "Finding a Footing," The Rockefeller Foundation: A Digital History, https://rockfound.rockarch.org/finding-a-footing. See also Joseph Kiger, *Philanthropists and Foundation Globalization* (New Brunswick, NJ: Transaction, 2008); and Olivier Zunz; *Philanthropy in America: A History* (Princeton, NJ: Princeton University Press, 2002).

28. "Dr. Klopsch's Vision," 1184; "Mr. Rockefeller's Greatest Gift," *CH*, March 16, 1910, 254; Sandison, "Story of the Christian Herald," 1120; and *The Rockefeller Foundation Annual Report, 1928* (New York: Rockefeller Foundation, n.d), 13, 16.

29. On the Rockefeller Foundation's support for the ARC, see Julia Irwin, *Making the World Safe: The American Red Cross and a Nation's Humanitarian Awakening* (New York: Oxford University Press, 2013), 57–60, 72–73.

30. Sandison, "Story of the Christian Herald," 1120; and Irwin, *Making the World Safe*, 61–63.

31. Irwin, *Making the World Safe*, 60, 66, 67, 75; and Marian Moser Jones, *The American Red Cross from Clara Barton to the New Deal* (Baltimore, MD: Johns Hopkins University Press, 2013),157.

32. Irwin, *Making the World Safe*, 67; and Sandison, "Story of the Christian Herald," 1120.

33. Sandison, "Story of the Christian Herald," 1120; and Pepper, *Life-work*, 357. The Bowery Mission also experienced an increase in giving from approximately $21,452 per year from 1894–1910 to about $34,045 annually from 1910–1928.

34. Sandison, "Story of the Christian Herald," 1120; and "Fifty Years Old and a New Birth for the Christian Herald," *CH*, October 27, 1928, 1118.

35. Stephen Board, "Moving the World with Magazines: A Survey of Evangelical Periodicals," in *American Evangelicals and the Mass Media: Perspectives on the Relationship between American Evangelicals and the Mass Media*, ed. Quentin James Schultze (Grand Rapids, MI: Zondervan, 1990), 128; and Martin Marty, "The Protestant Press," in *The Religious Press in America*, ed. Martin Marty, John G. Deedy, David Wolf Silverman, and Robert Lekachman (New York: Holt, Rinehart, and Winston, 1963), 12.

36. "A Bit of History," *CH*, October 1938, 2; and "Holiday Greetings," *CH*, November 30, 1910, 1119.

37. "Our History," Bowery Mission, https://www.bowery.org/about-us/purpose -goal/history.

38. "About the Bowery Mission," Bowery Mission http://www.bowery.org /about-us; "Faith-Based," Bowery Mission, http://www.bowery.org/about -us/faith-based.

39. Pepper, *Life-work*, 392, 380, 395.

EPILOGUE

1. "Men and Women Needing a Second Chance," Bowery Mission, https://www .bowery.org/homelessness/approach-second-chance; "The Purpose and Goal of the Bowery Mission," Bowery Mission, https://www.bowery.org /about-us/purpose-goal; and "Compassionate Care Programs," Bowery Mission, https://www.bowery.org/programs/compassionate-care.

2. David King, "Seeking a Global Vision: The Evolution of World Vision and American Evangelicalism" (PhD diss., Emory University, 2012); Gary F. VanderPol, "The Least of These: American Evangelical Missions to the Poor" (PhD diss., Boston University, 2010); and Melanie McAlister, *The Kingdom of God Has No Borders: A Global History of American Evangelicals* (New York: Oxford University Press, 2018).

3. David King, "The New Internationalists: World Vision and the Revival of American Evangelical Humanitarianism, 1950-2010," *Religions* 3, no. 4

(2012): abstract. For the history of nonprofit expansion in the twentieth century, see Peter Dobkin Hall, *Philanthropy, the Welfare State, and the Transformation of American Public and Private Institutions, 1945–2000* (Cambridge, MA: Hauser Center for Nonprofit Organizations, Harvard University, 2000); Peter Dobkin Hall, "Historical Perspectives on Nonprofit Organizations," in Robert D. Herman, ed., *The Jossey-Bass Handbook of Nonprofit Leadership and Management* (San Francisco: Jossey-Bass, 1994), 3–28; and Peter Dobkin Hall and Robert Wuthnow, quoted in Stephen M. King, "Nonprofit Organizations and Faith-Based Initiatives: What the Private Sector Can Contribute to the Pursuit of Public Interest," Policy Study No. 08-8, Public Interest Institute (November 2008), 10, 19.

4. "Quick Facts about Nonprofits," National Center for Charitable Statistics, http://nccs.urban.org/data-statistics/quick-facts-about-nonprofits. In 2016, there were also about 370,000 nonprofits of other types, including chambers of commerce, fraternal organizations, and civic leagues.

5. David King, "Religious Giving in America: Charity, Philanthropy, and Benevolence," in *Oxford Encyclopedia of Religion in America* (New York: Oxford University Press, forthcoming); see also Rachel McCleary, *Global Compassions* (New York: Oxford University Press, 2009); and Dobkin Hall and Wuthnow, quoted in King, "Nonprofit Organizations and Faith-Based Initiatives," 10, 19.

6. For a discussion of the humanitarian imagery in religious periodicals such as the *Christian and Missionary Alliance,* see Heather Curtis, "Depicting Distant Suffering: Evangelicals and the Politics of Pictorial Humanitarianism in the Age of American Empire," *MR* 8, no. 2 (2012): 153–182.

7. "Red Cross Magazine Becomes a Monthly," *ARCB* 10 (1915): 27; and Eliot Wadsworth, "An Improved Magazine to Upbuild the Red Cross," *ARCB* 11 (1916): 384. For this history of the ARC bulletin, see Julia Irwin, *Making the World Safe: The American Red Cross and a Nation's Humanitarian Awakening* (New York: Oxford University Press, 2013), 78–90; and Kevin Rozario, "'Delicious Horrors': Mass Culture, the Red Cross, and the Appeal of Modern American Humanitarianism," *AQ* 55, no. 3 (2003): 417–455.

8. Rozario, "'Delicious Horrors,'" 417–455.

9. Ibid., 419; and Louis Klopsch, "Please Regard This as a Personal Letter," *CH,* November 24, 1909, 993.

10. "America, the Almoner of the World," *CH,* June 26, 1901, cover, 565; *ARCB* 5, no. 3 (July 1910): cover; John F. Hutchinson, "Pictorial Essay," in *Champions of Charity: War and the Rise of the Red Cross* (Boulder, CO: Westview Press, 1996), 277–278; Irwin, *Making the World Safe,* 78–90; and Rozario, "'Delicious Horrors,'" 417–455.

11. On American exceptionalism, see Fabian Hilfrich, *Debating American Exceptionalism: Empire and Democracy in the Wake of the Spanish-American War* (New York: Palgrave, 2012); Godfrey Hodgson, *The Myth of American Exceptionalism* (New Haven, CT: Yale University Press, 2009); Martin Marty, *Righteous Empire: The Protestant Experience in America* (New York: Dial Books, 1970); Daniel T. Rodgers, "Exceptionalism," in *Imagined Histories: American Historians Interpret the Past,* ed. Anthony Mohlo and Gordon S. Wood (Princeton, NJ: Princeton University Press, 1998), 21–40; and Ian R. Tyrrell, "American Exceptionalism in an Age of International History," *AHR* 96, no. 4 (1991): 1031–1055, 1068–1072.

12. Robert D. Lupton, *Toxic Charity: How Churches and Charities Hurt Those They Help, and How to Reverse It* (New York: Harper One, 2012), 2.

13. Rosemary Corbett, "For God and Country: Religious Minorities Striving for National Belonging through Community Service," *RAAC* 26, no. 2 (2016): 227–259; and *Making Moderate Islam: Sufism, Service, and the "Ground Zero Mosque" Controversy* (Stanford, CA: Stanford University Press, 2017), 66, 190, 187.

14. "World Giving Index," Charities Aid Foundation, https://www.cafonline .org/docs/default-source/about-us-publications/worldgivingindex2809 2010print.pdf?sfvrsn=4.pdf.

15. On this point, see Marian Moser Jones, *American Red Cross: From Clara Barton to the New Deal* (Baltimore: Johns Hopkins University Press, 2013), 64–65; and Merle Curti, *American Philanthropy Abroad: A History* (New Brunswick, NJ: Rutgers University Press, 1963), 100, 107–108.

16. Alex de Waal, *Famine Crimes: Politics and the Disaster Relief Industry in Africa* (Bloomington: Indiana University Press, 1997); Michael Barnett and Thomas Weiss, eds., *Humanitarianism in Question: Politics, Power, Ethics* (Ithaca, NY: Cornell University Press, 2008), 25; and Michael Ignatieff, "The Stories We Tell: Television and Humanitarian Aid," in *Hard Choices: Moral Dilemmas in Humanitarian Intervention,* ed. Jonathan Moore (Lanham, MD: Rowman and Littlefield, 1988), quoted in Michael Barnett and Thomas G. Weiss, eds., *Humanitarianism Contested: Where Angels Fear to Tread* (New York: Routledge, 2013), 90.

17. Jean Bricmont, *Humanitarian Imperialism: Using Human Rights to Sell War,* trans. Diana Johnstone (New York: Monthly Review Press, 2005); Martha Finnemore, *The Purpose of Intervention: Changing Beliefs about the Use of Force* (Ithaca, NY: Cornell University Press, 2003); Conor Foley, *The Thin Blue Line: How Humanitarians Went to War* (New York: Verso, 2008); and Mahmoud Mamdani, *Saviors and Survivors: Darfur, Politics, and the War on Terror* (New York: Doubleday, 2010). For a helpful review of the literature on U.S. humanitarian imperialism, see Ashley Smith, "Humanitarian Imperialism and Its Apologists," *ISR,* http:// isreview.org/issue/67/humanitarian-imperialism-and-its-apologists.

18. Peter Buffett, "The Charitable-Industrial Complex," *NYT,* July 26, 2013, A19. See also Alain Finkielkraut, *In the Name of Humanity: Reflections on the Twentieth Century* (New York: Columbia University Press, 2000); David Kennedy, *The Dark Sides of Virtue: Reassessing International Humanitarianism* (Princeton, NJ: Princeton University Press, 2004); Michael Maren, *The Road to Hell: The Ravaging Effects of Foreign Aid and International Charity* (New York: Free Press, 1997); Linda Polman, *The Crisis Caravan: What's Wrong with Humanitarian Aid?* (New York: Metropolitan Books, 2010); and David Rieff, *A Bed for the Night: Humanitarianism in Crisis* (New York: Simon and Schuster, 2002).

19. Laura Sullivan, "Report: Red Cross Spent 25 Percent of Haiti Donations on Internal Expenses," NPR, http://www.npr.org/2016/06/16/482020 436/senators-report-finds-fundamental-concerns-about-red-cross -finances.

20. Denis Kennedy, "Selling the Distant Other: Humanitarianism and Imagery—Ethical Dimensions of Humanitarian Action," *JHA* 28 (February 2009): 1–25; Karen Halttunen, "Humanitarianism and the Pornography of Pain in Anglo-American Culture," *AHR* 100, no. 2 (1995): 303–334; David Morgan, "The Look of Sympathy: Religion, Visual Culture, and the Social Life of Feeling," *MR* 5, no. 2 (2009): 132–154; and Rozario, "'Delicious Horrors.'" On this point, see also Didier Fassin, *Humanitarian Reason: A Moral History of the Present* (Berkeley: University of California Press, 2012).

21. Heide Fehrenbach and Davide Rodogno, eds., *Humanitarian Photography: A History* (New York: Cambridge University Press, 2015).

22. Henrietta Lidchi, "Finding the Right Image: British Development NGOs and the Regulation of Imagery," in *Humanitarian Photography: A History,* ed. Heide Fehrenbach and Davide Rodogno (New York: Cambridge University Press, 2015), 297–321; and Sanna Nissinen, "Dilemmas of Ethical Practice in the Production of Contemporary Humanitarian Photography," in *Humanitarian Photography: A History,* ed. Heide Fehrenbach and Davide Rodogno (New York: Cambridge University Press, 2015), 297–321.

23. Dobkin Hall, "Historical Perspectives," 3–28; and Dobkin Hall, *Philanthropy.*

24. Thomas Piketty, *Capital in the Twenty-First Century,* trans. Arthur Goldhammer (Cambridge, MA: Belknap Press, 2014).

25. Buffett, "The Charitable-Industrial Complex," A19. On the debate over whether philanthropy can reduce inequality, see Bill Gates, "Why Inequality Matters," Gates Notes blog, October 13, 2014, https://www.gate snotes.com/Books/Why-Inequality-Matters-Capital-in-21st-Century-Review; and Bob Lord, "Can Philanthropy Fix Our Inequality?," Inequality.org, January 24, 2015, http://inequality.org/philanthropy-solution-inequality. See also Fassin, *Humanitarian Reason.*

26. Kent Annan, *Slow Kingdom Coming: Practices for Doing Justice, Loving Mercy, and Walking Humbly in the World* (Downer's Grove, IL: InterVarsity Press, 2016); Steve Corbett and Brian Fikkert, *When Helping Hurts: How to Alleviate Poverty without Hurting the Poor . . . and Yourself* (Chicago: Moody, 2009, 2012); and Lupton, *Toxic Charity.*

27. Pepper, *Life-work,* vii.

ACKNOWLEDGMENTS

This book is about how Christians have helped strangers. It would not have been written without the help of the women and men at the Christian Herald Association who welcomed me when I was a stranger and trusted me with their story. James Macklin first invited me to explore the archives, took me to serve at the Bowery Mission, and asked me a question that changed the direction of my research. Chapter 5 is dedicated to him. Ed Morgan granted ongoing access and approved the preservation of the *Christian Herald* for future generations of scholars. Julie Ramaine always made time for me when she did not have a moment to spare. James and Anna Winans provided thoughtful conversation and consistent encouragement. Although we only met during my final visit, Jason Storbakken offered inspiration that enabled me to bring the project to a close. Over the years, these strangers have all become friends. For their hospitality, and for the kindness I received from many other staff and volunteers at the CHA, I am grateful. I hope this book will make some contribution to their ministry. At the very least, I will donate any royalties from *Holy Humanitarians* to the mission.

Because so few records have survived from the *Christian Herald*'s earliest decades, I relied on archivists and librarians at numerous institutions to help find materials to flesh out the story. No research request was too obscure for my colleague Chris Strauber at Tufts University. Tisch Library's Christopher Barbour made possible the digitization of forty-four fragile volumes of the *Christian Herald* newspaper. I first discovered the CHA's humanitarian work through the assistance of Martha Smalley at Yale Divinity School's Day Missions Library. Jenn Whitemann from the Christian and Missionary Alliance National Archives located rare missionary records about the India famine. At the Flower Pentecostal Heritage Center and the Assemblies of God World Missions Archives, Darrin Rodgers, Glenn Gohr, and their supportive staff helped me navigate a complex set of collections. I also benefited from the expertise of archivists and researchers at the British Library; the Burke Theological Library at Union Seminary; the Houghton, Schlesinger, and Widener Libraries at Harvard University; the Library of Congress; the Marsten Memorial Historical Center and Archives at the Free Methodist Church of North America National Headquarters; the Massachusetts Historical Association; the National Archives and Records Administration; and the New York Public Library.

Sorting through the documents and images I collected at these many institutions took time, and I am especially indebted to the Louisville Institute for awarding me a Sabbatical Grant for Researchers. Tufts University provided funding through the Committee on Faculty Research Awards, the Faculty Fellows Program at the Jonathan M. Tisch College of Civic Life, and a Tufts Collaborates Grant spearheaded by my colleague David Ekbladh. I also received generous financial assistance in the form of a Protestant Missions Research Grant from the Institute for the Study of American Evangelicals, and through a Lake Institute Network of Emerging Scholars Research Award from the Indiana University Lilly Family School of Philanthropy.

For research support of another kind, I am grateful to my excellent student assistants: Megan Luce, Hannah Dorfman, and especially Niamh Doyle, whose assiduous work tracking down references enabled me to meet a crucial deadline. I owe particular thanks to Kip Richardson for help with obtaining images. Kaley Leshem and Joseph Philipson wrote exceptional senior theses on the history of humanitarianism. It was a privilege to learn from them while serving as their adviser.

While working on *Holy Humanitarians,* I participated in several collaborative research initiatives on related subjects. Colleagues in the Global History of American Evangelicalism Workshop (funded by the Henry Luce Foundation), the Religion and U.S. Empire Seminar (hosted by the Kripke Center at Creighton University), and the Secularization and Religious Innovation in the North Atlantic World project (sponsored by Harvard Divinity School) helped bring clarity to my thinking about the history of evangelical charity. During the early phase of my research, I had the good fortune to be selected as a Young Scholar in American Religion. Conversations with fellow participants and our mentors shaped my inquiry and have continued to provide insight and much needed encouragement.

Opportunities to share my work at colloquia and conferences offered occasions for honing my arguments. I owe thanks to Paul Lim for inviting me to speak at the Vanderbilt Divinity School Religious History Colloquium and to Gale Kenny for the chance to present at the Columbia University Religion in America Seminar. Participating in the Global Humanitarianism and Media Cultures Conference at the University of Sussex, England, introduced me to scholars from a range of disciplines who share concerns about the ethics and politics of representing suffering. Over the years, colleagues in the North American Religions Colloquium at Harvard University and the Boston Historians of American Religion Group have raised incisive questions about the *Christian Herald* and its role in the development of domestic philanthropy and foreign aid. I appreciate the welcome I received in these gatherings from conveners Catherine Brekus, Ann Braude, David Hempton, David Holland, and Jon Roberts.

Several colleagues deserve special mention. Edith Blumhofer, Mark Noll, and Dana Robert encouraged me to undertake the project to begin with and have continued to support me along the way. I am grateful to Uta Balbier, Rosemary Corbett, David King, Pamela Klassen, Melani McAlister, Eva Payne, and Davide Rodogno for instructive conversations about common interests in the histories of evangelicalism, humanitarianism, and missions. Members of the American Religious History Writing Group—Jonathan Ebel, Tracy Fessenden, Jennifer Graber, Alison Greene, and Kip Kosek—commented on numerous chapter drafts and cheered me on at every stage. Elizabeth Foster offered valuable recommendations on the entire manuscript. Martha Finch opened her home for extended periods during my visits to the Assemblies of God Archives. For unwavering moral support I thank Brandon Bayne, Anthea Butler, Linford Fisher, Candy Gunther-Brown, Katie Lofton, Michael McNally, Kristy Nabhan-Warren, Craig Townsend, and Tisa Wenger. I cannot imagine how I would have made it through the past few years without gracious and steady counsel from Adrian Weimer every week. Grant Wacker has also been a tireless proponent. He and two anonymous reviewers for Harvard University Press provided thoughtful and very helpful suggestions for making *Holy Humanitarians* a better book.

Kathleen McDermott shepherded this project through the publication process with patience and professionalism. Jill Uhlfelder and Judith Riotto offered critical assistance in cleaning up my prose. It has also been a pleasure to work with other Harvard University Press staff.

I am grateful to Cambridge University Press for permission to incorporate brief portions of my article "Popular Media and the Global Expansion of American Evangelicalism in an Imperial Age," *Journal of American Studies* 51, no. 4 (2017), 1043–1067, primarily in Chapter 3. I also acknowledge Taylor and Francis and Oxford University Press for providing excellent venues for the initial exploration of some themes and topics in my earlier writings, respectively: "Depicting Distant Suffering: Evangelicals and the Politics of Pictorial Humanitarianism in the Age of American Empire," *Material Religion* 8, no. 2 (2012): 153–182 and "'There Are No Secular Events': Popular Media and the Diverging Paths of British and American Evangelicalism," in *Secularization and Religious Innovation in the North Atlantic World*, ed. David N. Hempton and Hugh McLeod (New York: Oxford University Press, 2017), 80–102.

Charity suffereth long, and is kind (1 Corinthians 13:4). My family and friends have indeed suffered through many long years of waiting while I researched and wrote about evangelical benevolence. Their kindness and patience carried me through periods of doubt and discouragement. I thank especially my brother and sister-in-law, Tyler and Melissa Pakradooni, for hosting me during many visits to the Christian Herald Association headquarters. Redeemer Community Church provided a spiritual home; Eunice Schatz, spiritual companionship. Supper Club friends fed and prayed for me. Without the grace I receive from Clark, Jonathan, and David daily, I would lose sight of what really matters. It's true that charity begins at home. My parents taught me from the beginning about faith, hope, and love. The book is dedicated to them and to my mentor David D. Hall, whose steadfast honesty, guidance, and friendship have been for me a model of Christian charity.

INDEX

American Red Cross (*continued*)
expectations and, 101, 102; Geneva
Conventions and, 59, 107, 138, 140;
in Italy, 225, 248–249; in Japan,
217–218; in Johnstown, 21; Klopsch
as honorary member of, 225; in
Mexico, 250, 252–254; neutrality of,
59, 76, 80, 101, 226; presidents of
(*see* Barton, Clara; Taft, William
Howard); publications, 225, 283,
285; in Russia, 35, 75; in San
Francisco, 219–221; in World War I,
273, 283–284
American Relief Administration, 6
American Sunday School Union, 9,
188–189
anarchists, 13, 19, 182, 183, 184, 232
Anglo-Saxonism, 193, 209, 328n25.
See also race; racism
Anti-imperialist League, 128
anti-imperialists, 112, 120, 128–129,
131, 134, 138, 317n79; evangelical,
113, 126, 129
anti-Semitism, 244
antislavery movement: against slavery
in U.S., 29–30, 127, 305n27,
319–320n11; against slavery in
Africa, 204–206
Armenians: *Christian Herald* aids, 11, 58,
66, 70–79; ARC aids, 59, 74–77, 79; as
Christians or "Christian race," 66,
68–70, 72–73, 78, 80, 82; massacre or
oppression of, 11, 13, 57–59, 65–70,
72–74, 88; media coverage of, 66–70,
72, 74, 77–79; as refugees and
potential citizens, 11, 77–78, 81; U.S.
aid to Cuba and, 88
assimilation: of African Americans, 194,
195; of Armenians, 78; boarding
schools and, 198, 208 (*see also* Carlisle
Industrial Indian School); *Christian
Herald* and, 184–185, 187, 190, 209;
of Filipinos, 119; of immigrants,
182–185, 209, 211; of Jews, 184; into

labor economy, 195; legislation's role
in, 200–201, 209; narrative of, 190; of
Native Americans, 192, 194, 195, 198,
200–201, 208; opposition to,
183–184, 190, 198, 201; race or
racism and, 191; to white Protestant
culture, 182, 184–185, 329n38

Bacon, Robert, 248
Baker, Frazier, 206
Barton, Clara: in Armenia, 59, 67,
75–77, 80, 100; Boardman's conflict
with, 214–216; criticisms of,
105–106, 140, 141, 213–214; in Cuba,
92, 95, 100–104, 107, 126, 138; in
Johnstown, 21–22; Klopsch's conflict
with, 59, 67, 75–77, 79, 86, 100–108,
120, 138, 140, 145, 315n44; leaves
Cuba, 104, 138; resigns from ARC,
217; in Russia, 75
Barton, James, 12
Barton, Stephen E., 84, 99, 101–104,
106–108
Baxter, Michael Paget, 7–8
benevolence. *See* charity;
humanitarianism; philanthropy
benevolent organizations, 5, 12, 32, 43,
236, 266, 290
Bennett, James Gordon, 32
Bible, 17, 24; almsgiving or charity as
duty in, 2, 13, 45, 47, 149–150; "feed
the hungry" verse in, 2, 14, 33, 82, 83,
86, 89, 110, 128, 149, 150, 159, 264;
Golden Rule in, 45, 83, 109, 232;
Good Samaritan in, 27, 34, 63, 89,
109, 149; interpretation of, 47, 263,
266; Klopsch's Red Letter, 115, 117;
"neither Jew nor Greek" verse in, 127,
149, 192; redeemer motif from, 150;
Sermon on the Mount in, 232; used
to justify racism, 192; in U.S.
territories (or not), 114, 115, 118,
130
Bicknell, Ernest, 226

Boardman, Mabel: ARC and, 217, 225–227; Barton's conflict with, 214–216; Klopsch and, 224–225, 248, 250, 260; humanitarianism's professionalization and, 247; Italy aid and, 248; San Francisco aid and, 219–220; World War I aid and, 273

Booth, William, 12

Booth-Tucker, Frederick, 79, 143

Bowery Mission: acquisition of, 52, 231; breadline, 215, 228–231, 236–237, 246, 255; criticism of, 215, 228–231, 236; current work of, 3–4, 281; donors or finances of, 4; Free Labor Bureau, 231; Klopsch and, 3, 52–53, 231; pictures or photos of, 53, 229, 256; reputation of, 4; staff or volunteers, 3–4; Taft visits, 255, 257

Boxer Rebellion, 171–174, 177–178, 207, 326n2; Christians attacked during, 169, 172; European soldiers' atrocities or looting in, 172–174, 177; missionaries criticized for behavior during and after, 173–174, 177, 226

Bradford, Amory H., 202–204

Bread for the Hungry, 14

breadlines. See under Bowery Mission

British Empire, 57; in India, 124, 130, 135, 139, 142; Kaisar-i-Hind Medal awarded by, 3, 170; in South Africa, 135, 174; U.S. compared to, 135

Brooklyn Tabernacle, 7, 17, 18, 19, 26, 49; fire destroys, 25, 314n27; Christian Herald raises funds for, 25

brotherhood: Christian, 9, 36, 125, 147, 203; universal, 46, 63–65, 147, 149, 232, 261

Bryan, William Jennings, 247

Buffett, Peter, 289, 291

capitalism: exploitative, 37, 215, 237; laissez-faire, 19, 20, 37, 39; patrimonial, 291; regulation of, 37–38; spread of, 119

Carlisle Industrial Indian School, 198, 200, 208; Christian Herald page on, 199

Carnegie, Andrew, 5, 236, 237, 262, 272, 282, 291; on Social Darwinism, 38–40, 43

caste system, 146, 151, 163

Catholics: immigration of, 182, 184–185; Spanish-speaking, 110, 115, 154, 184–185; views of, 57, 154, 182, 184–185, 286

Cato, Will, 207

Central Cuban Relief Committee, 89, 92–93, 99–104, 107; established, 84, 87; fundraising by, 104; Klopsch resigns from, 86, 99, 108, 138; photo of, 85

charities: Christian Herald's, 26, 197, 227, 262, 274–277, 281; Christian or religious, 5, 83, 232, 282; corporate, 5; domestic, 4, 190, 275; evangelical, 14, 53, 190; tax code and, 282; public, 282; foreign, 125. See also names of individual charities

charity: biblical or theological support for, 21, 33, 35, 36, 38, 61, 63, 149, 223, 253; Christian Herald's role in evangelical, 28, 34, 59, 98, 246, 255, 262, 282; cosmopolitan vs. tribalist ethic of (see cosmopolitan ethic); debates about, 13, 43–46, 128, 144, 238, 262, 265 (see also philanthropy: preaching vs.); as elite vs. popular practice, 12, 30, 34, 236–238, 271–272; for enemies, 66; evangelism or missions advanced by, 141–143, 219, 223; as foreign policy (see humanitarianism: as foreign policy); grass-roots evangelical, 237, 249, 282; historiography or history of, 5, 13, 43, 57, 262, 293, 300n11; imperialism and, 86, 89, 112, 120, 130, 288; indiscriminate, 13, 43–46, 230–231, 238, 246; nationalism and, 59; peace charity (*continued*)

for world through, 13, 62, 65, 83, 84, 85, 86, 88, 89, 90, 91, 93. 95, 96–99, 108, 109, 110, 111, 113, 224; pentecostalism's impact on, 270; politicized, 59; pragmatic or strategic benefits of, 62, 189; race and, 149, 193, 195, 200, 201, 204, 207–208, 211; "scientific," 43–46, 221, 227, 292; as spiritual practice, 33–34, 149, 223; superiority of evangelical, 138–139, 141, 145; Winthrop sermon on, 88; world community forged by, 179, 211. *See also* humanitarianism; philanthropy

Charity Organization Societies, 43, 226, 336n35. *See also* New York Charity Organization Society

Chatelain, Héli, 204–206, 333n71

children: aid for Cuban, 89; American Sunday School Union's missions to, 188–189; in Appalachia or on frontier, 49, 188–190; ARC should focus on women and, 101–102; *Christian Herald* advocates for, 233–235; criticism of boarding schools for Native, 208; donations from, 34; immigrant, 185, 187; Klopsch's work with, 6, 51, 187; laws to protect, 233, 235, 261; "little white heathens," 188; marriage or sexual exploitation of, 151, 153; as menace, 187–190; orphans (*see under* Indian Famine *entries*). *See also* Christian Herald Children's Home

China: missionaries in, 172–177, 179, 185, 187–190, 266; orphanage in, 275; pentecostal revivals in, 269. *See also* Boxer Rebellion

China Relief Expedition, 172

Chinese Exclusion Act, 178

Chinese Famine of 1901, 175–177

Chinese Famine of 1906–1907, 221–225, 227, 248, 266

Chinese Famine of 1911–1912, 262

Chinese Famine of 1920–1921, 274

Chinese immigrants: aid for, 183, 187; assimilation of, 191; violence against, 178, 181–183

Christian and Missionary Alliance, 9, 132, 144, 168, 265–266, 269

Christian Endeavor, 9

Christian Herald: accounting or business practices of, 24–26, 30, 60, 87, 133, 140, 216, 218; advertisements in, 24, 140, 276; aid from (*see under* name of country receiving); art in, 2, 23, 29, 60, 87, 158, 159, 160, 167 (*see also under* photography); Bibles or gospels published by, 115, 117; British edition or editor of, 7, 22; circulation history of, 7, 9, 50, 86, 247, 257–258, 275, 276, 313n13; cover showing America as Almoner, 159–160, 284; criticism of relief efforts of, 20–21, 66, 127, 144–145; donors' names published by, 30, 32, 49, 60, 87, 133; economic issues covered in, 37–38, 40, 43, 232–233, 235–237; editorial policies, 9–10, 23–24, 47, 64, 129, 263–264, 274–275; editorial policies criticized, 24; end of publication of, 276; foreign aid methods or policies, 4, 11, 20, 28, 32–34, 36, 50, 53, 58, 67, 83, 120, 125, 127, 138, 140–141, 143, 227; foreign governments and, 11–12, 72, 73, 74, 88, 97, 124, 135, 139–140, 176, 216, 219, 249; fundraising by, 3, 11–12, 236, 283; fundraising for other organizations by, 49, 56, 59, 100, 247; fundraising statistics for, 11, 28, 58, 72, 83, 89, 124, 125, 216, 218, 219, 222, 223, 225, 249, 253, 266, 272–274; fundraising strategies of, 12, 28–30, 58–63, 145, 147, 161, 283; geographical scope of readers of, 6, 9, 32, 47, 50, 114, 132; humanitarian crises

Constantinople, 53, 55–62; *Christian Herald* aids, 53, 56–60, 65–66; significance of earthquake in, 57; riot in, 68

Conwell, Russell, 34

Corbett, Rosemary, 286

cosmopolitan ethic, 57, 147–148; abandoned, 80, 147, 280; tribalist ethic vs., 63–66, 79–80

Cottrell, Charles, 103–104, 106–107

Cuba: aid distribution problems in, 93, 94, 99, 100, 102, 104, 106, 126, 141; aid suspended in, 108; *Christian Herald* aids, 11, 84, 86–89, 93, 94, 95, 101, 103–106, 108, 120, 138; *Christian Herald* pamphlet on, 92, 93; debates over intervention in, 90, 96–97, 108–110, 141; humanitarian crisis in, 11, 13, 80, 82–89, 91–99, 101, 106, 110, 112, 113, 126; humanitarian leadership struggle in, 80, 85, 100, 101, 105, 108–109; Klopsch's visit to, 93–95, 99, 101–104, 106–107, 315n44; "negroes" in, 97; Proctor's visit to, 93; revolution in, 80, 82, 86, 97, 312n3; U.S. seizes, 110, 112–113; Weyler's policies in, 82, 85, 92

Cubans: citizenship for, 112; as immigrants, 184, 187

Curtis Act, 200, 208

Dawes Act, 195, 200, 208

Day, William, 96, 107

Devine, Edward, 220, 226, 228–232, 236, 246

de Waal, Alex, 288

Dixon, A. C., 143, 149, 152, 265–266

Dodge, William E., 236

Drexel, Morgan, & Co., 12, 56

Dwight, Henry Otis, 74–75

economic downturns: in 1873, 18; in 1893–1894, 13, 20, 37, 40, 44, 47, 185; in 1907, 227–228

Eddy, George Sherwood, 149–150

education, 6, 39, 48; industrial, 49, 184, 193, 195, 198, 204, 206

educational institutes, 49, 193, 204; Carlisle, 198–200, 208; *Christian Herald* and, 193–194, 196–198; Hampton, 193–195, 200; Mayesville, 197–198, 206, 274; Tuskegee, 195–196, 206

Eighth Avenue Mission, 40–42, 46, 48

Ely, Richard, 6

employment: of African Americans, 196; *Christian Herald*'s bureau for, 78, 191; farm colonies and, 49, 230; handouts vs., 161–162; of immigrants, 78, 196; training for, 276; urban ministries and, 48. *See also* unemployment

Enlightenment, 29, 60

ethics, sentimental, 29–30

Ethiopia, 290

evangelicals; African Americans and, 191–195, 198, 201, 203, 206–207; associations or organizations of, 34, 48; charity or humanitarian campaigns unite, 10, 21, 47–49, 50, 53, 56, 72, 114, 126, 128, 132, 144, 170, 264; cosmopolitan vs. tribalist aid ethic of (*see* cosmopolitan ethic); cultural authority of, 10; debates over future or identity of, 144, 215, 243, 262, 264; defined, 9, 301–302n22; foreign policy role of, 80, 83, 85, 91, 96, 109, 120, 136, 178, 214, 252; immigrants and, 182–183, 187–188, 191, 209, 211; in India, 128, 147, 163–164, 170; influence of, 85–86, 96, 108, 140, 207, 246, 255; as leaders in foreign aid, 83, 85, 109, 138, 139–141, 145, 250; mass media and, 21, 22; military conflict and, 86, 109, 119; nationalism or imperialism and, 59, 61, 86, 112–113, 119, 136, 175–176, 189, 327n12 (*see also* anti-imperialists: evangelical; United States: as "Christian nation"); Native Americans and, 191–195, 198, 200, 208; race or racism and, 192–195, 198, 200–201, 203–204, 206, 207, 209; racial and religious "others" and, 57, 63, 64, 127–128, 212; rhetoric of rescue used by, 156; tensions among U.S., 9–10, 21, 47–48, 113, 126, 129, 132, 212, 263, 271; as united front, 10, 21, 47–48, 302n23

evangelism, 308, 341; to immigrants, 183, 185; in India, 142–144, 151, 169, 266; pentecostal, 271; philanthropy as or vs., 62–63, 144, 264–267

exceptionalism, myth or narrative of American, 9, 83, 88, 111, 134, 135, 179, 204, 205, 283–287, 313n18, 328n25, 345n11; Ramabai's questioning of, 167; Twain's critique of, 174. *See also* United States: as "most generous nation"

Fairbanks, Charles, 248–249
Federal Council of Churches, 264
Fernie, J. B., 22
Finland, 215–216
Foley, Kevin, 288
foundations: ARC and, 225–227, 273, 336n27; Bill and Melinda Gates, 282; Carnegie's, 5, 237, 262, 272, 282; corporate, 5; faith-based, 282; Ford, 282; impact of, 227, 236, 262, 272; post–World War II, 282; Rockefeller, 4, 271–273, 276, 282; Russell Sage, 225, 237; secular, 282, 291; statistics about, 282

freedom: as American ideal or American expansionism and, 14, 57, 58, 66, 83, 121, 126, 130, 136, 168, 276; Armenian struggle for, 58, 68, 70, 78; *Christian Herald* on God establishing, 110, 113, 118; Cuban

struggle for, 87, 97, 110; Filipino struggle for, 118–119, 136, 152; religious, 60, 70, 72, 130; from slavery, 205

Fuller, Marcus B. and Jennie, 159, 161–163, 287, 290
fundamentalism, 262, 265–267, 271, 275, 341n16

Gates, Frederick Taylor, 4
gender: ARC or C. Barton and, 101, 102; evangelical humanitarianism and, 126; evangelical views of India and, 126, 152–153; evangelical views of Islam and, 68, 151, 153
Geneva Conventions, 59, 107, 138, 140
Gladden, Washington, 238
globalization, 4, 13, 17, 34, 58, 126
Guam, 86, 110, 115, 266

Haiti, 289
Hall, Peter Dobkin, 290
Hampton Normal and Industrial Institute, 193–195, 200
Hanna, Philip, 250, 252, 254
Hawthorne, J. B., 45–46
Hay, John, 125, 139, 176
Haymarket Affair, 19, 38
Hearst, William Randolph, 23–24, 90, 92, 155, 240, 338n57
"heathenism" or "heathendom," 110, 111, 118, 143; as threat, 188, 247
"heathens": in China, 223; gender and, 323n63; gospel preached to or conversion of, 264, 266; in India (*see under* India); "little white," 188; motif of rescue of, 150, 152; Native Americans as, 191; slaves as, 191; in Spanish colonies, 110
Hencke, Albert, 23
Hill, John Wesley, 255
Hindus, 127, 146, 147, 148, 153, 163, 267
Hoover, Herbert, 6
Hose, Sam, 174, 206

Howard, William Willard, 23, 72–74
Hull House, 6, 49
humanitarianism: *Christian Herald* as
leader in (*see* Christian Herald: as
humanitarian leader); *Christian
Herald*'s influence on, 4, 12, 28, 155,
276, 281–286; cosmopolitan vs. tribal
ethic of (*see* cosmopolitan ethic);
cultural imperialism and, 34, 289;
debates or doubts about, 144–146,
161, 228–230, 287–292, 322n48 (*see
also* philanthropy: preaching vs.);
defined, 300n11; divisions bridged by,
64–65, 67, 72, 132, 142, 147–148, 170,
261, 264; evangelical or faith-based,
14, 28, 85, 89, 125, 126, 143, 145, 170,
214, 217, 219, 227, 248, 249, 253, 260,
292; as foreign policy, 34, 58, 86,
88–89, 91, 96, 110–111, 140, 284;
history or historiography of, 4, 14, 28,
293; imperialism and (*see* imperialism:
charity or humanitarianism and);
"industrial" approach to, 162–163; as
industry, 5, 291, 293; local vs. foreign
leadership in, 128, 289; media and, 2,
5, 12, 21, 29, 30; military invasion as,
14, 86, 120, 284; military invasion vs.,
87; millennial expectations and, 22,
63; patronizing or paternalistic, 168;
pictorial representations and, 29, 155,
161–163, 283, 290; popular or
grassroots, 6, 216, 225, 227, 236, 253;
race or racism and, 76, 126–127, 145,
204; scientific or secular, 143, 146,
225, 227, 230; sensibilities or
sentiments of, 4, 29, 25; as spiritual
practice (*see* charity: biblical or
theological support for; charity: as
spiritual practice). *See also* charity;
philanthropy
hunger: affluent ignore, 131, 161–162,
228, 237, 239; causes of, 293;
Christian Herald coverage emphasizing, 27, 29, 30, 239; of children,

56; in India, 126, 148, 152–153, 163;
in New York, 3, 20, 40, 42, 44, 47, 50,
51, 228, 230, 231, 235, 237, 276, 281;
sexual exploitation and, 126,
152–153; Talmage on, 18, 148. *See
also* Bible: "feed the hungry" verse;
starvation

Ignatieff, Michael, 288
immigrants: Armenian, 78; Asian, 174,
181; assimilation of (*see under*
assimilation); Catholic, 182–184;
Chinese, 178, 191; *Christian Herald*
on, 178, 180–182, 209; as citizens (or
not), 182, 191, 211; European, 182,
187, 209; fear of, 181–182, 209;
Jewish, 44, 175, 183, 184, 211, 244; in
New York, 183, 185; policies
restricting, 178, 182, 209; Riis on,
209, 211, 333n85; rise in numbers of,
18, 187; violence against, 175,
180–181
imperialism: "benevolent," 118–120;
charity or humanitarianism and, 14,
86, 89, 112, 120, 130, 142, 286, 288,
345n17; of Christianity, 119;
civilizing mission of, 111–112,
119–120, 126, 179, 324n70; criticism
or debates about, 14, 86, 112–114,
118, 120, 126, 129–131, 134, 136,
174, 232, 288, 313n79, 320n17 (*see
also* anti-imperialists); cultural, 289;
divine mandate for, 109–112, 120;
evangelical views of, 14, 86, 119,
126–127, 129; images and, 127,
320n12; Klopsch, Talmage, or
Christian Herald supports, 86, 112,
113, 179, 232; NGOs and, 288; race
or gender and, 127, 319n10, 324n70
India: converts in, 127–128, 146, 151;
"heathens" in, 127, 143, 146, 147,
149–151, 161, 162; images or
depictions of, 127–128, 150–151;
Klopsch travels in, 156, 158, 162;

missionaries' views of, 150–151; women or widows in, 126, 151–153, 163–169

Indian Famine of 1876, 163

Indian Famine of 1896–1897, 11, 123, 318n2; *Christian Herald*'s aid for or coverage of, 132, 134, 135, 141, 144, 152, 154, 155, 156, 167; criticism of aid for or coverage of, 144–145; Indian Christians' aid work during, 163–164, 166 (*see also* Ramabai Sarasvati, Pandita); missionaries' aid work during, 124, 132, 141, 142, 146; orphans of, 123, 164; photos of sufferers in, 157, 163, 165; widows of, 163, 167

Indian Famine of 1899–1900, 161–163, 166; amounts raised for, 124, 125, 156; *Christian Herald*'s aid for or coverage of, 124–128, 132–136, 138–139, 143–150, 152–158; criticism of aid for or coverage of, 161–162; Indian Christians' aid work during (*see also* Ramabai Sarasvati, Pandita), 128, 166; missionaries' aid work during, 124, 125, 133, 141–142, 146, 161, 168; missionaries appeal for help for, 123–124, 131–132, 150, 153, 156, 162–163; orphans of, 125–126, 153–155; photos of sufferers in, 155–156, 158, 161–163; *Quito* sent to relieve, 124–125, 133, 136, 143, 152; Sheldon's concern with, 130–132; U.S.'s reputation and aid for, 126, 136, 138–139, 152, 159, 174; widows of, 126, 153–154

Indians. *See* Native Americans

industrial education. *See under* education

Industrial Missionary Association of Alabama, 196–197

Irish famine, 32

Islam. *See* Muslims

Italy, 225, 248–250, 254

James, Ollie M., 245

Jane Street Methodist Episcopal Church, 7, 40, 183. *See also* Eighth Avenue Mission

Japan, 3, 11–12, 187, 217–219, 266

Jesus Christ, 4, 38; "Asiatic," 148; charity as imitation of, 36, 42, 45, 49, 66, 150, 169, 215, 236; charity as service for or in name of, 33, 34, 50, 65, 91, 94, 124, 125, 141, 142, 150, 223, 258, 260, 262; kingdom or millennial reign of, 63, 83, 84, 85, 111, 118, 154, 174, 182, 211, 223, 228, 235, 238 (*see also* millennialism); love of, 53, 149; Spanish-language materials about, 115; universal brotherhood declared by, 232

Jews, 44, 60, 175, 183, 211, 286; anti-Semitism and, 244; assimilation of, 184; Forsyth Street Hebrew Christian Mission to, 184; as immigrants, 44, 175, 183, 184, 211, 244; public school controversy of, 244; as race, 184

Jim Crow. *See* segregation, racial

Johnstown Flood, 21–22, 62

journalism: sensational or yellow, 23–24, 90–91, 304n13; religious, 7, 9, 24, 83, 129, 156, 261, 275. *See also* newspapers and periodicals

Kennedy, Denis, 289

Kids With a Promise, 281

Kimball, Grace, 73–74, 79

King, David, 282

Klopsch, Louis: awards given to, 3, 219; Barton and (*see under* Barton, Clara); CCRC and (*see* Central Cuban Relief Committee); criticism of, 26, 97, 103; death or funeral of, 26, 259–261, 277; early years, 1–2; estate of, 26; as evangelical, 6–7, 21, 22; legacy or impact of, 4–6, 12, 261–262, 277;

modernism, Protestant, 262, 263–265, 271, 275, 302n23, 341n9

Monterey (Mexico), 250–254; *Christian Herald* cover on, 251

Mont-Lawn Children's Home. *See* Christian Herald Children's Home

Morgan, James Pierpont, 228, 273

Mormons: *Christian Herald* on, 215, 240–242; as threat, 212, 239–243; polygamy of, 240, 241

motto controversy, 215, 243–246

Muslims: ARC gives aid to, 59, 77; Armenians and, 67–70; in "brotherhood of man," 147; in Constantinople, 13, 58–60, 62–63, 65–66, 72, 127; in India, 146, 147, 153; as "Mohammedans," 13, 60, 67, 68, 69, 146; stereotypes of, 13, 60, 66, 72, 77, 146; stereotypes about gender and, 68, 151, 153

nationalism, 15, 57, 59, 73, 176, 293; evangelical, 175, 327n12

Native Americans: allotment of lands of, 195, 200–201, 208; boarding schools for, 198, 201, 208; *Christian Herald* coverage of, 193–194, 198–199, 200–201, 208; government mistreatment of, 130, 192–193, 200–201; labor of, 194; land seizures from, 192, 195, 208; missions to, 191, 198, 200; reservations for, 193, 200; Talmage on, 200; violence or wars against, 175, 193, 200. *See also* assimilation: of Native Americans; Dawes Act; Curtis Act

newspapers and periodicals: *American National Red Cross Magazine,* 283; *Brooklyn Daily Eagle,* 97–98; *Davenport Democrat,* 32, 33; evangelical or religious, 9, 22, 23–24, 50, 115, 202; *Frank Leslie's Illustrated Sunday Magazine,* 7; fundraising by, 32; lynching coverage in, 202, 206; *New*

York Evening Post, 32; *New York Herald,* 32, 33, 106; *New York Journal,* 23, 90, 92, 155, 240; New York *Sun,* 96, 173; *New York Times,* 107, 129, 173, 228, 230, 260, 291; *New York Tribune,* 32, 98, 173; *New York World,* 22, 23, 90, 92, 257; *North American Review,* 174, 176; *Northwestern Miller,* 28, 32, 33, 35; *Outlook,* 202; pentecostal, 271; as philanthropies, 32; secular, 9, 23–24; sensational or tabloid, 23–24, 90; *Sunday School Times,* 9. *See also* Christian Herald

Newton, Heber, 263

New York Charity Organization Society, 228–229, 232, 236

New York City: *Christian Herald* aids, 11, 20, 44, 46, 48, 50, 230; *Christian Herald* food fund, 20, 40, 46–47, 50, 51, 185; missions in, 4, 40–42, 183 (*see also* Bowery Mission; Eighth Avenue Mission); newspapers in (*see under* newspapers and periodicals); tenements in, 40, 51, 187–188, 260

NGOs, 282, 288

Nissinen, Sanna, 290

nonprofit sector, 4, 276, 282, 290, 344n3

Orientalism, 60

Ottoman Empire, 11, 56–58, 62, 65–67; American and European views of, 57, 60, 67–69; Bulgarian revolt against, 60; charity for Americans from, 62; Greek revolt against, 57; missionaries in, 73; violence in, 65, 68–69

pacifism, 86, 109, 280. *See also* charity: peace for world through

Palestine, 7, 19, 25, 60

Panic of 1907. *See under* economic downturns

Penney, J. C., 274–275

pentecostalism, 262, 275; periodicals, 271, 283; revivals, 267–271, 342n21; spread of, 269; tongues controversy, 269–271

periodicals. *See* newspapers and periodicals

Pew Charitable Trusts, 282

Philafrican Liberator's League, 204–206

philanthropy: agencies or organizations for, 35, 42, 226, 236, 227, 272, 276 (*see also* foundations); corporatization of, 274; critiques of robber barons', 237–239; debates about, 6, 13–14, 43–46, 100, 140, 287–289; defined, 300n11; divisions bridged by, 10, 34, 132, 133, 134, 263; evangelism and (*see under* evangelism); as foreign policy (*see* humanitarianism: as foreign policy); history or historiography of, 5, 13, 262–263, 300n11; Klopsch as "captain of," 6, 277; by newspapers, 32–33; paternalistic, 289; peace through (*see* charity: peace for world through); preaching vs., 143–146, 264–266; race or prejudice and, 6, 39, 145, 193, 196–197, 207; "scientific," 13, 21, 43–44, 215, 225–226, 230, 236, 238, 245–246, 249, 255, 274, 277; secularization of, 4, 5, 212, 227, 274. *See also* charity; humanitarianism

Philippine-American War, 118–121, 126, 136, 312n5; *Christian Herald* coverage of, 118–119, 129–130; Sheldon on, 129–130, 136, 288; Twain on, 174, 288; U.S. atrocities in, 126, 128–129, 136, 152, 159; U.S. atrocities in, and India aid, 136, 152, 154

Philippines: alcohol in, 129, 130; *Christian Herald* aids, 120, 266; civilized, 129; "comfortable homes" of converts in, 117–118; First Philippine Republic in, 118, 121,

126; gospel sent to, 115, 117; revolution in, 113, 118; as Spanish colony, 86; status or self-government of, 112–114, 119; U.S. imperialism in, 110, 130, 174, 179, 288

photography: active vs. passive aid recipients in, 162–163, 167, 289; *Christian Herald*'s use of, 2, 23, 30, 93, 127, 136, 155–158, 163, 164, 165, 283; ethics of, 161, 290; fundraising using, 127, 156, 158, 161; of "living skeletons," 155, 161, 163, 167, 290; technology of, 30, 155

Piketty, Thomas, 291

Plessy v. Ferguson, 202, 204

Poling, Daniel, 274–276

polygenesis. *See under* race

poverty: attitudes toward or debates about, 13, 18–19, 38, 46, 50, 229–232; causes of, 18, 20, 38, 45, 231–233; income inequality and, 13, 228, 230; Talmage on, 19; urban, 13; vice and, 13, 42–43, 229–230

Proctor, Redfield, 93–94

public schools, 212, 215; Christmas observances in, 244; religious diversity in, 243–244

Puerto Rico, 86, 110, 113–115, 117, 266; hurricane in, 115

Pulitzer, Joseph, 22–24, 90, 92

Quito, 124–125, 133, 136–137, 139, 143, 149, 152, 171

race: advancement of "American," 190, 209; amalgamation, 181, 201, 209, 328–329n25; "American," 181, 190, 207, 209; "Anglo-Saxon," 175, 193, 209; Armenians as Christian, 70, 73; "Aryan," 148; "Asiatic," 148, 177, 180, 191, 211; assimilation to white, 191, 211–212, 329–330n38 (*see also* assimilation); assumptions about, 14, 15, 126, 293; biblical views of, 65;

charity without distinction of, 12, 49, 57, 63, 65, 76, 127, 147, 149, 159, 167, 170, 179, 261 (*see also* cosmopolitan ethic); climactic conceptions of, 180; harmony of, 179, 180, 187, 198–202, 206, 208, 211; humanitarianism and, 126, 127; immigration, nationalism, and, 328–329n25; imperialism and, 127, 319n10, 320n12, 324n70; "Jewish," 184; photos displaying hierarchy of, 127, 159, 162, 289–290; polygenesis theory of, 65; prejudice against other, 58, 76, 68, 145, 148, 167, 170; science and, 65, 192–193; Talmage on (*see under* Talmage); theories of, 65, 180, 309n23, 323n56, 328n23; uplift of, 193, 195–197, 201, 204, 211

race relations, 10, 179, 192, 203, 207; Ramabai on U.S., 207–208, 239, 263; in south, 147, 203

race riots or racial violence, 175, 202–204, 206–207, 211. *See also* lynching

racism, 170, 176, 191–193, 201, 239; against African Americans, 193–195, 202; against immigrants, 174, 191, 208–211; intermarriage and, 201; against Native Americans, 194; against outsiders, 58, 76, 68, 145, 148, 167, 170; Ramabai on U.S.'s, 167–168, 170; "scientific," 65, 192–193. *See also* segregation, racial; Social Darwinism

Ramabai Sarasvati, Pandita, 128, 325n85; as Christian, 163; Chinese Christians aided by, 169; in famine of 1876, 163; in famine of 1897, 163–164; in famine of 1900, 166–170; fundraising by, 164, 166, 267; influence or reputation of, 128, 163–164, 168, 170, 326n92; Mukti mission of, 163, 166–170, 267, 271; orphans aided by, 164, 166, 168;

pentecostal revivals and, 268–269, 271; on racism in U.S., 167–168; rhetoric of rescue and, 164, 170, 290; Sharada Sadan of, 163, 166, 169; travels in U.S., 163; widows aided by, 163–168

Rauschenbusch, Walter, 6

reconcentrados, 85, 88, 91, 93–94, 96–98, 101–102, 106–108, 126, 138

Reed, Paul, 207

revivals: evangelical or Protestant, 9, 10, 29, 191; pentecostal, 267–271, 277

Riis, Jacob, 209, 211, 333n85

robber barons. *See* class: elite, millionaire, or wealthy

Roberts, Brigham H., 240

Rockefeller, John D., 4, 131, 236, 237, 238, 239, 262, 272, 291

Romanticism, 29

Roosevelt, Theodore: ARC and, 217–218, 220, 221, 248; *Christian Herald* and, 11, 125, 218–219, 222; motto controversy and, 243

Root, Elihu, 222

Rozario, Kevin, 283

Russell Sage Foundation, 225, 237

Russia: as American ally, 59; Klopsch and Talmage's trip to, 11, 28, 31, 64; tsars of, 27, 28, 287

Russian Famine of 1891–1892: *Christian Herald* aids, 11, 20, 27–28, 30–36, 58, 60, 287; extent of, 27; media coverage of, 28–32; ships sent to relieve, 27–28, 33; U.S. government response to, 35

Sage, Russell or Olivia, 225, 237, 272, 319

Salvation Army, 12, 14, 78, 132, 143, 266, 282; farm colonies of, 49, 79

Samoa, 86

Talmage, Thomas De Witt: criticism of, 7, 17–18, 25–26; death of, 207; as editor or editorials by, 20, 25, 37, 44–45, 64, 81–82, 90–91, 98, 178, 182; estate of, 25–26; *Frank Leslie's Illustrated Sunday Magazine* and, 7; on immigrants, 178, 180–182; millennial views of, 20, 22, 63, 179, 209; networking by, 7, 11–12, 92; as pastor, 7, 17–19, 25, 36, 49–50; as pastor of First Presbyterian Church, 92; photo of, 8; praise of, 18, 49–50; on race, 65, 148, 180–181, 194, 203–207, 309n23, 323n56, 328n23; sensationalist, 7, 17; sermons of, 7, 19, 25, 33, 38, 48, 65, 67, 68–69, 148, 180, 194; on war, 90–91, 98, 109, 179

Terrell, Alexander, 56

Thoburn, James M., 124, 132–133, 158

Turkish Relief Committee, 56

Turner, Henry McNeal, 207–208

Tuskegee Normal School, 195–196, 198, 206

Twain, Mark, 174, 176, 206, 287, 288

unemployment: debates over, 215, 229–232, 235; in 1873, 18; in 1893, 13, 20, 40, 42; farm colonies and, 49, 230; insurance, 37; missions or missionaries and, 48; in 1907, 227–228

United States: affluence demonstrated by foreign aid, 35, 134–135; as "Almoner of the World," 35, 126, 135, 159, 160, 170, 255, 283, 284, 293; *Christian Herald* as representative of, 98; as "Christian nation," 10, 35, 57, 58, 70, 73, 88–89, 99, 120, 126, 129, 130, 174, 190, 216, 239, 243, 244, 263; as "civilizer and evangelizer," 111; debates over global role of, 13, 14, 80, 82–83, 87, 98; diplomatic relations, 62; exceptionalism of (*see* exceptionalism); foreign aid vs. military intervention by, 58, 69, 83, 87–89, 118; foreign policy criticized, 129, 136; immigration policies in, 178, 182, 209; (manifest) destiny of, 86, 109, 111, 182, 188, 190, 192, 193, 200, 206, 211; military aids in humanitarian relief, 136; military interventions by, 82, 85, 86, 90, 96, 97, 108–110; as millennial kingdom's birthplace, 179, 190, 201, 206, 209; as "most generous nation," 35, 91, 159 (*see also* exceptionalism); motto controversy, 215, 243–246; Reconstruction-era, 193; as "redeemer nation," 2, 84, 86; religious diversity in, 226, 243, 263; reputation of, 10, 35, 88, 90, 98, 126, 129, 136, 138, 152, 174, 216, 226, 249; sectionalism/reunion of, 203; territories of, 110, 112–114, 120, 126; as welfare state, 5, 37; welfare policies, 14

urban ministries, 48–49

USS Maine, 85, 90–91

veterans, 36–37

Wanamaker, John, 12

war: holy, 66–67, 69, 70, 79, 109; humanitarian, 86, 120; just or righteous, 86, 109, 110, 120

Washington, Booker T., 195–196, 197, 332n52

wealth: attitudes toward, 18, 131, 168, 239; gospel of, 39; inequality of, 13, 37, 38, 39, 228, 230, 232, 290–291

Wells-Barnett, Ida B., 174–175, 327n9

Whitefield, George, 191

Willard, Frances, 12, 79, 163, 233

Willets, Gilson, 216